second edition

Technical Pascal
Using TURBO

ANDREW C. STAUGAARD, JR.

Department of Computer Science
The School of the Ozarks

ALT F brings up file
F6 WATCH
ALT F6 output screen (split)
to get out use ALT F6
F6
F6 again

Prentice Hall, Englewood Cliffs, New Jersey 07632

Library of Congress Cataloging-in-Publication Data

Staugaard, Andrew C.
    Technical Pascal: using Turbo / Andrew C. Staugaard, Jr. — 2nd ed.
        p.   cm.
    ISBN 0-13-901968-5
    1. Pascal (Computer program language)   2. Turbo Pascal (Computer
program)   I. Title.
QA76.73.P2S737   1990
005.13′3—dc19   89-16346
                                                                CIP

Editorial/production supervision and
  interior design: *bookworks*
Cover design: *Photo Plus Art*
Manufacturing buyer: *Gina Chirco-Brennan*

©1990, 1988 by Prentice-Hall, Inc.
A Division of Simon & Schuster
Englewood Cliffs, New Jersey 07632

Printed in the United States of America

10 9 8 7 6 5 4 3 2 1

ISBN 0-13-901968-5

Prentice-Hall International (UK) Limited, *London*
Prentice-Hall of Australia Pty. Limited, *Sydney*
Prentice-Hall Canada Inc., *Toronto*
Prentice-Hall Hispanoamericana, S.A., *Mexico*
Prentice-Hall of India Private Limited, *New Delhi*
Prentice-Hall of Japan, Inc., *Tokyo*
Simon & Schuster Asia Pte. Ltd., *Singapore*
Editora Prentice-Hall do Brasil, Ltda., *Rio de Janeiro*

To my family:
Jan, Ron, Dave, Zane, and Andrew III,
the five most important people in my life.

Contents

v

Preface

Welcome to the world of *Technical Pascal Using TURBO*. With this text, you will learn how to create Pascal programs to solve common problems found in mathematics, engineering, and technology. What's more, you will learn how to define technical problems in terms of computer input, output, and processing. Then you will create the problem solution using what is called an algorithm which can be easily converted to a Pascal program. In other words, this text not only will teach you the Pascal language, but more important, it will teach you how to define a technical problem and plan its solution so that it can be easily "coded" using Pascal, or any computer language for that matter.

Technical Pascal Using TURBO has been written to provide undergraduate students with a first exposure to technical programming using the Pascal language. The text is designed to be used at the introductory level, assuming that the students have no previous background in programming of any kind. However, it is assumed that the students are familiar with basic algebra and right-angle trigonometry concepts, such as might be found in a one-semester technical math course. In addition, it is assumed that the students have a general knowledge of basic electronic concepts, such as those found in introductory dc and ac circuits courses.

Each chapter includes numerous example programs and problems that specifically apply Pascal programming to simple problems in mathematics and technology. The emphasis is on electrical technology, since the largest number of students will be from this area or will have had an exposure to dc/ac circuits. Nevertheless, several problems from mechanical and civil technology have been included for students from these areas. The program examples and problems have been written in short, understandable modules that stress the fundamental concepts being discussed. I have added several application tasks as well as more programming problems to this new edition. The application tasks are included at the end of many of the chapters in an effort to tie things together and present a top-down design approach to technical problem solving using the Pascal language.

The text begins with a general overview of computer hardware and software technology in the first part of Chapter 1. This material can be covered rather rapidly if the students have already had some programming experience. However, the latter part of Chapter 1 discusses what I call the programmer's algorithm and should be covered thoroughly. The programmer's algorithm is a step-by-step procedure that I have used to get students started on the right programming track by considering good problem definition, solution planning, and documentation. Of particular importance is solution planning via algorithmic development. I feel that once students have defined the problem and planned a solution via an algorithmic structure, the actual program coding is secondary to the real problem-solving task. As a result, I stress good algorithmic development throughout the text. I have used a pseudocode algorithmic structure that is simple and very similar to Pascal. This approach allows for easy translation of the algorithm to the coded Pascal program.

Chapter 2 familiarizes students with concepts in Pascal that are missing in nonstructured languages such as BASIC. It is important here that students grasp the idea of data typing, since this is a primary feature of Pascal. In addition, the idea of program structure and the modular top-down design approach of a structured language are introduced in this chapter.

Students really begin to get their hands dirty in Chapter 3, where they learn how to get information in and out of a Pascal program. Special consideration is given to interactive user-friendly programming. The discussion in Chapter 3 is extended into Chapter 4, where students learn how to perform standard arithmetic, Boolean, and function operations in Pascal. Several simple program tasks are illustrated at the end of this chapter to illustrate these operations.

Up to this point, students have been writing simple straight-line programs. In Chapter 5, the **IF/THEN, IF/THEN/ELSE,** and **CASE** operations are discussed to introduce the decision-making element into the program. This is followed with a discussion of the Pascal iteration operations of **WHILE/DO, REPEAT/UNTIL,** and **FOR/DO** in Chapter 6.

In Chapter 7, students get the flavor of a structured language when they learn how to write their own functions and procedures in Pascal. From this point on, the idea of a modular top-down design approach to problem solving is emphasized. Such an approach using a structured language, such as Pascal, is mandatory if the students plan on tackling complex programming tasks such as those that are typically found in the industry. A discussion of recursion has been added to this new edition, along with associated examples and problems that demonstrate the characteristics of recursive versus iterative solutions. In addition, the last section of this chapter applies the Pascal language to the solution of series impedance circuits via vector analysis using polar and rectangular coordinates.

Chapter 8 begins with a discussion of user-defined data, another important feature of Pascal. Here, the technical student learns how to tailor a program to meet the application. This is followed by a discussion of arrays and how they are used to solve technical problems. In particular, arrays are applied using Cramer's rule to solve simultaneous equations. The resulting Pascal program is then applied to solve simultaneous loop equations resulting from Kirchoff's voltage law, as well as other technical problems that reduce to simultaneous equation solution.

I have added two new chapters to this edition which provide a discussion of records (Chapter 9) and files (Chapter 10). In Chapter 9 the student learns about the limitation of the array for storing different data types and discovers the record as the solution. The record data structure is covered thoroughly in this chapter using several real world applications.

Files are discussed in Chapter 10 to conclude the text. In this chapter the student first learns how to declare and access disk files through simple examples. Then the student learns how to construct general procedures that can be used to create, expand, read, and change disk files to meet just about any given file application. Several of the programming problems at the end of this chapter lead the student through the development of a comprehensive parts-inventory file, much like those which are found in industry.

The compiler employed is TURBO Pascal. TURBO Pascal was chosen due to its wide usage in the educational market. It is readily available at an affordable price and runs on just about any microcomputer, including the Apple Macintosh, IBM PC, IBM PS/2, and all compatables. This text is compatible with all current versions of TURBO Pascal. In addition, although TURBO Pascal is the primary vehicle for this text, the text is also appropriate for use with other versions of Pascal, such as Standard Pascal, UCSD Pascal, and MacPascal. I have made an effort to discuss the differences between TURBO and the others where appropriate.

Enjoy!

Andrew C. Staugaard, Jr.

chapter one

Getting Acquainted with Computers, Programs, and Pascal

INTRODUCTION

This first chapter has been written to provide you with an introduction to computers, computer programs, and Pascal in general. You will learn about the relationship between the computer system and the computer programs that operate the system. In particular, you will study the steps required to solve nearly any programming problem.

Of extreme importance is the last section of this chapter, which teaches you how to develop algorithms. Make sure that you understand this material and work the related problems at the end of the chapter. As you become more experienced in programming, you will find that the "secret" to successful programming is good planning through the use of algorithms.

Any computer system, regardless of its size, can be broken down into two major components: hardware and software. So let's begin with a comprehensive overview of each.

1-1 THE HARDWARE

You undoubtedly have seen some of the hardware components of a computer. These are the physical devices that you can see and touch, such as those shown in

Figure 1-1a. This typical microcomputer system has a keyboard for user input, a display screen for output, and magnetic disk drives for program and data storage. Two very important parts of the system that cannot be seen, because they are inside the console, are the ***central processing unit*** and its ***working memory***.

The block diagram in Figure 1-1b shows all the major hardware sections of the system. From this figure you see that the system can be divided into five functional parts: the central processing unit (CPU), main working or primary memory, secondary memory, input, and output.

The Central Processing Unit (CPU)

The central processing unit (CPU) is the brains of the entire system. This is where all the calculations and decisions are made. In a microcomputer system, the entire CPU is contained within a single integrated circuit (IC) chip called a ***microprocessor***. In fact, this is what distinguishes a microcomputer from a mini or mainframe computer. In mini and mainframe computers, several ICs make up the CPU, not just one as in a microcomputer. A typical microprocessor IC is pictured in Figure 1-2, along with a magnified view of the chip itself.

There are three basic functional regions within the CPU that you should know about. They are the ***arithmetic logic unit*** (ALU), the ***control unit,*** and the ***internal registers***.

The Arithmetic Logic Unit (ALU)

As its name implies, the arithmetic logic unit performs all the arithmetic and logic operations within the CPU. The arithmetic operations performed by the ALU include addition, subtraction, multiplication, and division. These four basic arithmetic operations can be combined to perform nearly any mathematical calculation, from simple arithmetic to calculus.

Logic operations performed by the ALU are comparison operations that are used to compare numbers, letters, and special characters. The three basic logic comparison operations are equal to ($=$), less than ($<$), and greater than ($>$). These three basic operations can be combined to form the three additional logic operations of not equal ($<>$), less than or equal to ($<=$), and greater than or equal to ($>=$).

Table 1-1 summarizes the arithmetic and logic operations performed by the ALU. Notice the operation symbols listed in the table. These are the symbols that you will use later to perform arithmetic and logic operations when writing Pascal programs.

The Control Unit

The control unit section of the CPU directs and coordinates the activity of the entire system. This section interprets program instructions and generates

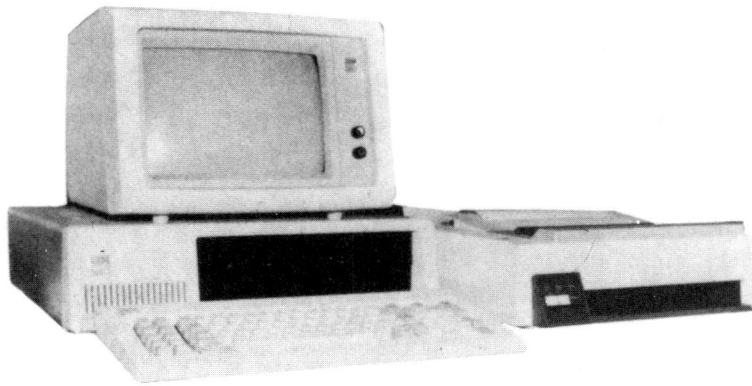

(a)

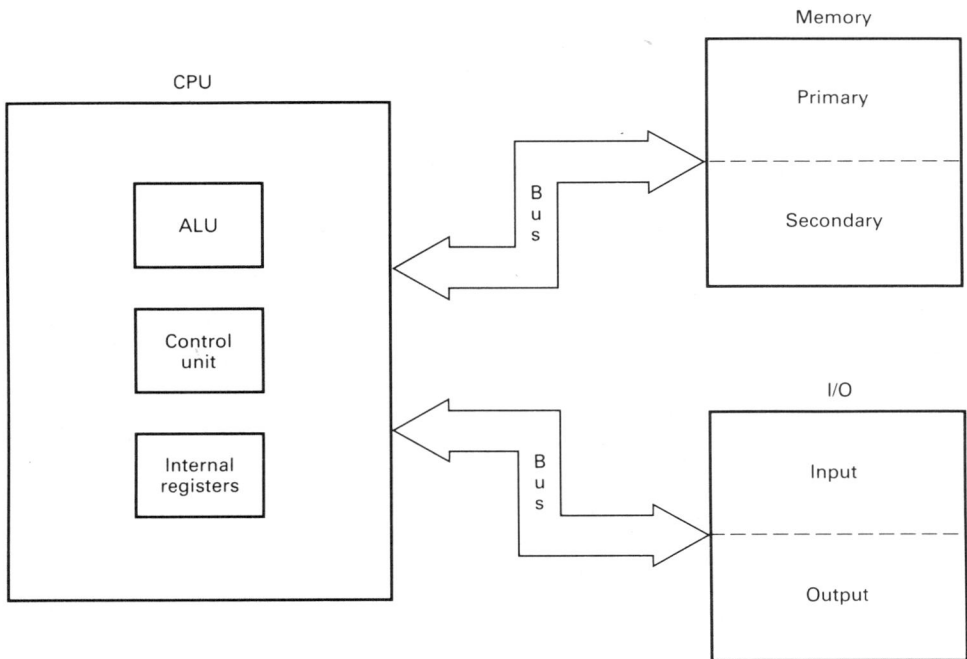

(b)

Figure 1-1   (a) A typical microcomputer system and (b) its hardware structure, or architecture.

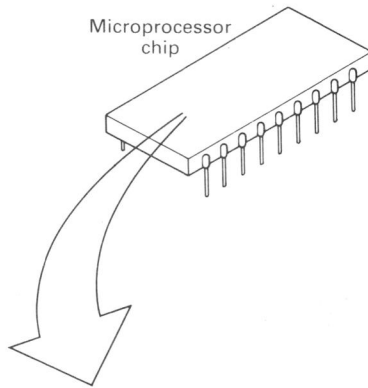

Figure 1-2   A microprocessor chip is the CPU of a microcomputer system.   (Copyright by Motorola, Inc.   Used by permission.)

TABLE 1-1   A SUMMARY OF
ARITHMETIC AND LOGIC OPERATIONS
PERFORMED BY THE ALU SECTION OF
THE CPU

Arithmetic operations	Symbol
Addition	+
Subtraction	−
Multiplication	*
Division	/

Logic operations	Symbol
Equal to	=
Not equal to	< >
Less than	<
Less than or equal to	< =
Greater than	>
Greater than or equal to	> =

electrical signals to the other parts of the system in order to execute those instructions. The control unit communicates with other sections of the CPU via internal signal paths called *buses*. The control unit is often likened to a traffic cop or orchestra leader because it directs the activity of the entire CPU.

Internal Registers

The internal register section of the CPU contains temporary storage areas for program instructions and data. In other words, these registers temporarily hold information while it is being processed by the CPU. Several different types of registers are employed. They include *accumulators, data registers, address registers,* and *general-purpose registers.* It is not important that you know the precise operation of each of these registers for high-level Pascal programming. However, they will become important to you if you ever do any assembly language programming (more about this later).

Primary Memory

Primary memory is often called main working memory. The reason for this is that primary memory is used to store programs and data while they are being "worked," or executed, by the CPU. As Figure 1-3 shows, there are two basic types of primary memory: *random access memory* (RAM) and *read-only memory* (ROM).

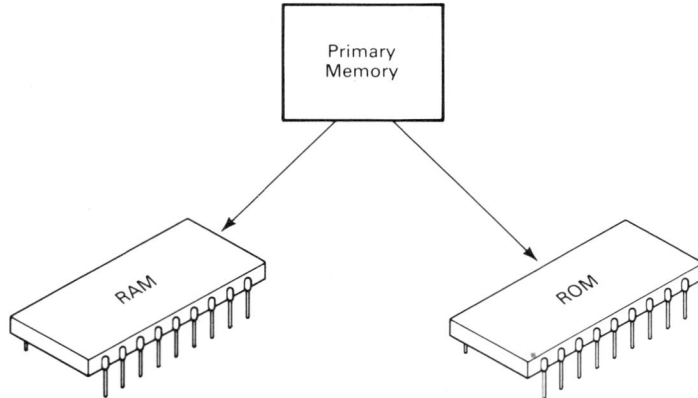

Figure 1-3 Primary memory consists of RAM (user memory) and ROM (system memory).

Random Access Memory (RAM)

Random access memory is memory for you, the user. When you enter a program or data into the system, it goes into RAM. This is why the amount of RAM is often quoted when you buy a computer system. You most likely have heard the terms *64K, 128K, 256K,* and so on, when describing a microcomputer system. This is the amount of RAM, or user memory, that the system contains. Here the letter K stands for the value 1,024. Thus, a 64K system has 64 $\times$ 1,024 = 65,536 *bytes* of RAM, a 128K system has 128 $\times$ 1,024 = 131,072 *bytes* of RAM, and so forth. The more bytes of RAM a system has, the more room there is for your programs and data. As a result, larger and more complex programs can be executed with larger amounts of RAM.

By definition, RAM is *read/write* memory. This means that information can be written into, or stored, into RAM and read, or retrieved, from it. When writing new information into a given area of RAM, any previous information in that area is destroyed. Fortunately, you don't have to worry about this when entering programs, since the system makes sure that the new program information is not written over any important old information.

Once information has been written into RAM, it can be read, or retrieved, by the CPU during program execution. A read operation is nondestructive. Thus, when data is read from RAM, the RAM contents are not destroyed and remain unchanged.

One final point about RAM: It is *volatile.* This means that any information stored in RAM is erased when power is removed from the system. As a result, any programs that you have entered in main working memory (RAM) will be lost when you turn off the system. You must remember to save your programs on a secondary memory device, such as a disk, before turning off the system power.

Read-Only Memory (ROM)

Read-only memory is often called *system memory,* since it stores system-related programs and data. These system programs and data take care of system-related tasks such as reset, cursor control, and binary conversions. All these system programs are part of a larger *operating system* program that is permanently stored in ROM or on a disk. We say that ROM and the operating system programs that it contains are "transparent" to you, the user. The word *transparent* is appropriate, since you do not "see" or concern yourself with the operating system programs during the course of programming in a high-level language, like Pascal.

As its name implies, read-only memory can only be read from and *not* written into. Consequently, information stored in ROM is permanent and cannot be changed. Since the information is permanent, ROM must be *nonvolatile.* This means that any information stored in ROM is not lost when power is removed from the system. Owing to this feature, ROM programs are often called *firmware.*

You might have heard the terms *mask-programmed ROM, EPROM,* or *EEPROM.* These are different forms of ROM that might be part of a system. Mask-programmed ROMs are programmed by the ROM chip manufacturer and can never be altered. EPROM stands for erasable, programmable read-only memory. Information stored in these chips can be erased using ultraviolet light. After erasure, the chip can be reprogrammed. EEPROM stands for electrically erasable, programmable read-only memory. These chips can be erased with electrical signals and reprogrammed.

Both EPROMs and EEPROMs usually are used during the initial development phases of a system. The reason is that any operating system *bugs* can be corrected by reprogramming the EPROM or EEPROM. Once the system is developed and all the bugs are removed, the EPROMs and EEPROMs usually are replaced with less expensive mask-programmed ROMs.

Secondary Memory

Secondary memory, sometimes called *mass storage,* is used to hold programs and data on a semipermanent basis. The most common type of secondary memory used in a microcomputer system is the magnetic floppy disk shown in Figure 1-4. The floppy disk in Figure 1-4 gets its name from the fact that it is flexible, rather than rigid or hard. The disk is coated with a magnetic material and enclosed within a plastic jacket. When inserted into a *disk drive,* the disk is spun by the drive at about 300 rpm. A read/write recording head within the drive reads and writes information on the disk through the access slot, or window, in the disk jacket.

Notice that there is a small write-protect notch on one side of the disk jacket. When covered with a small sticker or piece of tape, new information cannot be written, or recorded, on the disk. This feature is provided so that you can protect the disk from accidental erasure.

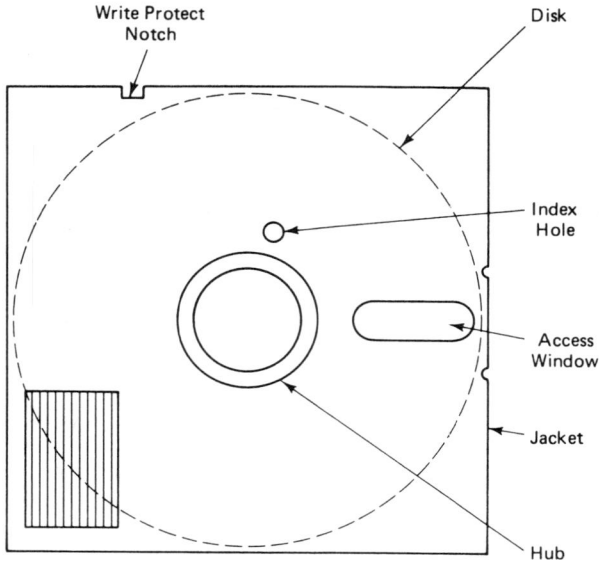

Figure 1-4   Floppy disk.

When writing programs, you will first enter the program code into the system primary memory, or RAM.   When entering TURBO Pascal programs, you must create a *work file* name for the program.   This work file name creates an area, or *file,* on the disk where your program will be saved.   As you enter and work with your program in RAM, you will periodically *save* the program on the disk so that it is permanently stored.   When you save the program, the system simply copies the program from RAM and saves it on the disk under the work file name that you created.   This process is illustrated in Figure 1-5a.

Saving a program on disk allows you to retrieve it easily later.   To read a program from a disk, you simply insert the disk in the disk drive and enter the work file name assigned to the program.   This tells the system to read the work file and transfer it into primary memory (RAM), as illustrated in Figure 1-5b. Once it is in working memory, the program can be executed (run) or changed (edited).   Of course, if any changes are made the program must be saved on disk again so that the changes are also made on the disk.   Refer to Appendix A for details on how to enter, save, and load programs using TURBO Pascal.

Input

Input is what goes into the system.   Input devices are hardware devices that provide a means of inputting programs and data into the system.   The major input device for a microcomputer system such as the one shown in Figure 1-1 is the keyboard.

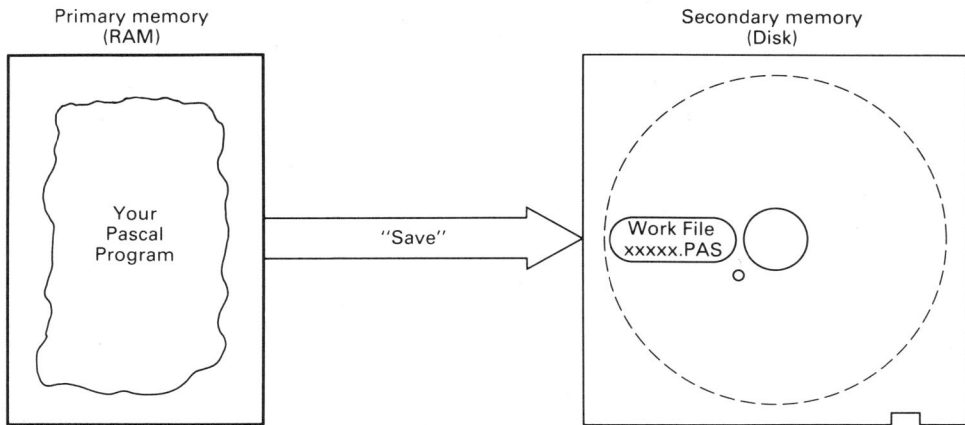

(a)

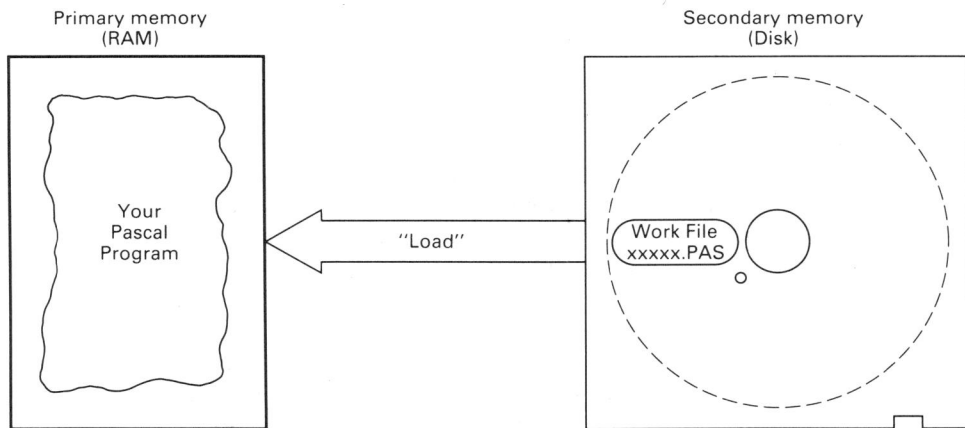

(b)

Figure 1-5   (a) Saving a program on disk and (b) loading a program from disk.

The computer keyboard contains all the characters that are commonly found on a typewriter keyboard.   In addition, there are also special control functions and special control keys that provide for cursor movement.   You should study the operating manual of your particular system so that you understand the function of all the keyboard keys.

The disk drive is another form of input device, since it also provides a means of inputting programs and data into the system.   There are many other types of input devices used with computer systems, but the keyboard and disk drive are the only two devices that you will be using when learning how to write Pascal programs.

CPU

ALU   Control Unit

Execute ③ ← ② Decode

Store ④ → ① Fetch

Main Working
(Primary)
Memory
Program Instructions
and Data

Bus   Bus

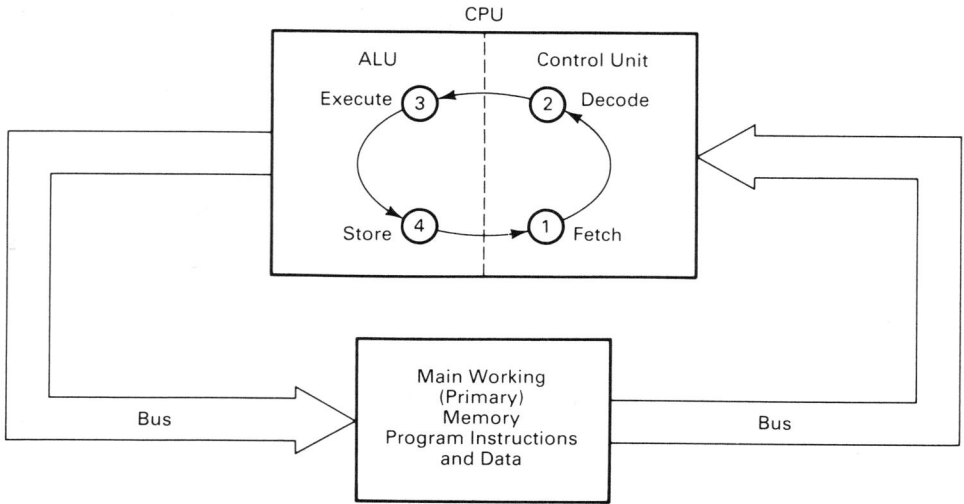

Figure 1-6   The fetch/execute cycle between the CPU and main working memory.

Output

Output is what comes out of the system. Output devices are hardware devices
that provide a means of getting data out of the system. The three major output
devices that you will be concerned with are the CRT screen, the printer, and the
disk drive. The cathode ray tube (CRT) screen allows you to observe programs
and data that are stored in primary memory (RAM).

A printer provides you with a *hard copy* of your programs and data. During
a printing operation, the system actually copies information from primary or secondary memory to the printer. Thus, any information to be printed must be stored
in primary or secondary memory.

Finally, a disk drive is also an output device, since information stored in
primary memory can be written to the disk. You could say that a disk drive is an
input/output (I/O) device, since it provides a means of getting information both in
and out of the system.

The Fetch/Execute Cycle

The *fetch/execute* cycle is what takes place when you *run* a program. To run a
program, you must first enter it into primary memory via the keyboard or load it
from disk. Once in primary memory, the program must be **compiled**. The compiling process is performed by a Pascal compiler, such as TURBO. The compiler
converts the Pascal instructions into a binary machine code that can be executed
by the CPU. In addition, the compiler checks the program for errors and generates

error messages to you via the CRT screen. Your program cannot be run, or executed, until it is free of errors and completely compiled.

Once compiled, the program is *fetched* from primary memory and *executed,* as shown in Figure 1-6. Observe the fetch/execute cycle within the CPU. The control unit first fetches a given program instruction from primary memory. The instruction is then decoded, or translated, to determine what is to be done. Next, the control unit makes available any data required for the operation and directs the ALU to perform the operation. The ALU performs the operation, and the control unit stores the operation results back into primary memory. The resulting data is temporarily stored in primary memory until it is used for another operation or sent to an output device such as a disk or printer. In summary, you can see from Figure 1-6 that the four basic fetch/execute cycle operations are *fetch, decode, execute,* and *store.* That's it in a nutshell!

1-2 THE SOFTWARE

If computer hardware can be likened to an automobile, computer software can be likened to the gas that makes the automobile go. Without this software gas, nothing happens. In other words, the computer hardware by itself can do nothing. The hardware system requires software that provides step-by-step instructions to tell the system what to do. A set of software instructions that tell the computer what to do is called a *computer program.* To communicate instructions to the computer, computer programs are written in different languages. In general, computer languages can be grouped into three major categories: *machine language, assembly language,* and *high-level language.*

Machine Language

All the hardware components in a computer system, including the CPU, operate on a language made up of binary 1s and 0s. They simply do not understand any other language. When a computer is designed, the CPU is designed to interpret a given set of instructions, called the *instruction set.* Each instruction within the instruction set has a unique binary code that can be translated directly by the CPU. This binary code is called *machine code,* and the set of all machine-coded instructions is called *machine language.*

A typical machine language program is provided in Figure 1-7a. To write such a program, you must determine the operation to be performed and then translate the operation into the required binary machine code from a list of instruction-set machine codes provided by the CPU manufacturer: As you might imagine, this is an extremely inefficient process. It is time-consuming, tedious, and subject to a tremendous amount of error. In addition, simple operations, such as multiplication and division, often require several lines of machine code. For these reasons, machine-language programming is rarely used.

```
                                                              •
                                                              •
          •                         •              x: = 2
                               MOVE D1,D2           IF x< = K THEN
    01011011                   ADD   D2,(A1)            x: = x + 1
    00011100                   MUL   D2,(A2)        ELSE
    11011011                   MOVE D2,(A5)             x: = x − 1
          •                         •              FOR Count: = 1 TO N DO
          •                         •                      •
                                                           •
         (a)                       (b)                    (c)
```

Figure 1-7   (a) Machine language, (b) assembly language, and (c) a high-level language.

Assembly Language

Assembly language is a step up from machine language. Rather than using 1s and 0s, assembly language employs alphabetic abbreviations called ***mnemonics*** that are easily remembered by you, the programmer. For instance, the mnemonic for addition is ADD, and the mnemonic for subtraction is SUB. A typical assembly language program is listed in Figure 1-7b.

The assembly language mnemonics provide us with an easier means of writing and interpreting programs. Although assembly language programs are more easily understood by us humans, they cannot be directly understood by the computer hardware. As a result, the assembly language program must be translated into machine code. This is the job of another program, called an ***assembler.*** The assembler program translates your assembly language programs into binary machine code that can be understood and decoded by the CPU.

Although programming in assembly language is easier than machine-language programming, it is not the most efficient means of programming. Assembly language programming is also tedious and prone to error, since there is usually a one-to-one relationship between the mnemonics and corresponding machine code. The solution to these inherent problems of assembly language is found in high-level languages.

High-Level Languages

High-level languages consist of instructions, or statements, that are similar to English and common mathematical notation. A typical series of high-level statements are shown in Figure 1-7c. High-level language statements are very powerful. A typical high-level language statement is equivalent to many machine-code instructions.

High-level languages were developed in the mid-1950s to take some of the work out of programming. When programming in a high-level language, you do not have to concern yourself with the specific instruction set of the CPU. Rather, you can concentrate on solving the problem at hand. Once you learn a given high-level language, you can program any computer that runs that language.

You must be aware that even when programming in a high-level language the system must still translate your instructions into machine code that can be understood by the CPU. Two types of system programs can be employed for this purpose: a *compiler* or an *interpreter*. A compiler is a program that accepts a high-level language program and translates the entire program into machine code all at one time, before it is executed by the CPU. On the other hand, an interpreter translates and executes one high-level statement at a time. Once a given statement has been executed, the interpreter then translates and executes the next statement, and so on, until the entire program has been executed. Although interpreters do have their advantages and are used with many microcomputers, TURBO Pascal employs a compiler. For this reason, let's look a little closer at the operation of a compiler.

The diagram in Figure 1-8 illustrates the basic function of a compiler. Notice that the compiler acts as the *interface* between your program and the machine. Here's how the TURBO Pascal compiler works. Once you have entered a Pascal-language program into the system, you must execute the TURBO compiler to translate your program. As the program is being translated, the compiler checks for certain errors. When a given error is detected, the translation process is halted and the compiler displays an error message. In addition, the compiler places the CRT cursor at the point in your program where the error was detected. You cannot compile your program past this point until the error is corrected. After you correct the error, you must execute the compiler again. Then, when the entire program has been successfully compiled, you can execute, or run, your program. When you run your program after it has been successfully compiled, you actually are executing the machine-language program generated by the compiler. One final point: Your high-level language program is sometimes referred to as a *source program*, and the corresponding machine language program generated by the compiler is called an *object program*.

As you are probably aware, there are several popular high-level languages, including COBOL, FORTRAN, BASIC, LISP, Ada, and Pascal. Each has been developed with a particular application in mind. For instance, COBOL, which stands for COmmon Business Oriented Language, was developed for business

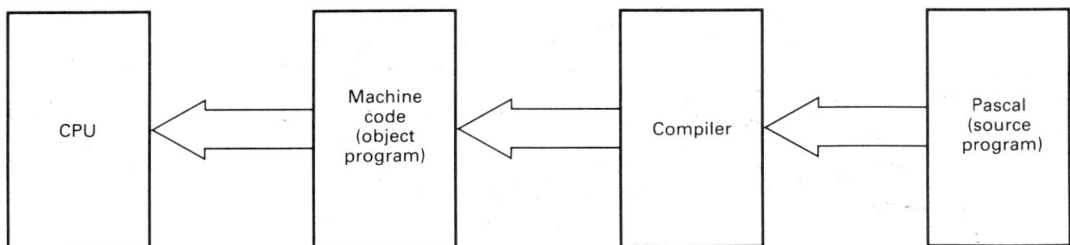

Figure 1-8   The Pascal compiler translates source code into object code to be executed by the CPU.

programming. FORTRAN, which means FORmula TRANslator, was developed for scientific programming. LISP was developed for artificial intelligence programming, and Pascal was developed primarily for education to teach the principles of programming. Let's take a closer look at the Pascal language in general, and TURBO Pascal in particular.

Why Pascal?

Pascal was developed around a need for a high-level programming language that would be efficient, complete, easy to learn, and well suited to *teach* all the fundamental concepts of computer programming. The *teaching* aspects of Pascal are probably the major reason you are presently using it in your classroom. The Pascal language provides an excellent vehicle for your instructor to teach you all the fundamental concepts of computer programming, from good programming style to complex data structures.

Other popular programming languages, such as BASIC, are also used to teach programming. The BASIC language is particularly attractive, since it is easy to learn, can be implemented on small computers, and only uses up a relatively small amount of memory. In fact, many nontechnical students are very proficient with the BASIC language. So you ask: "Why Pascal over BASIC?" The major reason is that BASIC has many limitations owing to its rules of usage, or syntax. It does not lend itself easily to modular, well-structured programs. This is particularly important when writing large, complex programs such as those that are used in industry.

On the other hand, the design of Pascal lends itself to **structured programming**. As you will soon find out, the rules that apply to Pascal force you to write well-organized modular programs that are easy to read, understand, modify, and maintain. Structured modular programs allow you to "divide and conquer" a large, complex programming problem. The idea is to break down the complex problem into a group of simpler subproblems, or modules. Individual program modules, called **subprograms,** are then written to solve the simpler subproblems. The subprogram modules can then be easily combined to solve the overall complex problem. This idea is illustrated by Figure 1-9. A nonstructured language, such as BASIC, provides simple solutions to simple problems. However, nonstructured languages require complex solutions to complex problems because of the lack of modularity, or structure.

You might be wondering how Pascal relates to other popular high-level languages that you might be familiar with. Well, you could say that Pascal loosely resembles FORTRAN or BASIC. However, it employs a much more powerful set of instructions, operates on more types of data, and is more flexible than either of these two languages. Pascal is more like PL/1 and ALGOL (ALGOrithmic Language). In fact, Pascal is a direct descendant of ALGOL.

Pascal was invented in 1970–71 by Professor Niklaus Wirth of the ETH Technical Institute in Zurich, Switzerland. He named the language Pascal in honor

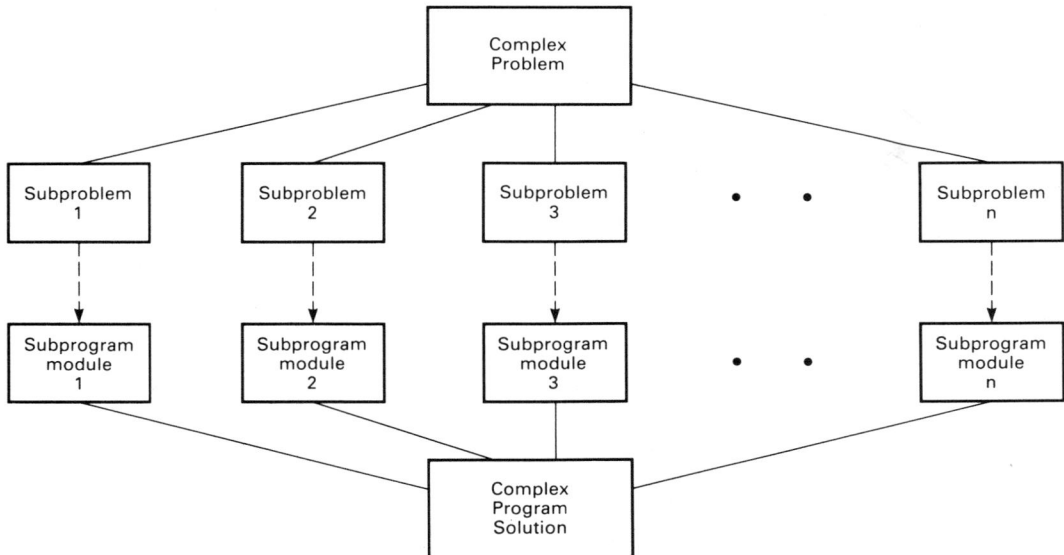

Figure 1-9   The "divide-and-conquer" idea behind a structured programming language, like Pascal.

of the famous seventeenth-century French mathematician Blaise Pascal. Since its introduction, Pascal has become one of the major languages used in the classroom and is catching on rapidly throughout industry, especially in the area of technical programming.

TURBO Pascal

As with any high-level language that survives the test of time, Pascal has many different versions. The original version developed by Professor Wirth is called *Standard Pascal.* All subsequent versions implement Standard Pascal but have included some additional features that might be suited to a particular group of computers, such as microcomputers. One popular version of Pascal is called *UCSD Pascal.* UCSD stands for the University of California at San Diego. Obviously, this is where UCSD was developed. UCSD Pascal is very similar to TURBO Pascal and was the primary version of Pascal used with small computers prior to the introduction of TURBO.

TURBO Pascal was developed by Frank Borland and marketed by his California firm, Borland International. I feel that TURBO is superior to other versions of Pascal because of its compiling efficiency and editing features. In addition, it was developed specifically for the microcomputer market. TURBO can be run on any microcomputer that uses the CP/M or MSDOS operating systems. This includes the majority of microcomputers on the market today, including the IBM

PC and all of its compatibles.   It is hoped that TURBO will also soon be available to run on microcomputers that employ the UNIX operating system.   If you are familiar with microcomputer operating systems, you know that most of the microcomputers on the market today use MSDOS, CP/M, or UNIX.

Just as there are different versions of Pascal, there are different versions of TURBO Pascal.   Each subsequent version provides additional improvements and features.   At this time, you might want to look at Appendix A, which provides an overview of TURBO and explains how to get started with TURBO.   Now, let's begin your learning adventure in programming.

1-3 THE PROGRAMMER'S ALGORITHM

Before we look at the programmer's algorithm, it might be helpful to define what is meant by an algorithm.   In technical terms:

An *algorithm* is a series of step-by-step instructions that produce a result within a finite amount of time.

Algorithms are not unique to the computer industry.   Any set of instructions, such as those you might find in a recipe or a kit assembly guide, can be considered an algorithm.   You will learn how to develop precise computer program algorithms in Section 1-4.   However, before you do this, let's look at a step-by-step procedure that you, the programmer, must use when developing computer programs.   For obvious reasons, I have chosen to call this the *programmer's algorithm*.   The algorithm is as follows:

Step 1: Define the problem.
Step 2: Plan the problem solution.
Step 3: Code the program.
Step 4: Test and debug the program.
Step 5: Document the program.

A graphical representation of an algorithm is called a *flowchart*. A flowchart for the programmer's algorithm is provided in Figure 1-10.

Defining the Problem

You might suggest that this is an obvious step in solving any problem.   However, it often is the most overlooked step, especially in computer programming.   The lack of good problem definition often results in "spinning your wheels," especially in more complex computer-programming applications.

```
┌─────────────────┐
│   Define the    │
│    problem      │
└─────────────────┘
         │
         ▼
┌─────────────────┐
│    Plan the     │
│ problem solution│
└─────────────────┘
         │
         ▼
┌─────────────────┐
│    Code the     │
│    program      │
└─────────────────┘
         │
         ▼
┌─────────────────┐
│  Test and debug │
│       the       │
│    program      │
└─────────────────┘
         │
         ▼
┌─────────────────┐
│  Document the   │
│    program      │
└─────────────────┘
```

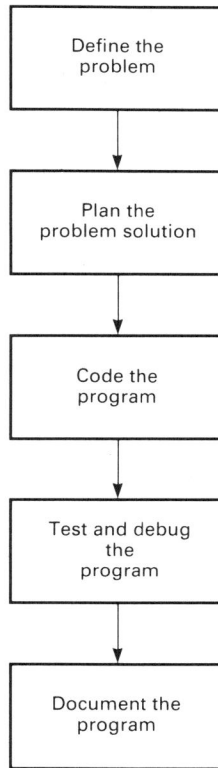

Figure 1-10   A flowchart of the "programmer's algorithm."

Think of a typical computer-programming problem, such as controlling the inventory of a large department store.   What must be considered as part of the problem definition?   The first consideration probably is what you want to get out of the system.   Will the output information consist of printed inventory reports or, in addition, will the system automatically generate product orders based on sales?   Must any information generated by a customer transaction be permanently saved on disk, or can it be discarded?   What type of data is the output information to consist of?   Will it be numerical data, character data, or both?   How must the output data be formatted?   All these questions must be answered in order to define the output requirements.

Careful consideration of the output requirements usually leads you to deciding what must be put into the system to obtain the desired output.   For instance, in our department store inventory example, a desired output would most likely be a summary of customer transactions.   How are these transactions to be input to the system?   Is the input to be obtained from a keyboard, or is product information to be input automatically via an optical character recognition (OCR) system that reads the bar code on the product price tags?   Does the input consist of all numerical data, character data, or a combination of both? What is the format of the input data?

The next consideration is processing. Will most of the customer processing be done at the cash register terminal, or will it be handled by a central store computer? What about credit card verification and inventory records? Will this processing be done by a local microcomputer, a minicomputer located within the store, or a central mainframe computer located in a different part of the country? What kind of programs will be written to do the processing, and who will write them? What sort of calculations and decisions must be made on the input data within individual programs to achieve the desired output?

All these questions must be answered when defining any computer-programming problem. In summary, you could say that problem definition must consider the application requirements of output, input, and processing. The department store inventory problem clearly requires precise definition. However, even with small application programs you must still consider the type of output, input, and processing that the problem requires. The application will always dictate the problem definition. I will discuss problem definition further, as we begin to develop computer programs to solve real problems.

Planning the Solution

The planning stage associated with any problem is probably the most important part of the solution, and computer programming is no exception. Two common ways of planning the solution to a programming problem are (1) to write an algorithm and (2) to construct a flowchart. As you already know, an algorithm is a series of step-by-step instructions that produce results to solve problems. When planning computer programs, algorithms are used to outline the solution steps using English-like statements, called *pseudocode* that require less precision than a formal programming language. A flowchart is simply a graphical representation of an algorithm. A good algorithm or flowchart should be independent of, but easily translated into, *any* formal programming language. You will learn how to develop algorithms and flowcharts in the next section.

Coding the Program

Coding the program should be one of the simplest tasks in the whole programming process, provided you have done a good job defining the problem and planning its solution. Coding involves the actual writing of the program in a formal programming language. The computer language you use will be determined by the nature of the problem, the programming languages available to you, and the limits of the computer system. Once a language is chosen, the program is written, or coded, by simply translating your algorithm steps into the formal language code. In this text you will code programs using the Pascal programming language.

I should caution you, however, that coding is a mechanical process and should be considered secondary to algorithm development. In the future, computers will generate their own program code from well-constructed algorithms. Research in the field of artificial intelligence has resulted in such computers. The thing to keep in mind is that computers might someday generate their own programming code from algorithms, but it takes the creativity and common sense of a human being to plan the solution and develop the algorithm.

Testing and Debugging the Program

You will soon find out that it is a rare and joyous occasion when a coded program actually "runs" the first time without any errors. Of course, good problem definition and planning will avoid many program mistakes, or "bugs." However, there always are a few bugs that manage to go undetected, regardless of how much planning you do. Getting rid of the program bugs (debugging) is often the most time-consuming job in the whole programming process. Industrial statistics show that over 50 percent of a programmer's time is often spent on program debugging.

When programming in Pascal, there are three things that you can do to test and debug your program: ***desk-checking*** the program, ***compiling*** the program, and ***running*** the program.

Desk-checking the Program

Desk-checking a program is similar to proofreading a letter or manuscript. The idea is to trace the program mentally to make sure that the program logic is workable. You must consider various input possibilities and write down any results generated during program execution. In particular, try to determine what the program will do with unusual data by considering input possibilities that "shouldn't" happen. Always keep Murphy's law in mind when desk-checking a program. If a given condition can't or shouldn't happen, it will!

For example, suppose a program requires the user to input a value whose square root must be found. Of course, the user "shouldn't" input a negative value, since the square root of a negative number is imaginary. However, what will the program do if he or she does? Another input possibility that should always be considered is an input of zero. This is especially important if the input value is to be used in a division operation.

When you first begin programming, you will be tempted to skip the desk-checking phase, since you can't wait to run the program once it is written. However, as you gain experience, you soon will realize the time-saving value of desk-checking.

Compiling the Program

Now you are ready to enter the program into the computer system. Once entered, the program must be compiled, or translated, into machine code. Fortunately, the compiler is designed to check for certain program errors. These usually are *syntax errors* that you have made when coding the program. A syntax error is any violation of the rules of the programming language, such as using a period instead of a semicolon.

During the compiling process, the TURBO Pascal compiler will generate error messages as well as position the CRT cursor to the point in the program where the error was detected. If you cannot understand a given error message, you will need to consult your compiler reference manual for further explanation of the message. In our case, the TURBO Pascal reference manual must be consulted. The program will not compile beyond the point of the error until it is corrected. Once an error is corrected, you must attempt to compile the program again. If another error is detected, it must be corrected, the program must be recompiled, and so on, until the entire program is successfully compiled.

Running the Program

Once compiled, you must execute, or run, the program. However, just because the program has been compiled successfully doesn't mean that it will run successfully under all possible conditions. Common bugs that occur at this stage include *infinite loops* and *run-time* errors. An infinite loop occurs when the program tells the computer to repeat an operation but does not tell it how to stop repeating. Such a bug will not cause an error message to be generated, since the computer is simply doing what it was told to do. The program execution must be stopped and debugged before it can run successfully.

A run-time error occurs when the program attempts to perform an illegal operation, as defined by the laws of mathematics or the particular system in use. Two common mathematical run-time errors are division by zero and attempting to take the square root of a negative number. A common error imposed by the system compiler is an integer value out of range. The TURBO Pascal compiler limits integers to a range of $-32,768$ to $+32,767$.

Fortunately, the program is automatically aborted and an error message is displayed when a run-time error occurs. Again, you should consult your compiler reference manual to determine the exact nature of the problem. The error must be located and corrected before another attempt is made to run the program.

A word from experience: Always go about debugging your programs in a systematic, common-sense manner. Don't be tempted to change something just because you "hope" it will work and don't know what else to do. Use your resources to isolate and correct the problem. Such resources include your algorithm, a program listing, your TURBO reference manual, this textbook, and your instructor, just to mention a few. Run-time errors are usually the result of a serious flaw in your program. They will not go away and cannot be corrected by blindly making changes to your program.

Documentation

This final step in the programmer's algorithm is often overlooked, but it probably is one of the more important steps, especially in commercial programming. Documentation is easy if you have done a good job of defining the problem, planning the solution, coding, testing, and debugging the program. The final program documentation is simply the recorded result of these programming steps. At a minimum, good documentation should include the following:

- A narrative description of the problem definition including the type of input, output, and processing employed by the program
- An algorithm or flowchart or both
- A program listing
- Samples of input and output data
- Testing and debugging results
- User instructions

The documentation must be neat and well organized. It must be easily understood by you as well as any other person who might have a need to use or modify your program in the future. What good is an ingenious program if no one can determine what it does or how to use it?

One final point: Documentation should always be an ongoing process. Whenever you work with the program or modify it, make sure the documentation is updated to reflect your experiences and modifications.

1-4 DEVELOPING ALGORITHMS

In the previous section, you learned that an algorithm is simply a sequence of step-by-step instructions that will produce a solution to a problem in a finite amount of time. It is now time for you to learn how to develop algorithms in preparation for coding Pascal programs.

You could say that nearly any sequence of step-by-step instructions can be classified as an algorithm. For instance, consider the following series of instructions:

> Apply to wet hair.
> Gently massage lather through hair.
> Rinse, keeping lather out of eyes.
> Repeat.

Look familiar? Of course, this is a series of instructions that might be found on the back of a shampoo bottle. But does it fit the technical definition of an algorithm?   In other words, does it produce a result in a finite amount of time? You might say yes, but look closer.   Since the algorithm requires that you keep repeating the procedure an infinite number of times, theoretically you would never stop shampooing your hair!   To fit our technical definition of an algorithm, the procedure must terminate in a finite amount of time.   The repeat instruction could be altered easily to make the shampooing algorithm technically correct:

> Repeat until hair is clean.

Now the shampooing process can be terminated.   Of course, you must be the one to decide when your hair is clean.

The foregoing shampoo analogy might seem a bit trivial.   You probably are thinking that any intelligent person would not keep on repeating the shampooing process an infinite number of times, right?   This obviously is the case when we humans are executing the algorithm, because we have some common-sense judgment.   But what about a computer?   Most computers do exactly what they are told to do via the computer program.   As a result, a computer would repeat the original shampooing algorithm over and over, an infinite number of times.   This is why the algorithms that you write for computer programs must be precise.

Now let's develop an algorithm for a process that is common to all of us: mailing a letter.   Think of the steps that are involved in this simple process.   You must first address an envelope, fold the letter, insert the letter in the envelope, and seal the envelope, right?   Next, you need a stamp.   If you don't have a stamp, you have to buy one.   Once a stamp is obtained, you must place it on the envelope and mail the letter.   The following algorithm summarizes the steps in this process:

> BEGIN
>   Obtain an envelope.
>   Address the envelope.
>   Fold the letter.
>   Insert the letter in the envelope.
>   Seal the envelope.
>   If you don't have a stamp, buy one.
>   Place the stamp on the envelope.
>   Mail the letter.
> END.

Does this sequence of instructions fit our technical definition of an algorithm? In other words, does the sequence of instructions produce a result in a finite amount of time?   Yes—assuming that each operation can be understood and carried out by the person mailing the letter.   This brings up two additional characteristics of good algorithms: each operation within the algorithm must be *well defined* and *effective*.   By well defined, I mean that each of the steps must be clearly understood by the person or machine executing the algorithm.   By effective, I mean that some means must exist to carry out the operation.   In other words, the person mailing the letter must be able to perform each of the algorithm steps.   In the case of a computer program algorithm, the machine must have the means of executing each operation in the algorithm.

In summary, a good computer algorithm must possess the following three attributes:

1. Employ well-defined instructions that can be easily understood by the machine executing the algorithm
2. Employ instructions that can be effectively carried out by the machine executing the algorithm
3. Produce a solution to the problem in a finite amount of time

To write computer program algorithms, we need to establish a set of well-defined, effective operations.   The set of operations listed in Table 1-2 will make up our *algorithmic language*.   We will use these operations from now on, whenever we write computer algorithms.

Notice that the operations in Table 1-2 are grouped into three major categories: *sequence, decision,* and *iteration*.   These categories are called *control structures*.   The sequence control structure includes those operations that produce a single action or result.   As its name implies, the decision control structure includes the decision-making operations.   Finally, the iteration control structure includes those operations that are used for looping, or repeating, operations within the algorithm.   Many of the operations listed in Table 1-2 are self-explanatory.   Those that are not will be discussed in detail as we begin to develop more complex algorithms.

TABLE 1-2 ALGORITHMIC LANGUAGE
OPERATIONS USED IN THIS TEXT

Sequence	Decision	Iteration
Begin	If/Then	While/Do
End	If/Then/Else	Repeat/Until
Set or Assign	Case of	For/Do
Read		
Write		
Calculate		
Add		
Subtract		
Multiply		
Divide		
Increment		
Decrement		
Print		

Flowcharts

You learned earlier that a flowchart is simply a graphical representation of an algorithm. In flowcharts, the algorithm is constructed by connecting boxes of different shapes. Each shape has a given meaning, as shown in Figure 1-11. These flowchart symbols are standardized throughout the industry and are called ANSI (American National Standards Institute) symbols. You should be aware that there are many more ANSI symbols than those shown in Figure 1-11; however, these are the most common.

The flowchart in Figure 1-12 is a graphical representation of the letter-mailing algorithm we developed earlier. Observe that the algorithmic instructions are simply repeated inside the corresponding flowchart symbol. As you can see, a rectangle is used to represent the sequence operations, and a diamond is used to represent the decision-making operation. The arrows in the chart indicate the direction of program flow. A circle, or connector, is used when any two or more paths must be connected together.

Your instructor will most likely choose which way you should construct your algorithms: using algorithmic language or flowcharts. I will use both methods in the beginning of this text, so that you can get comfortable with each. Then, as

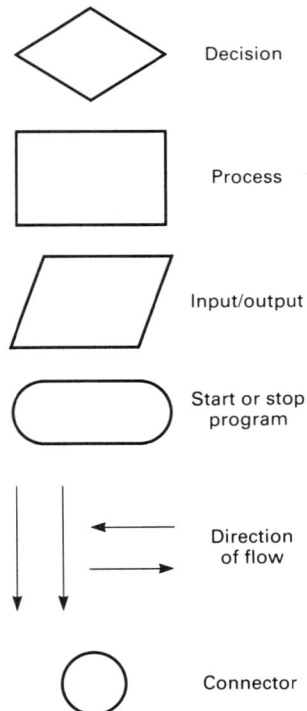

Decision

Process

Input/output

Start or stop
program

Direction
of flow

Connector   **Figure 1-11** The most common ANSI
flowchart symbols.

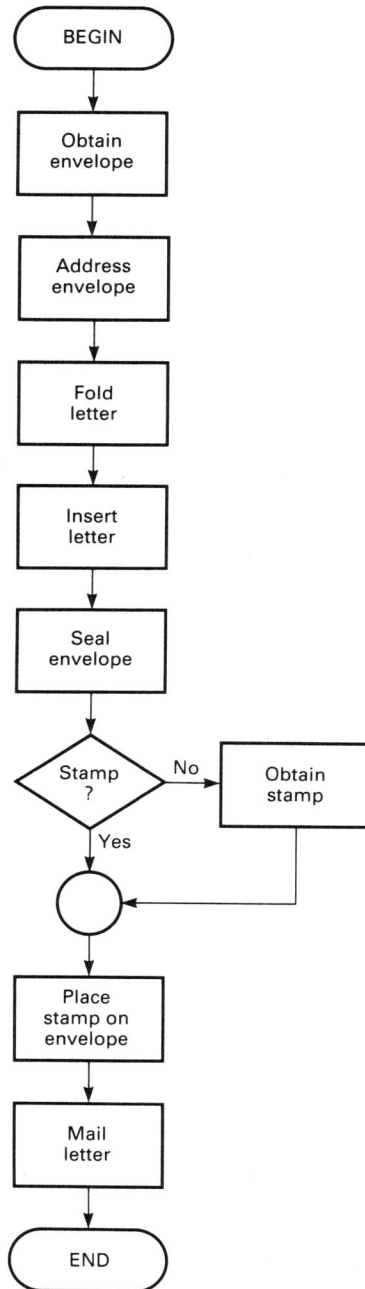

Figure 1-12 A flowchart of the letter-mailing algorithm.

the programming problems get more complex, I will only use algorithmic language. The reason for this is that Pascal programs can be very easily coded from algorithmic language. In addition, flowcharts begin to get a bit messy and extremely difficult to comprehend as programming problems get more complex.

Now, let's develop some algorithms for real programming problems through the following series of examples:

Example 1-1:

Develop an algorithm to find the hypotenuse of a right triangle using the Pythagorean theorem. Construct the algorithm using both the algorithmic instructions listed in Table 1-2 and the flowchart symbols shown in Figure 1-11.

Solution:

Defining the Problem
When defining the problem, you must consider three things: output, input, and processing as related to the problem statement. Recall that a right triangle has two right-angle sides and a hypotenuse. Let's label the two sides A and B, and the hypotenuse H. The problem requires us to find the hypotenuse (H), given the two sides (A and B). So, the output must be the hypotenuse (H). To obtain this output, the sides A and B must be input to the program.

The Pythagorean theorem states that the hypotenuse is equal to the square root of the sum of the squares of the two sides. In symbols,

$$H = \sqrt{A^2 + B^2}$$

This equation represents the processing that must be performed by the computer. Now that the problem has been defined in terms of output, input, and processing, it is time to plan the solution by developing an algorithm.

Planning the Solution: The Algorithm
In Table 1-2 you will find two sequence operations called read and write. The read operation is an input operation. We will assume that this operation will input data entered via a keyboard. The write operation is an output operation. We will assume that this operation causes information to be displayed on the CRT terminal. With this in mind, the algorithm for the right triangle problem is as follows:

BEGIN
    Write a program description message to the user.
    Write a user-prompt message to enter the first side of the triangle (A).
    Read (A).
    Write a user-prompt message to enter the second side of the triangle (B).
    Read (B).
    Square A and B.
    Calculate the hypotenuse: $H = \sqrt{A^2 + B^2}$.
    Write the hypotenuse (H).
END.

The corresponding flowchart is shown in Figure 1-13. Observe that the algorithm statements are simply abbreviated within the respective flowchart symbols.

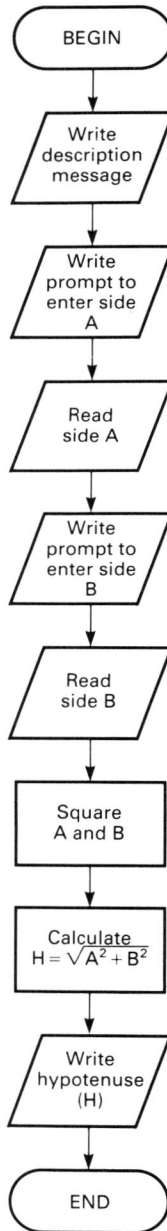

Figure 1-13 A flowchart for the right triangle problem in Example 1-1.

The foregoing example illustrates some operations that result in good programming style. Notice that the first write operation is to write a program description message to the person running the program—the user. It is good practice always to include such a message so that the user understands what the program will do. In addition, the second write operation will display a message to tell the user to "enter the first side of the triangle (A)." Without such a *prompt*, the user will not know what to do. You must write a user prompt message anytime the user must input data via the keyboard. Such a message should tell the user what is to be entered and in what format the information is to be entered. (More about this later.) Here's another example.

EXAMPLE 1-2:

Develop an algorithm to find the voltage output of the voltage divider circuit shown in Figure 1-14. Allow the user to input the source voltage (V_{source}) and the two resistors, R_1 and R_2. Use the algorithmic instructions listed in Table 1-2 and the flowchart symbols in Figure 1-11.

Solution

Defining the Problem

The problem requires us to find the voltage output of a voltage divider circuit. From the problem statement and circuit diagram in Figure 1-14, it is obvious that the program output must be the output voltage V_{out}, and the inputs must be the source voltage (V_{source}) and the two resistor values (R_1 and R_2). Now, from basic dc circuit analysis, you know that the output of a voltage divider can be found using the following voltage divider equation:

$$V_{out} = \frac{R_2}{R_1 + R_2} \times V_{source}$$

Thus, the computer must use this equation to process the input information.

Planning the Solution: The Algorithm

Using the foregoing problem definition, we are now ready to write the algorithm as follows:

BEGIN
    Write a program description message to the user.
    Write a user prompt to enter the source voltage value (V_{source}).
    Read (V_{source}).
    Write a user prompt to enter the first resistor value (R_1).
    Read (R_1).
    Write a user prompt to enter the second resistor value (R_2).
    Read (R_2).
    Calculate the output voltage:

$$V_{out} = \frac{R_2}{R_1 + R_2} \times V_{source}$$

    Write the output voltage (V_{out}).
END.

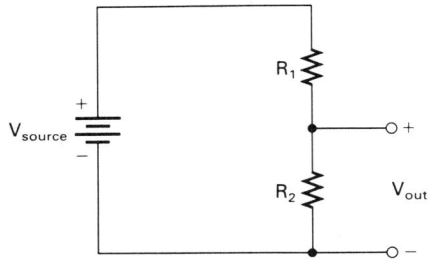

Figure 1-14 A voltage divider circuit for Example 1-2.

The corresponding flowchart is shown in Figure 1-15. As you can see, the algorithm and flowchart show three separate input operations to get the required data into the system. Separate operations are used for each input to make the program clearer and easier to use. Once the inputs have been obtained, they are processed using the voltage divider equation. The resulting voltage is then output to the CRT screen.

CHAPTER SUMMARY

Any computer system can be broken down into two major components: hardware and software. Hardware consists of the physical devices required to make up the machine, and software consists of the instructions that tell the hardware what to do.

There are five functional parts that make up the system hardware: the CPU, primary memory, secondary memory, input, and output. The CPU directs and coordinates the activity of the entire system as instructed by the software. Primary memory consists of user memory (RAM) and system memory (ROM). Secondary memory is usually magnetic and is used to store programs and data on a semipermanent basis. Input is what goes into the system via hardware input devices, such as a keyboard. Output is what comes out of the system via hardware output devices, such as a CRT screen or printer.

There are three major levels of software: machine language, assembly language, and high-level language. Machine language is the lowest level, since it consists of binary 1s and 0s that can only be easily understood by the CPU. Assembly language consists of alphabetic instruction abbrevations that are easily understood by the programmer but must be translated into machine code for the CPU by a system program called an assembler. High-level languages consist of English-like statements that simplify the task of programming. However, to be understood by the CPU, high-level language programs must still be translated to machine code using a compiler or interpreter.

The five major steps that must be performed when writing a program are (1) define the problem, (2) plan the problem solution, (3) code the program, (4) test and debug the program, and (5) document the program. When defining the

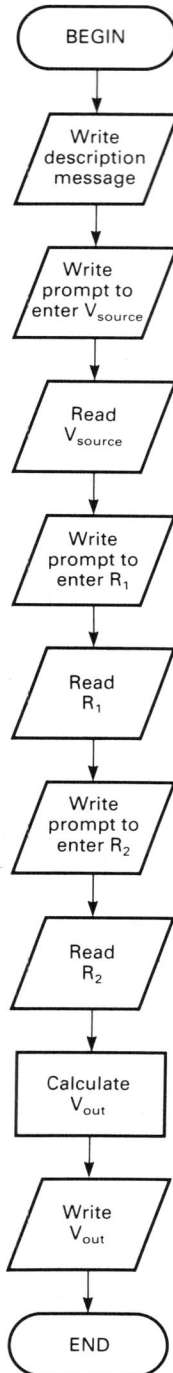

Figure 1-15 A flowchart for the voltage divider algorithm in Example 1-2.

problem, you must consider the output, input, and processing requirements of the application.   Planning the problem solution requires that you specify the problem solution steps via an algorithm or flowchart.   An algorithm is a series of step-by-step instructions that provide a solution to the problem in a finite amount of time. A flowchart is a graphical representation of an algorithm.   Once an algorithm or flowchart is constructed, it must be coded into some formal language that the computer system can understand.   The language used in this text is Pascal.   Once coded, the program must be tested and debugged through desk-checking, compiling, and execution.   Finally, the entire programming process, from problem definition to testing and debugging, must be documented so that it can be easily understood by you or anyone else working with it.

QUESTIONS AND PROBLEMS

Questions

1-1. Name the three operational regions of a CPU and explain their function.

1-2. Explain what is meant by the term *volatile* and how it relates to computer memory.

1-3. Another name for software located in read-only memory (ROM) is _____ _____ .

1-4. A floppy disk is a form of _____ memory.

1-5. Name the three levels of software and describe the general characteristics of each.

1-6. Explain the operational difference between a compiler and an interpreter.

1-7. An interpreter or compiler translates a _____ program into an _____ program.

1-8. What is a structured language and what advantages does such a language have over a nonstructured language?

1-9. Define an algorithm.

1-10. List the five steps of the programmer's algorithm.

1-11. What three things must be considered during the problem definition phase of programming?

1-12. What vehicle(s) are used for planning the solution to a programming problem?

1-13. The writing of a program is called _____ .

1-14. State three things that you can do to test and debug your programs.

1-15. List the minimum items required for good documentation.

1-16. What three attributes must a good computer algorithm possess?

1-17. A graphical representation of an algorithm is called a _____ .

1-18. The three major control structures of a structured programming language are _____ , _____ , and _____ .

Problems

1-1. Develop an algorithm to compute the sum, difference, product, and quotient of any two integers.

1-2. Revise the algorithm in problem 1 to protect it from a divide-by-zero run-time error.

1-3. Develop an algorithm to calculate voltage from input current and resistor values using Ohm's law.

1-4. Recall that the resistance of a conductor can be calculated based on its material composition and size using the following equation:

$$R = \rho \frac{l}{A}$$

where R is the conductor resistance in ohms.
  ρ is the resistivity of the conductor.
  l is the length of the conductor in meters.
  A is the cross-sectional area of the conductor in square meters.

Develop an algorithm to calculate the resistance of any size copper conductor, assuming that the user inputs the conductor length and cross-sectional area. (*Note*: The resistivity factor for copper is 1.72×10^{-8}.)

1-5. Revise the algorithm in problem 4, assuming that the user enters the conductor length in inches and cross-sectional area in square inches.

1-6. Develop an algorithm that will allow the input of three integer coefficients of a quadratic equation and output the roots of the equation. Provide for an error message if complex roots exist.

chapter two

Getting Acquainted with Pascal

INTRODUCTION

Now you are ready to begin learning the building blocks of the Pascal language. As you already know, Pascal is a very structured language—from the top down. Although it might seem cumbersome at first, this structure makes Pascal programs very readable, efficient, and powerful.

You will get your first exposure to the structure of Pascal in this chapter as you learn about the various data types that are operated upon by the language. Data is any information that must be processed by the Pascal program. However, before Pascal can process any information, it must know what type of data it is dealing with. As a result, any information processed by Pascal must be categorized into one of the legal data types defined for Pascal.

The data types that you will learn about in this chapter are the integer, real, character, string, and Boolean data types. It is important that you understand this idea of data typing, since it is one of the most important concepts in Pascal. Once you learn the general characteristics of each data type, you will learn how to declare, or define, different types of data for use in a Pascal program. Finally, you will look at the overall structure of a complete Pascal program and begin writing your own programs.

2-1 THE IDEA OF DATA TYPES

Just as Pascal programs are highly structured and modular, so are the data that the programs operate on. You might be thinking: "Data are data—how can there be different types of data?" First, you must think of data as any information that the computer might manipulate or perform operations on. So, let's define a *data element* to be any information item that is manipulated or operated on by the computer. Now, think about the types of information, or data elements, that the computer manipulates. Of course, a computer manipulates numbers, or *numeric data.* One of the primary uses of a computer is to perform calculations on numeric data, right? But what about letters, called *characters*? Isn't the computer operating with character data when it prints out your name? Thus, numeric data and character data are two different *types* of data. What makes them different? Well, numeric data consists of numbers, whereas character data consists of letters. In other words, each data type (numeric or character) consists of a set of data elements that more or less "belong with each other." This will form our definition of a *data type.*

Now for the big surprise: There are more than just numeric and character data types defined for Pascal. The diagram in Figure 2-1 shows all the various types of data that can be used in Pascal programming. First, observe that there are three major data-type classifications: *scalar, structured,* and *pointer.*

Scalar data types are those whose data elements are *ordered.* By ordering, I mean that given two elements in the data type, one element is either equal to (=), greater than (>), or less than (<) the other element. Numeric data, such as integer and real numbers, are clearly scalar data types, since all numbers have this ordering property. You will soon find out that characters are also ordered and are thus considered a scalar data type.

Observe also from the diagram that scalar data types can be *standard* or *user-defined.* Standard data types are those that are predefined, or "built-in," in the Pascal language. These consist of integer numbers and real numbers, as well as character and Boolean data. These built-in standard data types are all discussed in the next section.

User-defined data types are those that you, the user of Pascal, must define to meet a given application problem. In other words, a user-defined data type is a set of related data elements that you will create within your Pascal program for a specific purpose. For example, you might want to define the set of all the days of the week (Sun, Mon, Tue, Wed, Thur, Fri, Sat) as a user-defined data type in your program. Here, the data elements are the individual days and are ordered from Sunday through Saturday. As a result, these elements can be manipulated within your program similarly to the standard data types. At first, the idea of creating your own set of data elements might seem foreign to you, but you will soon see how this can be a powerful tool when programming in Pascal. You will learn more about user-defined data types later in this text.

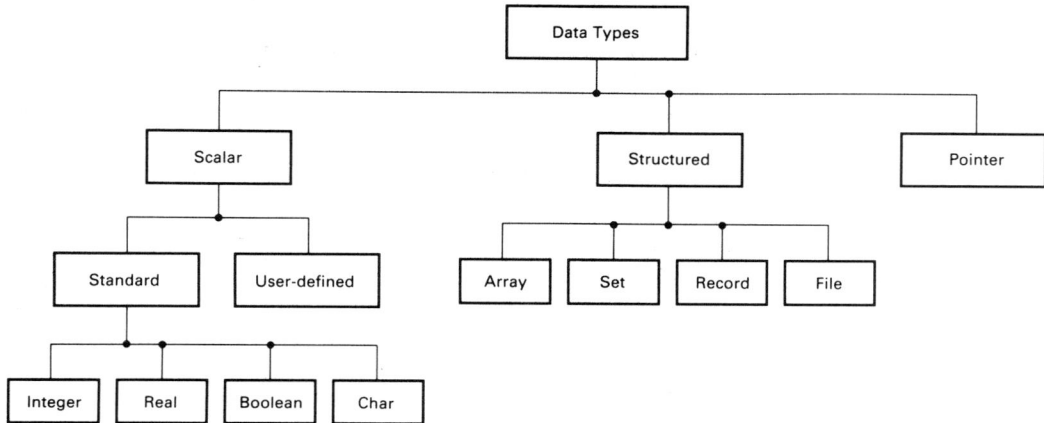

Figure 2-1 Data organization of a structured language.

The structured data-type category consists of data structures called **arrays, sets, records,** and **files.** These data types are complex data types, in the sense that they are made up of other data types. As an example, your name, address, and telephone number combine to form a record. This record obviously consists of integers and characters, both of which are simple data types. In other words, structured data types are formed using combinations of the simple scalar types as building blocks. In this text, you will learn about arrays, since they have many technical applications. In addition, you will learn about records and files.

Pointer data types are used to form data structures called **stacks, queues, linked lists,** and **trees.** These data structures are beyond the scope of an introductory text such as this one.

2-2 STANDARD DATA TYPES

Recall that standard data types are ordered, or scalar, data types that are built into Pascal. This built-in feature simply means that the Pascal compiler recognizes any legal elements contained in a standard data type. There are four standard data types that we need to discuss: **integer, real, character,** and **Boolean.**

The Integer Data Type

As you know, integers are the whole numbers. They may be positive, negative, or 0. In an algebra course, you most likely learned that there are no theoretical limits to the integers. They can range from minus infinity ($-\infty$) to plus infinity

$(+\infty)$. However, there are practical limits in the real world of computers. In Pascal, the largest possible integer value is called *MAXINT*, and the smallest possible integer value is $-MAXINT - 1$. The actual numeric value of *MAXINT* depends on the Pascal compiler being used. For example, in TURBO Pascal $MAXINT = +32767$ and $-MAXINT - 1 = -32767 - 1 = -32768$. So, the integer data type in TURBO Pascal consists of all the whole numbers from -32768 through $+32767$. In symbols:

INTEGERS IN TURBO **
$-32768, -32767, \ldots, 0, \ldots, 32766, 32767$
****

Example 2-1:

Which of the following are *not* legal integer data-type elements in TURBO Pascal?
a. $+35$
b. 35
c. -247
d. 0
e. 3.14
f. 32,767
g. 32768

Solution: The values in a, b, c, and d are all legal integer elements in Pascal, since they are all whole numbers within the defined range of integers. Notice that $+35$ and 35 are both legal representations of the integer value 35.

The values in e, f, and g are not legal integer elements in TURBO Pascal. The value 3.14 is not an integer because it is not a whole number. The value 32,767 is an integer within the predefined range but is not legal in Pascal, since it contains a comma. Commas are **not allowed** as part of numeric values in Pascal. Finally, the value 32768 is not a legal integer element in TURBO Pascal, since it is outside of the predefined integer range.

You must be especially aware of the integer range limits imposed by Pascal when performing integer calculations within your Pascal programs. For example, multiplying two integers could easily produce an integer result beyond this range, resulting in an incorrect result. This is called an *overflow* condition. Depending on where it occurs, an overflow condition might or might not generate an error message during program compiling or execution. Even if no overflow error message is generated, the operation will produce an incorrect result. The solution to this dilemma is found in the next standard Pascal data type: the reals.

Example 2-2:

Which of the following integer operations will generate an overflow condition in TURBO Pascal? (Assume that the * symbol means multiplication and the word **DIV** means division.)
a. 32 * 1000
b. 100 * 1000
c. (100 * 1000) **DIV** 5

Solution:
a. 32 * 1000 = 32000, which is within the predefined integer range. No overflow condition exists.
b. 100 * 1000 = 100000, which is outside the predefined integer range. The overflow condition will generate an incorrect integer result.
c. (100 * 1000) **DIV** 5 = 100000 **DIV** 5 = 20000. Although the final result is within the predefined integer range, an overflow condition will occur, thereby generating an incorrect result. Why? Because the multiplication operation in the numerator results in a value outside the integer range.

Integers in Later Versions in TURBO

Later versions of TURBO Pascal (beyond Version 3) actually support five different integer data types. They are ***byte, shortint, integer, word,*** and ***longint.*** The numeric ranges for these various integer data types are shown in Table 2-1. The byte and integer data types are available in most other versions of Pascal, including all versions of TURBO Pascal. In this text the standard integer data type will satisfy most of our applications. However, shortint, word, and longint are all new and unique to TURBO 4.0 and subsequent versions. The longint data type is especially advantageous in preventing overflow errors. If you are using a later version of TURBO, you will want to consider its use when the chance for an overflow error exists.

The Real Data Type

Real numbers include all the whole number integers as well as any value between two whole numbers that must be represented using decimal-point notation. Examples include the following:

$$3.14$$

$$-2.56$$

$$0.0$$

$$1.414$$

$$-3.0$$

All the foregoing numbers have been written using decimal-point notation. Decimal-point notation requires a sign, followed by an integer, followed by a decimal point, followed by another unsigned integer. This format is as follows:

DECIMAL FORMAT FOR A REAL NUMBER **
(+ or − sign) (integer)·(integer)
Note: The + sign is optional if the value is positive.
****

TABLE 2-1 INTEGER DATA TYPES IN
LATER VERSIONS OF TURBO

Type	Range
Byte	0 to 255
Shortint	−128 to 127
Integer	−32768 to 32767
Word	0 to 65535
Longint	−2147483648 to 2147483647

Another way to represent very large and very small real numbers is with scientific notation, sometimes called *exponential format*. With this notation, the real number is written as a decimal point value multiplied by a power of ten. The general format is as follows:

EXPONENTIAL FORMAT FOR A REAL NUMBER ✳✳✳✳✳✳✳✳✳✳✳✳✳✳✳✳✳✳✳✳✳✳✳✳✳✳✳✳✳✳✳✳✳✳✳✳✳✳
(+ or − sign)(decimal point value)E(integer exponent value)
Note: The + sign is optional if the value is positive.
✳✳✳

Examples of real numbers using this format include

$$1.32E3$$

$$0.45E-6$$

$$-35.02E-4$$

$$-1.333E7$$

Here, the letter E means "times 10 to the power of." The letter E is used because there is no provision on a standard computer keyboard to type above a line to show exponent values. Again, the + sign is optional for both the decimal-point value and the exponent value when they are positive.

Example 2-3:

Convert the following exponential values to decimal values.
a. 1.32E3
b. 0.45E−6
c. −35.02E−4
d. −1.333E7

Solution:

a. $1.32E3 = 1.32 \times 10^3 = 1320.0$
b. $0.45E-6 = 0.45 \times 10^{-6} = 0.00000045$
c. $-35.02E-4 = -35.02 \times 10^{-4} = -0.003502$
d. $-1.333E7 = -1.333 \times 10^7 = -13330000.0$

TABLE 2-2 COMMON
PREFIXES USED IN
ELECTRONICS

Prefix	Symbol	Meaning
pico-	p	10^{-12}
nano-	n	10^{-9}
micro-	μ	10^{-6}
milli-	m	10^{-3}
kilo-	k	10^{3}
mega-	M	10^{6}
giga-	G	10^{9}

You might be wondering if there is any practical limit to the range of real numbers that can be used in Pascal. In TURBO Pascal, the decimal-point value cannot exceed eleven digits. In addition, when using exponential notation, the exponent range is $1E-38$ through $1E+38$ (1×10^{-38} through 1×10^{38}). If an arithmetic operation results in a value smaller than $1E-38$, no error will occur, but the result is rounded-off to 0. If an arithmetic operation results in a value larger than 1E38, an overflow run-time error occurs and the program halts its execution.

Example 2-4:

In electronics, you often see electrical quantities expressed using the prefixes in Table 2-2. Given the following electrical quantities,

220 picofarads (pF)
1 kilohm (kΩ)
10 megohms (MΩ)
1.25 milliampere (mA)
25.3 microvolts (μV)
300 nanoamperes (nA)

a. Express each of the listed quantities in exponential form
b. Express each of the listed quantities in decimal form

Solution:

a. To express in exponential form you simply convert the prefix to its respective power of 10 using Table 2-2. Then use the E notation to write the value:
220 pF $= 220E-12$ F
1 kΩ $= 1E3$ Ω
10 MΩ $= 10E6$ Ω
1.25 mA $= 1.25E-3$ A
25.3 μV $= 25.3E-6$ V
300 nA $= 300E-9$ A

b. To express each in its decimal form simply move the decimal point according to the exponent value.

220 pF = 220E − 12 F = 0.000000000220 F

1 kΩ = 1E3 Ω = 1000.0 Ω

10 MΩ = 10E6 Ω = 10000000.0 Ω

1.25 mA = 1.25E − 3 A = 0.00125 A

25.3 μV = 25.3E − 6 V = 0.0000253 V

300 nA = 300E − 9 A = 0.000000300 A

Example 2-5:

Pascal includes two *standard functions* called *Sqr*(R) and *Sqrt*(R). A standard function is a predefined operation that the Pascal compiler will recognize and evaluate to return a result. The *Sqr*(R) and *Sqrt*(R) functions are used to find the square and square root, respectively, of a real number (R). Knowing this, determine the result of the following operations:

a. *Sqr*(25)
b. *Sqrt*(25)
c. *Sqrt*(− 25)
d. *Sqr*(4E20)
e. *Sqrt*(4E − 20)

Solution:

a. *Sqr*(25) = 25^2, or 625
b. *Sqrt*(25) = $\sqrt{25}$ = 5.0000000000E + 00
   Notice that this function generates a real-number result using exponential notation.
c. *Sqrt*(− 25) is imaginary and will generate a run-time error when encountered during a program execution.
d. *Sqr*(4E20) is beyond the predefined range for reals and will result in a run-time error during program execution.
e. *Sqrt*(4E − 20) = 2.0000000000E − 10

Reals in Later Versions of TURBO

TURBO 4.0 and subsequent versions employ five different real data types. They are *real, single, double, extended,* and *comp.* These differ according to the number of decimal, or significant, digits allowed as well as their exponential range. Table 2-3 summarizes the characteristics of each.

TABLE 2-3 REAL DATA TYPES IN LATER VERSIONS OF TURBO

Type	Decimal digits	Exponential range
Real	11	E-38 to E38
Single	7	E-38 to E38
Double	8	E-38 to E38
Extended	10	E-4931 to E4931
Comp	8	2^{63} to $2^{63} - 1$

The last four real data types in Table 2-3 are simply extensions of the standard real data type provided in Standard Pascal and earlier versions of TURBO Pascal. However, even if you are using TURBO 4.0 or a later version, you might not be able to use all these real data types. Consult your TURBO reference manual for the details. In this text we will stick with the standard real data type.

The Character Data Type

All of the symbols on your computer keyboard are characters. This includes all the upper- and lowercase alphabetic characters as well as the punctuation, numbers, and special symbols. Most Pascal compilers employ the ASCII (American Standard Code for Information Interchange) character set shown in Table 2-4.

As you can see from the table, each character has a unique numeric representation code. The reason for this is that, for the CPU to work with character data, the individual characters must be converted to a numeric (actually binary) code. When you press a character on the keyboard, the CPU "sees" the numeric representation of that character, not the character itself.

Example 2-6:

Pascal includes a standard function called *ordinal,* labeled *Ord*(C). This function is used to generate, or return, the numeric representation for any character (C). Determine the result of the following operations using Table 2-4.
a. *Ord*('A')
b. *Ord*('Z')
c. *Ord*('a')
d. *Ord*('z')
e. *Ord*('#')

Solution: Using Table 2-4, you get the following:
a. *Ord*('A') = 65
b. *Ord*('Z') = 90
c. *Ord*('a') = 97
d. *Ord*('z') = 122
e. *Ord*('#') = 35

The foregoing example points out several characteristics of character data. First, each character has a unique numeric representation inside the computer. Since each character has a unique numeric representation, the characters are ordered. This is why they are classified as scalar data types. For instance, 'A' < 'Z', since the numeric representation for 'A' (65) is less than the numeric representation for 'Z' (90). Likewise, '#' < 'a' < 'z', since 35 < 97 < 122. Next, notice that whenever a character is specified, it is always enclosed in single quotes like this, 'character'. This is a requirement of the Pascal compiler.

TABLE 2-4 ASCII CHARACTER CODE TABLE

DEC	CHAR	DEC	CHAR	DEC	CHAR	DEC	CHAR
0	^@ NUL	32	SPC	64	@	96	
1	^A SOH	33	!	65	A	97	a
2	^B STX	34	"	66	B	98	b
3	^C ETX	35	#	67	C	99	c
4	^D EOT	36	$	68	D	100	d
5	^E ENQ	37	%	69	E	101	e
6	^F ACK	38	&	70	F	102	f
7	^G BEL	39	'	71	G	103	g
8	^H BS	40	(	72	H	104	h
9	^I HT	41	)	73	I	105	i
10	^J LF	42	*	74	J	106	j
11	^K VT	43	+	75	K	107	k
12	^L FF	44	,	76	L	108	l
13	^M CR	45	-	77	M	109	m
14	^N SO	46	.	78	N	110	n
15	^O SI	47	/	79	O	111	o
16	^P DLE	48	0	80	P	112	p
17	^Q DC1	49	1	81	Q	113	q
18	^R DC2	50	2	82	R	114	r
19	^S DC3	51	3	83	S	115	s
20	^T DC4	52	4	84	T	116	t
21	^U NAK	53	5	85	U	117	u
22	^V SYN	54	6	86	V	118	v
23	^W ETB	55	7	87	W	119	w
24	^X CAN	56	8	88	X	120	x
25	^Y EM	57	9	89	Y	121	y
26	^Z SUB	58	:	90	Z	122	z
27	^[ESC	59	;	91	[	123	{
28	^\ FS	60	<	92	\	124		
29	^] GS	61	=	93	]	125	}
30	^ RS	62	>	94	^	126	~
31	^_ US	63	?	95	_	127	DEL

Strings

A *string* is simply a series of characters. Examples of strings include your name, address, and phone number, as well as the sentence you are now reading. TURBO Pascal treats strings as though they are a unique data type, even though they are made up of individual characters. This feature is not available on all versions of Pascal, such as Standard Pascal. You will soon discover that the inclusion of string data in TURBO makes the input and output of character information an extremely easy task, as compared with those versions of Pascal that do not allow strings. We will discuss more about strings later, when the need to use them arises.

The Boolean Data Type

The Boolean data type is the simplest data type utilized by Pascal. Only two elements make up the entire Boolean data type: TRUE and FALSE. This is an ordered, or scalar, data type, since Pascal specifies that FALSE is always less than TRUE (FALSE < TRUE).

Example 2-7:

Pascal employs a standard function called *Odd*(I), which returns a Boolean result. The function evaluates an integer (I) and returns the Boolean value TRUE if the integer is odd, and FALSE if the integer is even. Determine the results of the following operations:

a. *Odd*(3)
b. *Odd*(2)
c. *Odd*(0)
d. *Odd*(−135)
e. *Odd*(−134)
f. *Odd*(42537)
g. *Odd*(3.33)

Solution:

a. *Odd*(3) = TRUE, since 3 is odd.
b. *Odd*(2) = FALSE, since 2 is not odd.
c. *Odd*(0) = FALSE, since 0 is considered to be even.
d. *Odd*(−135) = TRUE, since −135 is odd.
e. *Odd*(−134) = FALSE, since −134 is even.
f. *Odd*(42537) will generate an error during the compiling process, since 42537 is outside the predefined range of integers.
g. *Odd*(3.33) will generate an error during the compiling process, since this function is only defined for integers, and the value 3.33 is a real value.

2-3 CONSTANTS AND VARIABLES

From mathematics, you know that a constant is a value that never changes, thereby remaining constant. A common example is the constant $pi(\pi)$. Here, the Greek symbol π is used to represent the real value 3.14. This value of π never changes, thus remaining constant regardless of where and how it might be used in a calculation.

On the other hand, a variable is something that can take on different values. In mathematics, the symbols x and y are often used to denote variables. Using the equation $y = 3x + 2$, you can substitute different values of x to generate different values of y. Thus, the values of x and y in the equation are variable.

In computers, the values of constants and variables are stored in main working memory for later use within a program. Each constant and variable has a symbolic name that locates its value in memory. This idea is illustrated in Figure 2-2. Here,

Main Working
Memory

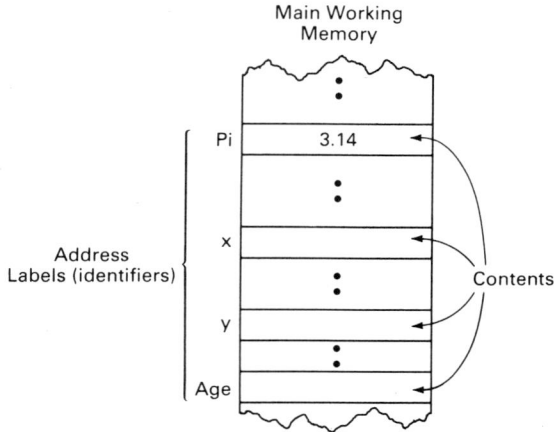

Address
Labels (identifiers)

Pi   3.14

x

y

Age

Contents

Figure 2-2 Each constant and variable has a label, or identifier, that locates its value in memory.

the word *Pi* locates the stored value 3.14.   This value will not be changed during the execution of the program, thereby making the symbol *Pi* a constant.   On the other hand, the memory contents located by the symbols *x*, *y*, and *Age* might change during the execution of the program.   As a result, these symbols are called variables.

Pascal requires you to *declare* any constants and variables that will be used in a given program prior to program execution.   The reason is twofold: First, the Pascal compiler must reserve memory locations to store the constants and variables.   Second, in the case of variables, the compiler must know the data type of the variables.   Now let's see how both constants and variables are declared in Pascal.

Declaring Constants

To declare a constant, you must use the word **CONST**, as follows:

```
CONSTANT DECLARATION  ***********************************************************
CONST
     constant identifier #1 = constant value;
     constant identifier #2 = constant value;
            :                      :
     constant identifier #n = constant value;
 **********************************************************************************
```

The constant *identifier* is the name of each respective constant that the compiler will use to locate the constant in memory.   The constant value is the actual value stored in memory for a given constant identifier.   Notice the syntax: The word **CONST** is followed by each constant declaration.   An equals sign (=) is used to separate the constant identifier from its declared value.   Finally, each constant declaration must be ended with a semicolon.

Example 2-8:

Suppose that you wish to use the current price of a first-class postage stamp in your Pascal program.   In addition, your program must calculate the sales tax required for a given sales item based on a sales-tax rate of 5 percent.   Declare appropriate constant identifiers to represent the current price of a stamp and the sales-tax rate.

Solution: Using the format given above, the postage price and sales-tax rate could be declared as follows:

```
CONST

     Postage = 0.25;

     TaxRate = 0.05;
```

With these declarations, you would simply use the words *Postage* and *TaxRate* when performing calculations within the program.   For instance, to find the tax on an item that costs $100, you would simply write the expression:

```
SalesTax := 100.00 * TaxRate;
```

When executing the expression, the computer simply substitutes the constant value 0.05 for the *TaxRate* identifier.

What about the word *SalesTax* in this expression?   Is it a constant or a variable? You're right—it's a variable identifier, since its value will change depending on the sales price of the item.   What data type must *SalesTax* be?   In other words, what type of data is generated as a result of the operation: integer, real, character, or Boolean?   Right again—real, since *SalesTax* might often result in a decimal value. Thus, *SalesTax* must be declared as a real variable.   You will find out how to do this shortly.

STYLE TIP ───

Pascal programs are structured to be very readable and self-documenting.   For this reason, you should always indent each constant definition two or three spaces underneath the word **CONST** as shown in Example 2-8.   You will find this indentation scheme used throughout this text to make programs easier to read and understand.

In addition, notice that the constant identifier *TaxRate* is made up of two words, *Tax* and *Rate*.   The Pascal compiler will not allow you to separate identifier words with a space. Thus, I have chosen to combine the two words into a single word, where the first letter of each word is capitalized.   This will be done throughout the text when using multiword identifiers.   How long can an identifier be?   This depends on the version of Pascal that you are using: with TURBO, identifiers can be any length, with the first 63 characters being significant.

Here are some other rules that govern the use of identifiers in TURBO Pascal:

- All identifiers must start with a letter.
- No spaces or punctuation, except the underscore character (_) are allowed.
- Lower- and uppercase characters are treated as identical. Thus, the identifiers *Tax* and *TAX* are seen as identical by the compiler.

You are probably wondering why we should declare constants using identifiers. Why not just insert the constant value into the expression whenever it is needed, as follows:

```
SalesTax := 100.00 * 0.05;
```

Have you ever known postage or sales-tax rates to change? Of course you have! You might say that these types of "constants" are not constant forever. So, when using constants such as these that might be subject to change in the future, it is much easier to define them in one single place at the beginning of the program. Then if they need to be changed, you only have to make a single change in your program. Otherwise, a change must be made each place that you use the constant within the program.

One final point: You probably have noticed that the word **CONST** is capitalized and set in bold type. Such a word in Pascal is called a *reserved word*. Reserved words have a specific meaning to the Pascal compiler and are used to perform a specific task. You cannot use a reserved word for anything else other than the specific operation for which it is defined. TURBO Pascal contains about forty-three reserved words, including **CONST**. You will learn about the other forty-two in subsequent chapters. In any event, from now on all reserved words will be printed in all caps and set in bold type so that you can recognize them.

Constants can also be declared as a string of characters. As a result, such constants are called *string constants*. Let's look at another example to illustrate this idea.

Example 2-9:

Define three constants that can be used to represent your name, address, and phone number.

Solution: Using the **CONST** declaration, the appropriate constants could be

```
CONST

    Name = 'Andrew C. Staugaard, Jr.';

    Address = 'Box 999, Pascal City, USA';

    PhoneNumber = '(012) 345-6789';
```

Observe that when defining string constants you must enclose the constant value within single quotes as shown.

You probably are wondering how and where string constants are used. One common use of string constants is to represent information that must be printed often, such as header information. For instance, each time you need to print your name in a report, you would simply insert an instruction into the program to print the constant identifier (*Name*). Since the value of *Name* is your name, the computer will print your name. You will see how this works when you learn about input and output operations in Chapter 3.

Declaring Variables

Before you can use a variable in a Pascal program, it must be declared. When you declare a variable, the compiler reserves a location inside the computer memory for the variable value. Variables are always declared at the beginning of your Pascal program, after the constant declarations. This is done by using the reserved word **VAR**, as follows:

```
VARIABLE DECLARATION  *****************************************************
VAR
    variable identifier #1 : variable data type;
    variable identifier #2 : variable data type;
            .                      .
            .                      .
            .                      .
    variable identifier #n : variable data type;
    ******************************************************************************
```

The foregoing format requires your variable identifiers, or names, to be listed under the reserved word **VAR.** In each instance, notice that the variable identifier (or name) is listed first, followed by a colon, followed by the data type of the variable (integer, real, char, or Boolean). Each variable declaration is ended with a semicolon. Here's the idea:

Example 2-10:

Suppose that you must write a Pascal program to calculate voltage from current and resistor values using Ohm's law ($V = I * R$). Declare the three variables (V, I, and R) using the **VAR** declaration.

Solution: The variable identifiers are given as V, I, and R. Now the question is: What data type must these variables be? You know that V, I, and R will be used to represent numeric data, so your decision as to their data type reduces to integer or real. If you declare V, I, and R as integers, you will be limited to using whole-number values for these variables within your program. However, this might create a problem, since voltage, current, and resistance values often are decimal values. Therefore, let's declare them as real variables, as follows:

```
VAR

    V : real;

    I : real;

    R : real;
```

Now, to save some typing, you can combine all variables of a given data type using a single line as follows:

```
VAR

    V, I, R : real;
```

Observe that the individual variables must be separated by commas. That's all there is to it!

STYLE TIP ──

In TURBO Pascal, variable identifiers, or names, can be any length. Thus, your programs will become much more readable and self-documenting if you use words, rather than letters and symbols, to represent variable values. For instance, the variable declaration in Example 2-10 would be much more readable to your nontechnical friend if you were to define voltage, current, and resistance as follows:

```
VAR

    Voltage, Current, Resistance : real;
```

Using this declaration, the actual words (*Voltage, Current*, and *Resistance*) would be used within your program when applying Ohm's law. The statement required to calculate voltage would therefore appear in your program as follows:

```
Voltage := Current * Resistance;
```

Notice the use of the := symbol in this equation. This is the way that you must equate things in Pascal. Also notice the use of the * symbol for multiplication. We will discuss this further later.

A word of caution: When using names as variable identifiers, you *cannot* use any punctuation within the name. For instance, the variable identifier *R*(total) to represent the total resistance in a circuit is an illegal identifier in Pascal because of the parentheses. Two legal identifiers are Rtotal or R_total. In the second case, the underline symbol _ is okay for use within Pascal identifiers.

───

Example 2-11:

You must write a program to calculate the sales tax of a sales item using a sales-tax rate of 5 percent. Declare the appropriate variables and constants.

Solution: First, you must decide what identifiers to use. Always use word identifiers that best describe the related constant or variable. Let's use the word *SalesTax* to identify the resulting calculation, the word *Price* to identify the cost of the item, and the word *TaxRate* to identify the sales-tax rate. Using these identifiers, the sales-tax calculation would be

```
SalesTax := Price * TaxRate;
```

Now the question is: Which are variables and which are constants? Obviously, the *SalesTax* and *Price* identifiers are variables, since they will change depending on the cost of the item. However, *TaxRate* will be constant, regardless of the cost of the item. So, we will declare *SalesTax* and *Price* as variable, and *TaxRate* as a constant, as follows:

```
CONST
    TaxRate = 0.05;
VAR
    SalesTax, Price : real;
```

Notice that both the variables are declared as real, since both will be decimal values. In addition, observe that the constant is declared before the variables. This is a requirement of Pascal and will be discussed shortly.

Example 2-12:

Choose an appropriate name and declare a variable that could be used to represent the days of the week. Assume that the days of the week are represented by the first letter of each day.

Solution: Let's pick a meaningful variable identifier such as: *DaysOfWeek*. Now, since the days of the week will be represented by the first letter of each day, the variable must be a character variable. When declaring character variables, you must use the word "char" in the variable declaration as follows:

```
VAR
    DaysOfWeek : char;
```

Do you see any problems with the declaration in Example 2-12? There are no syntax errors and it is perfectly legal as far as Pascal is concerned. But are there any problems associated with the usage of this variable? A character variable is limited to representing a *single* character at any given time. This is why each day of the week must be represented by a single letter. However, using the first letter of each day creates a problem. Does an 'S' represent Saturday or Sunday?

Likewise, does a 'T' mean Tuesday or Thursday? The solution to this dilemma is found in string variables.

Declaring String Variables

Recall that TURBO Pascal includes a string data type. Strings are simply a series of keyboard characters, including all the alphabetic characters as well as the numbers 0 through 9 and special symbols included on a terminal keyboard. Thus, a string variable can be used to represent a series, or string, of characters.

To declare a string variable, you must use the reserved word **STRING** within the variable declaration, as follows:

STRING VARIABLE DECLARATION **
VAR
    variable identifier : **STRING** [max string length];
****

As you can see, the format is basically the same, except for the reserved word **STRING** followed by brackets that must specify the maximum length of the string. Here are a couple of examples:

Example 2-13:

Using a character variable declaration in Example 2-12 presents a usage problem when representing the days of the week, because a character variable can only represent a single character at a time. Solve this problem by using a string variable declaration.

Solution: A string variable can be used to represent up to 255 characters in a string. Therefore, let's define *DaysOfWeek* as a string variable as follows:

```
VAR

    DaysOfWeek : STRING [9];
```

With this declaration, the variable *DaysOfWeek* can be used to represent the entire day of the week word (Sunday, Monday, Tuesday, etc.). Why did I choose 9 as the maximum length of the string? Because the longest day of the week word is Wednesday, which has 9 characters.

Example 2-14:

Suppose that you must write a Pascal program to instruct the user of the program to enter his or her name, address, and telephone number. Choose appropriate variable identifiers and declare three string variables to represent this information.

Solution: Let's call the variables *Name*, *Address*, and *PhoneNumber*, respectively. Now you must decide the maximum length of each string variable. Don't forget to include spaces and special symbols. A length of 30 should be sufficient for *Name*, 30 for *Address*, and 15 for *PhoneNumber*. If you are not sure, it is better to overestimate, rather than underestimate, its length.   The maximum length for a string in TURBO is 255 characters.

Using the foregoing variable identifiers and string lengths, the proper declaration is

```
VAR

    Name : STRING [30];

    Address : STRING [30];

    PhoneNumber : STRING [15];
```

Notice that the *Name* and *Address* variables have the same string length.   When this is the case, you can combine the two identifiers on a single line using commas, as follows:

```
VAR

    Name, Address : STRING [30];

    PhoneNumber : STRING [15];
```

Of course, *PhoneNumber* could also be combined with *Name* and *Address*, since its length (15) is less than 30.   However, this would reserve more memory space than is required to represent *PhoneNumber*, so we will keep it on a separate line.

You might be thinking that the declaration of variables is an unnecessary burden, especially if you are familiar with any other high-level languages.   For instance, BASIC does not require variables to be declared.   A variable in BASIC can be an integer value at one point and a real value at another point in the program.   Such a language is called *weakly typed,* while Pascal is a *strongly typed* language.   Strongly typed languages, like Pascal, provide for better program organization, or structure, since all the program variables and constants are collected together and shown at the beginning of the program.   This feature enhances the readability of the program by acting as a "table of contents" for the constants and variables used in the program.   In addition, strong data typing allows programs to be compiled more efficiently, requiring less memory space.   Moreover, one of the biggest benefits of a strongly typed language is its error-checking ability during program compilation and execution.

2-4 PROGRAM STRUCTURE—FROM BEGINNING TO END

You now have some of the basic ingredients to begin writing Pascal programs.   You will be doing this shortly, in the next chapter.   However, before we leave this chapter, let's put things into some perspective and take an initial look at the overall structure of a Pascal program.

Recall that the Pascal language is a modular, structured language.   This idea

```
        ⌈  PROGRAM program name (input, output);
        |
        |  CONST
        |
Declaration |     {Constant declarations go here}
Section  ⟨
        |  VAR
        |
        |     {Variable declarations go here}
        ⌊

        ⌈  BEGIN
        |
        |     Statement 1;
Statement |     Statement 2;
Section  ⟨        .
        |        .
        |     Statement n ◄──────────┐
        |                            |
        ⌊  END.

                          Note:   No ; required after the last
                                  program statement.
```

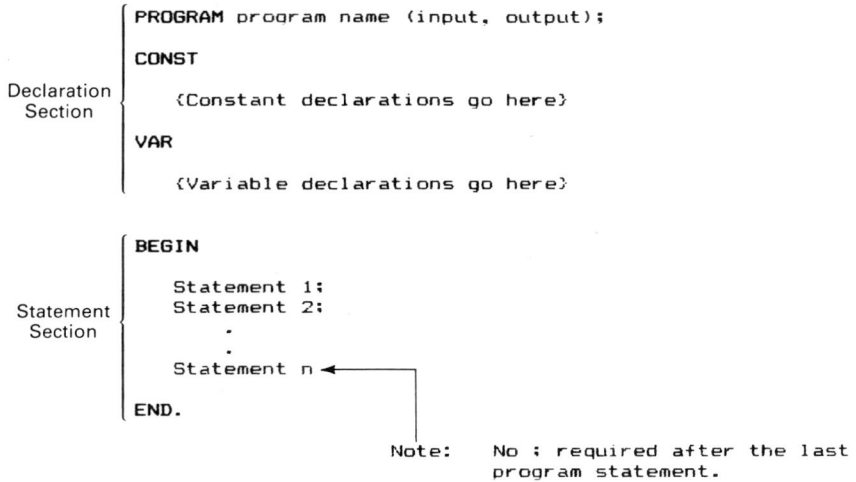

Figure 2-3   The general structure of a Pascal program.

is evident from the overall appearance, or structure, of a Pascal program.   Look at Figure 2-3.   Observe that any Pascal program consists of two fundamental sections: a ***declaration*** section and a ***statement*** section.

The declaration section contains all the things that the program will use during its execution.   It acts as a table of contents for the program.   Notice that the top line of this section begins with the reserved word **PROGRAM.**   This line provides a name for the entire program.   The program name must be one continuous word (no spaces or punctuation), and can be up to 127 characters long.   The program name is followed by a listing of files, enclosed in parentheses, that the program will use.   In this text we will only list two files in our program heading: input and output.   Thus, most of our program headings will look like this:

PROGRAM ProgramName (input, output);

The program heading is terminated using a semicolon.   You should be aware that TURBO Pascal does not require a program heading.   However, it is required for other versions of Pascal.   I will always use a program heading in this text, since the program name provides a means of referencing the program.   I suggest that you do the same when writing your own programs.   This will get you into the habit of using a program heading in case you ever write Pascal programs using a compiler other than TURBO.   By the way, the TURBO compiler simply ignores the program heading.

From Figure 2-3, you can see that the program heading is followed by any constant declarations, which in turn are followed by the program variable declarations, as discussed in Section 2-3.   If your program doesn't require any constants or variables, the reserved words **CONST** or **VAR** are not used in the declaration section.

We will add other things to the declaration section later on. For now, just remember that this is where the constant and variable declarations must appear.

The statement section of the program is the main executable body of the program. This section must begin with the reserved word **BEGIN** and end with the reserved word **END.** The program instructions, or statements, must go between these two reserved words. Each statement must be terminated with a semicolon as shown, except for the last statement. Observe from Figure 2-3 that a period must follow the reserved word **END.** The period signifies the end of the program just as it signifies the end of a sentence in English. Semicolons only designate the end of a statement within the program, just as they would within a sentence in English.

Example 2-15:

Use the program structure shown in Figure 2-3 and the declarations in Example 2-11 to write a program that will calculate the sales tax of a sales item.

Solution: In Example 2-11, we used the following relationship to calculate the sales tax of a sales item:

```
SalesTax :=  Price * TaxRate;
```

where *SalesTax* and *Price* were declared as real variables.

TaxRate was declared as a constant value of 0.05.

Putting this information into the required Pascal program structure shown in Figure 2-3, you get

```
PROGRAM FindSalesTax (input, output);

CONST
    TaxRate = 0.05;

VAR
    SalesTax, Price : real;

BEGIN

    SalesTax := Price * TaxRate

END.
```

The foregoing program's name is *FindSalesTax*, since that's what it does. Observe the structure: The program is very readable and everything used within the program is clearly defined. That's all there is to it! We have just written our first Pascal program!

The simple program in Example 2-15 will calculate the sales tax of an item, given the item price. But how does the actual price of the item (*Price*) get into the program so that the calculation can be performed?   Then, once the calculation is performed, how do you get the resulting sales-tax value (*SalesTax*) out of the program and displayed on a terminal or printed by a printer?   Getting things in and out of a Pascal program is called *reading* and *writing*—the topic of the next chapter.

CHAPTER SUMMARY

Pascal is a strongly typed language.   This means that all the data processed by a Pascal program must be part of a given data type that is declared at the beginning of the program.   There are three major data-type categories: scalar, structured, and pointer.   In this text we are primarily concerned with the scalar data type.

Scalar data elements are ordered and consist of standard and user-defined data.   Standard scalar data types include the integer, real, character, and Boolean data types.   The integer data type in TURBO Pascal includes all the whole numbers between -32768 and $+32767$.   In addition, later versions of TURBO include *shortint, longint*, and *word*.

The real data type consists of decimal values that can be represented in either decimal or exponential form.   In TURBO, a decimal-point value cannot exceed eleven digits.   In addition, the exponent range must be from $1E-38$ through $1E+38$ when using exponential notation.   Later versions of TURBO expand on this range by allowing the use of extended reals.

Character data includes all the symbols on your computer keyboard.   Characters are ordered, since they are represented internally using a numeric ASCII code.   A string is a series of characters.   TURBO Pascal treats strings as though they are a unique data type.   However, this feature is not available on all versions of Pascal.

Finally, the Boolean data type consists of only two elements, TRUE and FALSE.   The order is predefined such that FALSE is less than TRUE.

User-defined data types consist of elements that you, the programmer, define when constructing a program.   This data type will be discussed in Chapter 8.

All constants and variables used in a Pascal program must be declared in the declaration section of the program.   Constants are declared using the reserved word **CONST.**   The constant identifier is simply set equal to its constant value.   Variables are declared using the reserved word **VAR.**   Variables are declared by listing the variable identifier, followed by a colon, followed by the data type of that variable.

Pascal programs consist of two fundamental sections: the declaration section and the statement section.   The declaration section contains all the things that the program will use during its execution, including constants and variables.   This section begins with a program heading using the reserved word **PROGRAM.**   The statement section of the program is the main executable body of the program. This section follows the declaration section and must begin with the reserved word **BEGIN** and end with the reserved word **END.**

QUESTIONS AND PROBLEMS

Questions

2-1. Name the four standard data types defined in Pascal.

2-2. What characteristic does a scalar data type have over a nonscalar data type?

2-3. Which of the following are *not* legal integer values in TURBO Pascal? Explain why they are not valid. Assume the standard integer data type.
   a. −32.0
   b. +256
   c. 256
   d. 3,240
   e. 32000
   f. 40000

2-4. What is an integer overflow condition, and when will it generate incorrect results in TURBO Pascal?

2-5. Which of the following are *not* legal real values in TURBO Pascal? Explain why they are not valid. Assume the standard real data type.
   a. 35.7
   b. −35.7
   c. .456
   d. 1.25E − 9
   e. −2.5 − E3
   f. −0.375E − 3
   g. 25

2-6. Convert the following decimal numbers to exponential notation:
   a. −0.0000123
   b. 57892345.45
   c. 1.00004536
   d. +012.345

2-7. Convert the following exponential numbers to decimal notation:
   a. 3.45E − 7
   b. −0.0225E − 3
   c. 2.22E6
   d. −34.5E3

2-8. Three resistor values in a circuit are 4.7 kΩ, 2.2 MΩ, and 10 kΩ.
   a. Express each resistor as a real value in decimal form.
   b. Express each resistor as a real value in exponential form.
   c. Express each resistor as an integer value.

2-9. The following current and voltage values are measured in a circuit: 1 mA, 32 mV, 100 μV, and 125 nA.
   a. Express each current and voltage value in decimal form.
   b. Express each current and voltage value in exponential form.

2-10. What is the data type of each of the following?
   a. 250
   b. −250.0

   c. -16
   d. $-3.5E-4$
   e. 'x'
   f. '$'
   g. '2'
   h. '175'
   i. '1.25E-3'

Problems

2-1. Determine the result of each of the following operations:
   a. $Sqr(4)$ **b.** $Sqr(4.0)$ **c.** $Sqrt(16)$ **d.** $Sqrt(1.6E1)$
   e. $Sqrt(-4)$ **f.** $Ord(x)$ **g.** $Ord('y')$ **h.** $Ord('Y')$
   i. $Ord('5')$ **j.** $Odd(324)$ **k.** $Odd(-33)$ **l.** $Odd(2.75)$
   m. $Odd('Y')$

2-2. State the difference between a character and a string variable.

2-3. Choose appropriate names and declare constants to represent each of the following:
   a. A maximum value of 100
   b. The value required to represent the prefix *milli-*
   c. The value required to represent the prefix *kilo-*
   d. Your age
   e. A period
   f. Your birth date
   g. Your school

2-4. Declare a series of constants using a single **CONST** declaration that would represent the resistor color code.

2-5. Choose appropriate names and declare variables for each of the following:
   a. Grade point average (GPA)
   b. The grade for a course
   c. Gross pay on a paycheck
   d. The logic output of a digital gate
   e. The Thevenin resistance and Thevenin voltage of a dc circuit
   f. Student name, course name, and course number (assume that the course number is a seven-position alphanumeric number such as ENG-103).

2-6. The := symbol is used in Pascal to denote an assignment operation. For now, you can think of it as an equals sign, but you will find out later that it actually has a different meaning than just equals. Given the following program declarations,

```
PROGRAM Example (input, output);

CONST

    Value = 2.5;

VAR
    x, y : integer;
    a, b : real;
```

determine the results of each of the following program statements:

a. ```
BEGIN
    x := 25;
    b := Sqrt(x)
END.
```

b. ```
BEGIN
    y := 5;
    a := Sqrt(Sqr(y))
END.
```

c. ```
BEGIN
    x := 1;
    x := x + 1;
    y := Sqr(x)
END.
```

d. ```
BEGIN
    x := 2;
    y := x + x;
    a := (y + 1) * Value
END.
```

e. ```
BEGIN
    x := 2;
    y := x + x;
    a := y + 1* Value
END.
```

**2-7.** The *Write* instruction is used in Pascal to output a value from the program and display it on the CRT screen.   The format for this instruction is

```
Write (value or variable to output);
```

Notice that the value or variable to be written must be enclosed in parentheses.   Thus, to display the value of the variable x in a program, you simply use the following statement:

```
Write (x);
```

Add a *Write* statement to each of the program segments in problem 2-6 that will display the final results of the program.

2-8. Write a Pascal program that will find the total resistance in a series circuit and display the total resistance on the CRT screen.   Assume that the circuit has three variable resistance values.   Make sure to use the program structure given in Figure 2-3.
```

chapter three

Getting Things In and Out: Reading and Writing

INTRODUCTION

You are now ready to begin getting your hands dirty. In this chapter you will learn how to get information in and out of your system via Pascal. In Pascal, input is called *reading* and output is called **writing.** You will discover how to write information to your system CRT display and printer. Then you will learn how to read information from your system keyboard. Armed with this knowledge, you will be ready to write some simple Pascal programs. Make sure that you do the programming problems at the end of the chapter. You must get your hands dirty with some actual programming experience to *learn* how to program.

At the end of this chapter you will be asked to write, enter, and execute your first Pascal programs. As a result, it's probably a good idea for you to familiarize yourself with the operation of your system at this time. You should know how to load the Pascal compiler, enter and edit programs, compile programs, and run programs. Your instructor or lab assistant will most likely provide you with these system basics. A summary of the system procedures is provided in Appendix A, should you need a reference.

Now, let's get down to business.

3-1 GETTING THINGS OUT: WRITING

When executing your Pascal programs, you will usually want to output information to one of two hardware devices: a CRT or a printer. In fact, there will be occasions when you will need to output information to both of these devices during the execution of a program.

In Pascal getting information out of the system is called **writing.** You can write information to a CRT screen to be displayed, or write information to a printer to be printed. There are two commands in Pascal that are used for output. They are *Write* and *Writeln* (write line). Both these commands are used to output information to a CRT or a printer.

The words *Write* and *Writeln* are not considered reserved words within Pascal and, therefore, are not capitalized and set in bold type. Rather, *Write* and *Writeln* are commands that invoke a predefined procedure to accomplish the output task. You will learn more about procedures in Chapter 7. In this text you will see such words set in italics, with only the first letter capitalized. Now, let's learn how *Write* and *Writeln* are used for output. We will begin with the *Writeln* statement.

The *Writeln* Statement

The general format for the *Writeln* statement is

Writeln FORMAT ✱✱✱
              Writeln (item #1, item #2, item #3, ..., item #n);
✱✱

As you can see, the *Writeln* command is followed by a list of the items to be written. The items within the listing must be separated by commas. In addition, the item listing must be enclosed within parentheses and terminated with a semicolon (unless it is the last program statement).

The best way to understand how *Writeln* works is to look at the output generated by several different write line operations. Probably the simplest use of the *Writeln* statement is to output fixed, or constant, information. There are two types of fixed information that can be written: **numeric** or **character.**

Getting Out Fixed Numeric Information

When you want to output fixed numeric information, you simply list the numeric values within the *Writeln* statement. Thus, the statement

```
Writeln (250);
```

generates an output of

250

The statement

```
Writeln (-365);
```

generates an output of

```
-365
```

The statement

```
Writeln (1,2,3,4);
```

generates an output of

```
1234
```

The statement

```
Writeln (2.75);
```

generates an output of

```
2.7500000000E+00
```

Observe the last two outputs. When several individual items are listed and separated by commas within a single statement, the output does not generate any spacing between the items. This is why the statement *Writeln* (1,2,3,4) generates an output of 1234. Next, notice that when a decimal value is written, you get its exponential equivalent on the output. Both these conditions (item spacing and exponential output) can be altered using special formatting options within the *Writeln* statement. Output formatting will be discussed shortly.

Getting Out Fixed Character Information

To output character information, you must enclose the output information in single quotes. Consequently, the statement

```
Writeln ('HELLO');
```

generates an output of

```
HELLO
```

The statement

```
Writeln ('This is a great text!');
```

produces an output of

This is a great text!

Example 3-1:

Construct *Writeln* statements to generate the following outputs:
a. 2.75
b. 1 2 3 4 5

Solution:

a. One way to get a decimal output rather than an exponential output of a fixed value is to treat the numeric value as a character string and enclose it within quotes as follows:

Writeln ('2.75');

b. To get spacing in the output, use a character string that has blanks within the write line statement, as follows:

Writeln ('1   ','2   ','3   ');

Remember that blanks are also characters. As a result, the above statement generates blanks, or spaces, where they are inserted within the character string quotation marks.

Getting Out Variable Information

The next thing you must learn is how to output variable information. Again, this is a simple chore using the *Writeln* statement. You simply list the variable identifier(s) in the item listing. For instance, if your program has declared *Voltage*, *Current*, and *Resistance* as variables, you would output their respective values by listing them in the *Writeln* statement as follows:

Writeln (Voltage, Current, Resistance);

The foregoing statement would output the values stored in memory for *Voltage*, *Current*, and *Resistance*, in that order. The order of the output will be the same as the listing order within the *Writeln* statement. Let's see how this statement might be used within a complete program.

Example 3-2:

Write a Pascal program that will output a voltage value, given current and resistance values of 0.002A and 4700 Ω, respectively.

Solution: Of course, the program must use Ohm's law to calculate the voltage. So let's define three variables to represent voltage, current, and resistance. Then, we will assign the given current and resistance values and use Ohm's law to calculate the voltage. The resulting voltage will then be output via a *Writeln* statement. Here's the program:

```
PROGRAM OhmsLaw (input, output);

VAR
    Voltage, Current, Resistance : real;

BEGIN
    Current := 0.002;
    Resistance := 4700;
    Voltage := Current * Resistance;
    Writeln (Voltage)
END.
```

The output produced by the program is:

$$9.4000000000E+00$$

Again, notice that the output is in exponential form, since *Voltage* was defined as a real variable.

STYLE TIP ———

The output generated in Example 3-2 is simply the number 9.4000000000E + 00. What a bore! You need to "dress up" your program outputs so that the user of the program understands what's going on. First, you should always use a series of *Writeln* statements at the beginning of your program that tell the user what the program is going to do. This is called a ***program description message*** and might be coded as follows:

```
Writeln ('This program will calculate voltage, given a current');
Writeln ('and a resistance value.');
```

These two *Writeln* statements will generate the following output:

```
This program will calculate voltage, given a current
and a resistance value.
```

Observe that two *Writeln* statements are used to output two lines of character information. Does this give you a hint as to why the *Writeln* command is called "write line"? Such a program description message does two things:

1. It tells the user (the person running the program) what the program will do.
2. It provides documentation within the program listing as to what the program will do. As a result, the program listing becomes self-documenting.

Next, good style would dictate that the voltage output be more descriptive. In other words, the output should also be self-documenting. In Example 3-2, the voltage output statement could be modified as follows:

```
Writeln;
Writeln ('Given a Current value of ',Current,' and a');
Writeln;
Writeln ('Resistance value of ',Resistance,', the');
Writeln;
Writeln ('resulting voltage is ', Voltage, ' volts.');
Writeln;
```

These seven consecutive *Writeln* statements will generate the following output:

```
Given a Current value of 2.0000000000E-03 and a

Resistance value of 4.7000000000E+03 the

resulting voltage is 9.4000000000E+00.
```

Let's analyze this output.   First, observe that the single word *Writeln* has been inserted before, between, and after the individual output lines.   This generates a **line feed,** or **line space,** before, between, and after the output lines.   The first *Writeln* command generates a blank line prior to the program output to separate it from any previous output information, such as the program description message. The two *Writeln* commands inserted between the output lines provide for double spacing of the output, thereby making it easier to read.   Finally, the last *Writeln* command will separate this output from any subsequent output.

Next, look at the output lines themselves.   See how an output sentence is constructed using a *Writeln* statement.   The words within the sentence are simply character strings enclosed within single quotation marks.   The current, resistance, and voltage values are inserted in the sentence by listing the variables (*Current*, *Resistance*, and *Voltage*) when they are needed as part of the output.   Notice that each character string or variable item is separated by commas from the other items in the listing.   For instance, the first line of output is interpreted as follows:

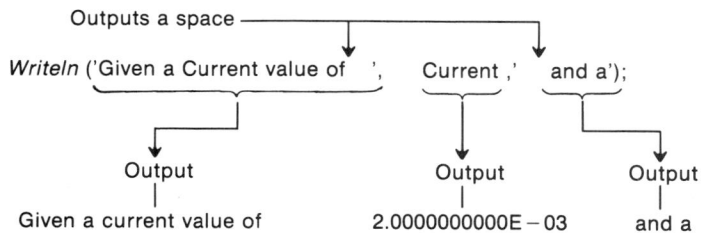

It is important that you see that the quotation marks are around the string information and not around the variables.

Of course, the variable output values are in exponential notation, since the variables have been declared as real.   You will learn how to output them in decimal notation shortly.

Example 3-3:

Insert the *Writeln* statements given in the above style tip into the program developed in Example 3-2 to form a complete program.

Solution:

```
PROGRAM OhmsLaw (input, output);

VAR
    Voltage, Current, Resistance : real;

BEGIN
    Writeln ('This program will calculate voltage, given a current');
    Writeln ('and a resistance value.');
    Current := 0.002;
    Resistance := 4700;
    Voltage := Current * Resistance;
    Writeln;
    Writeln;
    Writeln ('Given a Current value of ',Current,' and a');
    Writeln;
    Writeln ('Resistance value of ',Resistance,', the');
    Writeln;
    Writeln ('resulting voltage is ', Voltage, ' volts.')
END.
```

As you can see from Example 3-3, the general idea of using the *Writeln* statement is simple: You insert the *Writeln* statement in your program whenever you want to display information on your system CRT screen or print information on your system printer. Remember though, each *Writeln* statement results in a separate line of output. If there is no item listing within the statement, the single word *Writeln* will result in a line space, or blank line, on the output.

CRT versus Printer Output

All of the write line operations that you have seen up to this point will cause the output information to be displayed on your system CRT. So how can you get the information to be printed by your system printer? Simple: Add the acronym *lst* (which means list) to the beginning of the item listing.

Printer Output for Later Versions of TURBO

Version 4.0 and later versions of TURBO Pascal require an additional statement at the beginning of the program declaration section in order to output information to the printer. This required statement is the **USES** statement, and it must appear in the program as follows:

```
PROGRAM   program name (input, output);

USES
  Printer;

CONST

   {Constant declarations go here}

VAR

   {Variable declarations go here}


BEGIN

   ■
     {Program statements}
   ■

END.
```

The **USES** statement tells the TURBO compiler that the *lst* command within the program refers to the printer for output.

The **USES** statement is only required with TURBO 4.0 and later versions. It will cause a compiling error if included in earlier-version TURBO Pascal programs. For this reason, all the programs that follow will show the **USES** statement, when required, tinted lightly within the program. Simply ignore this statement if you are using a version of TURBO that is earlier than 4.0.

Example 3-4:

Revise the program in Example 3-3 so that the output information is printed on your system printer rather than to the CRT display.

Solution:

```
PROGRAM OhmsLaw (input, output);

USES
  Printer;

VAR
   Voltage, Current, Resistance : real;

BEGIN
   Writeln (lst,'This program will calculate voltage, given a current');
   Writeln (lst,'and a resistance value.');
   Current := 0.002;
   Resistance := 4700;
   Voltage := Current * Resistance;
```

(Continued)

```
Writeln (lst);
Writeln (lst);
Writeln (lst,'Given a Current value of ',Current,' and a');
Writeln (lst);
Writeln (lst,'Resistance value of ',Resistance,', the');
Writeln (lst);
Writeln (lst,'resulting voltage is ', Voltage, ' volts.')
```

END.

Now the program output will be generated on your system printer rather than on the CRT. Notice that the *lst* command must be the first item in the listing. In addition, to print a blank line, notice that the *lst* command appears as the only item within the listing.

How do you suppose that you could generate the program output on both the CRT and printer simultaneously? You're right if you thought to use duplicate *Writeln* statements. One statement would contain the *lst* command to print the information, and a duplicate statement, without the *lst* command, would be required to display the output information on your CRT.

The *Write* Statement

By now, you probably are wondering how the *Write* statement differs from the *Writeln* statement. Recall that each *Writeln* statement results in a separate output line. This is why it is called "write line." Now, think about what the CRT cursor or print head must do to execute this statement. Once the line has been displayed or printed, the CRT cursor or print head must return to the beginning of the next line. In other words, the *Writeln* statement tells the CRT or printer to return to the beginning of the next line after the current line has been displayed or printed. On the other hand, the *Write* statement does not cause this to happen.

Here's how it works. With a *Write* statement, the information is displayed or printed, and then the cursor or print head remains at the next position on the **current line.** A subsequent *Write* statement will cause its information to be output on the same line, where the previous *Write* statement left off. This idea is illustrated by Figure 3-1. Let's see how this works by looking at some examples.

Example 3-5:

Determine the output of the following program segments:

a.
```
Writeln ('Andrew C. Staugaard, Jr.');
Writeln ('Box 999');
Writeln ('Pascal City, USA');
```

b.
```
Write ('Andrew C. Staugaard, Jr.');
Write ('Box 999');
Write ('Pascal City, USA');
```

Writeln ('HELLO');

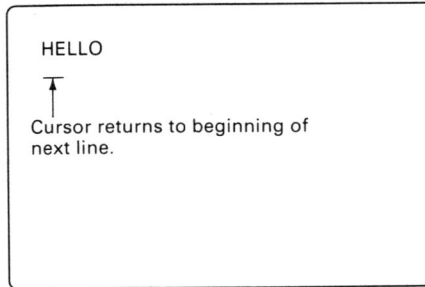

HELLO

Cursor returns to beginning of
next line.

(a)

Write ('HELLO');

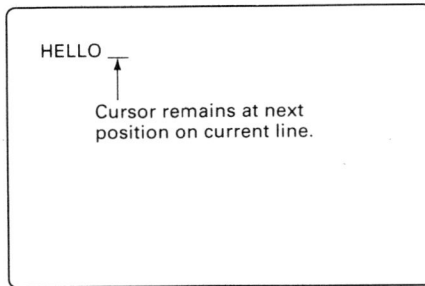

HELLO

Cursor remains at next
position on current line.

(b)

Figure 3-1   The difference between (a)
a *Writeln* statement and (b) a *Write*
statement.

Solution:

a. The three *Writeln* statements will generate three consecutive lines of output like
   this:

> **Andrew C. Staugaard, Jr.**
> **Box 999**
> **Pascal City, USA**

b. The three *Write* statements will generate a single line of output like this:

> **Andrew C. Staugaard, Jr.Box 999PascalCity,USA**

Example 3-6:

Notice in part b of Example 3-5 that the output is all jammed together.   When using
Write statements for output, you must be sure to format the output correctly by adding
any required spacing or punctuation.   Correct the *Write* statements in Example 3-5
to format the output properly.

a. Your English professor would require you to add spacing and punctuation so that the output would look like this:

```
Andrew C. Staugaard, Jr., Box 999, Pascal City, USA
```

The following three *Write* statements will accomplish this task:

```
Write ('Andrew C. Staugaard, Jr., ');
Write ('Box 999, ');
Write ('Pascal City, USA ');
```

Notice that a blank space has been added after the last character and just before the closing quote in each statement. This provides the required spacing between the consecutive statement outputs. In addition, the required punctuation has been added. Notice the comma that has been added after the last 9 in the second statement.

Formatting the Output

By formatting an output I mean structuring it to meet a given application. Pascal allows output formatting using special commands within the *Write* and *Writeln* statements. Before discussing the details, let's learn how the computer "sees" a CRT display or printed page.

Most systems, including the IBM PC, divide a page of output into 25 rows and 80 columns as shown by the ***layout chart*** in Figure 3-2. Layout charts are used to lay out, or format, your output. The layout chart allows you to align output information so that

- Proper margins are provided for header information
- Numeric and character data are properly aligned under column headings and evenly spaced across the page
- The output looks professional

The first thing to do when using a layout chart is to fill in the chart with the information to be output. For instance, suppose that you must create three columns of output: the first for a person's name, the second for the person's address, and the third for a person's phone number. Figure 3-3 shows how these three columns might be laid out on a layout chart. Looking at the figure, you can make the following observations:

- There are three headings located in row 4.
- There are dashes in row 5 to underscore each column heading.
- The NAME heading has a ***field width*** of 15.
- The ADDRESS heading has a ***field width*** of 22.
- The PHONE heading has a ***field width*** of 23.

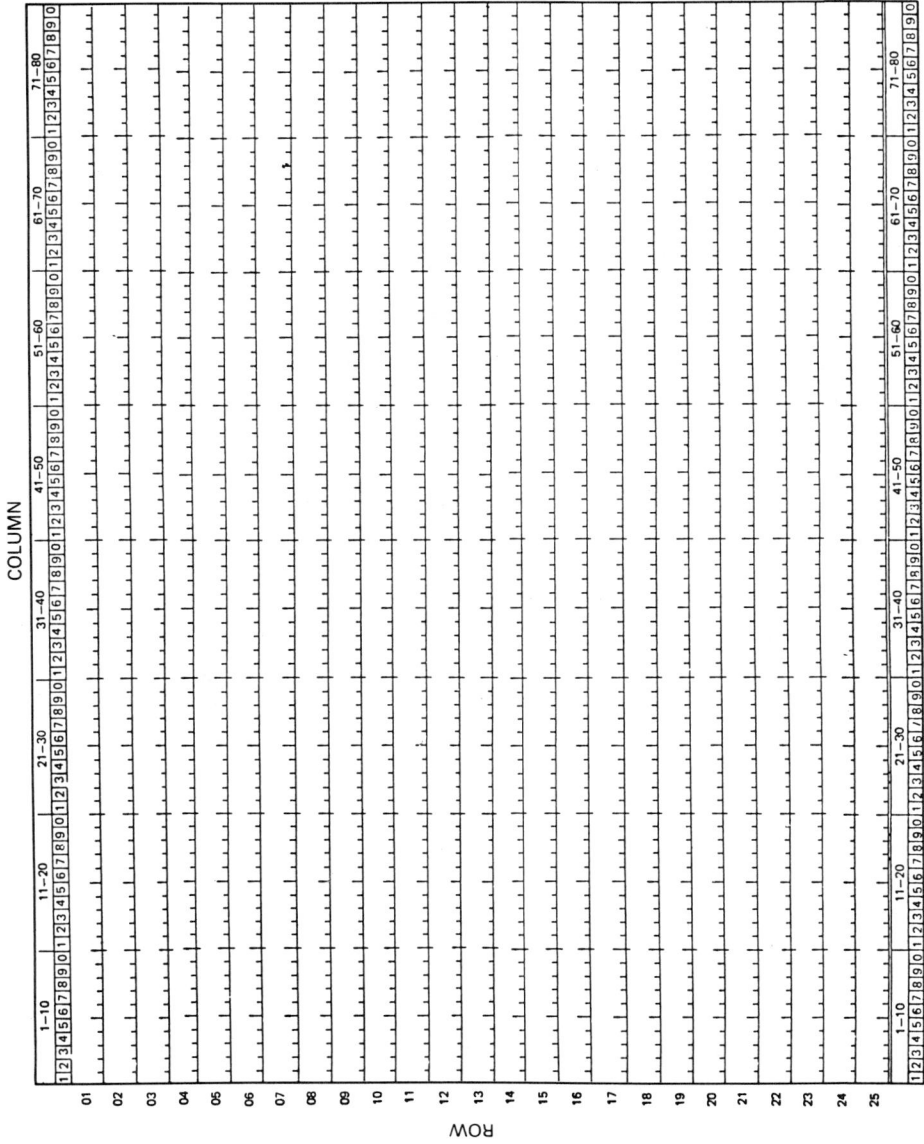

Figure 3-2 A typical layout chart.

69

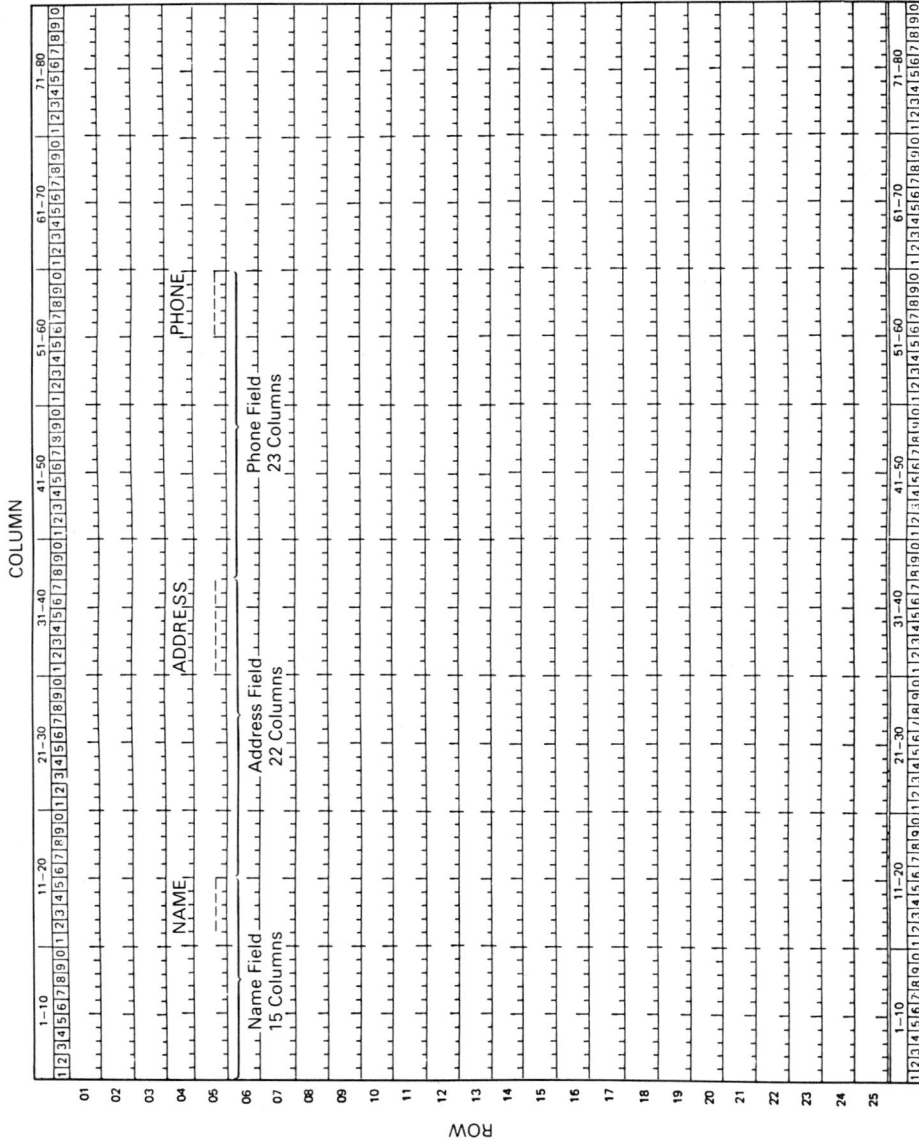

Figure 3-3 Laying out an output using a layout chart.

Using this information, let's write a program segment that will display the headings just as they appear on the spacing chart. Here it is:

```
Clrscr;
Writeln;
Writeln;
Writeln;
Writeln ('NAME':15,'ADDRESS':22,'PHONE':23);
Writeln ('----':15,'-------':22,'-----':23);
```

The first thing that you see in the foregoing program segment is the statement *Clrscr*. This is an abbreviation that means "clear screen." It does exactly what it says: It clears the CRT screen. You will often want to insert this statement at the beginning of your program so that a CRT output begins with a clean slate, or clear screen. Clearly, this statement has no effect on printer output.

Next, there are three consecutive *Writeln* statements. These three statements generate the three blank lines in rows 1, 2, and 3, respectively.

Now, looking at the layout chart in Figure 3-3, you see that each heading is designated by a ***field width***. The field width is the number of columns that Pascal will assign to the output item. All output items are ***right justified***. This means that the output item is positioned at the extreme right-hand side of the field. Observe that the first output, NAME, has a field width of 15. Thus, Pascal assigns the first 15 columns to the output item NAME. Since it is right justified, NAME is positioned at the extreme right-hand side of the field. And since the word NAME only requires four columns of output, Pascal generates $15 - 4$, or 11, spaces prior to NAME.

Next, count the number of columns from the NAME field to the last S in the ADDRESS field. You get 22, right? Thus, the ADDRESS field width is 22. Finally, counting the number of columns from the ADDRESS field to the last letter (E) in the PHONE field you get 23. Consequently, the PHONE field width is 23.

These field width values are used in the foregoing program segment to locate the output items. Notice that the output item is followed by a colon, which is followed by the field width required for the item. In general, the format for using field width designations is:

FIELD WIDTH FORMAT ***
Writeln
  or   (output item : field width, ...);
Write
  ****

Example 3-7:

Write a program segment that will format a three-column table for CURRENT, RESISTANCE, and VOLTAGE. Underscore each column heading.

Solution: Using a layout chart, you must first lay out the output headings. Such a layout is shown in Figure 3-4. Here, the table headings are located on row 5 and each heading has a field width of 20. In addition, each heading is underscored by using dashes in row 6. The dashes must also have a field width of 20 to locate them under their respective headings. The resulting program segment is as follows:

```
Clrscr;
Writeln;
Writeln;
Writeln;
Writeln;
Writeln ('CURRENT':20,'RESISTANCE':20,'VOLTAGE':20);
Writeln ('-------':20,'----------':20,'-------':20);
```

Example 3-8:

Given a current value of 0.0015 A and a resistance value of 10,000 Ω, write a program to calculate voltage using Ohm's law. Output the current, resistance, and voltage values using the format developed in Example 3-7.

Solution: The following program will do the job:

```
PROGRAM OhmsLaw (input, output);

USES
  Crt;

VAR
    Voltage, Current, Resistance : real;

BEGIN
    Clrscr;
    Current := 0.0015;
    Resistance := 10000;
    Voltage := Current * Resistance;
    Writeln;
    Writeln;
    Writeln;
    Writeln;
    Writeln ('CURRENT':20,'RESISTANCE':20,'VOLTAGE':20);
    Writeln ('-------':20,'----------':20,'-------':20);
    Writeln;
    Writeln (Current:20,Resistance:20,Voltage:20)

END.
```

This program will generate the following output:

CURRENT	RESISTANCE	VOLTAGE
-------	----------	-------
1.5000000000E-03	1.0000000000E+04	1.5000000000E+01

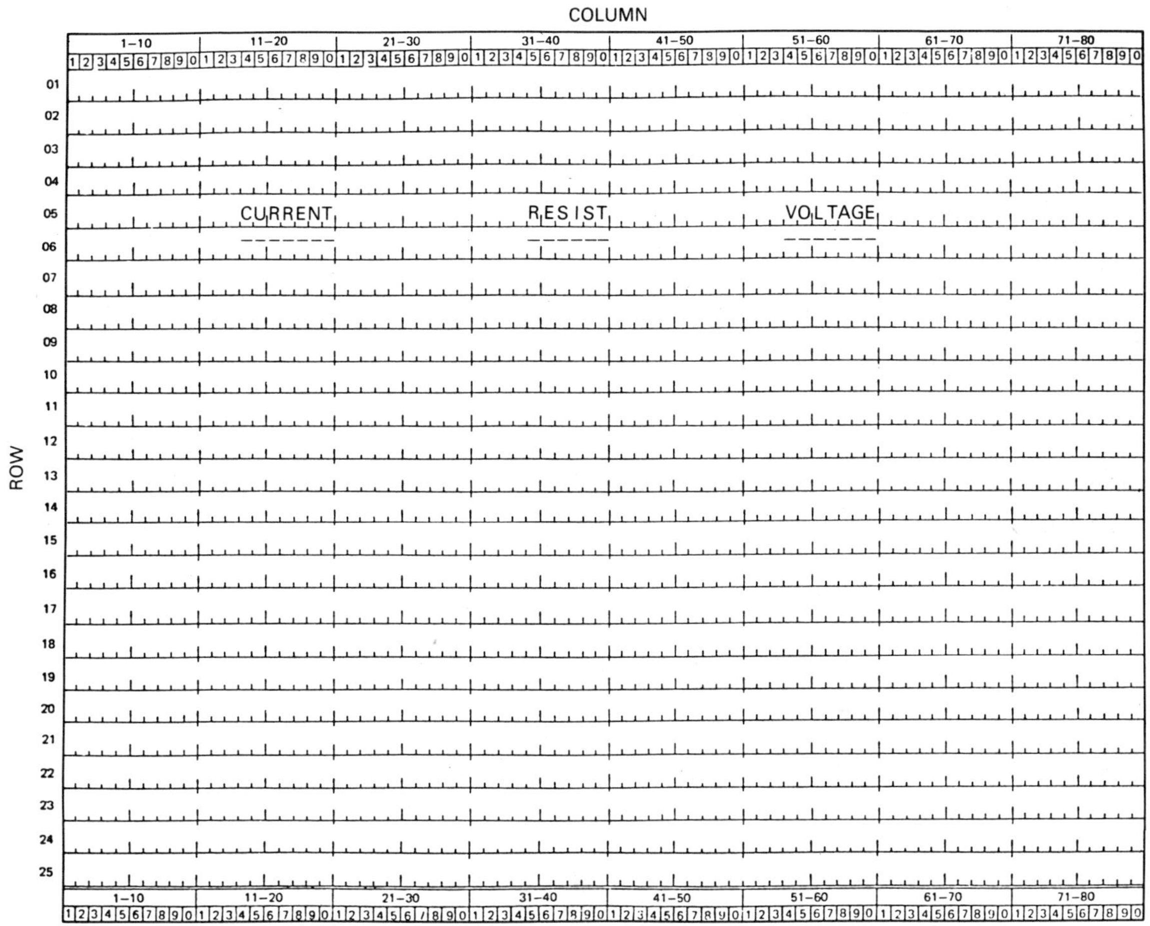

Figure 3-4 Layout for Example 3-7.

As you can see, the headings program segment from Example 3-7 was inserted to generate the required CURRENT, RESISTANCE, and VOLTAGE headings. Notice that the last *Writeln* statement in the program outputs the actual values of current, resistance, and voltage, respectively. Here, the variable identifier is listed along with the field width designation required to locate the value under the respective heading.

You also find a **USES** statement in this program. This statement is required by TURBO 4.0 or later versions whenever the *Clrscr* command is employed in a program. As you can see, the **USES** statement references the CRT. Of course, other versions of Pascal and earlier versions of TURBO Pascal do not require this statement and will not compile when it is present.

The output produced in Example 3-8 is easily understood by you and your technical friends. But what about a nontechnical friend? Would he or she understand the exponential notation? Wouldn't the output be easier for nontechnical people (or even technical people for that matter) to read if the values were in decimal, rather than exponential, form?

Getting Decimal Outputs

As you have seen, you get the exponential form of a real value when it is output via a *Writeln* or *Write* statement. However, there will be many times when you will want the decimal form to be output rather than the exponential form. To output a real value in decimal form, you must specify the number of decimal places in the output statement as follows:

DECIMAL OUTPUT FORMAT **
Writeln
   or   (real item : field width : number of decimal places, ...);
Write
  ****

As an example, recall that the statement

```
Writeln (2.75)
```

generates an output of

```
2.7500000000E+00
```

To generate an output of 2.75, you must alter the *Writeln* statement as follows:

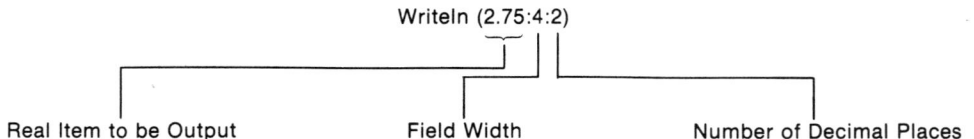

```
Writeln (2.75:4:2)
```

Real Item to be Output   Field Width   Number of Decimal Places

Notice that the real item is listed first, followed by the required field width, followed by the number of decimal places required.   A field width value of 4 is used, since there are four positions in the output, *including the decimal point.*   A larger field width value would result in blanks being generated prior to the output. A smaller field width value will not affect the output, even though the value 2.75 requires four columns of output.   Pascal simply adjusts and adds the minimum number of columns required to generate the correct output.

There are two places to the right of the decimal point.   Consequently, the value 2 is used to generate the required number of decimal places.   A value smaller than 2 will result in the output being rounded off.   For instance, a decimal place value of 1 will result in an output of 2.8 rather than 2.75.   On the other hand, a decimal place value larger than 2 will result in 0s being added to the output.   As an example, a decimal place value of 5 will result in an output of 2.75000 rather than 2.75.

Example 3-9:

Revise the program in Example 3-8 so that the values of current, resistance, and voltage are output in decimal form.

Solution: The following revised program will do it:

```
PROGRAM OhmsLaw (input, output);

USES
  Printer;

VAR
    Voltage, Current, Resistance : real;

BEGIN
    Clrscr;
    Current := 0.0015;
    Resistance := 10000;
    Voltage := Current * Resistance;
    Writeln;
    Writeln;
    Writeln;
    Writeln;
    Writeln ('CURRENT':20,'RESISTANCE':20,'VOLTAGE':20);
    Writeln ('-------':20,'----------':20,'-------':20);
    Writeln;
    Writeln (Current:20:4,Resistance:20:0,Voltage:20:4)

END.
```

This program will produce the following output:

CURRENT	RESISTANCE	VOLTAGE
-------	----------	-------
0.0015	10000	15.0000

As you can see, a decimal place value of 4 for the current generates the required four decimal places for the current value of 0.0015. Next, notice that a decimal place value of 0 for resistance generates the whole number integer representation for resistance (10000), completely eliminating the decimal point. You will want to remember this little trick when you only want to output the whole number portion of a real number. Finally, a decimal place value of 4 for voltage generates a voltage output with four positions to the right of the decimal point as shown.

3-2 GETTING THINGS IN: READING

In Pascal, getting information into a program for processing is called **reading**. In most present-day systems, information is read from one of two sources: from a keyboard or from a disk file. In this section you will learn how to read information that is being input via a keyboard by the system user.

There are two statements used in Pascal for input: *Read* and *Readln* (read line). Like *Write* and *Writeln*, the *Read* and *Readln* statements invoke predefined procedures to accomplish the input task. Now let's see how they work. We will begin with the *Read* statement.

The *Read* Statement

Before you can understand how this statement works, you must know a little bit about how the CPU sees a line of data. Suppose that you wish to enter a *line* of data consisting of three numeric values as follows:

75 92 88 `ENTER`

When typing in the foregoing data on a keyboard, you would type each number consecutively, separating them with one or more spaces. At the end of the line, you must press the `ENTER` or `RETURN` key, depending on your particular system. How do you suppose the system knows where one data item ends and another begins? You're right—the spaces, or blanks, define the separate data items. Next, how do you suppose the system knows where the line of data ends? Right again—by pressing the `ENTER` or `RETURN` key you are defining the end of the line. This operation places an **end-of-line (EOLN) marker** at the end of the line. In fact, as you might guess, the system does not actually take in any data until it sees the end-of-line marker produced by pressing the `ENTER` or `RETURN` key.

Now back to the *Read* operation. The general form for the *Read* statement is as follows:

Read FORMAT **
                Read (variable #1, variable #2, variable #3, ..., variable #n);
               ****

Notice that the word *Read* is followed by a variable listing enclosed within parentheses. Each variable is separated by a comma within the listing. Of course, the variables must be declared using the **VAR** statement prior to using them in the *Read* statement.

Suppose, for example, that you have declared three variables called *Test-Score1*, *TestScore2*, and *TestScore3*. Then, to read three scores into the system, you would insert a *Read* statement into your program as follows:

```
Read (TestScore1, TestScore2, TestScore3);
```

When the computer encounters the foregoing statement in your program, it *halts execution* until the user enters a line of data. Now suppose that the user enters the following via the system keyboard:

75 92 88   `ENTER`

What do you suppose happens? You're right again—the value 75 is assigned to *TestScore1*, the value 92 is assigned to *TestScore2*, and the value 88 is assigned to *TestScore3*. Thus, you can think of the *Read* operation as an assignment operation. The values entered on the keyboard are assigned on a one-to-one basis to the variables listed in the *Read* statement. The assignment order is the order of the respective data and variable listings. Once you press the `ENTER` or `RETURN` key, the system knows that the line has ended. It then makes the assignments, and execution of the program continues.

You're probably wondering what happens if the number of variables in the *Read* statement does not equal the number of data items entered by the user. Well, let's see: If the number of variables is greater than the number of data elements entered, no assignments are made to the excess variables. For instance, suppose that the user entered just two scores for the foregoing *Read* statement, as follows:

75 92   `ENTER`

Then the value 75 is assigned to *TestScore1* and the value 92 is assigned to *TestScore2*. No value is assigned to *TestScore3*. In fact, the actual value of *TestScore3* stored in memory will be random.

Next, suppose that the user enters more data than is required by the *Read* statement. In this case, only the required amount of data is used. Any excess data items are ignored. For instance, suppose that the user enters four scores, as follows:

75 92 88 67 `ENTER`

This results in the values 75, 92, and 88 being assigned to *TestScore1*, *TestScore2*, and *TestScore3*, respectively. The value 67 is ignored by this *Read* statement.

The *Readln* Statement

The general format for the *Readln* statement is as follows:

```
Readln FORMAT *************************************************************
          Readln (variable #1, variable #2, variable #3, ..., variable #n);
       *************************************************************
```

You can see that the *Readln* statement format is identical to the *Read* format, except for the command word itself. So, what's the difference? There is one subtle but important difference that you need to remember. After a *Readln* operation the CRT cursor is repositioned to the beginning of the next line. To illustrate this, consider the following program segment:

```
Write ('Please enter three test scores . . . ');
Read (TestScore1, TestScore2, TestScore3);
Write ('Thank You');
```

You will see the following on the CRT when the foregoing program segment is executed. (Of course, this assumes that you typed in the values 75 92 88 and pressed the **ENTER** key.)

```
Please enter three test scores . . . 75 92 88Thank You
```

Now suppose that you change the word *Read* to *Readln* in the foregoing program segment. Then the resulting CRT display will be

```
Please enter three test scores . . . 75 92 88
Thank You
```

Notice the difference between the two displays. With the *Read* statement, the words "Thank You" were displayed on the same line. However, the *Readln* causes the words "Thank You" to be displayed on the next line of output. The reason for this is that the *Readln* statement repositions the cursor to the beginning of the next line *after* the read operation is performed. In this text I will use the *Readln* statement much more frequently than the *Read* statement.

By the way, notice the *interaction* between the program and the user in the foregoing program segment. The program displays a *user prompt* to tell the user to enter three test scores. Once the scores are entered by the user, the program displays a "Thank You" message. This assures the user that his or her scores have been accepted by the computer. This is an example of *interactive programming* and will be discussed in more detail shortly.

Reading Different Data Types

Two cardinal rules apply when reading data:

Rule 1: All variables listed within the *Read* or *Readln* statements must be declared in the declaration section of the program.

Rule 2: The type of data entered for a given variable must match the
data type declared for that variable.

By now, the first rule should be obvious. You cannot use a variable in a
Pascal program unless it has been previously declared in the declaration section of
the program. The second rule needs to be explored a bit further. Consider the
following program:

```
PROGRAM TestScores (input, output);

VAR
    TestScore1 : integer;
    TestScore2 : real;

BEGIN
    Readln (TestScore1, TestScore2)
END.
```

Now suppose that the user enters the following line of data when the *Readln*
statement is encountered.

98.5 78   ▐ENTER▌

What happens? Notice that the program declares *TestScore1* as an integer
and *TestScore2* as a real. However, the user has entered a decimal value for
TestScore1 and an integer value for *TestScore2*. Thus, the computer attempts to
assign a decimal value (98.5) to an integer variable (*TestScore1*). This is called a
DATA TYPE MISMATCH and will result in an error when the user presses the
▐**ENTER**▌ key. At this point, the program must be aborted and run again.

Next, using the same program, suppose that the user enters the folowing line
of data:

98 78   ▐ENTER▌

Now there is no error. But how can this be, since the computer assigns an
integer value (78) to a real variable (*TestScore2*)? This is okay, since integer values
are also real. The computer simply converts the integer value to the real format.
Thus, the integer value 78 is converted to the real value 78.000000000E + 00 for
storage within main working memory. This is the **only** exception to the data type
mismatch rule (Rule 2).

DEBUGGING TIP ────────────────────────────────────

When you initially code a program, it is always wise to **echo** an input value back to the
display. This assures you that the program has performed the read operation and made
the correct variable assignment. To echo an input value back to the display, you simply
insert a *Writeln* statement after the *Read* or *Readln* statement. Within the *Writeln* statement,
you list the same variables that are listed within the *Read* or *Readln* statement. For instance,

to echo the test scores in the foregoing program, you would add a *Writeln* statement, as follows:

```
PROGRAM TestScores (input, output);

VAR
    TestScore1 : integer;
    TestScore2 : real;

BEGIN
    Readln (TestScore1, TestScore2);
    Writeln (TestScore1, TestScore2)
END.
```

Once the program has been debugged and is completely operational, you can remove the echoing *Writeln* statements.

___

Reading Character Data

Reading numeric data is straightforward, as long as you adhere to the two rules for reading data. However, there are three points that you will want to keep in mind when reading character data:

1. Only one character is read at a time.
2. Each blank space is treated as a separate character.
3. Numeric values can be read as characters, but each digit is read as a separate character.

Let's look at a simple program that illustrates most of these concepts. Consider the following:

```
PROGRAM TestGrades (input, output);

VAR
    TestGrade1, TestGrade2, TestGrade3 : char;

BEGIN
    Readln (TestGrade1, TestGrade2, TestGrade3);
    Writeln (TestGrade1, TestGrade2, TestGrade3)
END.
```

The foregoing program declares three variables (*TestGrade1*, *TestGrade2*, *TestGrade3*) as character variables. The program then reads the three character variables from the system keyboard and echoes the variables back to the system display. Now let's see what the program will do for several input cases.

Case 1

User types in: **Grade** `ENTER`
System displays: **Gra**
Here, the user has typed in the word "Grade" and pressed the `ENTER` key.
However, the system displays only the first three letters (Gra) of the entered word.
The reason is that character data is read only one character at a time. Only the
first three characters are echoed back, since only three character variables are read.
The character "G" is assigned to *TestGrade1*, the character "r" is assigned to
TestGrade2, and the character "a" is assigned to *TestGrade3*. The remaining two
characters (d and e) are excess and ignored.

Case 2

User types in: **A B C** `ENTER`
System displays: **A B**
In this case, the user has entered only three characters, right? Wrong! The
user has entered at least five characters. Remember that the computer interprets
each blank space as a separate character. Only the first three characters entered
are assigned and echoed back to the display. Thus, the character "A" is assigned
to *TestGrade1*, a **blank** character is assigned to *TestGrade2*, and the character "B"
is assigned to *TestGrade3*. The remaining characters (a blank and C) are excess
and are ignored by the program.

Case 3

User types in: **ABC** `ENTER`
System displays: **ABC**
This time, the user has entered three consecutive test grades with no spaces
or punctuation. As a result, the system assigns the character "A" to *TestGrade1*,
the character "B" to *TestGrade2*, and the character "C" to *TestGrade3*. This
assignment is verified by the display echo generated by the *Writeln* statement.

Case 4

User types in: **75 92 88** `ENTER`
System displays: **75**
In this case, the user has typed in three numeric test grades rather than letter
grades. However, since the variables are declared as character variables, the
system treats the numbers as characters during the read operation. Each digit
within a number is seen as a separate character. Thus, the digit 7 is assigned to
TestGrade1, the digit 5 is assigned to *TestGrade2*, and a blank is assigned to
TestGrade3. The remaining data (92 88) are excess and ignored by the program.
The lesson to be learned here is to always use numeric variables (integer or real)
to read numeric data. As you can see, data can be lost when using character
variables to read numeric data.

Case 5

User types in: `97.5 73 84` `ENTER`
System displays: `97.`

Again, the user has typed in three numeric test scores, which are treated as character data by the program. Thus, the first three characters are assigned, and the remaining information is ignored. As you can see from the echo, the digit 9 is assigned to *TestGrade1*, the digit 7 is assigned to *TestGrade2*, and the decimal point is assigned to *TestGrade3*.

As you can see, reading only one character at a time imposes a severe limitation on entering character data. A separate variable is required for each individual character to be input. This is why TURBO Pascal allows you to read string data.

Reading String Data

Recall that TURBO Pascal allows you to declare a string variable consisting of up to 255 characters, including spaces. This feature is extremely advantageous when reading variable data that consists of two or more characters. Here's an example program that illustrates the power of string variables.

```
PROGRAM StringInput (input, output);

VAR

    Name, Address : STRING [30];

    PhoneNumber :   STRING [15];

BEGIN
    Readln (Name);
    Writeln (Name);
    Readln (Address);
    Writeln (Address);
    Readln (PhoneNumber);
    Writeln (PhoneNumber)

END.
```

This program declares three string variables: *Name*, *Address*, and *Phone-Number*. After the declaration, each string variable is read via a *Readln* statement and subsequently echoed to the display via a *Writeln* statement. Here's how the program works:

User types-in: `Andrew C. Staugaard, Jr.`   `ENTER`
System displays: `Andrew C. Staugaard, Jr.`
User types-in: `Box 999, Pascal City, USA`   `ENTER`
System displays: `Box 999, Pascal City, USA`
User types-in: `(012) 345-6789`   `ENTER`
System displays: `(012) 345-6789`

Here, the string "Andrew C. Staugaard, Jr." is assigned to the string variable *Name*, the string "Box 999, Pascal City, USA" is assigned to *Address*, and the string "(012) 345-6789" is assigned to *PhoneNumber*. As you can see, string variables may consist of any of the keyboard characters, including numbers and punctuation. All the characters within the input string are assigned to their respective variable, as long as the length of the input string, including blanks, does not exceed the declared length of the variable. If an input string is longer than the declared length of the string variable, the excess characters are ignored.

You might also have noticed in the foregoing program that each string variable was input using a separate *Readln* statement. Although this is not required, it allows you (the programmer), the program user, and Pascal to keep the string variables separate. Using separate *Readln* statements to input individual variables avoids confusion and makes your program more user friendly.

Reading Information with Different Versions of TURBO

You should be aware that different verions of TURBO read keyboard data slightly different, due to the way that the compiler buffers the keyboard. Consult your TURBO reference manual concerning the *Read* and *Readln* statements if you don't get the exact program results expected.

3-3 USER-FRIENDLY PROGRAMS: INTERACTIVE PROGRAMMING

You must always strive to make your programs as user friendly as possible. By a user-friendly program, I mean a program that is easy to use and does not confuse the user. Such a program should always include the following (at a minimum):

1. A program description message that tells the user what the program is going to do.
2. Prompt messages prior to any read operations. These **user prompts** must tell the user what information to enter and how to enter it in clear, unconfusing terms.
3. Output information that is well formatted and whose meaning is easily understood by the user.

Let's see how we can make the name, address, and phone number program more user friendly. Suppose that we revise the program as follows:

```
PROGRAM StringInput (input, output);

USES
   Crt;

VAR

   Name, Address : STRING [30];

   PhoneNumber :   STRING [15];
```

(*Continued*)

```
BEGIN
  Clrscr;
  Writeln ('This program will ask you to enter your name, ');
  Writeln ('address, and phone number.  Please press the ');

  Writeln ('ENTER key after each entry.');
  Writeln;
  Writeln;
  Writeln;
  Write ('Please enter your name (first, middle initial, last):  ');
  Readln (Name);
  Writeln;
  Write ('Please enter your address:  ');
  Readln (Address);
  Writeln;
  Write ('Please enter your phone number, including area code:  ');
  Readln (PhoneNumber);
  Writeln;
  Writeln;
  Writeln ('Your name, address, and phone number are:');
  Writeln;
  Writeln (Name);
  Writeln (Address);
  Writeln (PhoneNumber)

END.
```

Here is what the user sees on the display after the program has run:

```
This program will ask you to enter your name,
address and phone number.  Please press the
enter key after each entry.



Please enter your name (first,  middle initial, last):  Andrew C.
Staugaard, Jr.

Please enter your address:  Box 999, Pascal City, USA

Please enter your phone number:  (012) 345-6789


Your name, address, and phone number are:

Andrew C. Staugaard, Jr.
Box 999, Pascal City, USA
(012) 345-6789
```

Notice that the information entered by the user is set in bold type so that you can distinguish it from the output information generated by the program. As you can see, the program description message tells the user what the program is about to do, as well as providing some general data-entry instructions.

Next, the program prompts the user to enter his or her name, indicating the required name format. A *Write* statement is used here rather than *Writeln* so that the user's name will be entered on the same line as the prompt. Remember this little trick! It makes for good interactive programming style. A *Readln* statement is required after the prompt to read the user entry and assign the entry to the string variable *Name*. The program then prompts the user for his or her address, and reads the address. The address entry is assigned to the variable *Address*. The third prompt asks the user for his or her phone number. The subsequent *Readln* operation assigns the entry to the variable *PhoneNumber*.

The program then echoes the input information back to the user to verify correct entry.

One final point: Notice how the single *Writeln* statements are used to provide output line spacing. This separates the output information, making it clear and easy to read—all in an effort to make the program more user friendly.

Example 3-10:

Write a user-friendly program that will calculate voltage from different values of current and resistance entered by the user. Format a three-column table for current, resistance, and voltage. Underscore each column heading and generate the respective outputs to four decimal places.

Solution: Let's first define the problem in terms of output, input, and processing as follows:

Output: The output must be a table showing the calculated voltage value along with the current and resistance values used in the calculation. Each output value must be in decimal form to four decimal places.

Input: The input must be a current and a resistance value entered by the user. Appropriate user prompts must be generated to instruct the user to enter the values.

Processing: Ohm's law → Voltage = Current *Resistance

The next step is to construct an algorithm from the problem definition. The following algorithm will do the job:

> BEGIN
> Clear the display screen.
> Write a program description message to the user.
> Write a user prompt to enter the current value (*Current*).
> Read (*Current*).
> Write a user prompt to enter the resistance value (*Resistance*).
> Read (*Resistance*).
> Calculate the voltage: *Voltage = Current * Resistance*.
> Write table headings for current, resistance, and voltage. Underscore the headings.
> Write the current, resistance, and voltage values under the respective headings to four decimal places.
> END.

Now, using the foregoing algorithm and your knowledge of Pascal, the program is coded as follows:

```
PROGRAM OhmsLaw (input, output);

USES
  Crt;

VAR
    Voltage, Current, Resistance : real;

BEGIN
  Clrscr;
  Writeln ('This program will calculate voltage from current and ');
  Writeln ('resistance values that you enter.');
  Writeln ('Please enter all values in decimal form.');
  Writeln;
  Writeln;
  Writeln;
  Write ('Enter a current value:  Current =  ');
  Readln (Current);
  Writeln;
  Write ('Enter a resistance value:  Resistance =  ');
  Readln (Resistance);
  Writeln;
  Voltage := Current * Resistance;
  Writeln ('CURRENT':20,'RESISTANCE':20,'VOLTAGE':20);
  Writeln ('-------':20,'_____':20,'-------':20);
  Writeln;
  Writeln (Current:20:4, Resistance:20:4, Voltage:20:4)
END.
```

You should now have no trouble understanding this program with the material presented in this chapter.

Now make a serious effort to complete all of the questions and problems that follow. It is time to get your hands dirty and to program your system to apply the program exercises that follow the chapter summary. This is where you will really learn how to program in Pascal.

CHAPTER SUMMARY

In Pascal getting information into your system is called reading, and getting information out of your system is called writing. There are two Pascal statements used for reading and two used for writing.

The two statements used for writing are *Write* and *Writeln*. The difference between the two is that *Writeln* causes the CRT cursor or printer head to return to the beginning of the next line after the current line has been output. The *Write* statement does not cause this to happen.

Each *Write* or *Writeln* statement must include a listing of the items to be written. The item listing must be enclosed in parentheses and the items within the listing must be separated by commas. The *Write* and *Writeln* statements can be used to output either fixed or variable information. When writing fixed character information, the information to be written must be enclosed within single quotes. When writing variable information, the variable identifier must be listed within the *Write* statement.

Information can be written to the system CRT display or printer. When writing to a printer, the *1st* command must be inserted at the beginning of the item listing. When no *1st* command is present, information is written to the system display.

To format an output, you must attach a field width designator to the item(s) to be output. The field width designator value specifies the number of columns of output that will be allocated to the item being written. Always use a layout chart to lay out your output and determine the correct field width values. When writing real values, you must specify the number of decimal places to be output; otherwise, the output will be in exponential form.

The two statements used for reading are *Read* and *Readln*. Like *Writeln*, *Readln* causes the cursor to be positioned at the beginning of the next line after the statement has been executed. The *Read* statement does not cause this to happen. This might not be the case in some versions of TURBO. If you don't get the results you expect, check your TURBO reference manual for the difference between *Read* and *Readln*.

Both the *Read* and *Readln* statements must include a listing of the variables to be input, or read. Input data are assigned sequentially to the variables listed in the *Read* or *Readln* statement as the data are entered on the system keyboard. All variables listed within the *Read* or *Readln* statement must be declared in the declaration part of the program. Moreover, the type of data entered for a given variable must match the data type declared for that variable.

User-friendly programs require interaction between the program and the user. At a minimum, a user-friendly program must

- Write a program description message to the user

- Prompt the user prior to any read operations
- Generate well-formatted outputs whose meaning is easily understood by the user.

QUESTIONS AND PROBLEMS

Questions

3-1. Indicate the output for each of the following:

```
a.  Writeln;
    Writeln;

b.  Writeln ('HELLO':40);

c.  Writeln (-36.2:12:3);

d.  Writeln (3.75);

e.  Writeln (1:5,2:5,3:5,4:5);

f.  Writeln ('My test score is :',97.6:5:2);

g.  Write ('TEST SCORE');
    Writeln (97.5:4:2);

h.  Writeln ('TEST SCORE');
    Writeln (97.5:4:2);

i.  Writeln (1st,'TEST SCORE');
    Writeln (1st,97.5:4:2);
```

3-2. Suppose that you define a constant as follows:

```
CONST
    Spaces = ' ';
```

What will the following *Writeln* statement do?

```
Writeln (Spaces:20,'HELLO');
```

3-3. What will the following statement do?

```
Writeln (' ':20,'HELLO');
```

3-4. What is the difference between the output produced by the following two program segments?

Program segment 1:

```
Writeln ('#');
Writeln ('#');
Writeln ('#');
```

Program segment 2:

```
Write ('#');
Write ('#');
Write ('#');
```

3-5. Consider the following program:

```
PROGRAM Problem_5 (input, output);

VAR
    A : integer;
    B : char;

BEGIN
    Readln (A,B);
    Writeln (A,B)

END.
```

What will be the output for the following user entries?

a. **6F**   ENTER

b. **6 F**   ENTER

c. **F 6**   ENTER

3-6. Suppose that while entering the program in question 3-5 you made the following typographical errors on the *Readln* statement:

a. **Readln (B,A);**
b. **Readln (AB);**
c. **Readln (A B);**

What will happen in each case?

3-7. What will the following statement do?

```
Writeln (1st.'              ');
```

3-8. What is a data type mismatch in Pascal?

3-9. Suppose that you must print two tables that are ten lines long on two separate pages of output.   Explain how to accomplish this task.

3-10. Explain what happens when the user inputs a string longer than the declared length of the respective string variable.

3-11. Explain what happens when the user inputs a string shorter than the declared length of the respective string variable.

Programming Problems

3-1. Using the layout chart in Figure 3-2, write a program to display your first name in the middle of the CRT screen.

3-2. Using the layout chart in Figure 3-2, write a program to display your first name in the upper left-hand corner of the display using characters that are six lines high, as follows:

```
    AA          NNN     NN    DDDDDDD    YY       YY
   AAAA         NN NN   NN    DD     DD  YY     YY
  AA  AA        NN  NN  NN    DD     DD   YY  YY
 AAAAAAAA       NN   NN NN    DD     DD     YYY
AA      AA      NN    NN NN   DD     DD     YYY
AA      AA      NN      NNN   DDDDDDD       YYY
```

3-3. Write a program that will generate a rectangle whose center is located in the middle of the display. Construct the rectangle using Xs eight lines high and twenty columns wide.

3-4. Write a program that will generate the following output in the middle of the display:

```
     STUDENT           SEMESTER AVERAGE
     -------           ----------------
        1                   84.5
        2                   67.2
        3                   77.4
        4                   86.8
        5                   94.7
```

3-5. Write a program to calculate simple interest on a $2,000 loan for two years at a rate of 12.5 percent. Format your output appropriately, showing the amount of the loan, time period, interest rate, and interest amount.

3-6. Write a program that will prompt the user to enter any four-letter word. Then display the word backwards. (Keep it clean!)

3-7. Write a program to calculate dc power from a voltage value of 12 V and a current value of 0.00125 A. Generate a tabular display of input and output values in decimal form.
Note: Power = Voltage × Current in a dc circuit.

3-8. Write a user-friendly program that will calculate power from voltage and current values entered by the user. Generate a tabular display of input and output values in decimal form.

3-9. Write a user-friendly program that will calculate the equivalent resistance of a series circuit from five resistances entered by the user. Generate a tabular display of input and output values in decimal form.
Note: The + symbol is used for addition in Pascal. Thus, in Pascal the equivalent resistance is

```
R_equiv := R1 + R2 + R3 + R4 + R5;
```

3-10. Write a user-friendly program that will calculate the equivalent resistance from two parallel resistances entered by the user. Generate a tabular display of values in decimal form.

Note: The / symbol is used for real-number division in Pascal. Thus, with two resistances, R1 and R2, the equivalent resistance is:

```
R_equiv := (R1 * R2) / (R1 + R2);
```

Observe the use of the parentheses to group the quantities. Why do you suppose this is necessary?

3-11. Write a user-friendly program that will allow a student to calculate his or her test average from four test scores. Generate a display of the student's name, course name, individual test scores, and test average.

chapter four

Writing Simple Pascal Programs

INTRODUCTION

You are now ready to begin learning how to write simple straight-line programs in Pascal. By a straight-line program, I mean a program that does not alter its flow; it simply executes a series of statements in a straight line, from beginning to end.

For your program to perform meaningful tasks, you must be familiar with several standard, or built-in, operations available to you in Pascal. The simplest of these are the standard arithmetic operations. By definition, an arithmetic operation generates a numeric result. Such operations are the topic of the first section of this chapter.

In addition to arithmetic operations, there are Boolean operations available in Pascal that generate a Boolean result. These operations are covered in the second section of the chapter.

To simplify the programming task, Pascal employs several standard functions. These functions allow you to easily implement many common operations, such as square, square root, sine, and cosine, without writing special routines. Standard functions are discussed in the third section of the chapter.

Finally, the last section of this chapter applies the material in the first three

sections to several real-world tasks.   Here you will learn by example.   I encourage
you to study these examples very closely, since they employ many of the ideas and
concepts presented in these first four chapters.   Now, let's go to it!

4-1 ARITHMETIC OPERATIONS

Arithmetic operations in Pascal include the common add, subtract, multiply, and
divide operations.   These operations can be performed on any numeric data type.
Recall that the standard numeric data types in Pascal are the integers and reals.
Although the simple arithmetic operations are similar for both integers and reals,
there are some distinct differences in Pascal, especially for the division operation.

Arithmetic Operations for Integers

As you might expect, you can add, subtract, multiply, and divide integers.   Table
4-1 lists these four basic arithmetic operations and the Pascal symbols used to
represent the operations.
   The addition $(+)$, subtraction $(-)$, and multiplication $(*)$ operations are
straightforward and do not need any further explanation.   However, you might
note that an asterisk $(*)$ is used for multiplication rather than a times symbol $(\times)$
so that the computer does not get multiplication confused with the letter x.
   Observe also that all these integer operations return an integer result.   This
is why there are two separate operations for integer division.   The **DIV** operation
returns the whole number, or integer, *quotient* when two integers are divided.   On
the other hand, the **MOD** operation returns the whole number *remainder* that
results when two integers are divided.   Both words **DIV** and **MOD** are reserved
words.

Example 4-1:

What integer value will be returned as the result of each of the following integer
operations?
a. $3 * (-5)$
b. $4 * 5 - 10$

TABLE 4-1   ARITHMETIC OPERATIONS FOR INTEGERS

Operation	Symbol	Example
Addition	+	$5 + 3 = 8$
Subtraction	−	$5 - 3 = 2$
Multiplication	*	$5 * 3 = 15$
Integer division (quotient only)	**DIV**	5 **DIV** $3 = 1$
Integer division (remainder only)	**MOD**	5 **MOD** $3 = 2$

c. 9 **DIV** 3
d. 9 **MOD** 3
e. −21 **DIV** (−2)
f. −21 **MOD** (−2)
g. 4 * 5 **DIV** 2 + 5 **MOD** 2

Solution:
a. 3 * (−5) returns the value −15.
b. 4 * 5 − 10 returns the value 10.
   Note that the multiplication operation is performed before the subtraction operation.
c. 9 **DIV** 3 returns the value 3.
d. 9 **MOD** 3 returns the value 0, since there is no remainder.
e. −21 **DIV** (−2) returns the integer quotient, 10.
f. −21 **MOD** (−2) returns the remainder, 1.
g. 4 * 5 **DIV** 2 + 5 **MOD** 2 =
   (4 * 5)**DIV** 2 + (5 **MOD** 2) =
   20 **DIV** 2 + (5 **MOD** 2) =
   10 + 1 =
   11

Notice that the multiplication, **DIV,** and **MOD** operations are performed first, from left to right. The addition operation is performed last.

Aside from showing how the individual integer operations work, the foregoing example illustrates the priority, or ordering, of the operations. When more than one operation is performed in an expression, you must know the order in which they will be performed to determine the result. Pascal performs integer operations in the following order:

- All operations within parentheses are performed first.
- If there are nested parentheses (parentheses within parentheses) the innermost operations are performed first.
- The *, **DIV,** and **MOD** operations are performed next, from left to right within the expression.
- The + and − operations are performed last, from left to right within the expression.

Arithmetic Operations for Reals

The arithmetic operations for reals are basically the same as those for integers, with the exception of division. The operations of **DIV** and **MOD** are defined *only* for integers, not reals. When dividing reals, you must use the slash (/) symbol. Table 4-2 lists the arithmetic operations used with real numbers.

TABLE 4-2 ARITHMETIC OPERATIONS FOR REALS

Operation	Symbol	Example
Addition	+	5.5 + 2.25 = 7.75
Subtraction	−	5.5 − 2.25 = 3.25
Multiplication	*	5.6 * 2.0 = 11.2
Division	/	5.6/2.0 = 2.8

When performing several real operations within an arithmetic expression, division and multiplication have the same priority. Thus, operations within parentheses are performed first, followed by multiplication and division, followed by addition and subtraction.

Example 4-2:

Evaluate each of the following expressions:
a. 4.6 − 2.0 + 3.2
b. 4.6 − 2.0 * 3.2
c. 4.6 − 2.0 / 2.0 * 3.2
d. −3.0 * ((4.3 + 2.5) * 2.0) − 1.0

Solution:
a. 4.6 − 2.0 + 3.2 =
    (4.6 − 2.0) + 3.2 =
    2.6 + 3.2 =
    5.8
b. 4.6 − 2.0 * 3.2 =
    4.6 − (2.0 * 3.2) =
    4.6 − 6.4 =
    −1.8
c. 4.6 − 2.0 / 2.0 * 3.2 =
    4.6 − ((2.0 / 2.0) * 3.2) =
    4.6 − (1.0 * 3.2) =
    4.6 − 3.2 =
    1.4
d. −3.0 * ((4.3 + 2.5) * 2.0) − 1.0 =
    −3.0 * (6.8 * 2.0) − 1.0 =
    −3.0 * 13.6 − 1.0 =
    −40.8 − 1.0 =
    −41.8

Notice that I have used parentheses in the solutions to indicate the order of the operations. As you can see, the parentheses clarify the expression. For this reason, I suggest that you always use parentheses when writing arithmetic expressions. This way you will always be sure of the order in which the computer will execute the operations within the expression. Keep in mind, however, that the computer will always perform the operations within parentheses from inside out, as shown in the last example problem.

4-2 BOOLEAN OPERATIONS

Boolean operations are those that will generate a Boolean result of TRUE or FALSE. There are two categories of Boolean operations: *relational* and *logical* operations.

Relational Operations

Relational operations allow two quantities to be compared. The six common relational operators available in Pascal are listed in Table 4-3.

The relational operators in Table 4-3 can be used to compare any two numbers or variable values. In general, you can only compare data of the same type. This means that integers must be compared with integers, reals with reals, and characters with characters. The one exception to this rule is that reals can be compared with integers, since integers are reals. In all cases the operation generates a Boolean result of TRUE or FALSE. Let's look at some examples.

Example 4-3:

Evaluate the following relational operations.
a. $5 = 5$
b. $0.025 > = 0.333$
c. $3 <> 3$
d. $-45.2 < -3$
e. $'A' < 'Z'$
f. $x := 25$
   $y := -10$
   $x <= y$

Solution:
a. TRUE, since 5 equals 5.
b. FALSE, since 0.025 is not greater than or equal to 0.333.
c. FALSE, since 3 equals 3.
d. TRUE, since -45.2 is less than -3.
e. TRUE, since Pascal considers the character 'A' to be less than the character 'Z'. Note that the characters must be enclosed within single quotes.
f. FALSE, since the value assigned to x (25) is not less than the value assigned to y (-10).

Relational operators can also be combined with arithmetic operations, as in the following:

$$5 + 3 < 4$$

Now the question is: How does the computer evaluate this expression? Does it perform the addition operation or the relational operation first? If it performs the addition operation first, the result is FALSE. However, if it performs the

TABLE 4-3 THE SIX RELATIONAL OPERATORS
AVAILABLE IN PASCAL

Mathematical symbol	Pascal operator	Meaning
=	=	Equal to
≠	<>	Not equal to
<	<	Less than
≤	<=	Less than or equal to
>	>	Greater than
≥	>=	Greater than or equal to

relational operation first, 3 is less than 4 and the result is TRUE.   As you might suspect, the addition operation is performed first, then the relational operation. Consequently, the result is FALSE, since 8 is not less than 4.   Remember, when relational operators are combined with arithmetic operators within an expression, the *relational operations are always performed last.*

In the next chapter, you will see how relational operators are used within a Pascal program to test data prior to making decisions.

Example 4-4:

Both arithmetic and relational operations can be part of an output statement to evaluate an expression.   Determine the output generated by the following:

a. **Writeln (3 + 4);**

b. **Writeln ('J' > 'K');**

c. **Writeln ('Janet' = 'Janet');**

d. **Writeln (3 * 10 MOD 3 - 2 > 20 DIV 6 + 4);**

e. **Writeln ((3 * 5)/(2 * 5):4:2);**

f. **Writeln (3 * 5 / 2 * 5 :4:2);**

Solution:

a. 7

b. FALSE

c. TRUE

d. Here, the evaluation process goes like this:
$(((3 * 10) \textbf{ MOD } 3) - 2) > ((20 \textbf{ DIV } 6) + 4)$
$((30 \textbf{ MOD } 3) - 2) > (3 + 4)$
$0 - 2 > 7$
$-2 > 7$
FALSE

Notice that the multiplication operation is performed first, followed by the **MOD** and **DIV** operations, from left to right.   Then the addition/subtraction operations are performed, and finally the greater-than operation.

e. 1.50
   Observe how the parentheses clarify the order of operations. Also notice how
   the decimal output is generated using the field width and decimal place designators
   discussed in the last chapter.
f. Here, without the use of parentheses, the evaluation process goes like this:
   3 * 5 / 2 * 5
   3 * 2.5 * 5
   7.5 * 5
   37.50
   Notice that without the use of parentheses the division operation is performed
   first, then the multiplication operations, from left to right. This is why you should
   always use parentheses when writing expressions. It's better to be safe than sorry!

Logical Operations

Logical operations also generate Boolean results. The four logical operators provided in Pascal are **NOT, OR, AND,** and **XOR** (TURBO only). The **NOT** operator
is used to negate, or invert, a Boolean value. Since there are only two possible
Boolean values (TRUE and FALSE), the negation of one results in the other.
For example, suppose we declare a Boolean variable A. Then the variable A can
take on only two values, TRUE or FALSE. If A is TRUE, **NOT** A is FALSE.
Conversely, if A is FALSE, **NOT** A is TRUE. This operation can be shown using
a *truth table*, as follows:

A	NOT A
TRUE	FALSE
FALSE	TRUE

The **OR** operation is applied to multiple Boolean variables. For instance,
suppose that A and B are both declared as Boolean variables. Then A and B can
be either TRUE or FALSE. The **OR** operator dictates that if either A *or* B are
TRUE, the result of the operation is TRUE. In terms of a truth table:

A	B	A OR B
FALSE	FALSE	FALSE
FALSE	TRUE	TRUE
TRUE	FALSE	TRUE
TRUE	TRUE	TRUE

Notice from the table that A **OR** B is TRUE whenever A is TRUE or B is
TRUE. Of course, if both A and B are TRUE, the result is TRUE.

The **AND** operator also operates on multiple Boolean values.   Here, if *A* and *B* are Boolean variables, the expression *A* **AND** *B* is TRUE only when both *A and B* are TRUE.   In terms of a truth table:

A	*B*	*A* **AND** *B*
FALSE	FALSE	FALSE
FALSE	TRUE	FALSE
TRUE	FALSE	FALSE
TRUE	TRUE	TRUE

Finally, the **XOR** (exclusive OR) operator is unique to TURBO Pascal.   We say that the **XOR** operator "recognizes" an odd number of TRUE inputs.   Thus, if the *number* of TRUE inputs is odd, the result of the **XOR** operation is TRUE. Here's the truth table:

A	*B*	*A* **XOR** *B*
FALSE	FALSE	FALSE
FALSE	TRUE	TRUE
TRUE	FALSE	TRUE
TRUE	TRUE	FALSE

As you can see, if there is only one TRUE input, the result is TRUE, since one is odd.   However, if there are two TRUE inputs, the operation result is FALSE, since two is even.

I should mention that the **OR, AND,** and **XOR** operators can be applied to any number of Boolean variables.   For instance, suppose that you have three Boolean variables: *A*, *B*, and *C*.   Then, *A* **AND** *B* **AND** *C* is TRUE only if *A* and *B* and *C* are all TRUE.

These logical operators can also be applied to Boolean expressions.   For example, consider the following:

$$(-6 < 0) \textbf{ AND } (12 > = 10)$$

Is this expression TRUE or FALSE?   Well, $-6 < 0$ is TRUE and $12 > =$ 10 is TRUE.   Consequently, the expression must be TRUE.   How about this one:

$$((3 - 6) = 3) \textbf{ OR } (\textbf{NOT } (2 = 4))$$

You must evaluate both sides of the expression.   If either side is TRUE, the result is TRUE.   On the left side, $3 - 6 = -3$, which is not equal to 3.   Thus, the left side is FALSE.   On the right side, $2 = 4$ is FALSE, but **NOT** $(2 = 4)$ must be TRUE.   Consequently, the right side of the expression is TRUE.   This makes the result of the ORing operation TRUE.

Observe in the two foregoing expressions that parentheses are used to define the expressions being operated on.   Remember to do this whenever you use a logical Boolean operator to evaluate two or more expressions.   In other words, *always* enclose the things you are ORing and ANDing within parentheses.

You will see in Chapter 5 how these logical operations are used to make decisions that control the flow of a program.   For example, using the **AND** operator, you can test to see if two conditions are TRUE.   If both conditions are TRUE, the program will execute a series of statements, while skipping those statements if one of the test conditions is FALSE.

4-3 THE STANDARD FUNCTIONS IN PASCAL

In Chapter 2 you were acquainted with several standard functions such as *Sqr*, *Sqrt*, and *Odd*.   Standard operations such as these are so common in programming that Pascal includes them as built-in functions.   To use, or *invoke*, a function within a program, you simply *assign* the function to a variable, as follows:

INVOKING A FUNCTION ∗∗
Variable Identifier : = Function Name (Argument);
∗∗∗

Thus, to find the square root of 256 you would assign the *Sqrt* function to a variable, say *X*, as follows:

```
X := Sqrt (256);
```

Here, the function name is *Sqrt* and the argument is 256.   Of course, *X* must be declared in the declaration section of the program.   Furthermore, the *Sqrt* function returns a real value.   Consequently, *X* must be declared as a real.   As a result, the foregoing statement will assign the value 16.0 to *X*.

Another way to invoke a function is to use it as part of a *Writeln* statement, as follows:

INVOKING A FUNCTION ∗∗∗
Writeln (Function Name (Argument));
∗∗∗

Using this idea, the statement

```
Writeln (Sqrt (25));
```

displays the value

```
5.0000000000E+00
```

Of course, you know how to get a decimal output if required.

There are arithmetic, scalar, and transfer functions.   I should caution you, however, that different versions of Pascal have available different standard functions. In this text you will learn about those standard functions available in TURBO Pascal. The following discussion will provide an overview of the standard TURBO functions. Space does not permit a detailed discussion of each function. However, you will observe the use of the more common functions in examples and problems that follow. If you're not sure how a given function works, refer to your TURBO reference manual.

Arithmetic Functions

Arithmetic functions perform an arithmetic operation. As a result, these functions require a numeric argument and return a numeric result. For this reason, they are sometimes called *numeric* functions. The standard arithmetic functions available in TURBO Pascal are listed in Table 4-4.

Most of the operations in Table 4-4 should be familiar to you from your background in mathematics. When using these functions in Pascal, you must make sure that the argument is the correct data type as specified by the function definition. In addition, any variable assigned to the function must be declared as the same data type returned by the function.

Scalar Functions

Scalar functions are those listed in Table 4-5 that deal with the ordered nature of scalar data types.

Transfer Functions

The transfer functions listed in Table 4-6 convert a value of one scalar data type to a value of another scalar data type.

There are a few more "miscellaneous" functions defined in TURBO. I have not shown them here, since they will not be used in this text. Consult your TURBO reference manual for a listing and explanation of these additional functions.

4-4 LEARNING BY EXAMPLE: SIMPLE PROGRAM TASKS

TASK 1: DIGITAL LOGIC

A common digital logic operator that is not available in Pascal is the NAND (not AND) operation. Given two Boolean variables, *A* and *B*, the NAND operation is defined as follows:

A	*B*	*A* **NAND** *B*
FALSE	FALSE	TRUE
FALSE	TRUE	TRUE
TRUE	FALSE	TRUE
TRUE	TRUE	FALSE

TABLE 4-4   THE STANDARD ARITHMETIC FUNCTIONS

Function name	Argument data type	Return data type	Operation
Abs	Real or integer	Same as argument	Returns the absolute value of the argument *Abs* (-5) returns 5
ArcTan	Real or integer	Real (radians)	Returns the angle, whose tangent is the argument *ArcTan* (1) returns 0.785
Cos	Real or integer (radians)	Real	Returns the cosine of the argument *Cos* (0) returns 1.0
Exp	Real or integer	Real	Returns $e^{(argument)}$ *Exp* (1) returns 2.718
Frac	Real or integer	Real	Returns the decimal portion of the argument *Frac* (3.14) returns 0.14
Int	Real or integer	Real	Returns the integer portion of the argument *Int* (3.14) returns 3.0
Ln	Real or integer	Real	Returns the natural logarithm of the argument *Ln* (2.718) returns 1.0
Sin	Real or integer (radians)	Real	Returns the sine of the argument *Sin* (0) returns 0.0
Sqr	Real or integer	Same as argument	Returns the square of the argument *Sqr* (5) returns 25
Sqrt	Nonnegative real or integer	Real	Returns the square root of the argument *Sqrt* (25) returns 5.0

Notice that the NAND operation is simply the opposite of the **AND** operation. In symbols, *A* **NAND** *B* = **NOT** (*A* **AND** *B*). Write a Pascal program that will display the NAND result of two Boolean values entered by the user.

Solution: Let's begin by defining the problem in terms of output, input, and processing.

The Problem Definition

Output: The program must display the Boolean result of the NAND operation as defined by the above truth table.

Input: The user must input Boolean values for the input variables, *A* and *B*.

TABLE 4-5   THE STANDARD SCALAR FUNCTIONS

Function name	Argument data type	Return data type	Operation
Odd	Integer	Boolean	Returns TRUE if argument is odd, and FALSE if argument is even *Odd* (−3) returns TRUE
Pred	Any scalar data type	Same as argument	Returns the predecessor of the argument *Pred* ('T') returns S
Succ	Any scalar data type	Same as argument	Returns the successor of the argument *Succ* ('S') returns T
Random	No argument	Real *decimal*	Returns a random real value between 0 and 1
Random	Integer	Integer	Returns a random integer value between 0 and the argument value

Processing: Although the NAND operation is not available in Pascal, you can implement it by using the **NOT** and **AND** operators, as follows:

$$A \text{ \textbf{NAND} } B := \textbf{NOT} \ (A \textbf{ AND } B);$$

Now the idea is to prompt the user to enter two Boolean values for *A* and *B* and apply the above relationship to generate a Boolean result.   However, there

TABLE 4-6   THE STANDARD TRANSFER FUNCTIONS

Function name	Argument data type	Return data type	Operation
Chr	Integer	Character	Returns the character whose ASCII value is the argument *Chr* (36) returns $
Ord	Any scalar type except real	Integer	Returns the internal ASCII representation of the argument *Ord* ('L') returns 76
Round	Real	Integer	Rounds the argument to the nearest integer value *Round* (3.5) returns 4
Trunc	Real	Integer	Returns the whole number portion of a decimal value *Trunc* (3.14) returns 3

is one minor difficulty. You *cannot* read Boolean values from the keyboard. Instead you must read character information, test the information for TRUE or FALSE, then make an assignment to the Boolean variables, *A* and *B*. Here's an algorithm that will do the job:

The Algorithm

BEGIN

    Write a program description message.

    Write a user prompt to enter a first Boolean value of *T* for TRUE or F for FALSE.

    Read the character entry.

    If entry is T then assign TRUE to *A*, else assign FALSE to *A*.

    Write a user prompt to enter a second Boolean value of T for TRUE or F for FALSE.

    Read the character entry.

    If the entry is T then assign TRUE to *B*, else assign FALSE to *B*.

    Assign **NOT** (*A* **AND** *B*) to NAND.

    Write NAND.

END.

The foregoing algorithm shows that a character (T or F) is read in, then tested to see if it is a T or an F. An assignment is then made to the Boolean variable, depending on the test. *If* the character is a T, *then* the Boolean variable is assigned to TRUE, *else* it is assigned to FALSE. This testing operation is called an *if/then/else* operation, for obvious reasons. You will learn more about this in Chapter 5. Once the two Boolean variables have been assigned, the NAND operation is performed and the result is output. Here's the program:

```
PROGRAM  NAND (input,output);

USES
   Crt;

VAR
   ENTRY : char;
   A, B : Boolean;

BEGIN
   Clrscr;
   Writeln ('This program will generate a NAND (not AND) result ');
   Writeln ('from two Boolean values that you must enter.');
   Writeln;
   Writeln;
   Writeln;
   Write ('Enter a Boolean value (T for TRUE or F for FALSE):  A = ')
   Readln (ENTRY);
```

```
IF ENTRY = 'T' THEN
   A := TRUE
ELSE
   A := FALSE;
Writeln;
Write ('Enter a second Boolean value (T for TRUE or F for ');
Write ('FALSE):  B = ');
Readln (ENTRY);
IF ENTRY = 'T' THEN
   B := TRUE
ELSE
   B := FALSE;
Writeln;
Writeln ('The NAND result is:    ',  NOT (A AND B))
                                          (A OR B))

END.
```

This program will generate the NAND (not AND) results, given two Boolean values entered by the user. Notice the use of the NAND expression in the final *Writeln* statement. This is where the operation is performed.

TASK 2: VOLTAGE DIVIDER

Write a Pascal program to calculate the output of the voltage divider circuit in Figure 4-1. Assume that the user will enter the source voltage and the two resistor values.

Solution: The problem solution begins with the problem definition phase.

The Problem Definition

Output: The program must display the calculated output voltage, V_{out}.
Input: The user must enter values for the source voltage and circuit resistances.

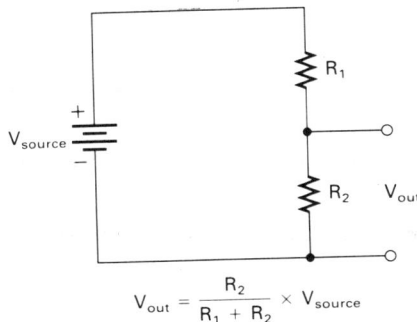

$$V_{out} = \frac{R_2}{R_1 + R_2} \times V_{source}$$

Figure 4-1   A general voltage divider circuit for Task 2.

Processing: The program must calculate the output voltage using the voltage divider equation as follows:

$$V_{out} = \frac{R_2}{R_1 \times R_2} \times V_{source}$$

BEGIN

Write a program description message.

Write a user prompt to enter the source voltage value, V_{source}.

Read (V_{source}).

Write a user prompt to enter the first resistor value, R_1.

Read (R_1).

Write a user prompt to enter the second resistor value, R_2.

Read (R_2).

Calculate the output voltage, V_{out}, using the voltage divider equation.

Write the output voltage, V_{out}.

END.

Now, by following the foregoing algorithm, the Pascal coding is easy.

The Program

```
PROGRAM VoltageDivider (input, output);

USES
   Crt;

VAR
    V_source, R1, R2, V_out : real;

BEGIN
    Clrscr;
    Writeln ('This program will calculate the voltage output of the ');
    Writeln ('voltage divider circuit in Figure 4-  .  You will be ');
    Writeln ('required to enter the source voltage and circuit');
    Writeln ('resistance values.');
    Writeln;
    Writeln;
    Write ('Enter the source voltage:  V_source = ');
    Readln (V_source);
    Writeln;
    Write ('Enter the first resistor value:  R1 = ');
    Readln (R1);
    Writeln;
    Write ('Enter the second resistor value:  R2 = ');
    Readln (R2);
    Writeln;
    Writeln;
    V_out := ( R2 / (R1 + R2) ) * V_source;
    Writeln ('The output voltage is : V_out = ', V_out:5:2, ' volts.')

END.
```

TASK 3: AC WAVEFORM ANALYSIS

Write a program to calculate the instantaneous voltage value of the ac waveform shown in Fig. 4-2.   The required equation is

$$v = V_{peak} \sin (2\pi ft)$$

where v = the instantaneous voltage at any point in time, t, on the waveform.

V_{peak} = the peak amplitude of the waveform in volts.

π = 3.14.

f = the frequency of the waveform in Hertz.

t = the time, in seconds, for v.

Have the user enter the peak voltage in volts, the frequency in kilohertz, and the time in milliseconds.

Solution: First, the problem definition:

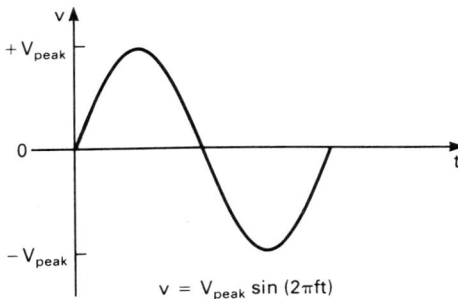

$$v = V_{peak} \sin (2\pi ft)$$

Figure 4-2.   The ac waveform of Task 3.

The Problem Definition

Output: The program must display the instantaneous voltage value, v, resulting from the above equation.

Input: The user must input the following information:
- The peak amplitude of the waveform, V_{peak}, in volts
- The frequency of the waveform, f, in kilohertz
- The point in time, t, in milliseconds for which the instantaneous voltage must be calculated

Processing: The program must calculate the instantaneous voltage value using the above equation.

The second step is to develop an algorithm.   Here's one that should work:

The Algorithm

BEGIN
  Write a program description message.
  Write a user prompt to enter the peak amplitude of the waveform, V_{peak}, in volts.
  Read (V_{peak}).
  Write a user prompt to enter the frequency of the waveform, f, in kilohertz.
  Read (f).
  Write a user prompt to enter the time, t, in milliseconds.
  Read (t).
  Calculate $v = V_{peak} \sin (2\pi ft)$.
  Write the instantaneous voltage value, v.
END.

Following the algorithm, the coded program is as follows:

The Program

```pascal
PROGRAM InstantaneousVoltage (input, output);

USES
  Crt;

VAR
  V, V_peak, f, t : real;

BEGIN
  Clrscr;
  Writeln ('This program will display the instantaneous voltage');
  Writeln ('value of an AC waveform.  You must enter the following');
  Writeln ('three quantities:');
  Writeln;
  Writeln ('        Peak Voltage of the waveform, V_peak.');
  Writeln;
  Writeln ('        Frequency of the waveform, f.');
  Writeln;
  Writeln ('        The point in time, t, for which the voltage');
  Writeln ('        must be calculated.');
  Writeln;
  Writeln;
  Write ('Enter the peak waveform voltage in volts:  V_peak = ');
  Read (V_peak);
  Writeln (' volts.');
  Writeln;
  Write ('Enter the waveform frequency in kilohertz:  f = ');
  Read (f);
  Writeln (' kilohertz.');
  Writeln;
```

```
Write ('Enter the time, t, in milliseconds: t = ');
Read (t);
Writeln (' milliseconds.');
v := V_peak * Sin ( 2 * Pi * f * t );
Writeln;
Writeln;
Write ('The instantaneous voltage at ',t:3:2, ' milliseconds ');
Writeln ('is ',v:5:3,' volts.')
```

END.

It's probably a good idea to take a closer look at some of the features of this program. Here is what you will see on the display after the program has been run:

```
This program will display the instantaneous voltage
value of an AC waveform.  You must enter the following
three quantities:

     Peak Voltage of the waveform, V_peak.

     Frequency of the waveform, f.

     The point in time, t, for which the voltage
     must be calculated.


Enter the peak waveform voltage in volts:  V_peak =  10 volts.

Enter the waveform frequency in kilohertz:  f =  1 kilohertz.

Enter the time, t, in milliseconds: t =  .125 milliseconds


The instantaneous voltage at 0.13 milliseconds is 7.071 volts.
```

As you can see, the program description message describes the purpose of the program. In addition, it tells the user what values must be entered and identifies the variables to be used for the entered values.

Now look at the first user-prompt line that tells the user to enter the peak waveform voltage. This line is formed by the following three lines in the program:

```
Write ('Enter the peak waveform voltage in volts:  V_peak = ');
Read (V_peak);
Writeln (' volts.');
```

Here, a *Write* statement is used to display the user-prompt message. A *Write* statement is used rather than a *Writeln* so that the user entry will appear on the same line as the user prompt. Next, a *Read* statement is used to input the user entry. A *Read* statement is used rather than a *Readln* statement so that the cursor **does not** return to the beginning of the next line after the read operation. Why, you ask, is this desired? Notice that the next statement is a *Writeln* statement that displays the word "volts." This statement adds the proper units to the numeric value entered by the user and completes the sentence. Furthermore, the *Writeln* statement will return the cursor to the beginning of the next line in preparation for the next operation. Note: TURBO 5 and later will not produce the same result due to the method the compiler buffers keyboard entries. With TURBO 5 and later, the word 'volts' will appear on the next line.

Observe also that the foregoing technique is used for each of the other variable entries (*f* and *t*). All this is good programming style and makes the display very user friendly and self-documenting. After the program has run and a result is generated, the user can easily check to see if he or she has made the correct entries.

Another observation from the program output is that the user must enter the waveform frequency in kilohertz and the time in milliseconds. These are typical units found in electronic circuits. Notice that the user prompts indicate this input requirement.

The calculation of the output voltage, *v*, is performed with this program statement:

```
v := V_peak * Sin ( 2 * Pi * f * t );
```

The equation does not have to be altered to accommodate *f* in kilohertz and *t* in milliseconds, since the product of these two units cancel each other out. Another thing that you see from the program statement is the use of "Pi" to represent the value 3.14159. However, this identifier is not declared as a constant at the beginning of the program. So how can it be used within the program? TURBO Pascal recognizes several *standard identifiers* that are used to represent constants. Another one is *Maxint*, which you learned about in Chapter 2. Recall that this identifier is used to represent the constant value 32767. All these standard identifiers are listed at the end of this text.

One final point: The *Sin* function is defined to evaluate angles in **radians**. Fortunately, the quantity (2 * *Pi* * *f* * *t*) produces radians and not degrees. If the value to be evaluated by the *Sin* function is in degrees, it must be converted to radians to obtain a correct result. You will see this shortly.

TASK 4: POLAR AND RECTANGULAR COORDINATES

Many times in technical problems you are required to convert between rectangular and polar coordinates. This is especially true in vector analysis, when applied to physics as well as electrical, mechanical, and civil technology.

The vector diagram in Figure 4-3 summarizes the conversion process. As you can see, a vector can be represented in one of two ways.

1. Polar coordinate:

$$M \angle \theta$$

where: *M* is the magnitude, or length, of the vector.

θ is the angle the vector makes with the horizontal axis.

2. Rectangular coordinate:

$$x + jy$$

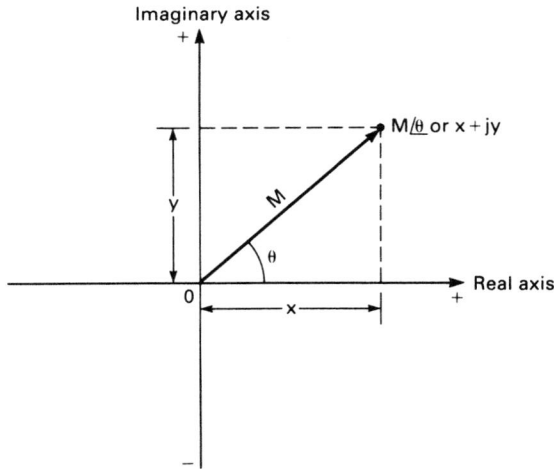

Rect. $\longrightarrow$ Polar	Polar $\longrightarrow$ Rect.	**Figure 4-3.** Polar/rectangular conver-
$M\underline{/\theta} = \sqrt{x^2 + y^2}/\text{Arctan } y/x$	$x + jy = M \cos \theta + jy \sin \theta$	sion for Task 4.

where: x is the real axis, or horizontal, coordinate for the tip of the vector.

y is the imaginary axis, or vertical, coordinate for the tip of the vector.

$j = \sqrt{-1}$, an imaginary number.

Using right angle trigonometry, you can convert between polar and rectangular coordinates. The conversion equations are shown in the figure.

Let's write a Pascal program that will convert from polar to rectangular coordinates using values supplied by the user. (A program to convert from rectangular to polar is left as a problem for you at the end of the chapter.)

Solution: First, the problem definition in terms of output, input, and processing:

The Problem Definition

Output: The output will be in tabular form, showing the input polar coordinate and the corresponding rectangular coordinate. The rectangular coordinate will be displayed using the format $x + jy$. The values of x and y will be in decimal form using two decimal places. The $+$ symbol and the j character will output as fixed character information.

Input: The user must enter the magnitude, M, of the vector and the angle, θ, it makes with the horizontal axis.

Processing: The program must calculate x and y as follows:

$$x = M \cos \theta$$

$$y = M \sin \theta$$

The angle, θ, must be converted to radians during the calculation.

Using this problem definition, an appropriate algorithm is as follows:

The Algorithm

BEGIN
    Write a program description message.
    Write a user prompt to enter the vector magnitude, *M*.
    Read (*M*).
    Write a user prompt to enter the vector angle, *Angle*, in degrees.
    Read (*Angle*).
    Calculate $x = M$ Cos (*Angle*).
    Calculate $y = M$ Sin (*Angle*).
    Write the table headings.
    Write the polar coordinate, $M \angle \theta$.
    Write the rectangular coordinate $x + jy$.
END.

Following this algorithm, the coded Pascal program is as follows:

```
PROGRAM Polar_To_Rectangular (input, output);

USES
  Crt;

VAR
   M, Angle, x, y : real;

BEGIN
   Clrscr;
   Writeln ('This program will convert polar vector coordinates');
   Writeln ('to rectangular vector coordinates.');
   Writeln;
   Writeln;
   Write ('Enter the magnitude of the vector:  M = ');
   Readln (M);
   Writeln;
   Writeln;
   Write ('Enter the vector angle in degrees:  Angle = ');
   Read (Angle);
   Writeln (' degrees.');
   Writeln;
   Writeln;
   x := M * Cos ( Pi/180 * Angle);
   y := M * Sin ( Pi/180 * Angle);
   Writeln ('POLAR COORDINATE':25,'RECTANGULAR COORDINATE':40);
   Writeln ('----------------':25,'----------------------':40);
   Writeln;
   Writeln (M:10:2, ' @ ', Angle:6:2,' degrees', x:23:2, ' + j', y:5:2)

END.
```

The Program

This program will generate the following display when executed. You should now have the knowledge required to write such a program. One thing that you should note is the conversion from degrees to radians within the *Cos* and *Sin* functions. You must multiply the *Angle* by the quantity (*Pi*/180) to get radians. Remember that the *Sin* function will only evaluate radians, not degrees.

```
This program will convert polar vector coordinates
to rectangular vector coordinates.


Enter the magnitude of the vector:  M = 5

Enter the vector angle in degrees:  Angle = 53.13 degrees.


        POLAR COORDINATE                RECTANGULAR COORDINATE
        ----------------                ----------------------

     5.00 @  53.13 degrees                 3.00 + j 4.00
```

TASK 5: THÉVÈNIN'S THEOREM

Write a program to accomplish the following tasks:

- Display the general circuit shown in Figure 4-4 when prompting the user for the circuit values.
- Calculate the Thévènin voltage of the circuit.
- Calculate the Thévènin resistance of the circuit.
- Calculate the load current.
- Calculate the load voltage.
- Display the Thévènin circuit showing the Thévènin and load values.

$$V_{th} = \frac{R_2}{R_1 + R_2} \times V_{source}$$

$$R_{th} = \frac{R_1 \times R_2}{R_1 + R_2} + R_3$$

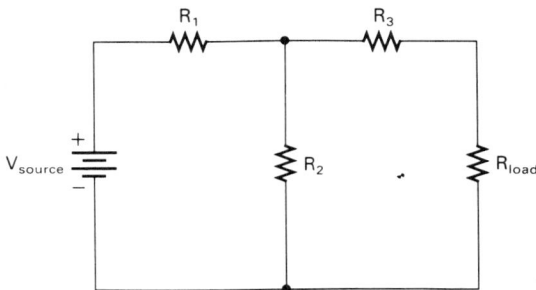

Figure 4-4 Circuit diagram for the Thévènin problem in Task 5.

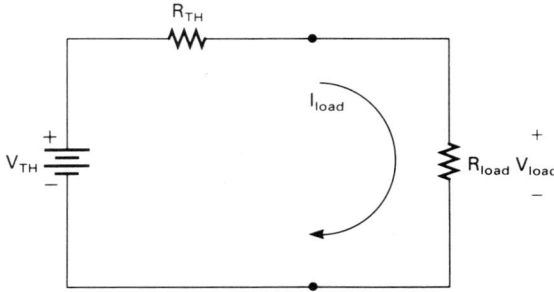

Figure 4-5 The Thévènin circuit for Task 5.

Solution:

The Problem Definition

Output: The output will be in two phases.

1. The program must display the general circuit shown in Figure 4-4. When the circuit is displayed, the user will be prompted to enter the circuit values.
2. Once the circuit values are entered, the program will then clear the screen and display the resulting Thévènin circuit and calculated load values.

Recall that a Thévènin circuit consists of the Thévènin voltage, V_{th}, in series with the Thévènin resistance, R_{th}, as shown in Figure 4-5. Thévènin's theorem says that the Thévènin circuit produces the same load voltage and current as the original circuit.

Input: The user must input the original circuit values, which include V_{source}, R_1, R_2, R_3, and R_{load}. The user will be asked to input the resistor values in kilohms.

Processing: The program must calculate the Thévènin and load values. The Thévènin values are V_{th} and R_{th}. For the circuit in Figure 4-4, these values are

$$V_{th} = \frac{R_2}{R_1 + R_2} \times V_{source}$$

$$R_{th} = \frac{R_1 \times R_2}{R_1 + R_2} + R_3$$

Once the Thévènin values are calculated, the program must calculate the load values as follows:

$$I_{load} = \frac{V_{th}}{R_{th} + R_{load}}$$

$$V_{load} = I_{load} \times R_{load}$$

The Algorithm

BEGIN
    Write a program description message to the user.
    Display the original circuit shown in Figure 4-4 using write operations.
    Write a user prompt to enter the source voltage, V_{source}.
    Read (V_{source}).
    Write a user prompt to enter the value of R_1 in kilohms.
    Read (R_1).
    Write a user prompt to enter the value of R_2 in kilohms.
    Read (R_2).
    Write a user prompt to enter the value of R_3 in kilohms.
    Read (R_3).
    Write a user prompt to enter the load resistance value, R_{load}.
    Read (R_{load}).
    Clear the screen.
    Calculate V_{th}.
    Calculate R_{th}.
    Calculate I_{load}.
    Calculate V_{load}.
    Display the Thévènin circuit shown in Figure 4-5, showing the calculated values.
END.

The Program

```
PROGRAM Thevenin (input, output);

USES
  Crt;

VAR
    R1, R2, R3 : real;
    V_source : real;
    R_th, V_th : real;
    R_load, I_load, V_load :real;
BEGIN
    Clrscr;
    Writeln ('This program will determine the load voltage and current');
    Writeln ('of the resistor circuit shown below using');
    Writeln  ('Thevenin','''','s',' Theorem.');
    Writeln;
```

(Continued)

```pascal
Writeln;
Writeln ('                              R1              R3');
Writeln ('                      --------XXXXXX----------XXXXXX-------');
Writeln ('                      :               :              :');
Writeln ('                      :               :              :');
Writeln ('                    -----             X              X');
Write   ('V_source            ---              X     R2       X');
Writeln (' R_load');
Writeln ('                    -----             X              X');
Writeln ('                     ---              X              X');
Writeln ('                      :               :              :');
Writeln ('                      :               :              :');
Writeln ('                      -----------------------------------');
Writeln;
Write ('Enter the  source voltage in volts:  V = ');
Read (V_source);
Writeln(' volts.');
Writeln;
Write  ('Enter the value of R1 in kilohms:  R1 = ');
Read (R1);
Writeln(' kilohms.');
Writeln;
Write ('Enter the value of R2 in kilohms:  R2 = ');
Read (R2);
Writeln(' kilohms.');
Writeln;
Write ('Enter the value of R3 in kilohms:  R3 = ');
Read (R3);
Writeln(' kilohms.');
Writeln;
Write ('Enter the load resistance in kilohms: R_load = ');
Read (R_load);
Writeln(' kilohms.');
Clrscr;
V_th := (R2 / (R1 + R2)) * V_source;
R_th := ((R1 * R2) / (R1 + R2)) + R3;
I_load := V_th / (R_th + R_load);
V_load := I_load * R_load;



Writeln;
Writeln;
Writeln ('             THEVENIN CIRCUIT');
Writeln;
Writeln;
Writeln;
Writeln ('                    R_th = ',R_th:5:2,'K');
Writeln ('              -------XXXXXX-----');
Writeln ('              :                :');
Writeln ('              :                : +');
Write   ('              :                X  R_load = ');
Writeln (R_load:5:2,' K');
Writeln ('            -----               X  ');
Write   ('V_th        ---                X  V_load = ');
Writeln (V_load:5:2,' V');
Writeln ('= ',V_th:5:2,' volts -----             X');
Write   ('            ---                X  I_load = ');
Writeln (I_load:5:2,' mA');
Writeln ('              :                : -');
Writeln ('              :                :');
Writeln ('              :                :');
Writeln ('              ------------------');
Writeln

END.
```

You should study the program to see how it performs the required display and calculation tasks. As you might guess, most of the "work" is in the formation of the *Writeln* statements that display the circuits.

Here is what the user will see:

```
This program will determine the load voltage and current
of the resistor circuit shown below using
Thevenin's Theorem.
                              R1                R3
                      --------XXXXX---------XXXXX-------
                      :                 :                :
                      :                 :                :
                      -----             X                X
        V_source      ---               X    R2          X  R_load
                      -----             X                X
                      ---               X                X
                      :                 :                :
                      :                 :                :
                      -----------------------------------
        Enter the   source voltage in volts:  V =   15 volts.
        Enter the value of R1 in kilohms:  R1 =   6 kilohms.
        Enter the value of R2 in kilohms:  R2 =   3 kilohms.
        Enter the value of R3 in kilohms:  R3 =   2 kilohms.
        Enter the load resistance in kilohms: R_load =   1 kilohms.
```

```
                    THEVENIN CIRCUIT


                    R_th =   4.00K
              -------XXXXX-----
              :                 :
              :                 :  +
              :                 X  R_load =   1.00 K
              -----             X
    V_th      ---               X  V_load =   1.00 V
  =  5.00 volts -----           X
              ---               X  I_load =   1.00 mA
              :                 :  -
              :                 :
              :                 :
              -------------------
```

CHAPTER SUMMARY

Arithmetic operations in Pascal include the common add, subtract, multiply, and divide operations that can be performed on any numeric data type. Addition, subtraction, and multiplication are basically the same for both the integer and real data types. However, there is a difference between integer and real division. Integer division employs the **DIV** and **MOD** operations. These two operations generate an integer quotient and remainder, respectively. They cannot be used to divide real numbers. Division of real numbers in Pascal requires the / operation.

Boolean operations are those that generate a Boolean result of TRUE or FALSE. The two categories of Boolean operations in Pascal are relational and logical operations. Relational operations allow two quantities to be compared.

These operations include $=$, $<>$, $>$, $<$, $<=$, and $>=$. Logical operators perform logic operations on Boolean values to generate a Boolean result. The standard logical operators available in Pascal are **NOT, OR, AND,** and **XOR.**

Finally, Pascal employs several standard functions that can be used to perform common tasks. There are arithmetic functions, scalar functions, and transfer functions. Arithmetic functions, such a *Sin* and *Cos*, perform an arithmetic operation. Scalar functions deal with the ordering of the scalar data types. They include *Odd*, *Pred*, *Succ*, and *Random*. Transfer functions convert a value of one scalar data type to a value of another scalar data type. These functions include *Chr*, *Ord*, *Round* and *Trunc*.

QUESTIONS AND PROBLEMS

Questions

4-1. What value will be returned for each of the following integer operations?
  a. $4 - 2 * 3$
  b. -35 **DIV** 6
  c. -35 **MOD** 6
  d. $-25 * 14$ **MOD** $7 * - 25$ **DIV** -5
  e. $-5 * 3 + 9 - 2 * 7$
  f. $(-13$ **DIV** $2)$ **MOD** 6

4-2. Evaluate each of the following expressions:
  a. $0.5 + 3.75 / 0.25 * 2$
  b. $2.5 - (1.2 + (4.0 - 3.0) * 2.0) + 1.0$
  c. $6.0E-4 * 3.0E+3$
  d. $6.0E-4 / 3.0E+3$

4-3. Which of the following expressions are valid and which are not valid in TURBO Pascal? Explain why a given expression is not valid.
  a. $5.0 - (6.0 / 3)$
  b. $200 * 200$
  c. $5.0 - (6.0$ **DIV** $3)$
  d. $5.0 - (6$ **DIV** $3)$
  e. $1 + 25$ **MOD** 5
  f. $-33000 + 2000$

4-4. Evaluate each of the valid expressions in question 4-3.

4-5. Evaluate each of the following relational operations:
  a. $7 <> 7$
  b. $-0.75 <= -0.5$
  c. $'m' > 'n'$
  d. $2 * 5$ **MOD** $3 - 7 < 15$ **DIV** $4 + 2$
  e. $'Janet   Smith' = 'Janet Smith'$

4-6. Determine the output generated by the following:
  a. ```Writeln ((2 MOD 5) DIV (5 MOD 2));```

  b. ```Writeln (3 * 6 / 3 + 6);```

    c.   `Writeln ((3 * 6) / (3 + 6));`

    d.   `Writeln (((3 * 6) / (3 + 6)));`

    e.   `Writeln (NOT (TRUE OR FALSE));`

    f.   `Writeln ((2 - 5/2 * 3) <= (8 MOD 2 - 6));`

    g.   `x := -7;`

         `y := 3;`

         `Writeln (NOT (3*x < 4*y) AND (5*x >= y));`

4-7. Develop a truth table for the following Boolean expression:

$$(A \text{ AND NOT } B) \text{ OR } (\text{NOT } A \text{ AND } B)$$

4-8. What standard logical operation is performed by the expression in question 4-7?

4-9. Develop a truth table for the following Boolean expression:

$$\text{NOT } A \text{ OR NOT } B$$

4-10. What standard logical operation is performed by the expression in question 4-9?

4-11. List the three categories of functions that are available in TURBO Pascal.

4-12. Determine the output generated by the following arithmetic functions:

    a.   `Writeln (Abs (-5));`

    b.   `Writeln (ArcTan (1))`

    c.   `Writeln ((ArcTan (1) * (180/3.14)):2:0);`

    d.   `Writeln (Sin (45));`

    e.   `Writeln (Sin (45 * (3.14/180)):4:3);`

    g.   `Writeln (Exp (1));`

    f.   `Writeln (Ln (2.72));`

4-13. Determine the output generated by the following scalar functions:

    a.   `Writeln (Pred (5));`

    b.   `Writeln (Succ ('a'));`

    c.   `Writeln (Pred (TRUE));`

    d.   `Writeln (NOT Odd (-3));`

4-14. Determine the output generated by the following transfer and miscellaneous functions:

    a.   `Writeln (Chr (65));`

    b.   `Writeln (Ord ('A'));`

    c.   `Writeln (Round (3.475));`

    d.   `Writeln (Trunc (-4.3678));`

    e.   `Writeln (Random);`

    f.   `Writeln (Random (100));`

4-15. Prove or disprove via truth tables that

$$NOT\ A\ AND\ NOT\ B\ =\ NOT\ (A\ AND\ B)$$

Programming Problems

4-1. Write a program that will allow a user to convert a temperature in degrees Fahrenheit to degrees centigrade using the following relationship:

$$C\ =\ 5/9\ \times\ (F\ -\ 32)$$

4-2. Write a program that will allow a user to convert a measurement in inches to centimeters.

4-3. Write a program that will allow a user to find the total current in the parallel circuit in Figure 4-6. Assume that the user will enter values for V_{source}, R_1, and R_2.

4-4. Write a program that will allow a user to find the hypotenuse of a right triangle using the Pythagorean theorem.

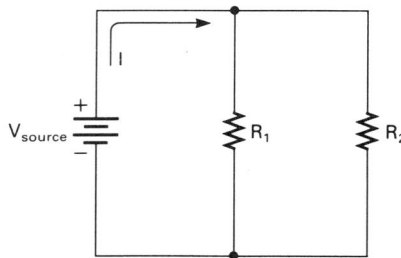

Figure 4-6 Parallel circuit for problem 4-3.

4-5. Write a program to solve the following equation for x:

$$3x\ -\ 5y\ +\ 2\ =\ 35$$

Assume that values for y will be entered by the user.

4-6. Write a program to generate a truth table for a **NOR** operation. A **NOR** operation is a **NOT OR** operation. Thus,

$$A\ NOR\ B\ =\ NOT\ (A\ OR\ B)$$

Assume that Boolean values for A and B will be entered by the user.

4-7. Write a program to convert from rectangular to polar coordinates. Generate a tabular output of the rectangular versus polar coordinate.

4-8. The kinetic energy of a moving object is found using the following equation:

$$K\ =\ 1/2\ (mv^2)$$

where K = the kinetic energy in kgm/s
   m = mass in kilograms
   v = velocity in meters per second

Write a program that accepts inputs of mass and velocity of an object and determines its kinetic energy.

4-9. Look at the circuit in Figure 4-7.   When the switch is closed, the capacitor will charge-up to the source voltage potential after five time constant periods.   A time constant period is defined as the product of R times C, or simply RC.   At any given point

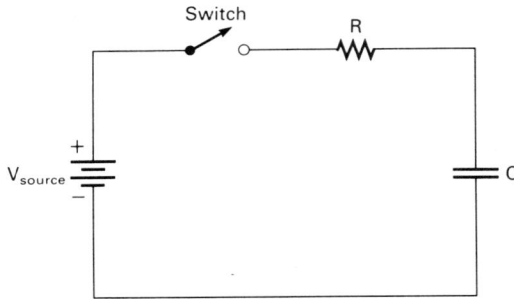

Figure 4-7   RC charging circuit for problem 4-9.

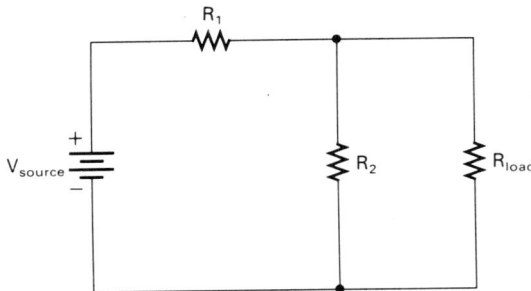

Figure 4-8   Resistor circuit for problem 4-10.

during this time, you can calculate the percent charge across the capacitor using the following exponential equation:

$$\% \ charge = (1 - e^{-t/RC}) \times 100$$

where e is the base of natural logarithms and has a value of approximately 2.718
     t is any given point in time, in milliseconds, during the charge cycle
     R is the resistance, in kilohms, that is in series with the capacitor, C
     C is the capacitor value in microfarads

Write a program to display the $\%$ *charge* across the capacitor at any given point in time.   Assume that the user will enter the resistance in kilohms, the capacitance in microfarads, and the time in milliseconds.   (*Hint:* Use the *Exp* function available in Pascal [see Table 4.4].)

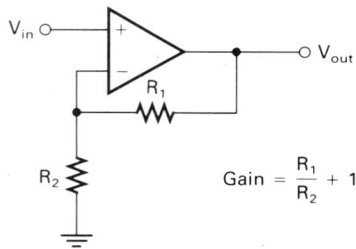

Figure 4-9 Op-amp circuit for problem 4-11.

$$Gain = \frac{R_1}{R_2} + 1$$

4-10. Write a program to accomplish the following tasks:

  - Display the circuit shown in Figure 4-8 when prompting the user to enter the circuit values.
  - Calculate the Thévènin voltage of the circuit.
  - Calculate the Thévènin resistance of the circuit.
  - Calculate the load current.
  - Calculate the load voltage.
  - Display the Thévènin circuit showing the Thévènin and load values.

4-11. The gain of the operational amplifier circuit in Figure 4-9 is found using the following relationship:

$$Gain = (R_1/R_2) + 1$$

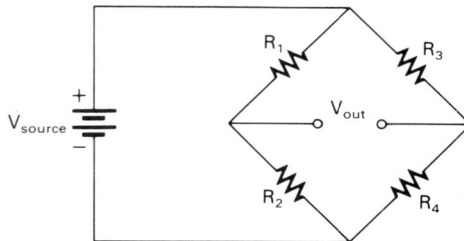

$$V_{out} = \left(\frac{R_2}{R_1 + R_2} - \frac{R_4}{R_3 + R_4}\right) \times V_{source}$$

Figure 4-10 A dc Wheatstone bridge for problem 4-12.

Write a program to calculate the gain of the circuit from values of R_1 and R_2 entered by the user. Display the general circuit shown in Figure 4-9 when asking for the user to enter values. Then display the circuit again, labeling the user values and showing the calculated gain.

4-12. Write a program to calculate the output voltage of the Wheatstone bridge circuit in Figure 4-10 from voltage and resistance values entered by the user. Display the general bridge circuit shown in Figure 4-10 when asking the user to enter the circuit values. Then display the circuit again, labeling the user values and the calculated output voltage.

chapter five

Making Decisions:
Selection

INTRODUCTION

As I stated earlier, Pascal is a ***structured*** programming language. As you will begin to find out, structured programming languages, such as Pascal, make programs easier to write, check, read, document, and maintain. A major reason for this is the modularity feature of a structured programming language. Program modularity simply means that any program, no matter how complex, can be broken down into simpler independent program modules. In fact, any complex program can be broken down into modules that conform to one of three fundamental patterns called ***control structures***. A control structure is simply a pattern for controlling the flow of a program module.

The three fundamental control structures of a structured programming language are ***sequence, selection,*** and ***iteration***. The sequence control structure is illustrated in Figure 5-1. As you can see, there is nothing fancy about this control structure, since program statements are executed sequentially, one after another, in a straight-line fashion. This is called ***straight-line programming*** and is what you have been doing in Pascal up to this point.

The second two control structures, selection and iteration, allow the flow of the program to be altered, depending on one or more conditions. The selection

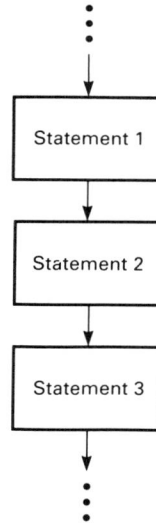

Figure 5-1 The sequence control structure is a series of sequential step-by-step statements.

control structure is a decision-making control structure. It is implemented in Pascal using the **IF/THEN, IF/THEN/ELSE,** and **CASE** statements. These are the topics of this chapter.

The iteration control structure is a looping control structure. It is implemented in Pascal using the **WHILE/DO, REPEAT/UNTIL,** and **FOR/DO** statements. These operations are discussed in Chapter 6.

Now, let's explore the selection control statements available in Pascal.

5-1 THE IF/ THEN STATEMENT

The operation of the **IF/THEN** statement is illustrated by the flow diagram in Figure 5-2. Observe that the flow of the program is altered, depending on the result of a Boolean test. If the test result is TRUE, the TRUE statements are executed. However, if the result of the test is FALSE, the TRUE statements are bypassed and the program flow continues. This is known as a selection, or decision-making, operation since the program selects, or decides, between one of two possible routes, depending on the conditions that are tested. In summary, the **IF/THEN** operation can be stated in words as follows: "**IF** the Boolean test result is TRUE, **THEN** execute the TRUE statements." Of course, this implies that the TRUE statements are not executed but are bypassed if the Boolean test result is FALSE.

Before we look at the Pascal format for the **IF/THEN** statement, let's take a

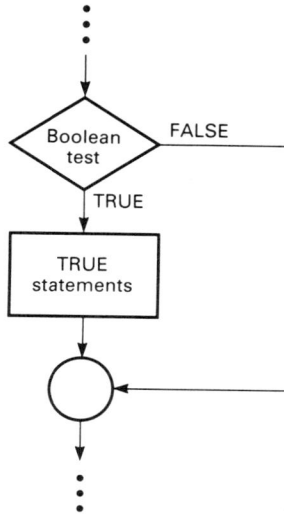

Figure 5-2   The flow of **IF/THEN**.

closer look at the Boolean test operation.   The Boolean test is a conditional test. This means that one or more conditions are tested to generate a TRUE or FALSE result.   To test a single condition, you will use the relational Boolean operators of $=$, $<>$, $<$, $>$, $<=$, and $>=$.   For instance, a typical test might be **IF** $x = y$ **THEN.**   Here, the single condition, $x = y$, is tested.   If x does in fact equal y, the result of the test is TRUE and the TRUE statements will be executed.

To test multiple conditions, you must use the logical Boolean operators of **OR** and **AND.**   For example, a test such as **IF** $(x <> y)$ **AND** $(a < b)$ tests two conditions.   If x does not equal y and if a is less than b, the test result is TRUE and the TRUE statements will be executed.

The Format

The Pascal format for the **IF/THEN** operation is as follows:

```
IF/THEN FORMAT *********************************************************
IF Boolean test THEN
    BEGIN
        statement 1;⎫
        statement 2;⎬   Compound Statement
            ⋮        ⎭
        statement n ⎭

    END;
    **********************************************************************
```

```
IF Boolean test THEN

  |BEGIN
  |
  |  |Statement 1;
  |  |
  |  |Statement 2;                    Compound
Indent ──►|                               TRUE
  └─►|  .                           statement
  |  |
  |  |  .
  |  |
  |  |Statement n
  |
  |END;
```

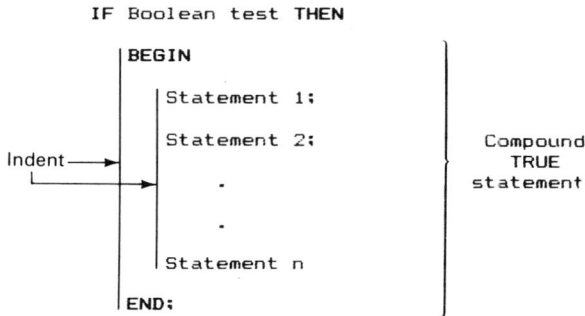

Figure 5-3 The **IF/THEN** statement
structure in Pascal.

First, notice the overall structure of this format. The **IF/THEN** clause is written on the first line of the statement. The words **IF** and **THEN** are both reserved words in Pascal. The first line is followed by a *compound statement*. A compound statement in Pascal is nothing more than a series of statements that are *framed* with the reserved words **BEGIN** and **END**. When a compound statement is encountered within a Pascal program, the entire group of statements between the **BEGIN** and **END** is treated like a single statement. As a result, a compound statement is sometimes called a **BEGIN/END** *block*. Notice from Figure 5-3 that the compound statement is made up of the statements that will be executed if the Boolean test result is TRUE.

In addition, look at the indentation scheme shown in the figure. The reserved words **BEGIN** and **END** are usually indented two or three spaces from the **IF/THEN** line. Furthermore, the individual statements that make up the compound statement are indented two or three spaces from the **BEGIN** and **END** lines. This indentation scheme obviously enhances the readability of the program. When this structure is part of a complex program, there is no question which statements belong to the **IF/THEN** operation.

Finally, look at the punctuation syntax of the **IF/THEN** statement. Notice that there is *no* semicolon after the reserved word **THEN** in the first line. However, each statement within the compound statement is terminated by a semicolon, *except* the last statement. The last statement does not need to be terminated by a semicolon, since the reserved word **END** terminates the compound statement. It's similar to writing a sentence in English where several clauses are separated by semicolons. Each clause is terminated by a semicolon except for the last clause, which is terminated by a period. With the **IF/THEN** syntax, the last statement is terminated by the reserved word **END**. Finally, a semicolon must follow the **END**, since you only use a period after an **END** at the end of the program.

It's probably a good idea to look at some example exercises and programs to get a "feel" for the **IF/THEN** operation.

Example 5-1:

Determine the output for each of the following program segments.   Assume that x and y have the following assignments prior to the execution of each **IF/THEN** operation:

```
x := 2;

y := 3;
```

a. **IF** x < y **THEN**
       BEGIN
          Writeln (lst, 'x = ', x);
          Writeln (lst, 'y = ', y)
       END;

b. **IF** y < x **THEN**
       BEGIN
          Writeln (lst, 'x = ', x);
          Writeln (lst, 'y = ', y)
       END;

c. **IF** x < y **THEN**
       BEGIN
          Temporary := y;
          y := x;
          x := Temporary;
          Writeln (lst, 'x = ', x);
          Writeln (lst, 'y = ', y)
       END;

d. **IF** (x < y) **AND** (y <> 10) **THEN**
       BEGIN
          Sum := x + y;
          Writeln (lst, 'x = ', x);
          Writeln (lst, 'y = ', y);
          Writeln (lst, 'Sum = ', Sum)
       END;

e. **IF** (x > y) **OR** (x - y < 0) **THEN**
       BEGIN
          x := x + 1;
          y := y - 1;
          Writeln (lst, 'x = ', x);
          Writeln (lst, 'y = ', y)
       END;

(Continued)

```
f. IF (x > y) OR ( x * y < 0) THEN
     BEGIN
       x := x + 1;
       y := y - 1;
       Writeln (lst, 'x = ', x);
       Writeln (lst, 'y = ', y)
     END;
   Writeln (lst, 'x = ', x);
   Writeln (lst, 'y = ', y);


g. IF x MOD y = 0 THEN
     Writeln (lst,'x is divisible by y.');
     Writeln (lst,'x is not divisible by y.');
```

Solutions:

a. The value of x is less than the value of y. Thus the output is:

```
x = 2
y = 3
```

b. The value of y is not less than x. Thus, the *Writeln* statements are bypassed and there is no output.

c. The value of x is less than y, so the compound statement is executed and the output is

```
x = 3
y = 2
```

Notice that the values of x and y have been swapped using a *Temporary* variable. Why is this temporary variable required?

d. The value of x is less than y and the value of y is not equal to 10. As a result, the two values are added and the output is

```
x = 2
y = 3
Sum = 5
```

e. Here the value of x is not greater than the value of y, but $x - y$ is less than 0. Thus, the compound statement is executed and the output is

```
x = 3
y = 2
```

Notice that the compound statement increments x and decrements y.

f. This time the Boolean test is FALSE. Thus, the compound statement is bypassed. As a result, the values of x and y remain unchanged and the output is

```
x = 2
y = 3
```

g. This is a tricky one. Here, the Boolean test is FALSE, since y does not divide evenly into x. So what happens? Since there is no **BEGIN** and **END,** the compiler takes only the first *Writeln* statement to be the TRUE statement. As a result, the first *Writeln* statement is bypassed and the second one is executed to produce an output of

x is not divisible by y.

The moral of this example is to *always frame your TRUE statements using* **BEGIN** *and* **END.**

Now let's look at a program example that employs the **IF/THEN** control structure.

Example 5-2:

Write a Pascal program to read in an employee's total weekly work hours and rate of pay. Determine the gross weekly pay using time and a half for anything over forty hours.

Solution: First the problem definition:

The Problem Definition

Output: The program will output the employee's name, hours worked, pay rate, and gross pay.

Input: The user will be prompted to enter the employee's name, hours worked, and pay rate.

Processing: *Case 1 (Hours worked less than or equal to 40.)* Gross pay = hours × rate

Case 2 (Hours worked greater than 40.) Gross pay = (40 × rate) + [(hours − 40) × 1.5 × rate]

The Algorithm

Here is where you must think out the problem in terms of the program logic and flow. Notice from the problem definition that the gross pay is calculated using one of two cases, depending on the number of hours worked. Thus, a decision must be made to use processing case 1 or case 2. One approach is to test to see if the hours worked is less than or equal to 40. If so, use processing case 1. Then test to see if the hours worked is greater than 40. If this is the case, use case 2. This approach suggests two **IF/THEN** operations. Here's the algorithm:

> BEGIN
> Write a program description message.
> Write a user prompt to enter the employee's *Name.*
> Read (*Name*).
> Write a user prompt to enter the *Rate* of pay.
> Read (*Rate*).
> Write a user prompt to enter the weekly *Hours* worked.

Read (*Hours*).

If *Hours* $\leq$ 40 then

Calculate *Gross Pay* = *Hours* $\times$ *Rate*.

If *Hours* > 40 then

Calculate *Gross Pay* = (40 $\times$ *Rate*) + [(*Hours* $-$ 40) $\times$ 1.5 $\times$ *Rate*]

Write appropriate output headings.

Write employee *Name*, *Rate* of pay, *Hours* worked, and *Gross Pay*.

END.

You might be wondering why two **IF/THEN** operations are required. You say that if the hours worked are *not* less than or equal to 40, you know the hours must be greater than 40, right? However, suppose that the second **IF/THEN** operation were eliminated. In addition, suppose that the hours worked is less than 40. Then the gross pay would be calculated twice, right? This would result in an erroneous gross pay figure. In fact, if you were the employee I'm sure that you would complain, since you would be getting cheated. (Why?)

One final point about the algorithm: Notice how indentation is used to show those steps that are executed if the test is TRUE. Using an indentation scheme such as this makes your algorithms readable. In addition, it makes your Pascal programs much easier to code. Now simply follow the algorithm to code the program as follows:

The Program

```
PROGRAM GrossPay  (input, output);

USES
  Crt;

VAR
    Name : STRING [30];
    Hours, Rate, Gross : real;

BEGIN
    Clrscr;
    Writeln ('This program will calculate the weekly gross pay of');
    Writeln ('an employee, given his/her rate of pay and hours worked.');
    Writeln;
    Writeln;
    Write ('Enter employee name:  Name = ');
    Readln (Name);
    Writeln;
    Write ('Enter the hourly rate of pay for ',Name,':  Rate = $');
    Readln (Rate);
    Writeln;
    Write ('Enter the number of hours that ',Name,' has worked ');
    Write (' this week:  Hours =  ');
    Readln (Hours);
    Writeln;
    Writeln;
    IF Hours <= 40 THEN
       BEGIN
          Gross := Hours * Rate
       END;
    IF Hours > 40 THEN
       BEGIN
          Gross := (40 * Rate) + ((Hours - 40) * 1.5 * Rate)
```

```
    END;
Write ('EMPLOYEE':15, 'HOURS WORKED':15, 'HOURLY RATE':15);
Writeln ('GROSS PAY':15);
Write ('_____':15, '_____':15, '_____':15);
Writeln ('_____':15);
Writeln;
Writeln (Name:15, Hours:15:1, '$':10, Rate:5:2, '$':10, Gross:5:2)
```
END.

5-2 THE IF/THEN/ELSE STATEMENT

The operation of the **IF/THEN/ELSE** statement is illustrated by the flowchart in Figure 5-4.   Here you see that there are two sets of statements that can be executed, depending on whether the Boolean test result is TRUE or FALSE.   If the test result is TRUE, the TRUE statements are executed.   Conversely, if the test result is FALSE, the FALSE statements are executed.   In words, "**IF** the Boolean test result is TRUE, **THEN** execute the TRUE statements, **ELSE** execute the FALSE statements."   As compared with the **IF/THEN** operation, you could say **IF/THEN/ELSE** is a *two-way selection* operation, whereas **IF/THEN** is a *one-way selection* operation.

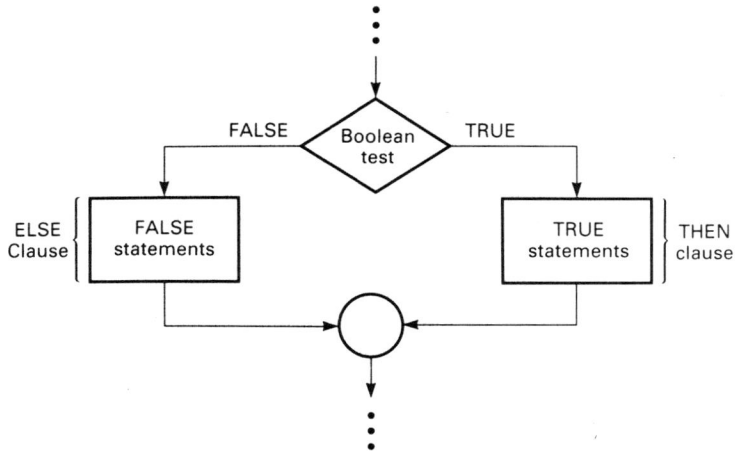

Figure 5-4   The flow of **IF/THEN/ELSE**.

The Format

The Pascal format for the **IF/THEN/ELSE** operation is as follows:

IF/THEN/ELSE FORMAT **
IF Boolean test **THEN**

```
BEGIN
    statement 1;
    statement 2;
       ⋮
    statement n
END
ELSE
    BEGIN
        statement 1;
        statement 2;
           ⋮
        statement n
    END;
```

****

As you can see, the **ELSE** option is included after the **THEN** option. If the Boolean test is TRUE, the **THEN** statements are executed and the **ELSE** statements are ignored. However, if the Boolean test is FALSE, the **THEN** statements are ignored and the **ELSE** statements are executed.

A few words about syntax: First, observe that both the **THEN** and **ELSE** statements are "framed" using the reserved words **BEGIN** and **END.** It's always a good idea to do this, since there is never any question where the respective statements begin and end. Second, notice that there is *no* semicolon preceding the reserved word **ELSE.** A semicolon after the last statement prior to an **ELSE** will always create an error condition. The reason is that a semicolon prior to **ELSE** causes the compiler to treat the **IF/THEN** portion as one operation, and the **ELSE** portion as a separate operation. This generates an error, since an **ELSE** operation cannot stand alone without a related **IF/THEN** operation. Finally, notice the indentation scheme. Again, such a scheme makes your programs self-documenting and readable.

Now let's see how the **IF/THEN/ELSE** operation can be applied to the gross pay problem.

Example 5-3:

Revise the gross pay program in Example 5-2 to employ a single **IF/THEN/ELSE** operation in place of the two **IF/THEN** operations.

Solution: The problem definition does not require any alteration. Only the algorithm and Pascal coding must be changed as follows to employ the **IF/THEN/ELSE** operation.

The Algorithm

```
BEGIN
    Write a program description message.
    Write a user prompt to enter the employee's Name.
```

Read (*Name*).

Write a user prompt to enter the *Rate* of pay.

Read (*Rate*).

Write a user prompt to enter the weekly *Hours* worked.

Read (*Hours*).

If *Hours* <= 40 then

    Calculate *Gross Pay* = *Hours* × *Rate*.

Else

    Calculate *Gross Pay* = (40 × *Rate*) + [(*Hours* − 40) × 1.5 × *Rate*]

Write appropriate output headings.

Write employee *Name*, *Rate* of pay, *Hours* worked, and *Gross Pay*.

END.

As you can see, the **ELSE** operation replaces the second **IF/THEN** operation of Example 5-2. If the hours worked are less than or equal to 40, the Boolean test is TRUE and the gross pay is calculated without overtime. However, if the hours worked are greater than 40, the Boolean test is FALSE and the **ELSE** operation is performed to include the overtime calculation. Notice that the indentation scheme clearly shows the two selection options. Now for the coding:

The Program

```
PROGRAM GrossPay  (input, output);

USES
  Crt;

VAR
   Name : STRING [30];
   Hours, Rate, Gross : real;

BEGIN
   Clrscr;
   Writeln ('This program will calculate the weekly gross pay of');
   Writeln ('an employee, given his/her rate of pay and hours worked.');
   Writeln;
   Writeln;
   Write ('Enter employee name:  Name = ');
   Readln (Name);
   Writeln;
   Write ('Enter the hourly rate of pay for ',Name,':  Rate = $');
   Readln (Rate);
   Writeln;
   Write ('Enter the number of hours that ',Name,' has worked ');
   Write (' this week:  Hours =  ');
   Readln (Hours);
   Writeln;
   Writeln;
   IF Hours <= 40 THEN
```

(Continued)

```
   BEGIN
      Gross := Hours * Rate
   END
ELSE
   BEGIN
      Gross := (40 * Rate) + ((Hours - 40) * 1.5 * Rate)
   END;
Write ('EMPLOYEE':15, 'HOURS WORKED':15, 'HOURLY RATE':15);
Writeln ('GROSS PAY':15);
Write ('_____':15, '_____':15, '_____':15);
Writeln ('_____':15);
Writeln;
Writeln (Name:15, Hours:15:1, '$':10, Rate:5:2, '$':10, Gross:5:2)

END.
```

Comparing this program with the program in Example 5-2, you find that the second **IF/THEN** statement is simply replaced by the **ELSE** clause.

5-3 NESTED IF'S

Up to this point, you have witnessed one-way and two-way selection using the **IF/THEN** and **IF/THEN/ELSE** statements, respectively. You can achieve additional selection options by using *nested IF* statements. A nested **IF** statement is simply

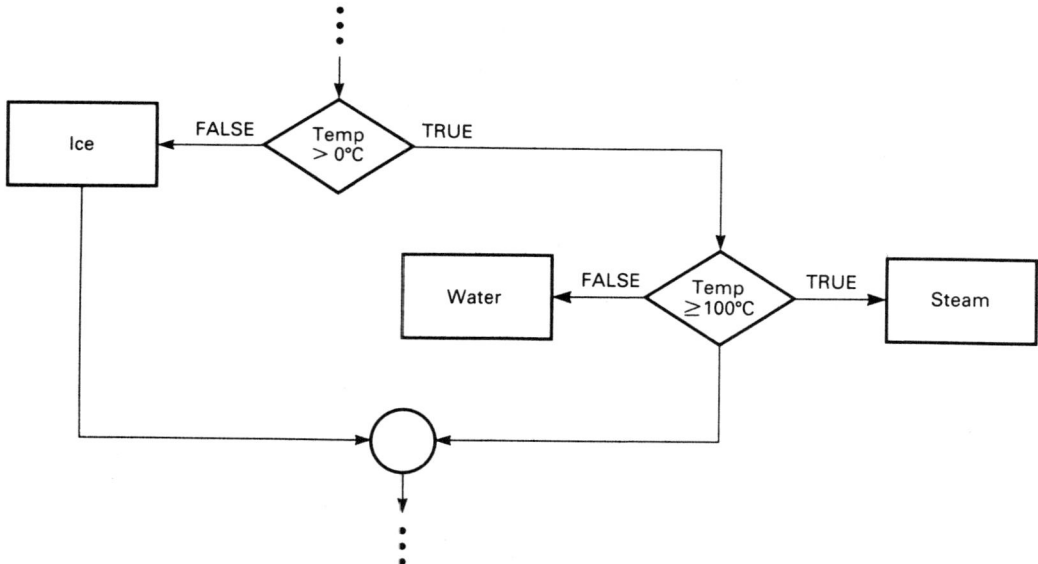

Figure 5-5 A nested **IF** operation.

an **IF** statement within an **IF** statement.   To illustrate this idea, consider the flowchart in Figure 5-5.   Here, a temperature is being tested to see if it is within a range of 0 to 100 degrees Celsius.   If it is within this range, you get water. However, if it is outside the range you get steam or ice, depending on whether it is above or below the range, respectively.

Let's follow through the flowchart.   The first Boolean test operation checks to see if the temperature is greater than 0°.   If the test is FALSE, the temperature must be less than or equal to 0°, resulting in ice.   However, if the test is TRUE, a second test is made to see if the temperature is greater than or equal to 100°. If this test is TRUE, you get steam.   However, if this second test is FALSE, you know that the temperature must be somewhere between 0° and 100°, resulting in water.   Notice how the second test is "nested" within the first test.   The first test result must be TRUE before the second test is performed.

Example 5-4:

Write an algorithm and code a Pascal program to perform the nested **IF** operation shown in Figure 5-5.   Assume that the temperature is to be read in via a keyboard and the result is to be written to the display.

Solution:

The Algorithm

```
BEGIN
    Write a program description message.
    Write a user prompt to enter the Temperature in degrees Celsius.
    Read (Temperature).
    If Temperature > 0 then
      If Temperature > = 100 then
        Write "STEAM".
      Else
        Write "WATER".
    Else
      Write "ICE".
END
```

This algorithm is constructed by simply following the flowchart in Figure 5-5. Notice how the second **IF/THEN/ELSE** operation is nested within the first **IF/THEN/ ELSE** operation.   If the *Temperature* is not greater than 0°, the nested **IF** operation is not performed.   However, if the *Temperature* is greater than 0°, the nested **IF** operation is performed to see if the *Temperature* results in steam or water.

To code the program you simply follow the algorithm as follows:

The Program

```
PROGRAM  Ice_Water_Steam (input, output);  ➊

USES
  Crt;

VAR
   Temperature : real;

BEGIN
   Clrscr;
   Writeln ('This program will evaluate a temperature to see if');
   Writeln ('produces ice, water, or steam.');
   Writeln;
   Writeln;
   Write ('Enter a temperature in degrees Celsius:  Temp. = ');
   Read (Temperature);
   Writeln (' degrees Celsius.');
   Writeln;
   Writeln;
   IF Temperature > 0 THEN
      BEGIN
         IF Temperature >= 100 THEN
            BEGIN
               Writeln ('STEAM')
            END
         ELSE
            BEGIN
               Writeln ('WATER')
            END;
      END
   ELSE
      BEGIN
         Writeln ('ICE')
      END;
END.
```

Notice how the program flow can be seen by the indentation scheme. Each **THEN** and **ELSE** clause is framed with the reserved words **BEGIN** and **END**.

STYLE TIP ─────────────────────────────

As you begin to frame more operations using **BEGIN** and **END,** it often becomes difficult to determine where a given operation ends. This can be seen from the program in Example 5-4. The indentation scheme helps, but a *commenting technique* is also used. You can insert a comment within your program by using braces { }. Any information contained within the braces is ignored by the compiler. *Note:* Some systems do not have braces { } available on the keyboard. If you are using such a system, enclose your comments within a combination parenthesis/asterisk like this (* comment *). Using this idea, comments can be used to designate when a given operation ends as follows:

```
PROGRAM Ice_Water_Steam (input, output);

VAR
   Temperature : real;

BEGIN


      .
      .
      .


   IF Temperature > 0 THEN
      BEGIN
         IF Temperature >= 100 THEN
            BEGIN
               Writeln ('STEAM')
            END  {nested then clause}
         ELSE
            BEGIN
               Writeln ('WATER')
            END; {nested else clause}
      END {outer then clause}
   ELSE
      BEGIN
         Writeln ('ICE')
      END; {outer else clause}
END.  {program}
```

Here, the comments are an aid to anyone reading the program.   Notice how they indicate which program segments are being ended.   One final point: You are not required by Pascal to begin and end *single-line statements*.   As a result, you can actually eliminate most of the **BEGIN** and **END** statements like this:

```
PROGRAM Ice_Water_Steam (input, output);

VAR
   Temperature : real;

BEGIN


      .
      .
      .


   IF Temperature > 0 THEN
      IF Temperature >= 100 THEN
         Writeln ('STEAM')
      ELSE
         Writeln ('WATER')
   ELSE
      Writeln ('ICE')
END.  {program}
```

As you can see, this requires less coding. But a word of caution: Although single-line statements do not need to be framed, compound statements must *always* be framed. If you are in doubt, frame all the **THEN** and **ELSE** clauses to avoid ambiguity and protect against any possible errors. This often pays off in the long run, just as does using parentheses to clarify arithmetic expressions.

5-4 THE CASE STATEMENT

This last category of selection enables the program to select one of many options, or *cases*. The selection of a particular case is controlled by a *matching* process, as illustrated in Figure 5-6. Here, a *selector* is first evaluated to produce a value.

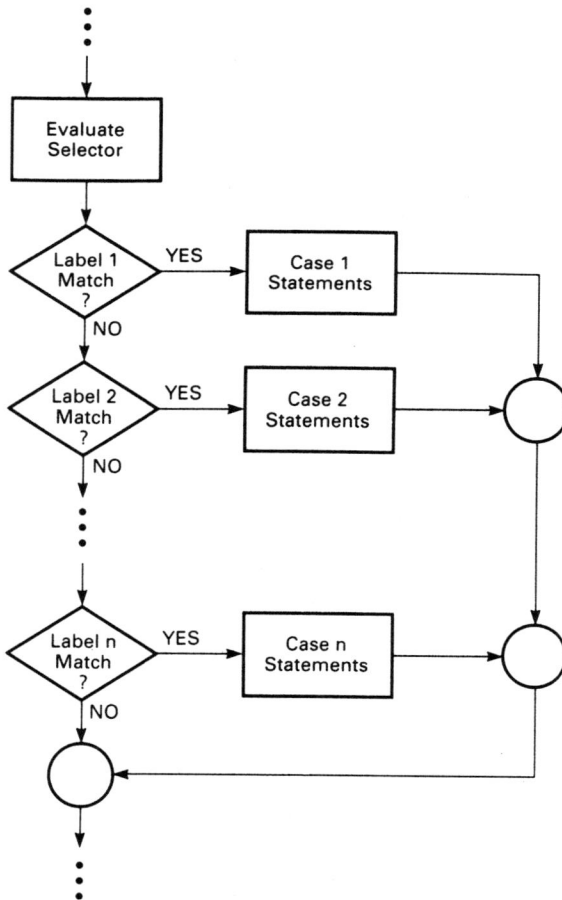

Figure 5-6 The flow of **CASE**.

The selector value is then compared with a series of ***labels***. If the selector value matches one of the labels, the corresponding case is executed. After a given case is executed, the program continues with the first statement following the **CASE** operation. If no match is made, the program simply continues in a straight-line fashion, with the first statement following the **CASE** operation.

The Format

The Pascal format for the **CASE** operation is as follows:

```
CASE FORMAT ***************************************************************
CASE selector OF
     label 1 : statement 1;
     label 2 : statement 2;
        ⋮           ⋮
     label n : statement n
END;
***********************************************************************
```

Again, the idea behind the **CASE** statement is easy, if you simply think of it as a matching operation. Some simple examples should demonstrate this idea.

Suppose the selector is the letter grade you made on your last quiz. Assuming that the variable *LetterGrade* is declared as a character variable in the declaration part of the program, a typical **CASE** statement might go something like this:

```
CASE LetterGrade OF

    'A' : Writeln ('Excellent');

    'B' : Writeln ('Superior');

    'C' : Writeln ('Fair');

    'D' : Writeln ('Poor');

    'F' : Writeln ('Try again')

END;
```

Here, the selector is the variable *LetterGrade*. The labels are 'A', 'B', 'C', 'D', and 'F'. The selector value is compared with the label list. If a match is found, the corresponding label statement is executed. For instance, if the value of *LetterGrade* is 'B', the program generates an output of

```
Superior
```

Next suppose that you wish to match a numeric test score to a letter grade. Many instructors consider scores of 90 through 100 to be an A, 80 through 89 a

B, and so on.   Assuming that the variable *Score* has been declared as an integer, you can use a **CASE** operation to convert a numeric score to a letter grade as follows:

```
CASE Score OF

    90 .. 100 : Writeln ('A score of ', Score, ' is an A.');

    80 .. 89  : Writeln ('A score of ', Score, ' is a B.');

    70 .. 79  : Writeln ('A score of ', Score, ' is a C.');

    60 .. 69  : Writeln ('A score of ', Score, ' is a D.');

     0 .. 59  : Writeln ('A score of ', Score, ' is an F.')

END;
```

Here the selector is an integer and the labels are integer subranges.   So if the value of *Score* is 73, for example, the **CASE** operation would produce an output of

```
A score of 73 is a C.
```

What happens if the score is not within the label ranges?   The program simply bypasses all the cases and continues on to the next sequential statement following the **CASE.**

You also can list several labels on a single line.   For instance, suppose that you wish to prompt the program user to respond to a simple yes/no question with a Y or N.   You can use a **CASE** statement to match the user's response, as follows:

```
Writeln ('Do you like this text? (Y/N)');
Readln (Answer);
CASE Answer OF

    'Y','y' : Writeln ('This is an excellent choice --- Thanks!.');

    'N','n' : Writeln ('Sorry, better luck next time.')
END;
```

Here, the prompt has asked the user to enter an uppercase *Y* for yes or an uppercase *N* for no.   However, what do you think the user is likely to do?   You're right!   Often the user will respond with a lowercase *y* or *n*.   The program must react to either response.   To do this, you can list both the upper- and lowercase labels on the same label line as shown.   When this is done, a user response of either *Y* or *y* will produce an output of

```
This is an excellent choice --- Thanks!
```

Now that you have the idea behind the operation of the **CASE** statement, we had better consider some rules that govern its use.

Rule 1: The selector variable must be declared as any data type *except* real or string.

Rule 2: Label values can only appear once in the label listing. Consequently, the statement

```
CASE Score OF

    98, 99 : Writeln ('A');

    97, 98 : Writeln ('Excellent')

END;
```

generates an error, since the label 98 applies to two different cases.

Rule 3: Syntax
  - Commas are used between labels for the same case.
  - A colon is used between the label and its respective statement.
  - Semicolons are used after each statement within a given case, except the last statement just prior to **END**.

Rule 4: The reserved word **END** is used to conclude the **CASE** operation. No corresponding **BEGIN** is used.

Rule 5: Compound statements can be used within any case option. However, they must be framed with **BEGIN** and **END.**

The application of rules 1 through 4 can be seen in the foregoing **CASE** examples.   I might caution you about rule 4.   This is the first (and one of the very few) times that you use an **END** without a corresponding **BEGIN** in Pascal.   The reserved word **END** must be used to conclude the **CASE** operation.   However, the use of **BEGIN** at the beginning of the **CASE** operation will always produce an error.

Compound Cases

Now, what about using compound statements within a **CASE** option (Rule 5)? Recall that a compound statement is a group of individual statements that are framed with a **BEGIN** and **END.** Here's the format:

```
COMPOUND CASE FORMAT  *************************************************
CASE selector OF
    label 1 : BEGIN
                statement 1;
                statement 2;
                   ⋮
                statement n
             END; {end of label 1 compound statement}
    label 2 : BEGIN
                statement 1;
                statement 2;
                   ⋮
                statement n
             END; {end of label 2 compound statement}
     ⋮         ⋮
    label n : BEGIN
                statement 1;
                statement 2;
                   ⋮
                statement n
             END {end of label n compound statement}
END; {end of case}
*****************************************************************************
```

Observe the syntax and indentation scheme. Each compound statement is framed with the reserved words **BEGIN** and **END.** The word **BEGIN** is placed after the label colon. Then the individual statements that make up the compound statement are listed sequentially and indented two or three spaces. The compound statement is concluded with an **END.** Thus, when a given label is matched, the entire compound statement is executed, from beginning to end. Of course, a final **END** must be used as before to end the **CASE** operation. You will see an example of using compound **CASE** statements shortly.

The ELSE Option

The last thing we need to discuss is the use of the **ELSE** option within a **CASE** statement. The **ELSE** option is used within a **CASE** statement as follows:

```
ELSE OPTION FORMAT  *********************************************************
CASE selector OF
    label 1 : statement 1;
    label 2 : statement 2;
       ⋮         ⋮
    label n : statement n
```

ELSE
    statement 1;
    statement 2;
     ⋮
    statement n
END; {end of case}
****

The **ELSE** option allows a series of statements to be executed if no match occurs within the **CASE.**   On the other hand, if a match does occur, the **ELSE** statements are skipped.   This provides a valuable protection feature within your program, as you will see shortly.   A word about syntax: There cannot be a semicolon preceding the **ELSE.**   You do not have to frame the **ELSE** statements with **BEGIN** and **END.**   However, the **CASE** must be ended as shown.   Finally, you should be aware that not all versions of Pascal allow the use of the **ELSE** option. This is true of Standard Pascal and some UCSD versions.   Fortunately, TURBO Pascal includes this feature.

5-5 PUTTING IT ALL TOGETHER

Let's take a look at a comprehensive example that employs several of the selection operations discussed in this chapter, in particular the **CASE** statement.
    CASE statements are often used to create menu-driven programs.   I'm sure that you have seen a menu-driven program.   It's one that asks you to select different options during the execution of the program.   For instance, suppose that you must write a menu-driven program that will allow the user to calculate dc voltage, current, or resistance.   By Ohm's law ($V = I \times R$), you know that any one of these can be found by knowing the other two.

Problem Definition

Output: A program menu that prompts the user to select either a voltage (V), a current (I), or a resistance (R) option.
            Invalid entry messages as required.
            A voltage, a current, or a resistance value, depending on the program option that the user selects.
   Input: A user response to the menu (V, I, or R).
            If V is selected: User enter values for I and R.
            If I is selected: User enter values for V and R.
            If R is selected: User enter values for V and I.
Processing: Calculate the selected option.
            Case V: $V = IR$.
            Case I: $I = V/R$.
            Case R: $R = V/I$.

The Algorithm

BEGIN

Write a program description message.

Display a program menu that prompts the user to select either a voltage
(V), a current (I), or a resistance (R) option.

Read (Selection).

Case Selection of

   V: Write a user prompt to enter a current value (I).
   Read (I).
   Write a user prompt to enter a resistance value (R).
   Read (R).
   If $R < 0$ then
       Write an invalid entry message and ask the user to run the
       program again.
   Else
       Calculate $V = I \times R$.
   Write (V).

   I: Write a user prompt to enter a voltage value (V).
   Read (V).
   Write a user prompt to enter a resistance value (R).
   Read (R).
   If $R <= 0$ then
       Write an invalid entry message and ask the user to run the
       program again.
   Else
       Calculate $I = V/R$.
   Write (I).

   R: Write a user prompt to enter a voltage value (V).
   Read (V).
   Write a user prompt to enter a current value (I).
   Read (I).
   If $I = 0$ then
       Write an invalid entry message and ask the user to run the
       program again.
   Else
       Calculate $R = V/I$.
   Write (R).

   Else
       Write an invalid entry message and ask the user to select again.
END.

Taking a close look at the algorithm, you find several protection features.
First, the menu-driven options are provided by a **CASE** statement. If the user

selects an option not provided by the **CASE**, the last **ELSE** clause is executed, which instructs the user to select again.   When a proper option is selected, the **IF/ THEN/ELSE** statements within each **CASE** option protect against invalid data entries.   A negative resistance value is invalid, since there is no such thing as negative resistance.   In addition, you cannot divide by 0.   As a result, the algorithm checks for zero entries if the value is to be used as a divisor.   Using the above algorithm, the Pascal program is as follows:

The Program

```
PROGRAM Ohms_Law (input, output);

USES
  Crt;

VAR
  V, I, R : real;
  Choice : char;

BEGIN
  Clrscr;
  Writeln ('This program will calculate DC voltage, current, or');
  Writeln ('resistance given the other two values.');
  Writeln;
  Writeln;
  Writeln;
  Writeln ('                        Enter V to find voltage':30);
  Writeln;
  Writeln ('                        Enter I to find current':30);
  Writeln;
  Writeln ('                        Enter R to find resistance':30);
  Writeln;
  Write ('          Please enter your choice:  ');
  Readln (Choice);
  Clrscr;
  CASE Choice OF

     'V','v' : BEGIN
                Write ('Enter the current value in milliamps');
                Write (':  I = ');
                Read (I);
                Writeln (' milliamps.');
                Write ('Enter the resistance value in kilohms');
                Write (':  R = ');
                Read (R);
                Writeln (' kilohms.');
                Writeln;
                IF R < 0 THEN
            BEGIN
              Write ('This is an invalid entry, press R');
              Writeln (' to run the program again.');
            END {end then clause}
```

(*Continued*)

```
            ELSE
               BEGIN
                 V := I * R;
                 Writeln ('The voltage value is ',V:4:2,' volts.')
               END   {end else clause}
           END;  {V case}


 'I','i' : BEGIN
              Write ('Enter the voltage value:  V = ');
              Read (V);
              Writeln (' volts.');
              Writeln;
              Write ('Enter the resistance value in kilohms:  R = ');
              Read (R);
              Writeln (' kilohms.');
              Writeln;
              IF R <=0 THEN
                 BEGIN
                   Write ('This is an invalid entry, press R');
                   Writeln (' to run the program again.');
                 END   {then clause}
                   ELSE
                     BEGIN
                       I := V/R;
                       Writeln ('The current is ',I:4:2,' milliamps.');
                     END   {else clause}
                 END;  {I case}

    'R','r' : BEGIN
                 Write ('Enter the voltage value:  V = ');
                 Read (V);
                 Writeln (' volts.');
                 Writeln;
                 Write ('Enter the current value in milliamps:  I = ');
                 Read (I);
                 Writeln (' milliamps.');
                 Writeln;
                 IF I = 0 THEN
                    BEGIN
                      Write ('This is an invalid entry, press R');
                       Writeln (' to run the program again.');
                     END   {then clause}
                    ELSE
                      BEGIN
                        R := V/I;
                        Write ('The resistance value is ',R:4:2);
                        Writeln (' kilohms.');
                      END   {else clause}
                  END {R case}
   ELSE
      Write('This is an invalid entry, press R');
      Writeln (' to run the program again.');
   END    {case}
END.   {program}
```

Now look at the program closely and you will find that it incorporates most of the things that you learned about in this chapter. You will find the **CASE** operation with compound statements and the **ELSE** option. In addition, notice the **IF/THEN/ELSE** operations embedded within each case. In particular, you should observe the beginning and ending of the various sections, along with the associated indentation and commenting scheme. As you can see, the program is very readable and self-documenting.

The following output shows what you will see on the display screen when the program is executed. The first output is the menu. When the user enters his or her choice, the screen is cleared and the user is prompted to enter the required values as shown in the second output. The result is then calculated and displayed as shown.

```
This program will calculate DC voltage, current, or
resistance given the other two values.



                    Enter V to find voltage

                    Enter I to find current

                    Enter R to find resistance

            Please enter your choice:  I

Enter the voltage value:  V =  12 volts.

Enter the resistance value in kilohms:  R =  10 kilohms.

The current is 1.20 milliamps.
```

CHAPTER SUMMARY

In this chapter you learned about the selection, or decision-making, operations available in Pascal. These include the **IF/THEN, IF/THEN/ELSE,** and **CASE** statements. Each of these operations alters the flow of a program, depending on the result of a Boolean test or matching condition.

The **IF/THEN** statement executes the **THEN** clause of the statement "if" the Boolean test is TRUE. The **THEN** clause can be a single-line statement, or a compound statement composed of a series of single-line statements. When using a compound statement, you must frame the clause with the reserved words **BEGIN** and **END.**

The **IF/THEN/ELSE** statement consists of two separate clauses: a **THEN** clause and an **ELSE** clause. If the Boolean test is TRUE, the **THEN** clause is executed; otherwise, the **ELSE** clause is executed when the test is FALSE. Thus, you could say that **IF/THEN/ELSE** is a two-way selection operation. Additional selection options can be achieved using nested **IF/THEN** or **IF/THEN/ELSE** statements.   Again, compound statements can be used within the **THEN** or **ELSE** clauses; however, they must be framed with **BEGIN** and **END.**

The **CASE** statement achieves selection using a matching process.   Here, a selector is compared with a series of labels.   If the selector matches one of the labels, the corresponding label statements are executed.   If no match is made, the program simply continues in a straight-line fashion (TURBO only).   In addition, TURBO Pascal provides an **ELSE** option with the **CASE** statement.   When using the **ELSE** option, the **ELSE** statements are executed if no match is made.   However, if a match does occur, the corresponding label statements are executed and the **ELSE** statements are skipped.   Remember, you must always **END** a **CASE** statement.   However, you do not **BEGIN** the statement.

QUESTIONS AND PROBLEMS

Questions

5-1. When will X be written as a result of the following **IF/THEN** operation?

```
IF ( X <= 0) AND NOT (X MOD 5 = 0) THEN
   Writeln (X);
```

5-2. Convert the single **IF/THEN** statement in question 5-1 to two nested **IF** statements.

5-3. Consider the following program segment:

```
IF X > 0 THEN
   BEGIN
      IF Y > 0 THEN
         Y = Y - 1
   END;
ELSE
   X := X + 1
```

    a. Are there any syntax errors in the above code?   If so, where are they?
    b. Assuming that any syntax errors are corrected, when will Y be decremented?
    c. Assuming that any syntax errors are corrected, when will X be incremented?

5-4. Consider the following segment of code:

```
IF X > 0 THEN
   BEGIN
      IF Y > 0 THEN
         Y := Y - 1
      ELSE
         X := X + 1
   END;
```

    a. Are there any syntax errors in the code?   If so, where are they?

    b. Assuming that any syntax errors are corrected, when will *Y* be decremented?

    c. Assuming that any syntax errors are corrected, when will *X* be incremented?

5-5. True or False: You must always begin and end a **CASE** statement.

5-6. True or False: **ELSE** conditions are not allowed as part of **CASE** statements in Standard Pascal.

5-7. True or False: When using a **CASE** statement in TURBO Pascal, a no-match condition results in an error.

5-8. Consider the following segment of code:

```
IF X >= 0 THEN
   IF X < 10 THEN
      BEGIN
         Y := Sqr(X);
         IF X <= 5 THEN
            X := Sqrt(X)
      END
   ELSE
      Y := 10 * X
ELSE
   Y := X * X * X;

Writeln ('X = ', X:5:2);
Writeln ('Y = ', Y:5:2);
```

What will be displayed by the program for each of the following initial values of *X*? Assume that *X* and *Y* have been declared as real.

    a. `X := 0;`

    b.

        `X := 4;`

    c.

    d. `X := -5;`

5-9. Consider the following **CASE** statement:

```
X := 2;
CASE Power OF
   0 : Writeln ('1');
   1 : Writeln (X);
   2 : Writeln (Sqr(X));
   3 : Writeln (X * X * X);
   4 : Writeln (Sqr(X) * Sqr(X))
ELSE
   Writeln ('No match exists for this Power.')
END;
```

What will be displayed by the program for each of the following values of *Power*? Assume that *X* and *Power* are declared as integer.

    a. `Power := 0;`

    b. `Power := 1;`

    c. `Power := 2;`

    d. `Power := 3;`

    e. `Power := 4;`

    f. `Power := 5;`

5-10. Consider the following nested **CASE** statements:

```
CASE M OF
   2,4,6 : CASE N OF
             1, 2, 3 : M := M + N;
             -1,-2,-3 : M := M - N
           END;
   1,3,5 : CASE N OF
             2, 4, 6 : M := M * N;
             -2,-4,-6 : M := N * N
           END
END;
Writeln ('M = ', M);
Writeln ('N = ', N);
```

What will be displayed by the program for each of the following values of *M* and *N*?

```
a.  M := 4;
    N := -2;

b.  M := 3;
    N := 6;

c.  M := 1;
    N := -4;

d.  M := 7;
    N := -2:

e.  M := 2;
    N := 5;
```

5-11. Rewrite the following program segment using a single **CASE** statement.

```
IF Score >=60   THEN
   IF Score >= 70 THEN
      IF Score >= 80 THEN
         IF Score >= 90 THEN
            LetterGrade := 'A'
         ELSE
            LetterGrade := 'B'
      ELSE
         LetterGrade := 'C'
   ELSE
      LetterGrade := 'D'
ELSE
   LetterGrade := 'F';
```

Programming Problems

5-1. The output of a commercial power supply is tested after final assembly to determine if it is within an acceptable range. The supply specification requires the output to be 5 V $\pm$ 10 percent.

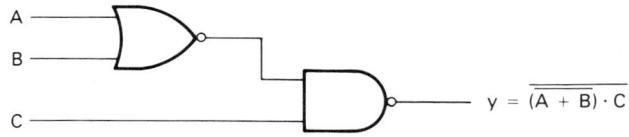

Figure 5-7   Digital logic circuit for programming problem 5-3.

Write a program that will allow an inspector to enter the measured output value. Generate a display of "ACCEPTABLE" if the voltage meets the specification and "UNACCEPTABLE" if the voltage is out of the specification range.   (*Hint:* Use nested **IF** statements.)

5-2. Using your algorithm from problem 1-6 (Chapter 1), code a Pascal program to find the roots of a quadratic equation.

5-3. Write a program that will simulate the digital circuit shown in Figure 5-7.   In other words, the program must generate a logic 1 or 0 output given logic inputs for A, B, and C entered by the user.

(*Hints:* Write the Boolean expression for the circuit and implement the expression in

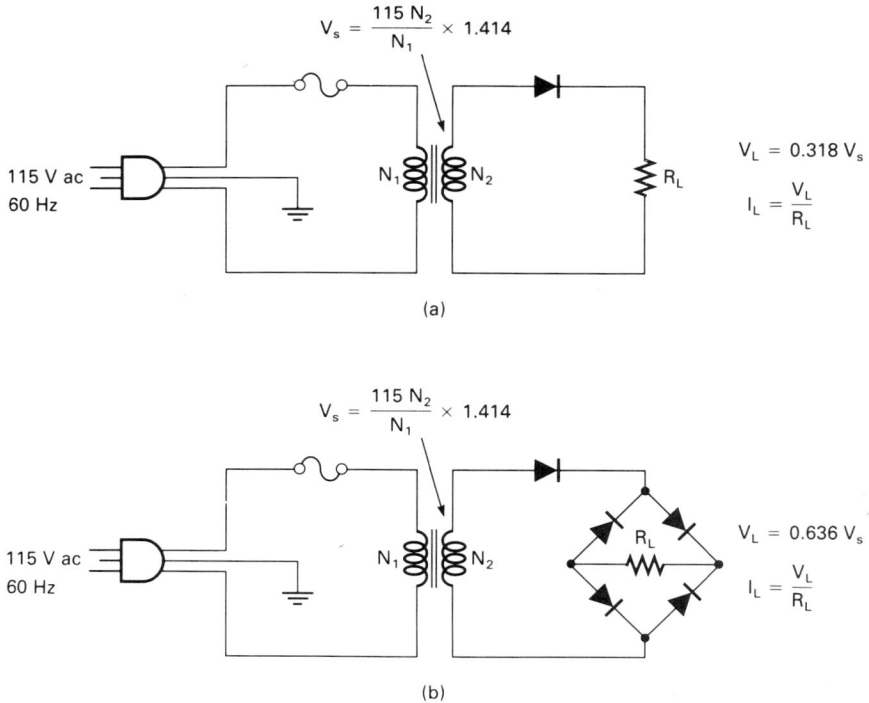

(a)

(b)

Figure 5-8   (a) Half-wave power supply and (b) full-wave power supply circuits for programming problem 5-7.

Pascal. A logic 1 must be represented in your program by the Boolean value TRUE, and a logic 0 is represented by the Boolean value FALSE.)

5-4. Write a program that will display the corresponding name of a month for an integer entry from 1 to 12. Protect for invalid entries.

5-5. Using the resistor color code, write a program that will display the color that corresponds to an integer entry from 0 to 9. Protect against invalid entries.

5-6. Write a menu-driven program that will allow a user to find either dc power, voltage, or current given the other two values. Protect against invalid entries. (*Note:* $P = VI$).

5-7. Two typical power supply circuits are shown in Figure 5-8. A half-wave supply is shown in Figure 5-8a and a full-wave bridge supply is shown in Figure 5-8b. Each circuit is labeled with the equations necessary to calculate the load voltage and current. Write a Pascal program that will allow the user to choose a given supply, then calculate the dc load voltage and current. (*Note:* The user must enter the transformer turns and load resistor value.)

5-8. Five different op-amp configurations are shown in Figure 5-9, along with their respective output equations. Write a menu-driven program that will allow a user to select a given op-amp configuration and calculate the output voltage. Assume that the user will enter the required circuit input and component values.

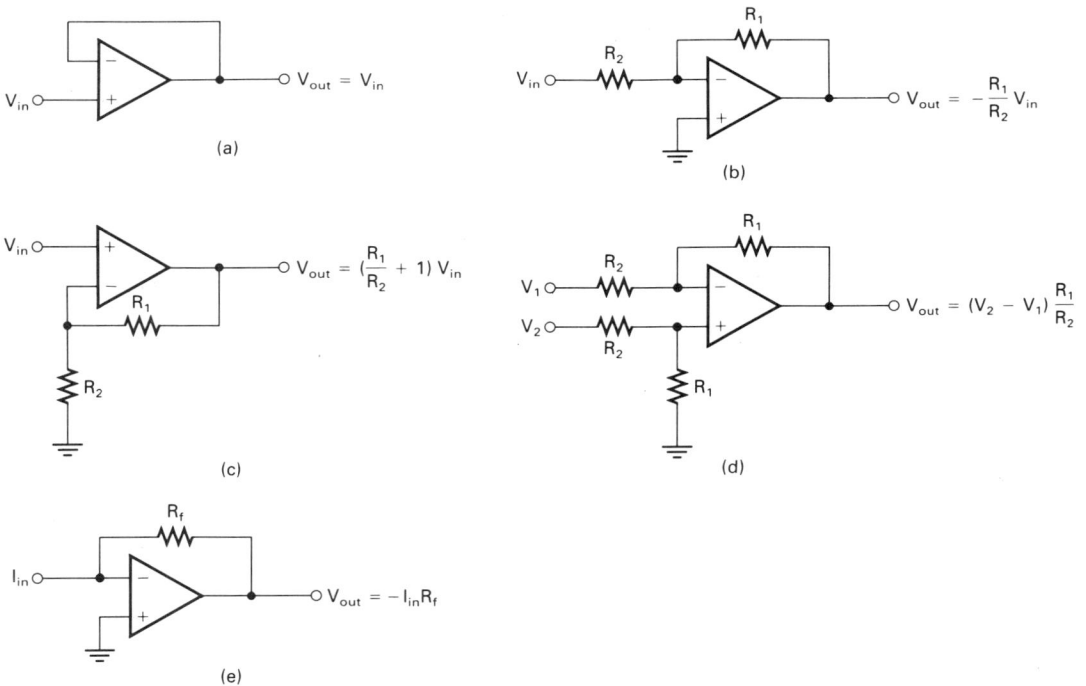

Figure 5-9 (a) Voltage follower, (b) inverting amplifier, (c) noninverting amplifier, (d) difference amplifier, and (e) current-to-voltage converter for problem 5-8.

chapter six

Looping Operations: Iteration

INTRODUCTION

In Chapter 5 you learned about the selection control structure. It is now time to explore the third and final control structure employed by Pascal: *iteration.* Iteration simply means to do something repeatedly. In programming, this is called *looping* because the iteration control structure causes the program flow to go around in a loop. Of course, there must be a way to get out of the loop or the computer would theoretically loop forever. Such a situation is called an *infinite loop*, for obvious reasons. To prevent infinite looping, all iteration control structures test a condition to determine when to exit the loop. *Pretest loops* test a condition each time before the loop is executed. *Posttest loops* test a condition after each loop execution. And finally, *fixed repetition loops* cause the loop to be executed a predetermined number of times.

The three iteration control structures employed by Pascal are the **WHILE/ DO, REPEAT/UNTIL,** and **FOR/DO.** As you will learn in this chapter, each provides a means for you to perform repetitive operations. The difference between them is found in the means by which they control the exiting of the loop. The **WHILE/DO** is a pretest loop, the **REPEAT/UNTIL** is a posttest loop, and the **FOR/ DO** is a fixed-repetition loop. Let's begin our discussion with the **WHILE/DO** loop.

6-1 THE WHILE/DO LOOP

You can see from Figure 6-1 that the **WHILE/DO** loop is a pretest loop because a Boolean test is made before the loop statements are executed. If the test is TRUE, the loop is executed. If the test is FALSE, the loop statements are bypassed and the next sequential statement after the loop is executed. As long as the test is TRUE, the program continues to go around the loop. In other words, the loop is repeated "while" the test is TRUE. To get out of the loop, something must change within the loop that makes the Boolean test result FALSE. If such a change does not take place, you have an infinite loop. In addition, the flowchart shows that if the first Boolean test is FALSE, the loop statements will never be executed. This is an important characteristic of the **WHILE/DO** control structure.

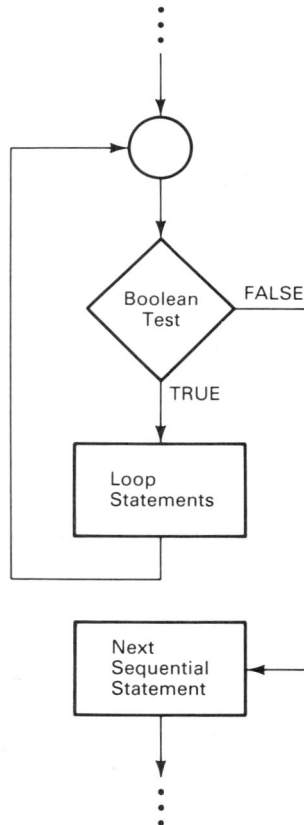

Figure 6-1 The flow of **WHILE/DO.**

The Format

The Pascal format for the **WHILE/DO** statement is as follows:

```
WHILE/DO FORMAT ************************************************************
WHILE Boolean test DO
   BEGIN
       statement 1;
       statement 2;      Loop Statements
          ⋮
       statement n
   END;
*****************************************************************************
```

The first line of the statement contains the reserved words **WHILE** and **DO**. A Boolean test expression must be inserted between these two reserved words. To test a single condition, you will often use the Boolean operations of $=$, $<>$, $<$, $>$, $<=$, $>=$, and **NOT**. To test multiple conditions, you must use the logical operators of **OR** and **AND**.

Notice that the loop statements are framed using the reserved words **BEGIN** and **END**. This forms a compound statement, which consists of the individual loop statements. An indentation scheme is also used so that the loop portion of the statement can be easily identified. Finally, you should be aware that the loop does not have to be framed if it consists of only a single statement. However, the CPU will only execute this single statement during the loop. Any additional statements are considered to be outside the loop structure. Let's see how the **WHILE/DO** loop works by looking at a few simple examples.

Example 6-1:

What will be displayed by the following segments of code? Assume that the variables employed in each segment have been appropriately declared.

```
a. Number := 5;
   Sum := 0;
   WHILE Number > 0  DO
     BEGIN
        Sum := Sum + Number;
        Number := Number - 1
     END;    {while}
   Writeln ('The sum is ', Sum);

b. Number := 5;
   Sum := 0;
   WHILE Number > 0  DO
     BEGIN
        IF Odd(Number)  THEN
           Sum := Sum + Number;
        Number := Number - 1
     END;    {while}
   Writeln ('The sum is ', Sum);
```

(Continued)

```
c.  Number := 5;
    Sum := 0;
    WHILE Number > 0  DO
      BEGIN
         IF NOT Odd(Number) THEN
            Sum := Sum + Number;
         Number := Number - 1
      END;   {while}
    Writeln ('The sum is ', Sum);

d.  MaxNumber := 5;
    Number := 0;
    Sum := 0;
    WHILE Number <> MaxNumber  DO
      BEGIN
        Sum := Sum + Number
      END;   {while}
    Write ('The average of the first ', MaxNumber);
    Writeln (' positive integers is ', Sum/MaxNumber:4:2);

e.  MaxNumber := 5;
    Number := 0;
    Sum := 0;
    WHILE Number <> MaxNumber  DO
      BEGIN
        Number := Number + 1;
        Sum := Sum + Number
      END;   {while}
    Write ('The average of the first ', MaxNumber);
    Writeln (' positive integers is ', Sum/MaxNumber:4:2);
```

f. What would happen if *Number* were incremented by 2 in the foregoing loop?

Solutions:

a. Here, the variable *Number* is first assigned the value 5 and the variable *Sum* is assigned the value 0. The **WHILE/DO** loop statements will be executed as long as *Number* is greater than 0. Observe that each time the loop is executed, the value of *Number* is added to *Sum*. In addition, the value of *Number* is decremented by 1. Let's trace through each iteration to see what is happening, keeping track of the values of *Number* and *Sum* after each iteration:

1st Iteration
    Sum is 5
    Number is 4

2nd Iteration
    Sum is 9
    Number is 3

3rd Iteration
    Sum is 12
    Number is 2

4th Iteration
     Sum is 14
     Number is 1
5th and Final Iteration
     Sum is 15
     Number is 0

The looping stops here, since the test *Number* > 0 is FALSE. As a result, the **WHILE/DO** loop is bypassed and the *Writeln* statement is executed, producing a display of:

```
The sum is 15
```

In summary, you could say that the program segment computes the sum of integers from 1 through 5.

b. Here, an **IF/THEN** statement has been included within the loop so that *Number* is only added to *Sum* if *Number* is odd. Thus, the program segment computes the sum of odd integers from 1 through 5, resulting in a display of

```
The sum is 9
```

c. This time, the program computes the sum of even integers from 1 through 5, since *Number* is only added to *Sum* if *Number* is *not* odd. As a result, the display is

```
The sum is 6
```

d. This is an infinite loop. Notice that the loop is executed as long as *Number* and *MaxNumber* are *not* equal. The initial value of *Number* is 0, and the initial value of *MaxNumber* is 5. However, these values are never changed within the loop. Thus, *Number* is always not equal to *MaxNumber*, resulting in an infinite loop. No display is generated, and with many systems you must turn off the computer to get out of the loop.

e. Now the loop in part d has been modified so that the value of *Number* is incremented by 1 with each iteration. When *Number* reaches 5, it reaches the value of *MaxNumber*, the iterations stop, and the resulting display is

```
The average of the first five positive integers is 3.00
```

f. This modification would also result in an infinite loop, since the value of *Number* would skip over the value of *MaxNumber* and the two would always be unequal.

Data Input Using WHILE/DO

There are many situations in which you will want to use a looping operation to input data. One common example is to input strings of data. The idea is to read a single data element, such as a character, each time the loop is executed, then break out of the loop when the data string is terminated. For instance, consider the following program:

```
PROGRAM Count_the_Characters (input, output);

CONST
  Period = '.';

VAR
  Count : integer;
  InChar : char;

BEGIN
  Writeln ('Input a string of characters and terminate');
  Writeln ('with a period.  Press ENTER after each character.');
  Writeln;
  Count := 0;
  Readln (InChar);
  WHILE (InChar <> Period) DO
    BEGIN
      Count := Count + 1;
      Readln (InChar);
    END;    {while}
  Writeln;
  Writeln ('The number of characters entered was ',Count)
END.    {program}
```

The general idea of this program is to input a string of characters until a period (.) is encountered. The period is called a *delimiter*, since it ends, or delimits, the input string but is not part of that string. The input variable is *InChar*. The **WHILE/DO** loop is executed as long as *InChar* is not equal to a period. With each iteration, a counter (*Count*) is incremented to count the number of characters that were input before the period. Here is what you will see when the program is executed:

```
Input a string of characters and terminate
with a period.  Press ENTER after each character.

a
b
c
d
e
.

The number of characters entered was 5
```

Now let's look at the program a bit closer. First, notice that a character is read just prior to the **WHILE/DO** statement. The reason is that the **WHILE/DO** statement tests the variable *InChar* to see that it is not a period. Without the first *Read* operation, *InChar* would not have a value and, therefore, could not be tested. Remember that the variable being tested in the **WHILE/DO** statement must always have a value prior to the first test. This is a common source of error when writing **WHILE/DO** loops.

6-2 THE REPEAT/UNTIL LOOP

The flow of the **REPEAT/UNTIL** loop can be seen in Figure 6-2. If you compare it with the flow of **WHILE/DO** in Figure 6-1, you will find that the Boolean test is made at the end of the loop, rather than at the beginning of the loop. This is why the **REPEAT/UNTIL** loop is referred to as a posttest loop. In other words, the loop "repeats until" the Boolean test result is TRUE. On the other hand, the **WHILE/DO** loop repeats until the Boolean test result is FALSE. (Think about it!)

By looking at Figure 6-2, you can see another important characteristic of the **REPEAT/UNTIL** operation: The loop is always executed *at least once*. It continues to repeat as long as the Boolean test result is FALSE. To break the loop, the Boolean test result must become TRUE. Thus, if the test condition is initially FALSE, something must happen within the loop to change the condition to TRUE; otherwise, you have an infinite loop.

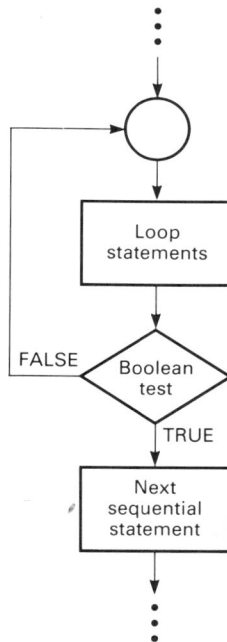

Figure 6-2   The flow of **REPEAT/UNTIL.**

The Format

The Pascal format for the **REPEAT/UNTIL** statement is as follows:

REPEAT/UNTIL FORMAT **
REPEAT
        statement 1;
        statement 2;   Loop Statements
          ⋮
        statement n

UNTIL Boolean test;

****

The format shows that the operation must begin with the single reserved word **REPEAT.** This is followed by the actual loop statements, which are followed by the reserved word **UNTIL** and the Boolean test expression. You do not have to **BEGIN** and **END** the loop statements, since they are naturally framed by the reserved words **REPEAT** and **UNTIL.** Look at the program segments in Example 6-2 and see if you can predict their results.

Example 6-2:

What will be displayed by the following segments of code? Assume that the variables and constants employed in each segment have been appropriately declared.

a.
```
Number := 5;
Sum := 0;
REPEAT
    Sum := Sum + Number;
    Number := Number - 1
UNTIL Number = 0;
Writeln ('The sum is ', Sum);
```

b.
```
Number := 0;
Sum := 0;
REPEAT
    Sum := Sum + Number;
    Number := Number + 1
UNTIL Number = 5;
Writeln ('The sum is ', Sum);
```

c.
```
MaxNumber := 5;
Number := 0;
Sum := 0;
REPEAT
    Number := Number - 1;
    Sum := Sum + Number
UNTIL Number = MaxNumber;
Write ('The average of the first ', MaxNumber);
Writeln (' positive integers is ', Sum/MaxNumber:4:2);
```

d.
```
MaxNumber := 5;
Number := 0;
Sum := 0;
REPEAT
    Number := Number + 1;
    Sum := Sum + Number
UNTIL Number = MaxNumber;
Write ('The average of the first ', MaxNumber);
Writeln (' positive integers is ', Sum/MaxNumber:4:2);
```

e.
```
Writeln ('Input a string of characters, ending them');
Writeln ('with a period.  Press ENTER after each character.');
Writeln;
Count := 0;
REPEAT
   Count := Count + 1;
   Readln (InChar)
UNTIL InChar = '.';
Writeln;
Writeln ('The number of characters entered was ',Count - 1);
```

Solutions:

a. In this segment, the value of *Number* is initially set to 5 and the value of *Sum* to 0. Each time the loop is executed, the value of *Number* is added to *Sum*. In addition, the value of *Number* is decremented by 1. The looping will end when *Number* has been decremented to 0. The resulting display is

```
The sum is 15
```

Notice that this **REPEAT/UNTIL** loop computes the sum of integers 1 through 5, as did the **WHILE/DO** loop in Example 6-1a.

b. In this segment, both *Number* and *Sum* are initially 0. Again, you might suspect that the loop computes the sum of the integers 1 through 5. But it actually computes the sum of integers 1 through 4. Why? Notice that *Number* is incremented after *Sum* is calculated. Thus, when *Number* increments to 5, the loop is broken and the value 5 is never added to *Sum*. The resulting display is

```
The sum is 10
```

How would you change the loop to sum the integers 1 through 5? One way is to change the **UNTIL** statement to **UNTIL** *Number* = 6. Another, more preferred way is to reverse the two loop statements so that *Number* is incremented prior to the *Sum* calculation.

c. In this segment *MaxNumber* begins with the value 5, and both *Number* and *Sum* are initialized to 0. The loop is broken when the value of *Number* equals the value of *MaxNumber*. How many times will the loop execute? If you said five, you are wrong! Notice that *Number* is *decremented* each time the loop is executed. Theoretically, the loop will execute an infinite number of times. However, since the range of integers in TURBO Pascal is from $-32,768$ to $32,767$ the loop will execute 65,531 times. How did I get this figure? Well, 32,768 loops will have executed when *Number* reaches $-32,768$. The next looping operation will decrement *Number* to 32,767. It then takes 32,762 loops to decrement *Number* to 5. Notice that $32,768 + 1 + 32,762 = 65,531$. Of course, this is infinite for all practical purposes.

d. Here, the loop in part c has been corrected so that the value of *Number* is incremented by 1 with each iteration.   When *Number* reaches 5, it equals the value of *MaxNumber* and the loop is broken.   The resulting display is

```
The average of the first five positive integers is 3.00
```

    e. This program segment shows how a delimiter can be employed to break a **REPEAT/ UNTIL** loop.   Notice that each iteration reads a single character from the terminal keyboard until the period key is entered.   The character *Count* must be decremented by 1 in the last *Writeln* statement, since the test is made at the end of the loop, after the *Count* has been incremented.   Observe that *Count* will be incremented, even for the last loop that reads the period delimiter.   Assuming that the user inputs the characters "abcd." the display would be

```
Input a string of characters, ending them
with a period.  Press ENTER after each character.

a
b
c
d
.


The number of characters entered was 4
```

6-3 THE FOR/DO LOOP

The flow of this final iteration control structure is illustrated in Figure 6-3.   The **FOR/DO** loop is called a fixed-repetition loop because the loop is repeated a fixed number of times.   As you can see, the first thing that takes place before the loop statements are executed is the ***initialization*** of a counter.   Initialization simply means to set a counter variable to some initial, or beginning, value.   The counter value is then tested to see if it is *less than or equal* to some predetermined final value.   If it is, the test result is TRUE and the loop statements are executed. Each time the loop statements are executed, the counter value is *automatically* incremented by 1.   The counter is tested again before the loop statements are executed another time.   The loop is repeated as long as the counter value remains less than or equal to the final value.   In other words, the counter is incremented, tested, and the loop is repeated until the counter *exceeds* the final value.   When this occurs, the loop statements are not executed again, and the loop is broken. Control of the program then goes to the next sequential statement following the loop.   Here's the Pascal format:

FOR/DO FORMAT **
FOR Counter : = initial value **TO** final value **DO**
    BEGIN
        statement 1;
        statement 2;   Loop Statements
          ⋮
        statement n

    END;

****

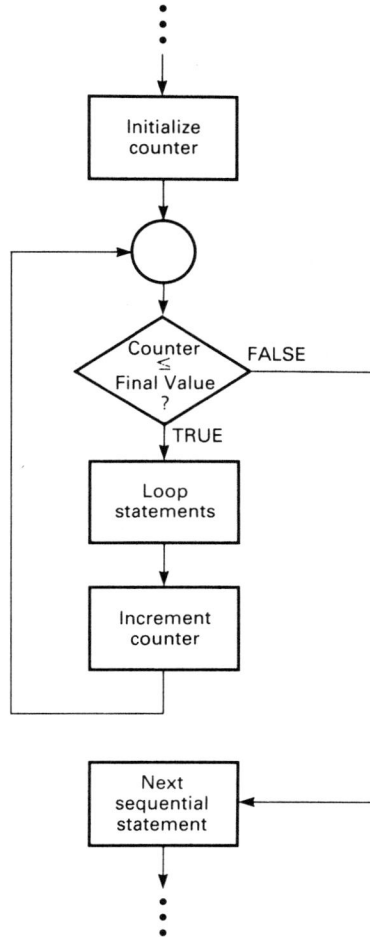

Figure 6-3   The flow of **FOR/DO**.

The statement begins with the three reserved words **FOR . . .   TO . . .   DO.** The loop counter is initialized by assigning the variable *Counter* to an initial value. Observe that the assignment symbol (: =) must be used here.   A common source of error is to use an equals sign (=) rather than the required assignment symbol.

I have chosen to call the counter variable *Counter*, for obvious reasons. Actually, you can use any simple scalar variable *except* real.   Of course, the variable must be declared in the declaration part of the program.   Most applications require an integer variable, and many times you will see the variables *I*, *J*, or *K* used. Regardless of the variable used, the initial counter value must be the same data type as the variable or an error will result.

The final counter value is inserted between the reserved words **TO** and **DO.** Again, the data type of this value must be the same as that of the counter variable.

Each time the loop is executed, the counter value is automatically incremented by 1, from its initial value to its final value. The loop is not broken until the counter value *exceeds* the final value. Thus, the loop statements are executed one more time after the final value is reached. After the loop is broken, the counter value is lost and cannot be used reliably in subsequent operations unless it is reinitialized.

One last point about the counter variable: *Never* alter the counter variable within the loop. The counter variable can be used within the body of the loop, but its value cannot be altered. In other words, never use the counter variable on the *left side* of the assignment symbol (: =) within the loop.

Finally, notice from the above format that the loop statements are framed within the reserved words **BEGIN** and **END.** This is always required when there are more than one loop statement. The framing can be eliminated when there is only a single loop statement. Here are a few examples. See if you can predict their results.

Example 6-3:

What will be displayed by the following segments of code? Assume the following constant and variable declarations:

```
CONST

    MaxCount = 100;

VAR
    Count, Sum, I, Row, Col, : integer;
    Average : real;
    Character : char;
```

a. ```
FOR Count := 1 TO 10 DO
    Writeln (Count);
```

b. ```
FOR Count := 50 TO 1 DO
    Writeln ('This statement is within the loop.');
Writeln ('This statement is outside the loop.');
```

c. ```
FOR Count := -5 TO 5 DO
    Writeln (Count);
```

d. ```
Writeln ('Number':12, 'Square':10, 'Cube':10);
FOR Count := 1 TO 10 DO
    Writeln (Count:10, Sqr(Count):10, Count * Sqr(Count):10);
```

e. ```
FOR Character := 'A' TO 'Z' DO
    Write (Character, ' ');
```

f. ```
Sum := 0;
FOR Count := 1 TO MaxCount DO
    Sum := Sum + Count;
```

```
Average := Sum / MaxCount;
Writeln;
Write ('The average of the first ', MaxCount, ' positive ');
Writeln ('integers is ', Average:4:2);
```

g.
```
FOR  I := 1 TO MaxCount DO
   IF I MOD 17 = 0   THEN
          Writeln ('The value ',I,  ' is divisible by 17.');
```

Solutions:

a. This first loop is straightforward. The loop counter variable, *Count*, ranges from 1 to 10. Each time the loop is executed, the *Writeln* statement displays the value of *Count* as follows:

```
                    1
                    2
                    3
                    4
                    5
                    6
                    7
                    8
                    9
                    10
```

b. Recall that the counter value is tested *before* the loop statements are executed. As a result, the loop statement in this loop is never executed, since the initial value of *Count* is greater than its final value. The resulting output is

```
          This statement is outside the loop.
```

c. Here, *Count* ranges from −5 to 5. How many times will the loop be executed? Ten, right? Wrong! There are eleven integers between −5 and 5, *including 0*. As a result, the loop is executed eleven times to produce an output of

```
                   −5
                   −4
                   −3
                   −2
                   −1
                    0
                    1
                    2
                    3
                    4
                    5
```

d. This **FOR/DO** loop is being used to generate a table of square and cubes for the integers 1 through 10. Notice how the counter variable, *Count*, is squared and cubed using the *Sqr* function. However, observe that at no time is the value of *Count* altered within the loop. The resulting display is

Number	Square	Cube
1	1	1
2	4	8
3	9	27
4	16	64
5	25	125
6	36	216
7	49	343
8	64	512
9	81	729
10	100	1000

e. The counter variable in this loop is the character variable *Character*. Recall that the character data type is ordered such that 'A' is smaller than 'Z'. Consequently, the loop is executed twenty-six times as *Character* ranges from 'A' to 'Z'. The value of *Character* is displayed each time using a *Write* statement to produce an output of

```
A B C D E F G H I J K L M N O P Q R S T U V W X Y Z
```

f. Here, the counter value is being added to the integer variable *Sum* each time through the loop. Thus, the loop adds all the positive integers within the defined range of the counter variable. The range of *Count* is from 1 to *MaxCount*. Notice that *MaxCount* has been declared a constant with a value of 100. Therefore, *Count* will range from 1 to 100 resulting in a *Sum* of all integers within this range. After the loop is broken, the value of *Sum* is divided by *MaxCount* to calculate the *Average* of all integers from 1 to 100. Here's what you would see:

```
The average of the first 100 positive integers is 50.50
```

You should be aware that constants are often used in this way for the initial or final counter values in a **FOR/DO** loop. The reason is this: If the constant value needs to be changed for some reason, you only need to change it in one place, at the beginning of the program within the **CONST** declaration. This changes its value any place it is used within the program.

g. An **IF/THEN** statement is used in this loop to determine when the counter value, *I*, is divisible by 17. Thus, the loop displays all the values between 1 and *MaxCount* (100) that are divisible by 17. Notice that the loop is not framed, since the **IF/THEN** statement, with its *Writeln* statement, is treated as a single statement. Here is what you would see when it is executed:

```
The value 17 is divisible by 17.
The value 34 is divisible by 17.
The value 51 is divisible by 17.
The value 68 is divisible by 17.
The value 85 is divisible by 17.
```

Nested Loops

Many applications require looping operations within loops. This is called ***nested looping.*** To get the idea, think about the seconds, minutes, and hours of a twelve-hour digital stopwatch. Isn't each a simple counter? The seconds count from 0 to 59, the minutes from 0 to 59 and the hours from 0 to 11. For every sixty seconds, the minutes counter is incremented. Likewise, for every sixty minutes, the hours counter is incremented. Thus, the seconds count is "nested" within the minutes count and the minutes count is "nested" within the hours count. Here's how a digital stop watch might be coded in a Pascal program using nested **FOR/DO** loops:

```
FOR Hours := 0 TO 11 DO
   BEGIN
      Write (Hours);
      FOR Minutes := 0 TO 59 DO
         BEGIN
            Write (Minutes);
            FOR Seconds := 0 TO 59 DO
               Write (Seconds)
         END   {Minutes for}
   END;   {Hours for}
```

As you can see, the seconds **FOR/DO** loop is part of the minutes loop, which is part of the hours loop. The program segment begins by initializing the *Hours* counter to 0 and writing the hours. Then the next statement in the hours loop initializes the *Minutes* counter to 0 and writes the minutes. This leads to the seconds loop, where the *Seconds* counter is initialized to 0. Once the *Seconds* counter is initialized, the seconds loop is executed sixty times. Each time the seconds loop is executed, the *Seconds* count is displayed. After the seconds loop is executed sixty times, the *Minutes* count is incremented and displayed. Then the seconds loop is entered again and executed sixty more times.

Thus, the seconds loop is executed sixty times for each iteration of the minutes loop. Likewise, since the minutes loop is nested within the hours loop, the minutes loop is executed sixty times for each iteration of the hours loop. After sixty iterations of the minutes loop (3,600 iterations of the seconds loop) the *Hours* count is incremented and displayed. The hours loop is not broken until it has been executed twelve times. Of course, this requires $12 \times 60 = 720$ iterations of the minutes loop, and $12 \times 60 \times 60 = 43,200$ iterations of the seconds loop. We say that the seconds loop is the ***innermost*** loop, while the ***outermost*** loop is the hours loop.

Notice the use of the **BEGIN**s and **END**s to frame the loops. The hours loop must be framed, since it consists of the minutes and seconds loop statements. In the same way, the minutes loop must be framed, since it consists of the seconds loop statements. The seconds loop is not framed, since it consists of only a single *Write* statement. Here is where an indentation scheme and commenting become important for program readability. Observe how the indentation scheme actually shows the nesting, while the commenting indicates the end of the respective loop structures.

To make the digital stopwatch work, the seconds counter must be incremented precisely once every second. This requires a nested loop within the seconds loop to slow down, or delay, the seconds count accordingly. This will be left as a programming exercise at the end of the chapter. You will actually execute a Pascal program that will turn your computer into a digital stopwatch.

Before we leave the topic of nested loops, you should be aware that **WHILE/DO** and **REPEAT/UNTIL** loops can also be nested. You will find examples of this in the questions at the end of the chapter.

DOWNTO Loops

In all the **FOR/DO** loops you have seen so far, the loop counter has been *incremented* from some initial value to some final value. You can also make the loop counter *decrement* from the initial to the final value using the reserved word **DOWNTO** within the loop statement, as follows:

DOWNTO LOOP FORMAT **
FOR Counter : = initial value **DOWNTO** final value **DO**
    BEGIN
        statement 1;⎤
        statement 2;⎟ Loop Statements
           ⋮   ⎟
        statement n ⎦

    END;
****

The digital stopwatch program segment could be easily revised to employ **DOWNTO** loops, as follows:

```
FOR Hours := 11 DOWNTO 0 DO
    BEGIN
        Write (Hours);
        FOR Minutes := 59 DOWNTO 0 DO
            BEGIN
                Write (Minutes);
                FOR Seconds := 59 DOWNTO 0 DO
                    Write (Seconds)
            END  {Minutes for}
    END;  {Hours for}
```

The only difference here is that the initial and final values of the respective loop counters have been reversed. The **DOWNTO** command causes the counter value to be decreased by 1, or decremented, with each loop iteration. The net effect is still the same: There are sixty iterations of the seconds loop for each iteration of the minutes loop, and sixty iterations of the minutes loop for each iteration of the hours loop.

6-4 AN APPLICATION TASK: PARALLEL CIRCUIT ANALYSIS

Let's close this chapter by writing several programs that will allow a user to find the total equivalent resistance of a circuit for any number of resistors in parallel. We will solve the task three different ways, using each of the three iteration control structures discussed in this chapter.   First, let's define the task at hand in terms of output, input, and processing.

The Problem Definition

Output: The program must first prompt the user to enter the number of resistors in the parallel circuit.   A prompt will then be generated to enter each resistor value separately.   The final output will be a display of the equivalent parallel resistance.

Input: The number of resistors in the circuit and the individual resistor values in kilohms.

Processing: Each time a resistor value (R) is entered, the equivalent parallel resistance (R_equiv) will be recalculated using the "product-over-sum" rule as follows:

$$R\_equiv = \frac{R\_equiv \times R}{R\_equiv + R}$$

Now, using the above problem definition, we are ready for the algorithm. Let's first employ the **WHILE/DO** iteration control structure to recalculate the equivalent parallel resistance each time a resistor value is entered.

The Algorithm

BEGIN
    Write a program description message.
    Write a user prompt to enter the number of resistors in the circuit.
    Read *(Number)*.
    Set *Count* = 0.
    While *Count* < *Number*
      Set *Count* = *Count* + 1;
      Write prompt to enter resistor #*(Count)*.
      Read *(R)*.
      If *Count* = 1 Then
        Set *R_equiv* = *R*
      Else
        Calculate *R_equiv* = (*R_equiv* × *R*) / (*R_equiv* + *R*).
    Write *R_equiv*.
END.

As you can see, this is a rather simple algorithm employing the *While/Do* control structure. Each time the loop is executed, an additional resistor value is entered and the equivalent resistance of the circuit is calculated. You probably are wondering why the *If/Then/Else* statement is used within the loop. Well, the first resistor value is entered the first time through the loop. Since *Count* = 1 during the first iteration, the *Then* clause of the *If/Then/Else* statement is executed and *R_equiv* is set to this first resistor value. In subsequent iterations, the *Else* clause is executed to calculate *R_equiv* using the product-over-sum rule. Without setting *R_equiv* to the first resistor value the first time through the loop, *R_equiv* would have no beginning value for subsequent calculations and the results would be unpredictable. Think about it!

So, you say to set the value of *R_equiv* equal to 0 prior to the loop. But this will result in the numerator of the product-over-sum equation being 0, which makes the value of *R_equiv* 0 in each loop iteration. The easiest solution is to set *R_equiv* to the value of the first resistor during the first loop iteration. Then the value of *R_equiv* is recalculated with each subsequent loop iteration. Of course, if there is only one resistor in the circuit (*Number* = 1), the loop is only executed once, with the value of *R_equiv* being set to this single resistor value.

Notice also that a counter (*Count*) must be initialized to 0 prior to the loop. The value of *Count* must then be incremented with each loop iteration to prevent an infinite loop. The looping continues until the value of *Count* equals the number of resistors in the circuit (*Number*). When this happens, the loop statements are not executed again and the equivalent resistance is displayed.

Following the algorithm, you can code a Pascal program as follows:

The Program

```
PROGRAM Parallel_Resistance (input, output);

USES
  Crt;

VAR
  Number, Count : integer;
  R_equiv, R1, R : real;
BEGIN
  Clrscr;
  Writeln ('This program will calculate the total resistance');
  Writeln ('of a  parallel circuit.');
  Writeln;
  Writeln;
  Write ('Enter the number of resistors in the circuit:  Number = ');
  Readln (Number);
  Writeln;
  Count := 0;
  WHILE  Count < Number DO
    BEGIN
      Count := Count + 1;
      Write ('Enter resistor value #',Count,' in ');
```

```
      Write ('kilohms:  R',Count,' = ');
      Read (R);
      Writeln (' kilohms.');
      Writeln;
      IF Count = 1 THEN
        R_equiv := R
      ELSE
        R_equiv := (R_equiv * R) / (R_equiv + R)
    END;  {while}
  Write ('The equivalent resistance of the parallel circuit');
  Writeln (' is ', R_equiv:6:2,' kilohms.')
END.  {program}
```

Here is what you would see on the display when the program is executed:

```
This program will calculate the total resistance
of a  parallel circuit.


Enter the number of resistors in the circuit:  Number = 2

Enter resistor value #1 in kilohms:  R1 = 10 kilohms.

Enter resistor value #2 in kilohms:  R2 = 10 kilohms.

The equivalent resistance of the parallel circuit is   5.00 kilohms.
```

Next suppose that you want to use the **REPEAT/UNTIL** control structure to perform the same task.   Remember the major difference is that the **REPEAT/ UNTIL** loop statements are always executed at least once.

The Algorithm

BEGIN

    Write a program description message.

    Write a user prompt to enter the number of resistors in the circuit.

    Read (*Number*).

    Set *Count* = 0.

    Repeat

      Set *Count* = *Count* + 1.

      Write prompt to enter resistor #(*Count*).

      Read (*R*).

      If *Count* = 1 then

        Set *R_equiv* = *R*.

      Else

        Calculate *R_equiv* = (*R_equiv* × *R*) / (*R_equiv* + *R*).

      Until *Count* = *Number*.

    Write *R_equiv*.

  END.

Here, you can see that the only difference between this algorithm and the previous **WHILE/DO** algorithm is the Boolean test on the loop counter. With **WHILE/DO**, the loop is executed as long as the value of *Count* is less than *Number*. In other words, the **WHILE/DO** loop is repeated until *Count* = *Number*. This requires a Boolean test of While *Count* < *Number*. However, to achieve the same result with a **REPEAT/UNTIL** loop the test must be Until *Count* = *Number*. Here's the resulting program.

The Program

```
PROGRAM Parallel_Resistance (input, output);

USES
  Crt;

VAR
  Number, Count : integer;
  R_equiv, R1, R : real;

BEGIN
  Clrscr;
  Writeln ('This program will calculate the total resistance');
  Writeln ('of a  parallel circuit.');
  Writeln;
  Writeln;
  Write ('Enter the number of resistors in the circuit:  Number = ');
  Readln (Number);
  Writeln;
  Count := 0;
  REPEAT
      Count := Count + 1;
      Write ('Enter resistor value #',Count,' in ');
      Write ('kilohms:  R',Count,' = ');
      Read (R);
      Writeln (' kilohms.');
      Writeln;
      IF  Count = 1 THEN
        R_equiv := R
      ELSE
        R_equiv := (R_equiv * R) / (R_equiv + R)
  UNTIL Count = Number;
  Write ('The equivalent resistance of the parallel circuit');
  Writeln (' is ', R_equiv:6:2,' kilohms.')
END.   {program}
```

The output of this program is the same as that of the **WHILE/DO** program.

Finally, lets rewrite the algorithm and code a program to employ the **FOR/DO** iteration control structure. Remember that with the **FOR/DO** structure, the loop is executed a fixed number of times as the loop counter ranges from its initial to final values. So why not set the initial counter value to 1 and the final value to the number of resistors in the parallel circuit.   Here's the idea in the form of an algorithm:

The Algorithm

BEGIN
  Write a program description message.
  Write a user prompt to enter the number of resistors in the circuit.
  Read (*Number*).
  For *Count* = 1 to *Number*
    Write prompt to enter resistor #(*Count*).
    Read (*R*).
    If *Count* = 1 then
      Set *R_equiv* = *R*.
    Else
      Calculate *R_equiv* = (*R_equiv* × *R*) / (*R_equiv* + *R*).
    Write *R_equiv*.
END.

Here, the loop executes as *Count* ranges from 1 to *Number*.   The counter is automatically incremented and tested as part of the *For/Do* control structure.   An *If/Then/Else* is used as before to initialize the value of *R_equiv* to the first resistor value during the first loop iteration.   Here's the program:

The Program

```
PROGRAM Parallel_Resistance (input,output);

USES
  Crt;

VAR
  Number, Count : integer;
  R_equiv, R : real;

BEGIN
  Clrscr;
  Writeln ('This program will calculate the total resistance');
  Writeln ('of a parallel circuit.');
  Writeln;
  Writeln;
  Write ('How many resistors are in parallel?  Number = ');
  Readln (Number);
  Writeln;
  Writeln;
```

(Continued)

```
FOR Count := 1 TO Number DO
  BEGIN
    Write ('Enter resistor value #',Count,' in ');
    Write ('kilohms:  R',Count,' = ');
    Read (R);
    Writeln (' kilohms.');
    Writeln;
    IF Count = 1 THEN
      R_equiv := R
    ELSE
      R_equiv := (R_equiv * R) / (R_equiv + R)
  END;  {for}
Write ('The total resistance of the parallel circuit');
Writeln (' is ', R_equiv:6:2,' kilohms.')
END.
```

The output of this program is the same as that for the previous two programs.

CHAPTER SUMMARY

In this chapter you learned about the three iteration control structures employed by Pascal: **WHILE/DO, REPEAT/UNTIL,** and **FOR/DO.** The **WHILE/DO** is a pretest looping structure, the **REPEAT/UNTIL** is a posttest looping structure, and the **FOR/DO** is a fixed-repetition looping structure. As a result, the following general guidelines should be considered when deciding which looping structure to use in a given situation:

- Use **WHILE/DO** whenever there is a possibility that the loop statements will not need to be executed.
- Use **REPEAT/UNTIL** when the loop statements must be executed at least once.
- Use **FOR/DO** when it can be determined exactly how many times the loop statements must be executed.

QUESTIONS AND PROBLEMS

Questions

6-1. Name the three iteration control structures employed by Pascal.

6-2. Which of the iteration control structures will always execute the loop at least once?

6-3. Which of the iteration control structures performs the Boolean test before the loop is executed?

6-4. Which of the iteration control structures is employed when it is determined exactly how many times the loop must execute?

6-5. When must a **REPEAT/UNTIL** loop be framed?
  a. Always
  b. You only end, not begin it
  c. You only begin, not end it
  d. Never

6-6. Using the choices in question 6-5, when must you frame a **WHILE/DO** loop?

In questions 6-7 through 6-17, determine the output generated by the respective program segment. Assume that the variables employed within the program segments have been appropriately declared.

6-7.
```
A := 1;
WHILE (17 MOD A) <> 5 DO
    BEGIN
        Writeln (A,'   ', 17 MOD A);
        A := A + 1
    END;
```

6-8.
```
B := 2;
REPEAT
    Writeln (B,'   ', B DIV 5);
    B := B * 2
UNTIL B = 20;
```

6-9.
```
B := 2;
REPEAT
    Writeln (B,'   ', B DIV 5);
    B := B * 2
UNTIL B = 32;
```

6-10.
```
Number := 1;
Product := 1;
REPEAT
    Number := Number + 1;
    Product := Product * Number
UNTIL Number = 5;
Writeln ('The product is ', Product);
```

6-11.
```
Writeln ('Enter a string of characters, ending them with');
Writeln ('an asterisk.  Press the ENTER key after each entry.');
Writeln;
Readln (Input);
Count := 0;
WHILE Input <> '*' DO
  BEGIN
    Count := Count + 1;
    Readln (Input)
  END;
Writeln;
Writeln ('The character count is ',Count,'.');
```

(Continued)

```
6-12. FOR Number := 10 TO 1 DO
         Writeln (Number);
      Writeln ('That',''''','s all folks!');
```

```
6-13. FOR Number := 10 DOWNTO 1 DO
         Writeln (Number);
      Writeln ('That',''''','s all folks!');
```

```
6-14. Writeln (1st,'Angle':12, 'Sin':10, 'Cos':10);
      Writeln (1st,'-----':12, '---':10, '---':10);
      FOR Angle := 0 TO 90  DO
         BEGIN
            Write (1st,Angle:10, Sin(Angle * Pi/180):12:3);
            Writeln (1st,Cos(Angle * Pi/180):10:3)
         END;
```

```
6-15. FOR Row := 1 TO 5 DO
         BEGIN
            Writeln;
            FOR Col := 1 TO 10 DO
               Write (Row, ',' , Col, '    ')
         END;
```

```
6-16. Count := 0;
      MaxCount := 5;
      WHILE Count < MaxCount DO
         BEGIN
            FOR I := 1 TO MaxCount  DO
               Write (I);
            Writeln;
            Count := Count + 1
         END;
```

```
6-17. Times := 0;
      MaxCount := 5;
      REPEAT
         Count := 0;
         WHILE Count < MaxCount DO
            BEGIN
               FOR  J := 1 TO Count DO
                  Write (J);
               Count := Count + 1;
               Writeln
            END;
         Writeln;
         Times := Times + 1
      UNTIL Times = 3;
```

Programming Problems

6-1. Write a program that will compute the average of any number of test scores using a **WHILE/DO** loop.

6-2. Revise the program in problem 6-1 to employ a **REPEAT/UNTIL** loop.

6-3. Revise the program in problem 6-1 to employ a **FOR/DO** loop.

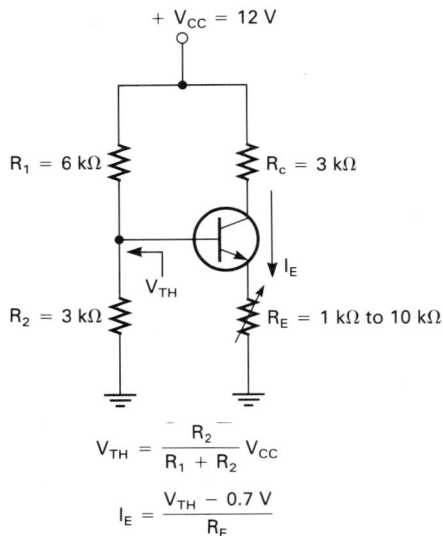

$$V_{TH} = \frac{R_2}{R_1 + R_2} V_{CC}$$

$$I_E = \frac{V_{TH} - 0.7\ V}{R_E}$$

Figure 6-4 The voltage divider bias circuit for problem 6-10.

6-4. Write a Pascal program that will calculate the equivalent resistance of any number of resistors in series.   Employ the **WHILE/DO** control structure.

6-5. Revise the program in problem 6-4 to employ the **REPEAT/UNTIL** control structure.

6-6. Revise the program in problem 6-4 to employ the **FOR/DO** control structure.

6-7. Write a menu-driven program that will allow the user to calculate the equivalent resistance of any number of resistors in a series *or* parallel circuit.

6-8. Write a program that will allow the user to find the equivalent resistance of a series-parallel circuit of any arbitrary configuration.

6-9. Using the formula $C = 5/9(F - 32)$, generate a Celsius conversion table for all even temperatures from 32° to 212° degrees Fahrenheit.

6-10. Write a program to generate a table of emitter current (I_E) versus emitter resistance (R_E) for the voltage divider bias circuit shown in Figure 6-4.   Assume that the emitter resistance (R_E) ranges from 1 kΩ to 10 kΩ.

6-11. Write a program to generate a table of voltage gain (A) versus feedback resistance (R_1) for the op-amp circuit in Figure 6-5.

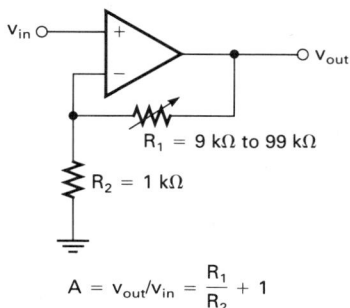

$$A = v_{out}/v_{in} = \frac{R_1}{R_2} + 1$$

Figure 6-5 The op-amp circuit for problem 6-11.

6-12. There are occasions when you will need to interrupt, or break, a loop before the counter reaches its final value. An example of this can be found in the digital stopwatch program discussed in this chapter. Here's the program again:

```
FOR Hours := 0 TO 11 DO
    BEGIN
        Write (Hours);
        FOR Minutes := 0 TO 59 DO
            BEGIN
                Write (Minutes);
                FOR Seconds := 0 TO 59 DO
                    Write (Seconds)
            END    {Minutes for}
    END;   {Hours for}
```

Assuming that the *Seconds* counter increments precisely once every second, the clock routine will require twelve hours to execute. But suppose that you wish to break the program execution before the twelve-hour period expires? In other words, suppose that you want to stop the clock from a keyboard command without resetting or turning off your system? There is a way, but it violates the fundamental modularity concept of structured programming. Pascal includes a **GOTO** command that causes the program to unconditionally branch, or go to, a designated place within the program. Here's a complete clock program that incorporates the **GOTO** command to stop the clock:

```
PROGRAM Clock (output);

LABEL
   10;

VAR
   Hours, Minutes, Seconds, Delay : integer;

BEGIN
   Clrscr;
   Writeln ('This program turns your computer into a digital');
   Writeln ('stop watch. Press any key to stop the clock.');
   Writeln;
   Writeln;
   Writeln;
   Writeln ('The Hours are:   ');
   Writeln;
   Writeln ('The Minutes are:   ');
   Writeln;
   Writeln ('The Seconds are:   ');
   FOR Hours := 0 TO 11 DO
      BEGIN
         GotoXY (16,6);
         Write (Hours);
         FOR Minutes := 0 TO 59 DO
            BEGIN
               GotoXY (18,8);
               Write (Minutes:2);
               FOR Seconds := 0 TO 59 DO
                  BEGIN
                     GotoXY (18,10);
                     Write (Chr(7),Seconds:2);
                     FOR Delay := 1 TO 7500 DO
                        Write;
                     IF KeyPressed THEN
                        GOTO 10
```

```
                              END  (seconds for)
                        END  (minutes for)
            END;    (hours for)

      10 :
         Writeln;
         Writeln;
         Writeln ('TIME OUT --> PRESS THE R KEY TO START THE CLOCK AGAIN.')
      END.  (program)
```

Let's examine several features of this program. First, notice the **LABEL** declaration at the top of the program and the **GOTO** 10 statement within the seconds loop of the program. The 10 is called a *label*, since it labels the place to go to when the **GOTO** 10 statement is executed. Pascal requires you to declare all labels using the reserved word **LABEL** in the declaration section of the program, as shown. When executed, the **GOTO** 10 statement causes the program to branch to the 10 label at the bottom of the program and resume execution at that point. Notice that when the program goes to 10, a TIME OUT message is displayed and the program ends.

Now the question is: When will the **GOTO** 10 statement be executed? Well, notice that it is part of the **IF** *KeyPressed* **THEN** statement within the seconds loop. *KeyPressed* is a built-in Boolean function available in TURBO Pascal. It returns the value TRUE when any keyboard key is pressed. The **IF** *KeyPressed* **THEN** statement calls this function once every second. If a keyboard key is pressed, the function is TRUE and the **GOTO** 10 statement is executed, breaking the nested loop structure.

CAUTION ───

As mentioned earlier, the **GOTO** statement violates the fundamental concept of modularity in structured programming. In other words, **GOTO** statements defeat the purpose of the modular block structure of Pascal. This can result in unworkable programs that are very difficult to read and debug, especially for complex programming tasks such as those that might be found in an industrial application. For these reasons, many Pascal texts do not even mention the **GOTO** statement. I have obscured it within this program and only mention it here owing to a reasonable application for its use.

───

Next notice that there are four nested loops: hours, minutes, seconds, and delay. Why the delay loop? The delay loop is required to slow down the seconds loop so that the *Seconds* counter is incremented precisely once every second. Observe that the delay loop does not perform any meaningful operation. It simply increments a counter from 1 to 7,500 and executes a *Write* command with each iteration. The *Write* command doesn't write anything; it is there simply to complete the **FOR/DO** loop.

Finally, another interesting feature of this program is the *GotoXY* command. This command does *not* cause the program to alter its execution like the **GOTO** instruction. Rather, the *GotoXY* command is a standard procedure available in TURBO Pascal that positions the CRT display cursor at position (X,Y) on the screen. Think of the CRT screen as an (X,Y) coordinate system, where X is the column, or horizontal, coordinate and Y is the row, or vertical, coordinate. The upper left-hand corner of the CRT screen is position $(1,1)$. Since most CRT terminals have 80 columns and 25 rows, the lower right-hand cursor position is $(80,25)$. Your system might be different, but regardless of the system, the upper left-hand corner position is always

(1,1). By substituting the appropriate coordinate in the *GotoXY* command, you can position the cursor at any desired location on the screen to write a message. This is done in the foregoing stopwatch program to update the hours, minutes, and seconds display. The *GotoXY* command is also ideal for use in programs that generate graphical outputs. Again, a **USES** *Crt* statement must be added to TURBO 4.0 and later-version programs in order to use *GotoXY*.

Now that you have been introduced to the program, your task is simple: enter, execute, and observe its operation on your system. You might have to change the final value of the delay loop counter so that the seconds counter increments precisely once every second. The value 7,500 worked on my system (Zenith Z-90), but since other systems operate with different internal clock frequencies, your system might require a different final count value.

6-13. Using the ideas that you saw in problem 6-12, write a Pascal program to display the output of the binary counter shown in Figure 6-6. Use the *GotoXY* command to update the counter output lines each time the user presses the **ENTER** key. Thus, the **ENTER** key simulates the application of a clock pulse by the user to the circuit. (*Hints:* You will need four nested **FOR/DO** loops, one for each counter output line. Insert a single *Readln* statement into the innermost loop to stop the program execution until the user presses the **ENTER** key, thus simulating the application of a clock pulse.)

6-14. Write a program that will calculate the mean ($\bar{x}$) and standard deviation (σ) of a series of numbers. The mean of a series of numbers is the same as the average of the

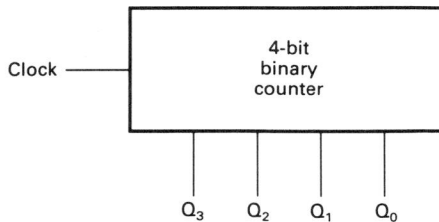

State	Q_3	Q_2	Q_1	Q_0
0	0	0	0	0
1	0	0	0	1
2	0	0	1	0
3	0	0	1	1
4	0	1	0	0
5	0	1	0	1
6	0	1	1	0
7	0	1	1	1
8	1	0	0	0
9	1	0	0	1
10	1	0	1	0
11	1	0	1	1
12	1	1	0	0
13	1	1	0	1
14	1	1	1	0
15	1	1	1	1

Figure 6-6 The binary counter for problem 6-13.

numbers. The standard deviation of a series of numbers is found using the following formula:

$$\sigma = \sqrt{\frac{(x_1 - \bar{x})^2 + (x_2 - \bar{x})^2 + \cdots + (x_n - \bar{x})^2}{n}}$$

6-15. Some programming languages, like BASIC, allow you to use a *STEP* command within a **FOR/DO** statement as follows:

FOR Counter : = initial value **TO** final step *STEP N* **DO**

The *STEP* command allows the loop counter to increment by some value (*N*), other than the value 1, with each loop iteration. In Pascal the **FOR/DO** statement only allows the counter to be incremented or decremented by 1.

Write a **FOR/DO** loop in Pascal that will emulate this *STEP* operation. Provide for user input of any desired step value. To demonstrate its operation, use your step loop to display every fifth integer, from 1 to 100.

(*Hint*: Use an auxiliary counter variable within the loop that increments by the *STEP* value. Display this auxiliary counter variable with each loop iteration.)

chapter seven

Subprograms: Functions and Procedures

INTRODUCTION

Up to this point, you have been working with Pascal programs that consist of two sections: a declaration section and a statement section. Any and all operations to be performed were executed as part of the statement section of the program. Now suppose that you needed to perform a given operation several times at different locations within the program. For instance, suppose that you must print your name more than once during the program execution. With your present knowledge of Pascal, you would simply code a statement such as

```
Writeln (lst,'My name  is:  George Washington');
```

Then insert this statement each time your name must be printed, right? However, there is a simpler way to do it! Suppose that you could write a ***subprogram*** that will print your name. Let's call the subprogram *PRINTNAME*. Then each time your name must be printed, you simply insert the statement *PRINTNAME*, rather than repeating the above *Writeln* statement.

Of course, this is a rather simple example. But even here you can see that the amount of coding is reduced, especially if you must print your name many times during the execution of the program.   Clearly, your coding efficiency is enhanced even more when the subprogram task gets more complex.

A subprogram is simply a block of statements that are written to perform a specific task required by you, the programmer.   The subprogram is given a name and *called,* or *invoked,* using its name each time the task is to be performed within the main program.   The program that calls, or invokes, a subprogram is often referred to as the *calling program.*

Subprograms eliminate the need for duplicate statements within a program. Given a task to be performed more than once, the statements are written just once for the subprogram.   Then the subprogram is called each time the task must be performed.   In addition, the use of subprograms enhances the program listing clarity and readability.   And most important, subprogramming within a structured language like Pascal allows you to solve very large complex tasks using a *top/down* program design approach.   The meaning of a top/down program design should become clear by the end of this chapter.

There are two ways that you can develop subprograms in Pascal: by writing *functions* or *procedures.*   Let's learn how to do both, beginning with functions.

7-1 FUNCTIONS

You have already had some experience with functions in Pascal.   Recall the *standard functions* that you learned about in Chapter 4 such as *Sqr, Sqrt, Cos,* and *Odd,* just to mention a few.   You found that Pascal included several standard arithmetic, scalar, transfer, and miscellaneous functions.   But suppose that you wish to perform some operation, such as *Cube,* that is not a standard function in Pascal.   Since Pascal does not include any standard function for cube, you could code the cube operation as follows:

$$Cube := X * X * X$$

Then insert this statement into your program each time the value of X must be cubed.   However, wouldn't it be a lot easier to simply insert the command $Cube(X)$ each time X is to be cubed, where Pascal knows what to do just like it knows how to execute $Sqr(X)$?   You can do this by declaring your own *Cube* function.   Such a function is called a *user-defined* function, for obvious reasons.

A function is a subprogram that, when invoked, returns a *single* value to the calling program.   Thus, if *Cube* is a user-defined function that will cube a value, say X, the statement *Writeln (Cube (X))* will invoke the function and cause the cube of X to be displayed.   Now you need to learn how you can create such user-defined functions.

The Format

Here is the format that you must use when declaring your own functions:

```
USER-DEFINED FUNCTION FORMAT ***************************************************
FUNCTION function name (parameter listing):function data type;
CONST
        local function constants
VAR
        local function variables
BEGIN
        function statement #1;
        function statement #2;
                 ⋮
        function statement #n
END;
********************************************************************************
```

Notice that the structure of a user-defined function is just like that of a Pascal program. This is why a function is called a subprogram. As you can see, the format includes a declaration section and a statement section. The declaration section begins with the function heading.

The Function Heading

In the function heading the reserved word **FUNCTION** is followed by the function identifier, or name, a parameter listing, and the function data type.

The Function Identifier

The function identifier, or name, can be any legal identifier in Pascal. The name should be descriptive of the operation that the function performs, such as *Cube* to cube a value. When you invoke the function within your calling program, you will use this name.

In addition, some value must be assigned to the function name within the statement section of the subprogram. With the *Cube* function, you would need a statement such as

```
Cube := X * X * X;
```

within the statement section of the function.

Two things to remember:

1. The function identifier can never be used on the right side of the assignment symbol inside the function. In other words, the following statement inside the cube function will generate an error:

```
Cube := Cube * X;
```

There is one exception to this rule, called ***recursion,*** which will be discussed soon.

2. The function identifier can never be used on the left side of the assignment symbol *outside* the function. Thus,

`Cube := X * X * X;`

is *legal within* the function, but *illegal outisde* the function.

The Parameter Listing

The function ***parameter listing*** includes things that will be passed from the calling program and evaluated by the function. With the *Cube* function, the parameter is *X*. Think of this as a function variable waiting to receive a value from the calling program when the function is invoked. As a result, the appropriate parameter listing for the cube function would be

`(X : integer)`

Notice that the data type of the parameter must also be specified as part of the parameter listing.

The Function Data Type

The last thing in the function header line is the function data type. Since, by definition, a function returns a *single* value to the calling program, the function header must specify the data type of the returned value. If we cube an integer with our *Cube* function, the function will return an integer. Therefore, the *Cube* function data type is integer and the complete function heading is

`FUNCTION Cube (X : integer) : integer;`

Example 7-1:

Suppose that you wish to write a user-defined function to calculate the voltage in a dc circuit using Ohm's law. Write an appropriate function heading.

Solution: Let's call the function *Voltage*, since this is what the function must return to the calling program each time the function is invoked. Now the next question is: What must the function parameters be? Well, think about what the function must evaluate. To calculate voltage using Ohm's law, the function must evaluate two things: current and resistance. So let's use the words *Current* and *Resistance* as our parameters. What data type should the parameters be? The obvious choice is real. Thus, the function parameter listing becomes

`(Current, Resistance : real)`

Finally, you must decide on the function data type.   Again, this Ohm's law application requires that the function return a real voltage value to the calling program.   Consequently, the complete function heading is

FUNCTION Voltage (Current, Resistance : real) : real;

| function | parameter | function |
| identifier | listing | data type |

The Function Constants and Variables

Look at the general format for a user-defined function again.   As you can see, the function heading is followed by any constants and variables that will be used within the function.   Any constants or variables listed here are called *local*, since they are only defined for local use, within the function itself.   Local variables have no meaning outside the subprogram, or function, in which they are declared. You *must not* duplicate any of your function parameters here.   You only list any additional constants or variables that the function might require during its execution.   In fact, many simple functions do not even require local constants or variables.   When this is the case, you simply omit the reserved word **CONST** or **VAR,** as required, from the declaration section of the function.

The Statement Section

Finally, the statement section of the function includes those operations that the function must perform to return a value to the calling program.   Remember, the function identifier must be assigned a value within this statement section. Observe that the statement section is framed using the reserved words **BEGIN** and **END.**   In addition, notice that a semicolon follows the **END;** rather than a period. A period is only used to end the main program, not a subprogram.   Now, putting everything together, we can complete our *Cube* function as follows:

```
FUNCTION Cube (X : integer) : integer;

BEGIN

    Cube := X * X * X

END;
```

Example 7-2:

Complete the *Voltage* function whose header was developed in Example 7-1.

Solution: This function does not require any local variables in addition to the two parameters *Current* and *Resistance*.   So the reserved word **VAR** is omitted from the function declaration section.   Ohm's law requires the function to multiply *Current*

times *Resistance* to get *Voltage*.   Thus, the only statement required in the function is

```
Voltage := Current * Resistance;
```

Putting it all together, the complete function becomes

```
FUNCTION Voltage (Current, Resistance : real) : real;

BEGIN

    Voltage := Current * Resistance

END;
```

Example 7-3:

Write a function to return the sum of all integers from 1 to some maximum integer value, called *Max*.   The function must obtain the value of *Max* from the calling program.

Solution: Let's call this function *Sum*.   Now, the parameter must be *Max*, since the function must receive this value from the calling program.   The parameter data type must be integer and the sum must return an integer.   (Why?) Using these ideas, the function heading becomes

```
FUNCTION Sum (Max : integer) : integer;
```

The next step is to determine if there are any local variables required by the function statements.   You can use a **FOR/DO** loop to calculate the sum of integers from 1 to *Max*.   However, the **FOR/DO** statement requires a counter variable.   This is a classic application for a local variable.   Let's call this local counter variable *Count*.   Next you also need a temporary variable within the **FOR/DO** to keep a running subtotal of the sum each time the loop executes.   Let's call this local variable *SubTotal*.   Using these ideas, the complete function is as follows:

```
FUNCTION Sum (Max : integer) : integer;

VAR
    SubTotal, Count : integer;

BEGIN

    SubTotal := 0;
    FOR Count := 1 TO Max DO
       SubTotal := SubTotal + Count;
    Sum := SubTotal

END;
```

Why can't you use *Sum* instead of *SubTotal* within the function **FOR/DO** loop?   This would cause an error during compilation.   The reason?   *Sum* is the function identifier and cannot appear on the right side of an assignment statement.

Invoking a Function

You invoke a user-defined function just as you invoke a standard function in Pascal: using an assignment statement or a *Write/Writeln* statement such as the following:

```
K := Cube (2);
```

or

```
Writeln (Cube(2));
```

In both cases, the value 2 is **passed** to the function to be cubed. Thus, in our *Cube* function, the parameter X takes on the value 2. The function will return the cube of 2, which is 8. With the assignment statement, the variable K will be assigned the value 8, and the *Writeln* statement causes the value 8 to be displayed on the CRT terminal.

Here's another way that our *Cube* function can be invoked:

```
A := 2;
K := Cube(A);
```

or

```
Writeln (Cube(A));
```

In these cases, the function is cubing the variable A, where A has been previously assigned the value 2. Thus, the value of A, or 2, is passed to the function to be cubed. In our *Cube* function, the parameter X takes on the value of A.

Functions can also be invoked as part of arithmetic expressions or relational statements. For instance, our *Cube* function can be invoked as part of an arithmetic expression such as the following:

```
A := 2;
K := 1 + Cube(A) * 2;
```

What will be assigned to K? Well, Pascal evaluates the *Cube* function first to get 8, then performs the multiplication operation to get 16, and finally adds 1 to 16 to get 17.

You can also use functions as part of relational operations as follows:

```
IF Cube(A) >= 27 THEN
```

When will the relationship be TRUE?   When *A* is greater than or equal to 3.   This makes *Cube(A)* greater than or equal to 27.

Actual versus Formal Parameters

Some terminology is appropriate at this time.   In the foregoing *Cube* example, the variable *A* used in the calling program is called an ***actual parameter.***   On the other hand, the corresponding variable *X* used in the function is called a *formal parameter.* Actual parameters are variables used within the subprogram call, whereas formal parameters are variables used within the subprogram header.   Thus, the formal parameter in our *Cube* function (*X*) takes on the value of the actual parameter (*A*).   Here are some things that you will want to remember about actual and formal parameters:

- Actual parameter variables must be declared in the calling program.   This will be the main program, unless subprograms are nested within subprograms.
- The data type of the corresponding actual and formal parameters must be the same.
- Formal parameters are placeholders for the actual parameter values during the execution of the subprogram.   Formal parameters are always listed in the parameter section of the subprogram heading.
- The number of actual parameters used during the subprogram call must be the same as the number of formal parameters listed in the subprogram heading.
- The correspondence between actual and formal parameters is established on a one-to-one basis according to the respective listing orders.
- Although the actual and formal parameter variables often have different variable names, they can be the same.   When this is the case, the variable must still be declared in the declaration part of the calling program as well as appear in the parameter listing of the subprogram.

Placement of the User-Defined Function

Now that you know how to write and invoke a function, where do you place it within the main program listing?   Since a function is a subprogram of the main program and declared by you, the user, it must be placed in the declaration section of the main program as illustrated in Figure 7-1.   Notice the ***block structure*** of the overalll program.   The main program is the ***outer block,*** and the subprograms, or functions, form the ***inner blocks.***   This is why Pascal is called a ***block-structured language.***   In other words, the function blocks are nested within the declaration section of the main program block.   In particular, the function blocks are part of the main program ***VAR*** declarations.   The statement section of the main program

```
PROGRAM Main (input, output);

CONST
  {global constants go here}

VAR
  {actual parameters and global variables go here}


  FUNCTION One (parameter listing) : function data type;

  CONST
    {local function One constants go here}

  VAR
    {local function One variables go here}

  BEGIN {function One statements}

    {function One statements go here}

  END; {function One}


  FUNCTION Two (parameter listing) : function data type;

  CONST
    {local function Two constants go here}

  VAR
    {local function Two variables go here}

  BEGIN {function Two statements}

    {function Two statements go here}

  END; {function Two}


BEGIN {main program}

  {main program statements and function calls go here}

END. {main program}
```

Figure 7-1 Location of functions within the main program.

*BEGIN*s after all the user-defined function declarations.   You will see this idea of block structure again when you learn about procedures in the next section.

Of course, when the main program calls, or invokes, a function, the invocation is within the statement part of the main program.

STYLE TIP ──

When listing subprograms within the main program declaration section, it is good documentation to precede the function with a comment block that explains what the function does.   For example:

```
{**************************************************************

          This function cubes an integer value.

**************************************************************}

FUNCTION  Cube (X : integer) : integer;

  BEGIN
    Cube := X * X * X
  END;
```

Remember that the comment must be enclosed within braces { }, as shown, to be ignored by the compiler.

───

Now, let's put it all together in the form of an example.

Example 7-4:

Write a menu-driven program that employs three user-defined functions to calculate dc voltage, current, or resistance, respectively, at the user's option.

Solution: First, let's write the functions.   We will identify the functions by *Voltage*, *Current*, and *Resistance*.   For a given function, the parameters must be the other two quantities.   Thus, the parameters must be *Current* and *Resistance* for the *Voltage* function.   We will assume that all values must be real.   As a result, the function headers are

```
    FUNCTION Voltage (Current, Resistance : real) : real;

    FUNCTION Current (Voltage, Resistance : real) : real;

    FUNCTION Resistance (Voltage, Current : real) : real;
```

Next, there are no local variables to be declared and the statement section of each function is simply the Ohm's law expression to solve for the required quantity.   Thus, the three complete functions are as follows:

```
    FUNCTION Voltage (Current, Resistance : real) : real;
      BEGIN
        Voltage := Current * Resistance
      END;
```

```
FUNCTION Current (Voltage, Resistance : real) : real;
  BEGIN
    Current := Voltage / Resistance
  END;


FUNCTION Resistance (Voltage, Current : real) : real;
  BEGIN
    Resistance := Voltage / Current
  END;
```

Now let's place them in the main program declaration section with the appropriate comments, as follows:

```
PROGRAM Ohms_Law (input, output);

VAR
  V, I, R : real;
  Answer : char;

{*************************************************************

          This function will calculate DC voltage.

*************************************************************}
FUNCTION Voltage (Current, Resistance : real) : real;
  BEGIN
    Voltage := Current * Resistance
  END;



{*************************************************************

          This function will calculate DC current.

*************************************************************}
FUNCTION Current (Voltage, Resistance : real) : real;
  BEGIN
    Current := Voltage / Resistance
  END;



{*************************************************************

          This function will calculate DC resistance.

*************************************************************}
FUNCTION Resistance (Voltage, Current : real) : real;
  BEGIN
    Resistance := Voltage / Current
  END;
```

Finally, we will use a **CASE** statement to provide the user with menu-driven options and include the required function calls within the case.   The complete program is then as follows:

```
PROGRAM Ohms_Law (input, output);

USES
  Crt;

VAR
  V, I, R : real;
  Answer : char;


{***************************************************************

        This function will calculate DC voltage.

***************************************************************}
FUNCTION Voltage (Current, Resistance : real) : real;
  BEGIN
    Voltage := Current * Resistance
  END;



{***************************************************************

        This function will calculate DC current.

***************************************************************}
FUNCTION Current (Voltage, Resistance : real) : real;
  BEGIN
    Current := Voltage / Resistance
  END;



{***************************************************************

        This function will calculate DC resistance.

***************************************************************}
FUNCTION Resistance (Voltage, Current : real) : real;
  BEGIN
    Resistance := Voltage / Current
  END;

             {end main program declaration section}

BEGIN  {main program statement section}
   Clrscr;
   Writeln ('This program will calculate DC voltage, current, or');
   Writeln ('resistance using Ohms Law functions.');
```

(Continued)

```
Writeln;
Writeln;
Write ('Do you wish to find Voltage (V), Current (I), or ');
Write ('resistance? ');
Readln (Answer);
Writeln;
CASE Answer OF

   'V', 'v' : BEGIN
                Write ('Enter the current in milliamps:  I = ');

                Read (I);
                Writeln (' milliamps');
                Writeln;
                Write ('Enter the resistance in kilohms:  R = ');
                Read (R);
                Writeln (' kilohms');
                Writeln;
                Write ('The voltage is ', Voltage(I,R):5:2);
                Writeln (' volts')
              END; {voltage case}

   'I', 'i' : BEGIN
                Write ('Enter the voltage in volts:  V = ');
                Read (V);
                Writeln (' volts');
                Writeln;
                Write ('Enter the resistance in kilohms:  R = ');
                Read (R);
                Writeln (' kilohms');
                Writeln;
                Write ('The current is ', Current(V,R):5:2);
                Writeln (' milliamps')
              END; {current case}

   'R', 'r' : BEGIN
                Write ('Enter the voltage in volts:  V = ');
                Read (V);
                Writeln (' volts');
                Writeln;
                Write ('Enter the current in milliamps:  I = ');
                Read (I);
                Writeln (' milliamps');
                Writeln;
                Write ('The resistance is ', Resistance(V,I):5:2);
                Writeln (' kilohms')
              END   {resistance case}

  END   {case}
END.   {program}
```

You should observe the following in the foregoing program:

- The functions are invoked as part of a *Write* statement within their respective case operation.
- The actual parameters are *V*, *I*, and *R*. They are declared using **VAR** in the main program declaration section. These actual parameters are then used as

needed when the functions are invoked. Notice that the listing order of the actual parameters within the function call *must* be the same as the listing order of the corresponding formal parameters in the function heading. For instance, the *Current* function must be invoked as follows,

$$\texttt{Current(V,R)}$$

since the listing order of the formal parameters is (*Voltage, Resistance*) within the *Current* function heading. Reversing the actual parameter listing, as follows,

$$\texttt{Current(R,V)}$$

will result in an erroneous current calculation, since the function would divide *Resistance* by *Voltage* to get *Current*.

- Finally, notice that since the functions return a real value, the appropriate field designators follow the function call like this

$$\texttt{Current(V,R):5:2}$$

to produce a decimal output.

7-2 PROCEDURES

As you learned in the chapter introduction, Pascal provides two ways of writing subprograms, by using functions or procedures. Recall that a function is a subprogram that returns a single value to the main program. A procedure, on the other hand, does not have this restriction. Procedures can be used to return a complete set of values to the calling program, as well as to perform some specific task such as input or output.

As with functions, there are both standard and user-defined procedures. You have already used several standard procedures such as *Clrscr*, *GotoXY*, *Read*, *Readln*, *Write*, and *Writeln*. These are all predefined operations within Pascal, designed to perform a specific task. (Check your TURBO reference manual for additional standard procedures.) There are many applications in which you will want to write your own procedures. These are called ***user-defined procedures.*** Writing user-defined procedures is very much like writing user-defined functions. Here's how you do it.

The Format

Like a function, a procedure is a program in itself. It consists of a declaration section and a statement section just like the main program. The general format is as follows:

USER-DEFINED PROCEDURE FORMAT **
PROCEDURE procedure name (parameter listing);
CONST
        local procedure constants
VAR
        local procedure variables
BEGIN
        procedure statement #1;
        procedure statement #2;   ,
              ⋮
        procedure statement #n
END;
        ****

The Procedure Header

The first line of the procedure is the header line. This line begins with the
reserved word **PROCEDURE,** which is followed by a procedure name and an
optional listing of the formal parameters. The formal parameter listing, if required,
is followed by a semicolon to end the procedure header. Notice that you *do not*
specify a procedure data type at the end of the header, as you must with functions.

The Formal Parameter Listing

This listing is optional, depending on whether or not the procedure must
receive any values from the calling program. Some procedures do not receive any
values from the calling program and, therefore, do not require any parameter
listing. When this is the case, the procedure name is simply followed by a semicolon, to indicate the end of the header line. For instance, here's a simple procedure to print your name:

```
PROCEDURE PRINTNAME;

BEGIN
    Writeln ('My name is George Washington.')
END;
```

Since the procedure does not need to evaluate any parameters, the parameter
listing is omitted.

When parameters are required, they must be listed in one of two ways: as
value parameters or *variable parameters.*

Value Parameters

Value parameters allow for *one-way communication* of data from the calling
program to the procedure. This concept is illustrated in Figure 7-2a. Observe
that the actual parameter values in the calling program are passed (by value) to

Calling Program
(Main)

Actual
parameters

Subprogram
(Procedure)

Formal
parameters

(a)

Calling Program
(Main)

Actual
parameters

Subprogram
(Procedure)

Formal
parameters

(b)

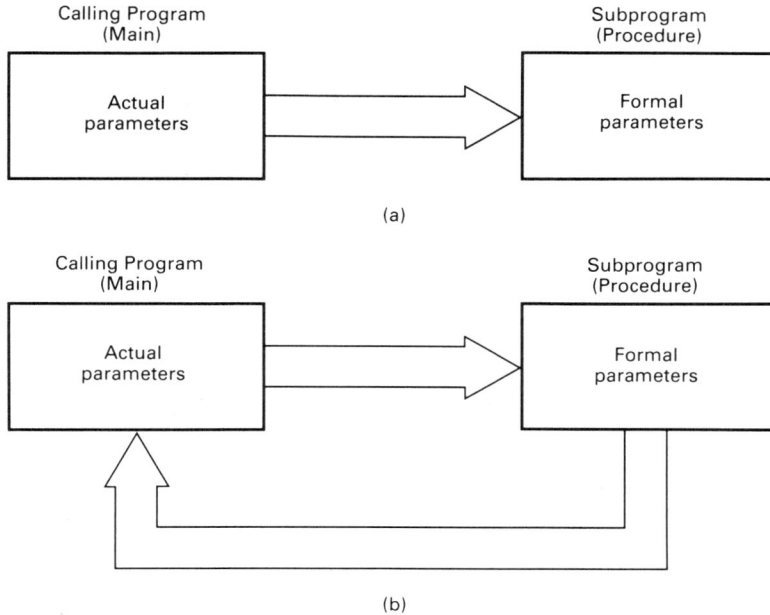

Figure 7-2   (a) Passing parameters by value and (b) by variable.

the formal parameters in the procedure.   The important thing to remember is that any manipulation of the formal parameters within the procedure *does not affect* the actual parameter values in the calling program.   For instance, consider the following procedure:

```
PROCEDURE Pass_By_Value (X,Y : integer);

BEGIN  {procedure}
  X := X + 1;
  Y := Y - 1;
  Writeln ('X = ',X);
  Writeln ('Y = ',Y)
END;  {procedure}
```

Here, the parameters X and Y are value parameters.   Notice that within the procedure, the value of X is incremented and the value of Y is decremented.   Then the resulting values are displayed using *Writeln* statements.   Now suppose that the above procedure is called by the following main program (assume that A and B have been declared as integer variables within the main program declaration section):

```
BEGIN {main program}
  A := O;
  B := O;
  Pass_By_Value (A,B);
  Writeln ('A = ',A);
  Writeln ('B = ',B)
END.  {main program}
```

First, notice how the procedure is called.   It is simply a statement in the main program.   You do not use an assignment or *Write* statement to call the procedure as you must when calling a function.   The procedure name is simply listed, followed by the required actual parameters.   The actual parameters are A and B, since they are listed in the procedure call.   When the procedure call is executed, the value of A is passed to the formal parameter X and the value of B is passed to the formal parameter Y.   Notice that before the procedure call, the main program assigns both A and B the value 0.   As a result, both X and Y receive the value 0 from the main program.   Now, within the procedure, X is incremented and Y is decremented as follows:

$$X := X + 1 := 0 + 1 := 1$$

$$Y := Y - 1 := 0 - 1 := -1$$

The procedure then displays these values of X and Y.   However, the operations on X and Y have no effect on the actual parameters (A and B) in the main program.   The values of A and B remain 0.   Notice that after the procedure call the main program displays the values of A and B.   What would you see on the display by executing the main program?   Well, the procedure dislays X and Y, while the main program displays A and B.   Therefore, the resulting display is

```
X = 1
Y = -1
A = O
B = O
```

Variable Parameters

Variable parameters differ from value parameters in that they provide *two-way communication* between the calling program and the procedure, as illustrated in Figure 7-2b.   Observe the two-way communication path: the actual parameter values are passed to the formal parameters in the procedure, then the formal parameter values are passed back to the actual parameters.   This allows the procedure to change the actual parameter values in the calling program.   To accomplish this, you simply insert the reserved word **VAR** prior to the appropriate parameters in the procedure heading, as follows:

```
PROCEDURE procedure name (VAR parameter listing);
```

Let's change our preceding example to use variable parameters, as follows:

```
PROCEDURE Pass_By_Variable (VAR X,Y : integer);

BEGIN  {procedure}
  X := X + 1;
  Y := Y - 1;
  Writeln ('X = ',X);
  Writeln ('Y = ',Y)
END;   {procedure}

BEGIN {main program}
  A := 0;
  B := 0;
  Pass_By_Variable (A,B);
  Writeln ('A = ',A);
  Writeln ('B = ',B)
END.   {main program}
```

The major change that I have made is to insert the reserved word **VAR** prior to X and Y in the procedure heading.   Of course, I have also changed the procedure name to reflect the application.   What would you see on the display as a result of executing the above program?   How about this:

```
X = 1
Y = -1
A = 1
B = -1
```

As you can see, the new values of X and Y are passed back to A and B, respectively.

Example 7-5:

What will be displayed as a result of the following program?

```
PROGRAM Example7_5 (output);

VAR
  A. B : integer;

{****************************************************************

       This procedure displays the parameter values.

****************************************************************}

   PROCEDURE Display_Param (VAR X : integer; Y : integer);

   BEGIN  {procedure}
     X := X + 1;
     Y := Y - 1;
```

(Continued)

```
   Writeln ('X = ',X);
   Writeln ('Y = ',Y)
END;  {procedure}

         {end main program declaration section}

BEGIN {main program statement section}
  A := 0;
  B := 0;
  Display_Param (A,B);
  Writeln ('A = ',A);
  Writeln ('B = ',B)
END.  {main program}
```

Solution: Here you see an entire program that incorporates a procedure. Like a function, the procedure is located in the declaration section of the main program. The procedure is then called within the statement section of the main program by simply listing its name followed by a listing of the required actual parameters. Notice that the actual parameters (A and B) are declared as integer variables in the declaration section of the main program. Now look at the procedure heading. The formal parameters are X and Y. Both are integers; however, X is a variable parameter, whereas Y is a value parameter. Observe the use of the reserved word **VAR** prior to X. This declares X as a variable parameter. However, a semicolon follows X, ending this declaration. Then, Y is declared separately as a value parameter. As a result, the value of X is passed back to the main program, but the value of Y is not. Here's what you would see on the display:

$$X = 1$$
$$Y = -1$$
$$A = 1$$
$$B = 0$$

You should be aware that variable parameters can also be employed for functions, although it is not common to do so.

Placement and Calling of User-Defined Procedures

As you can see from Example 7-5, user-defined procedures are located in the declaration section of the main program along with any user-defined functions. There is no limit on the number of user-defined functions or procedures that can be used in a program. However, good style dictates that you should use asterisks within comment braces {********} to identify the separate functions and procedures.

To call a user-defined procedure, you simply list its name as a statement within the calling program. Of course, any actual parameters required by the procedure must be listed within parentheses after the procedure name. In addition, the number of actual parameters used in the procedure call must be the same as the number of formal parameters declared in the respective procedure heading.

7-3 SCOPING OUR VARIABLES: BLOCK STRUCTURE

In the last two sections, you observed the use of local variables. Recall that a local variable is a variable that is declared within a subprogram (function or procedure). Don't get local variables confused with the variable parameters listed in the subprogram heading. Local variables are declared in the declaration section of the subprogram, using the reserved word **VAR.** Variable parameters are declared using the word **VAR** in procedure headings.

A local variable is only defined for use within the subprogram block and has no meaning outside the respective subprogram. On the other hand, a *global variable* is a variable that can be used by all subprograms of a given program. Thus, a variable declared within the main program declaration section is a global variable that can be used by any subprograms of that program.

To illustrate the use of local and global variables, look at the block structure in Figure 7-3. Here, the local variable is *X1* and the global variable is *X0*. The subprogram can perform operations on both *X0* and *X1*. However, the main program can only operate with *X0*, since *X1* is not defined outside the subprogram block. Any attempt to use *X1* outside the subprogram will result in an error. In addition, any value assigned to *X1* during the subprogram execution is destroyed and cannot be retrieved for subsequent executions of the subprogram.

Now look at Figure 7-4. This time there are two subprograms, both of which declare *X1* as a local variable. Again, the global variable is *X0* and can be used

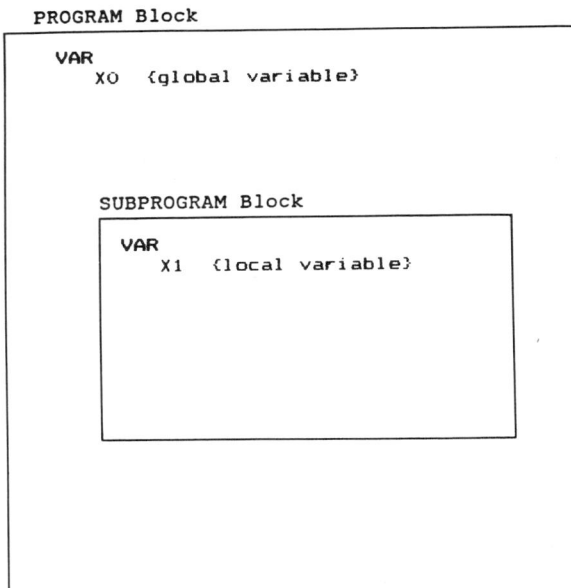

```
PROGRAM Block
┌─────────────────────────────────────────────────┐
│  VAR                                             │
│      X0   {global variable}                      │
│                                                  │
│                                                  │
│      SUBPROGRAM Block                            │
│      ┌───────────────────────────────────┐      │
│      │  VAR                               │      │
│      │      X1   {local variable}         │      │
│      │                                    │      │
│      │                                    │      │
│      │                                    │      │
│      │                                    │      │
│      └───────────────────────────────────┘      │
│                                                  │
│                                                  │
│                                                  │
└─────────────────────────────────────────────────┘
```

Figure 7-3 Local versus global variables.

Main Program Block

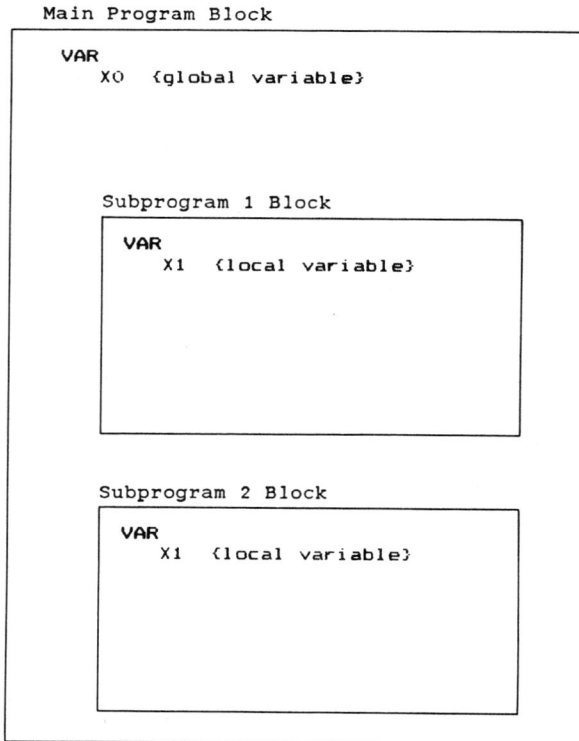

Figure 7-4 Local versus global variables.

within the main program as well as within all the subprograms.   The variable *X1* can only be used within the two subprograms.   However, any operations on *X1* within subprogram 1 do not affect the value of *X1* in subprogram 2, and vice versa. In other words, the *X1* in subprogram 1 is considered a separate variable from the *X1* in subprogram 2.   It's as if they are two completely different variables!   This provides a very important feature of structured programming, called ***modularity***.

To realize the importance of modularity, suppose that you are a member of a programming team that must develop the software to solve a very complex industrial task.   The easiest way to solve any complex problem is to break the problem down into simpler, more manageable subproblems, then solve the sub-problems and combine their solutions to solve the overall complex problem.   This is called ***top/down design***.   Using the top/down design approach, your team leader breaks the complex programming problem down into simpler subprograms, then asks each member of the team to write a subprogram (procedure) to solve a given subproblem.   How does this relate to the use of local variables?   Well you can write your subprogram using any local variables you wish, without worrying that another team member might use the same local variables.   Even if two team members use the same local variable identifiers, the subprograms will still execute independently when they are combined in the main program. This allows a top/down team approach to software design, something that is not available in non-structured languages like BASIC. The subprograms in a structured language act as modular building blocks to form the overall program. This is why a structured language, like Pascal, is often referred to as a modular, block-structured language.

Scope of Identifiers

To conclude this section, look at the block structure in Figure 7-5. The *scope* of a variable identifier refers to the largest block in which a given variable is accessible. In Figure 7-5, the scope of *X0* is the entire program, since it is accessible, or global,

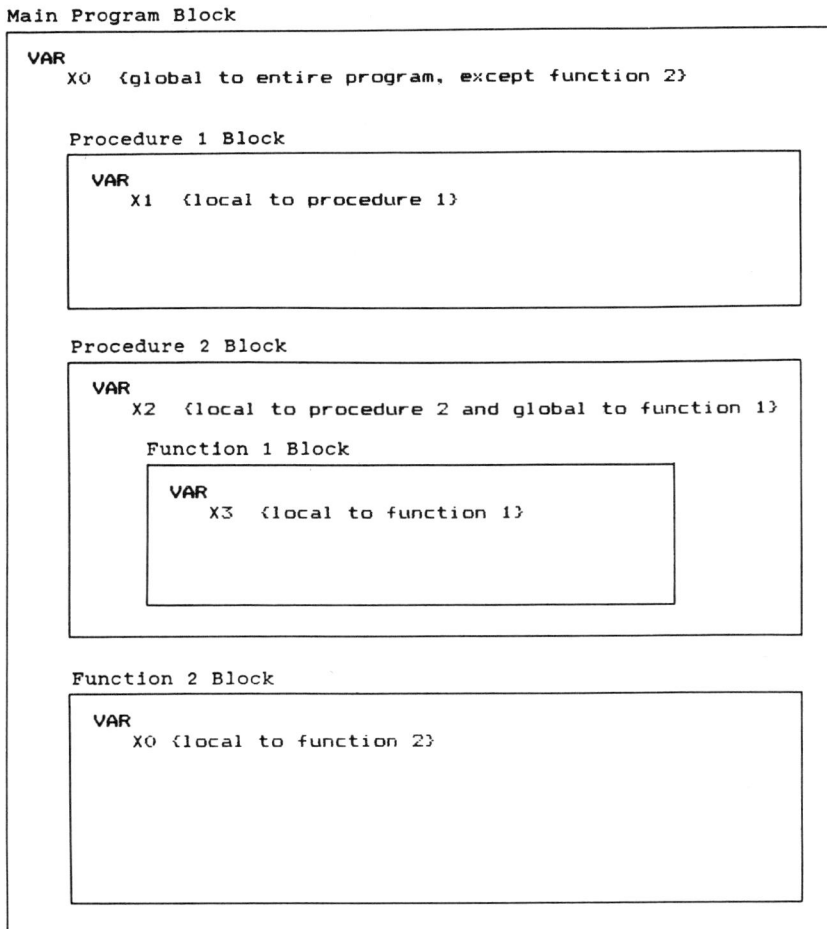

```
Main Program Block

VAR
    X0   {global to entire program, except function 2}

    Procedure 1 Block

    VAR
        X1   {local to procedure 1}




    Procedure 2 Block

    VAR
        X2   {local to procedure 2 and global to function 1}

        Function 1 Block

        VAR
            X3   {local to function 1}




    Function 2 Block

    VAR
        X0 {local to function 2}
```

Figure 7-5   Scope of identifiers.

to all blocks in the program. However, the scope of *X1* is only procedure 1, since it is local to this procedure.

How about *X2*? The scope of *X2* is procedure 2 and function 1, since it is declared in procedure 2 and function 1 is a subprogram of this procedure. In other words, function 1 is **nested** within procedure 2. Thus, we say that *X2* is local to procedure 2 and global to function 1. In addition, notice that *X3* is declared as a local variable in function 1. As a result, *X3* is only available within this function and undefined outside the function.

Finally, notice that the variable *X0* is also declared in function 2. Is there a problem here, since *X0* is also global to the entire program? No! The *X0* in function 2 is considered independent of the *X0* declared in the main program. Since *X0* is declared locally in function 2, any operations on *X0* within this function will not affect the global variable *X0* in the main program. It's as if they are two unique variables.

In summary, we could make the following statements concerning the scope of the variables in Figure 7-5:

- *X0* is global to the entire program, except in function 2 where it is a local variable.
- *X1* is local to procedure 1.
- *X2* is local to procedure 2 and global to function 1.
- *X3* is local to function 1.

As you can see, the terms *local* and *global* are very relative terms.

In Figure 7-5, all the subprograms except function 2 have access to the global variable *X0*. As a result, the value of *X0* can be altered by any of these subprograms. The altering of a global variable by a subprogram is referred to as a **side effect**. In most cases, side effects are undesirable. It is not good practice to alter global variables within a function or procedure, since it defeats the modularity characteristic of a structured language. Therefore, *always declare your variables as locally as possible within a given subprogram block.*

One exception to this rule is when you wish to save a value from one call of a subprogram to the next subsequent call of the same subprogram. A global variable must be used for this purpose, since the value of a local variable is destroyed after the subprogram execution is complete. Another instance when global variables are appropriate is when several functions or procedures need to share a common variable or data structure. You will observe this application when you learn about arrays in the next chapter.

The Scope of Constants

Constants, like variables, can also be termed global or local. In other words, you can declare constants globally within the main program declaration section, or locally within the function or procedure declaration sections. The scope of a constant works just like that of a variable. Its scope is the largest block in which it is available. However, the general rule for declaring constants is just the opposite of declaring variables: *you should declare constants as globally as possible.* In other words, all constants should be declared in the main program declaration section if possible.

Declaring constants globally allows all subprograms access to a given constant. Moreover, constants are not always constant. Remember the *Postage* and *Sales Tax* constants we used in Chapter 2? These constants are subject to change over a period of time. When they must be changed, you need to make a change in only one place in the program if they are declared globally. However, if they are declared locally, a change must be made in each subprogram in which they are declared.

7-4 RECURSIVE FUNCTIONS AND PROCEDURES

Pascal supports a very powerful operation called **recursion.** Recursion allows a function or procedure to call itself. That's right, with the power of recursion a given function or procedure can actually contain a statement that calls, or invokes, the same function or procedure, thereby calling itself.

To get the idea of recursion, consider a typical compound-interest problem. Suppose that you deposit $1,000 in the bank at a 12 percent annual interest rate, but that it is compounded monthly. What this means is that the interest is calculated and added to the principle on a monthly basis. Thus, each time the interest is calculated, you get interest on the previous month's interest. Let's analyze the problem a bit more closely.

Your initial deposit is $1,000. Now, the annual interest rate is 12%, which translates to a 1 percent monthly rate. Since interest is compounded monthly, the balance at the end of the first month will be

Month 1 balance = $1,000 + (0.01 × $1,000) = $1,010.00

As you can see, the interest for month 1 is 0.01 × $1,000, or $10.00. This interest amount is then added to the principle ($1,000) to get a new balance of $1,010.00. Using a little algebra, the same calculation can be made as follows:

Month 1 balance = 1.01 × $1,000 = $1,010.00

Now how would you calculate the interest for the second month? You would use the balance at the end of the first month as the principle for the second month's calculation, right? So the calculation for month 2 would be

Month 2 balance = 1.01 × $1,010.00 = $1,020.10

For month 3 the calculation would be

Month 3 balance = 1.01 × $1,020.10 = $1,030.30

Do you see a pattern? Notice that to calculate the balance for any given month, you must use the balance from the previous month. In general, the calculation for any month becomes

$$Balance = 1.01 \times previous\ balance$$

Let's let B_i represent the balance of any given month and B_{i-1} the previous month's balance. Using this notation, the balance for any month, B_i, is

$$B_i = 1.01 \times B_{i-1}$$

Let's use this relationship to calculate what your balance would be after four months. Here's how you must perform the calculation:

First, the balance for month 4 is

$$B_4 = 1.01 \times B_3$$

However, to find B_4 you must find B_3 as follows:

$$B_3 = 1.01 \times B_2$$

Then B_2 must be found like this

$$B_2 = 1.01 \times B_1$$

Finally, B_1 must be found like this

$$B_1 = 1.01 \times B_0$$

Now, you know that B_0 is the original balance of \$1,000. This is really the only thing known, aside from the interest rate. Therefore, working backwards you get

$$B_1 = 1.01 \times \$1,000.00 = \$1,010.00$$

$$B_2 = 1.01 \times \$1,010.00 = \$1,020.10$$

$$B_3 = 1.01 \times \$1,020.10 = \$1,030.30$$

$$B_4 = 1.01 \times \$1,030.30 = \$1,040.60$$

This is a classic example of recursion, since to solve the problem you must solve the previous problem condition, and so on, until you encounter a known condition (in our case the initial \$1,000 deposit). This known condition, or state, is called a ***primitive state.*** Thus, a recursive operation is an operation that calls itself until a primitive state is reached. Likewise, a recursive function or procedure is one that calls, or invokes, itself until a primitive state is reached.

Now, suppose that we wish to express the preceding compound-interest calculation as a recursive function. The function would be

$$B_0 = 1,000\ and\ B_i = 0.01 \times B_{i-1}\ (for\ i > 0)$$

This mathematical function can be expressed in algorithmic form as follows:

$$\text{If } i = 0 \text{ Then}$$

$$B_i = 1000$$

$$\text{Else}$$

$$B_i = 1.01 \times B_{i-1}$$

Next, if a programming language allows recursive operations, a software function can be coded directly from the above algorithm. Since Pascal employs the power of recursion, the Pascal code is as follows:

```
FUNCTION  Balance (i : integer) : real;

BEGIN

    IF i = 0 THEN
        Balance := 1000
    ELSE
        Balance := 1.01 * Balance (i - 1)

    END;
```

That's all there is to it! This function will calculate the balance at the end of any month, i, passed to the function. Notice how the function calls itself in the **ELSE** clause. Here's how it works: When the computer encounters the recursive call in the **ELSE** clause, it must temporarily delay the calculation to evaluate the recursive function call, just as we did as part of the compound-interest calculation. When it encounters the **ELSE** clause a second time, the function calls itself again, and keeps calling itself each time the **ELSE** clause is executed until the primitive state is reached. When this happens, the **IF** clause is executed and the recursive calling ceases.

During any recursive call, all information required to complete the calculation after the recursive call is saved by the computer in a memory area called a *stack*. As the recursive calls continue, information is saved on the memory stack, until the primitive state is reached. Then the computer works backwards from the primitive state, retrieving the stack information to determine the final result. The process that the computer goes through is identical to what we did when working the compound-interest problem.

One word of caution: There must always be a primitive state for the recursive function. If not, the function will keep calling itself forever, resulting in a run-time error.

Example 7-6:

Write a recursive Pascal function to find the sum of all integers from 1 to some number, *N*.

Solution: Think about this operation for a minute. Isn't it a classic recursive operation? To find the sum of integers 1 to, say, 5, couldn't you add 5 to the sum of integers from 1 to 4? Then, to find the sum of integers from 1 to 4, you add 4 to the sum of integers from 1 to 3, and so on, right? Expressed in symbols:

$$Sum\ 5 = 5 + Sum\ 4$$

$$Sum\ 4 = 4 + Sum\ 3$$

$$Sum\ 3 = 3 + Sum\ 2$$

$$Sum\ 2 = 2 + Sum\ 1$$

$$Sum\ 1 = 1$$

Notice that *Sum 1* is the primitive state. Now, translating this to a recursive function you get

$$Sum\ 1 = 1 \text{ and } Sum\ N = N + Sum\ (N - 1) \text{ (for } N > 1)$$

This function can be expressed as an algorithm as follows:

If $N = 1$ Then

$$Sum = 1$$

Else

$$Sum = N + Sum\ (N - 1)$$

The Pascal function is then coded directly from the algorithm as follows:

```
FUNCTION  Sum (N : integer) : integer;

BEGIN

  IF N = 1 THEN
    Sum := 1
  ELSE
    Sum := N + Sum (N - 1)

END;
```

Although recursion is a very powerful feature of any language, you should be aware that it is not always the most efficient method of solving a problem. Whenever we talk about computer efficiency, we must consider two things: *execution speed* and *memory usage*. When using recursion, the computer must keep track of each recursive call so that it can work backwards to obtain a solution. This requires large amounts of both memory and time. As a result, a recursive solution to a problem is not always the most efficient solution. Many recursive problems can also be solved nonrecursively using iteration. For instance, consider the sum of integers from 1 to *N*. This problem can be solved using an iterative function, as follows:

```
FUNCTION  Sum (N : integer) : integer;

VAR
  Count, Temp : integer;
```

```
BEGIN
   Temp := 0;
   FOR Count := 1 TO N DO
      Temp := Temp + Count;
   Sum := Temp
END;
```

So why use recursion? Probably the main reason to use recursion is that many recursive solutions are much simpler than iterative solutions. In addition, there are some problems and data structures, such as binary trees, that do not lend themselves to iterative solutions. Here are two guidelines that should help you decide when to use recursion:

1. Consider a recursive solution only when a simple iterative solution is not possible.
2. Use a recursive solution only when the execution and memory efficiency of the solution is within acceptable limits, considering the system limitations.

7-5 AN APPLICATION TASK: SERIES IMPEDANCE ANALYSIS

Let's end this chapter by writing a comprehensive program to analyze the series impedance circuit shown in Figure 7-6. Notice that the circuit consists of any number of impedances in series. Our program must find the total impedance and total current in the circuit, given the individual impedances and the source voltage. Here's the problem definition:

The Problem Definition

Output: The program must first prompt the user to enter the number of impedances in series. A prompt will then be generated to enter each impedance magnitude and angle separately. The user will then be prompted to enter the source voltage magnitude and angle. The final output will be a display of the total circuit impedance and current in polar form.

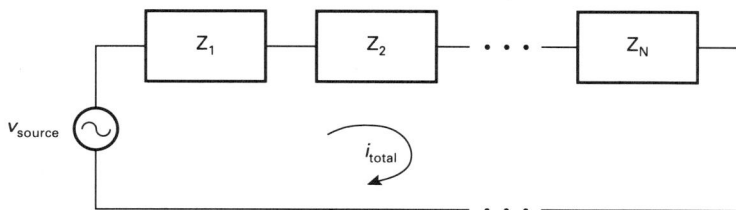

Figure 7-6 A series impedance circuit is a candidate for structured programming.

Input: The number of impedances in the circuit and the individual impedances in polar form.   The source voltage value in polar form.

Processing: Each time an impedance is entered, the total impedance values will
be recalculated using the following series impedance relationship:

$$Z_{total} = Z_1 + Z_2 + Z_3 + \ldots + Z_n$$

Since the individual impedances will be entered in polar form, the
program must convert them to rectangular form to find their sum.
The sum must then be converted back to polar form for output as
the total circuit impedance.

Once the total circuit impedance is known, the total circuit current
is found as follows:

$$I_{total} = V_{source} / Z_{total}$$

The Algorithm

We are at the point now where our programming task is getting a bit complex.
So let's employ a good top/down design approach to our algorithm and develop
several *levels* of algorithms.

The Top Level

The top algorithm level will represent the main program.   Here is where you must
decide the overall structure of the program.   I have decided to write three procedures: one to find total circuit impedance, another to find the circuit current,
and a final procedure to display the circuit values.   Sound reasonable?   The top-
level algorithm simply shows these procedure calls, as follows:

    PROGRAM Series Impedance
    BEGIN
        Write a program description message.
        Call *Z_Total* procedure.
        Call *I_Total* procedure.
        Call *Display* procedure.
    END.

The Second Level

The second level of our program-design task is to develop an algorithm for each
of the top-level procedures.

The *Z_Total* procedure must read-in the individual impedance values and sum them to find the total circuit impedance. Here's an algorithm that should do the job:

PROCEDURE *Z_Total*
BEGIN
  Write a user prompt to enter the number of impedances in the circuit.
  Read (*Number*).
  Set *x_total* and *jy_total* to 0.
  For *Count* = 1 to *Number*
      Write prompt to enter *Z(Count)* magnitude.
      Read (*Magnitude*).
      Write prompt to enter *Z(Count)* angle.
      Read (*Angle*).
      Calculate *x_total* = *x_total* + FUNCTION *x*.
      Calculate *jy_total* = *jy_total* + FUNCTION *jy*.
  Set *Z_Magnitude* = FUNCTION *Mag*.
  Set *Z_Angle* = FUNCTION *Angle*.
END.

The first part of the algorithm is straightforward. The user is asked to enter the number of impedances in series. Then a *For/Do* loop is entered to add the impedances as they are entered. However, recall that the impedances are to be entered in polar form. Thus, the user must be prompted for the magnitude and angle of each impedance. In addition, the polar values must be converted to rectangular values to be added, since polar values cannot be added directly.

Recall that to add rectangular values you must sum the individual real (*x*) and imaginary (*jy*) parts to get a total *x* and a total *jy* coordinate. I have labeled these totals as *x_total* and *jy_total* in the preceding algorithm.

The values of *x_total* and *jy_total* are calculated by adding the *x*- and *jy*-coordinates of a given impedance to the previous *x_total* and *jy_total* values. Since the individual impedances are being entered in polar form, they must be converted to rectangular coordinates to be added as they are entered by the user. To do this I have created two functions (FUNCTION *x* and FUNCTION *jy*) that will find the *x* and *jy* coordinates, respectively, for a given polar value. More about these functions shortly.

Finally, since the total impedance must be expressed in polar form, the algorithm calls two more functions, FUNCTION *Mag* and FUNCTION *Angle*, to calculate the total impedance magnitude and angle, respectively, from the *x_total* and *jy_total* values obtained in the loop.

The *I_Total* procedure algorithm is straightforward. It must obtain the source voltage and use the total circuit impedance found in the *Z_Total* procedure to calculate the total circuit current. Here it is:

PROCEDURE *I_Total*
BEGIN
  Write a prompt to enter the source voltage magnitude.
  Read (*V_Mag*).
  Write a prompt to enter the source voltage angle.
  Read (*V_Ang*).
  Calculate $I\_Mag = V\_Mag / Z\_Mag$.
  Calculate $I\_Ang = V\_Ang - Z\_Ang$.
END.

Notice that the current magnitude is found by dividing the voltage magnitude by the impedance magnitude. However, the current angle must be obtained by subtracting the impedance angle from the voltage angle. This is polar division, right?

The third procedure must display the circuit values calculated by the two previous procedures. Here's an algorithm that will work:

PROCEDURE *Display*
BEGIN
  Write the total circuit impedance in polar form.
  Write the total circuit current in polar form.
END.

The Third Level

This program requires a third algorithm level. Why? Because the *Z_Total* procedure must convert between polar and rectangular values. This is an ideal application for functions. In fact, we will write four functions as follows:

FUNCTION *x* to calculate the real part of a rectangular coordinate from a polar coordinate

FUNCTION *jy* to calculate the imaginary part of a rectangular coordinate from a polar coordinate

FUNCTION *Mag* to find the magnitude of a polar coordinate from a rectangular coordinate

FUNCTION *Angle* to find the angle of a polar coordinate from a rectangular coordinate

Here are algorithms that simply apply the required conversion techniques:

FUNCTION *x*
BEGIN
  Calculate $x = Magnitude * Cos(Angle)$
END.

FUNCTION *jy*
BEGIN
  Calculate *jy* = *Magnitude* * *Sin(Angle)*
END.

FUNCTION *Mag*
BEGIN
  Calculate *Mag* = *Sqrt(Sqr(x)* + *Sqr(y))*
END.

FUNCTION Angle
BEGIN
  Calculate *Angle* = *Arctan(y/x)*
END.

We are now ready to code the program. However, before we do, look at Figure 7-7. This pyramid structure summarizes the top/down design that we just performed. That's structured programming! Notice how we have taken a complex problem and broken it down into a series of simpler subproblems, whose solution provides the complex problem solution.

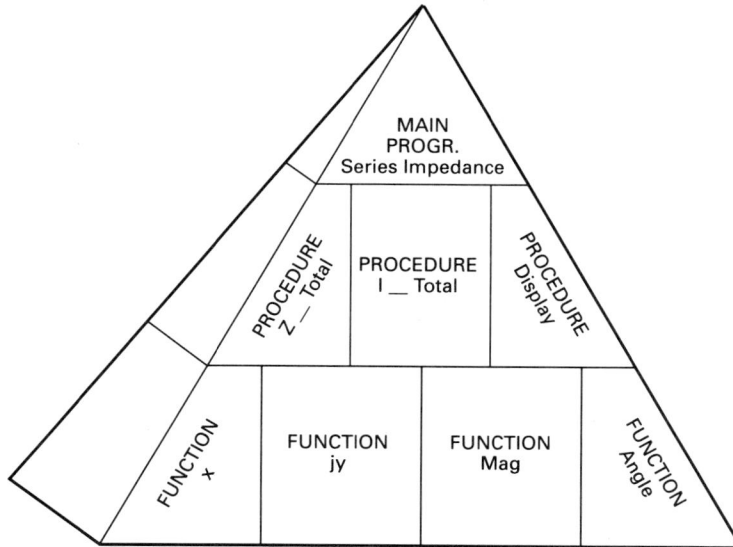

Figure 7-7   A structured top/down program design resembles a pyramid.

The Program

Coding all the foregoing algorithms into a single structured Pascal program we get the following:

```
PROGRAM Series_Impedance (input,output);

  USES
    Crt;

VAR
  Z_Magnitude, Z_Angle : real;
  I_Magnitude, I_Angle : real;




{*************************************************************

  This function converts a polar coordinate to an x-coordinate.

 *************************************************************}

FUNCTION x (M, A : real) : real;


BEGIN
   x := M * Cos( Pi/180 * A);
END;




{*************************************************************

  This function converts a polar coordinate to a jy-coordinate.

 *************************************************************}

FUNCTION jy (M, A : real) : real;

BEGIN
   jy := M * Sin( Pi/180 * A)
END;
{*************************************************************

  This function converts an x/y coordinate to a polar magnitude.

 *************************************************************}
```

```
FUNCTION Mag (x, y : real) : real;

BEGIN
   Mag :=  Sqrt(Sqr(x) + Sqr(y))
END;



{***********************************************************************

  This function converts an x/y coordinate to a polar angle.

  ***********************************************************************}

FUNCTION Angle (x, y : real) : real;

BEGIN
    Angle := (Arctan (y/x)) * (180/Pi)
END;



{***********************************************************************

          This procedure calculates total series impedance.

  ***********************************************************************}

PROCEDURE  Z_Total  (VAR Z_Mag, Z_Ang : real);

VAR
  Number, Count : integer;
  Z_M, Z_A : real;
  x_total, jy_total : real;

BEGIN
  Write ('Enter the number of series impedances:  ');
  Readln (Number);
  Writeln;
  Writeln;
  Writeln;
  x_total := 0;
  jy_total := 0;
  FOR Count := 1 TO Number DO
    BEGIN
      Write ('Enter Z',Count,' magnitude:  ');
      Readln (Z_M);
      Writeln;
      Write ('Enter Z',Count,' angle:  ');
      Readln (Z_A);
      Writeln;
```

(Continued)

```
      Writeln;
      x_total := x_total + x(Z_M,Z_A);
      jy_total := jy_total + jy(Z_M,Z_A)
   END;   {for}
   Z_Mag :=  Mag(x_total,jy_total);
   Z_Ang :=  Angle(x_total,jy_total)
END;   {procedure}


{***************************************************************

      This procedure calculates total circuit current.

***************************************************************}

PROCEDURE I_Total (Z_Mag,Z_Ang : real; VAR I_Mag, I_Ang : real);

VAR
  V_Mag, V_Ang : real;

BEGIN
  Write ('Enter the source voltage magnitude:  ');
  Readln (V_Mag);
  Writeln;
  Write ('Enter the source voltage angle:  ');
  Readln (V_Ang);
  I_Mag := V_Mag / Z_Mag;
  I_Ang := V_Ang - Z_Ang
END;


{***************************************************************

This procedure displays the total circuit impedance and current.

***************************************************************}

PROCEDURE Display (Z_Mag,Z_Ang,I_Mag,I_Ang : real);

BEGIN
  Writeln;
  Writeln;
  Writeln ('The total impedance for this circuit is ',
           Z_Mag :4:2, ' kilohms @ ', Z_Ang:4:2,' degrees');
  Writeln;
  Writeln;
  Writeln ('The total current for this circuit is ',
           I_Mag:4:2, ' milliamps @ ', I_Ang:4:2,' degrees');
  Writeln;
  Writeln;
```

```
  Writeln ('NOTE: The above polar coordinate angles are the
          reference');
  Writeln ('angles in the given quadrant.')
END;




BEGIN   {main}
  Clrscr;
  Z_Total (Z_Magnitude,Z_Angle);
  I_Total (Z_Magnitude,Z_Angle,I_Magnitude,I_Angle);
  Display (Z_Magnitude,Z_Angle,I_Magnitude,I_Angle)
END.   {main}
```

First, look at the order in which the functions and procedures are declared. In general, the rule is that a subprogram must be declared prior to it's being called. Here, our four functions are called within the *Z_Total* procedure and, therefore, must be declared prior to this procedure. You should be aware, however, that there is a compiler directive available in TURBO Pascal that allows forward referencing. Forward referencing allows you to declare subprograms in any arbitrary order. Consult your TURBO reference manual for the details.

Next, let's take a close look at the subprogram parameters. FUNCTION *x* and FUNCTION *jy* must evaluate a polar coordinate magnitude and angle to return the *x* and *jy* parts of a rectangular coordinate, respectively. Thus, the formal parameters for these two functions are *M* and *A*. All the parameters as well as the individual functions are declared as real, for obvious reasons.

The *Mag* and *Angle* functions must evaluate the real (*x*) and imaginary (*y*) parts of a rectangular coordinate to find the polar magnitude and angle, respectively. As a result, the formal parameters for these two functions are *x* and *y*. These parameters are declared as real, as are the individual functions.

The *Z_total* procedure parameters are *Z_Mag* and *Z_Ang*. When declaring procedure parameters you must ask yourself two questions:

1. What must be received by the procedure from the calling program?
2. What must be returned by the procedure to the calling program?

The answer to the first question will determine the value parameters, and the answer to the second question will determine the variable parameters. In our case, the *Z_Total* procedure does not receive anything from the calling program, since the individual impedance values are obtained within the procedure. Thus, there are no value parameters. However, the procedure must return the total circuit impedance (in polar form) to the calling program. Consequently, there are two variable parameters: *Z_Mag* for the total impedance magnitude and *Z_Ang* for the angle.

Now look at the *I_Total* procedure parameters. This procedure must receive the total impedance values from the calling program. Thus, *Z_Mag* and *Z_Ang* are declared as real value parameters. What must this procedure return to the calling program? You're right—the total circuit current in polar form. As a result, *I_Mag* and *I_Ang* are declared as real variable parameters.

Finally, look at the *Display* procedure parameters. This procedure simply receives the circuit values from the calling program and displays them. Therefore, *Z_Mag*, *Z_Ang*, *I_Mag*, and *I_Ang* are declared as value parameters. There are no variable parameters, since the procedure does not return anything to the calling program.

Now let's look at the variable declarations within the program. First, you see that there are only four global variables declared in the main program. These are required to receive the total circuit impedance and current from the *Z_Total* and *I_Total* procedures.

In the *Z_Total* procedure, you find several local variables declared. These are temporary variables that are only required within the procedure itself. That's why they are declared locally within the procedure, rather than globally in the main program. Remember to declare your variables as locally as possible.

In the *I_Total* procedure, there are two local variables. These are the source voltage values that are obtained within the procedure to calculate the circuit current. They are declared locally, since the source voltage values are not needed any other place in the program.

The last thing we need to do is to take a look at how the functions and procedures are called. Look at the simplicity of the main program statement section. All that needs to be done here is to clear the CRT screen and call the three main procedures. The *Z_Total* procedure is called using the actual parameters *Z_Magnitude* and *Z_Angle*. These parameters must be listed in the procedure call to correspond with *Z_Mag* and *Z_Ang*, respectively, in the procedure heading. Recall that *Z_Magnitude* and *Z_Angle* are the global variables that receive the total circuit impedance values from the procedure.

To call the *I_Total* procedure, you must list *Z_Magnitude*, *Z_Angle*, *I_Magnitude*, and *I_Angle*. The actual impedance parameters (*Z_Magnitude* and *Z_Angle*) must be listed to pass the total impedance values to *Z_Mag* and *Z_Ang*, respectively, in the procedure heading. The actual current parameters (*I_Magnitude* and *I_Angle*) must be listed to receive the total circuit current from the procedure.

To call the *Display* procedure, you list all four total impedance and current variables, since the procedure must receive them from the calling program to perform the display operation.

Do you see how the functions are called within the *Z_Total* procedure? FUNCTION *x* and FUNCTION *jy* are called within the **FOR/DO** loop, as we discussed in the algorithm to convert from polar to rectangular while the impedances are being summed. FUNCTION *Mag* and FUNCTION *Angle* are called at the end of the procedure to convert the total impedance from rectangular back to polar.   Notice how the local procedure variables are used as actual parameters within the function calls.

Here is what you would see for a sample run of the program:

```
Enter the number of series impedances:   3

Enter Z1 magnitude:   3.00
Enter Z1 angle:   60.00

Enter Z2 magnitude:   4.00
Enter Z2 angle:   45.00

Enter Z3 magnitude:   5.00
Enter Z3 angle:   -30.00

Enter the source voltage magnitude:   10.00
Enter the source voltage angle:   0.00

The total impedance for this circuit is 9.14 kilohms @ 18.67 degrees

The total current for this circuit is 1.09 milliamps @ -18.67 degrees

NOTE:   The above polar coordinate angles are the reference
angles in the given quadrant.
```

That's it!   However, before going on, make sure that you have a good understanding of this program, since you will be asked to write similar programs in the chapter problems. '

CHAPTER SUMMARY

In this chapter you learned how to write and use subprograms in Pascal.   There are two vehicles provided within Pascal for subprogramming: functions and procedures. A function is a subprogram that returns a single value to the calling program.   It is called, or invoked, using an assignment ($:=$) or *Write/Writeln* statement.   A procedure, on the other hand, can be used to return a set of values to the calling program as well as perform some specific task, such as input or output.

Parameters are variable data passed between the calling program and subprogram.   Actual parameters are part of the subprogram call within the calling program. Formal parameters are defined within the subprogram heading and take on the value(s) of the actual parameters when the subprogram is called.   Furthermore, parameters can be passed between the calling program and subprogram by value or variable. When passing parameters by value, the actual parameters in the calling program are not affected by operations on the formal parameters within the subprogram. When passing parameters by variable, the actual parameters in the calling program will reflect any changes to the formal parameters within the subprogram.   Thus, passing parameters by value is one-way communication of data from the calling program to the subprogram.   Passing parameters by variable is two-way communication of data from the calling program to the subprogram and back to the calling program.   In Pascal, variable parameters are declared using the reserved word **VAR** in the parameter listing within the subprogram heading.

In addition to parameters, subprograms can operate with local variables that are declared within the subprogram declaration section.   Such local variables are only available for use within the subprogram in which they are declared.   Global variables, on the other hand, are usually declared in the main program and are available for use by any subprograms called by the main program.   The scope of a variable refers to the largest block in which a variable is accessible.   A side effect occurs when a subprogram changes the value of a global variable.   Variables should always be declared as locally as possible, whereas constants should be declared as globally as possible.

A recursive operation is an operation that calls itself until a primitive state is reached.   Pascal supports both recursive functions and procedures.   There must always be a primitive state to terminate a recursive function or procedure call. Otherwise, a run-time error will occur.

Recursive operations can be performed as part of an **If/Then/Else** statement. The primitive state forms the **Then** clause, while the recursive call is part of the **Else** clause of the statement.

Many recursive operations can also be performed using iteration.   Since recursion eats up time and memory as compared to iteration, you should only consider recursion when a simple iterative solution is not possible, and when the execution and memory efficiency of the solution are within acceptable limits.

QUESTIONS AND PROBLEMS

Questions

7-1. A subprogram used to return a single value is a _____ .

7-2. Explain the difference between an actual and a formal parameter.

7-3. Which of the following are invalid function headings?   Explain why they are invalid.

```
a. FUNCTION Average (Num1,Num2);
b. FUNCTION Largest (X,Y : integer);
c. FUNCTION XNOR (A,B : Boolean) : Boolean;
d. FUNCTION Result (Num : real; Character : char) : Boolean;
```

7-4. Write the appropriate headings for the following functions:
   a. Calculate dc power.
   b. *tan (x)*
   c. 2-bit NAND
   d. Converting degrees Fahrenheit to degrees Celsius.
   e. The output of a voltage divider circuit.
   f. Compute the average of 3 integer test scores.

7-5. True or False: A procedure data type must always be specified in a procedure heading.

7-6. Explain the difference between a value parameter and a variable parameter.

7-7. When passing parameters to a subprogram by variable,
   a. The actual parameter takes on the formal parameter value before the subprogram execution
   b. The formal parameter takes on the local variable value
   c. The actual parameter is altered after the subprogram execution
   d. None of these

7-8. An assignment statement is used to call a _____ .

7-9. Which of the following are invalid procedure headings? Explain why they are invalid.
   a. PROCEDURE PrintHeader;
   b. PROCEDURE Error (Num1 : real; Answer :char) : Boolean;
   c. PROCEDURE GetData (Amount : integer; VAR x : char);
   d. PROCEDURE OutData (X, VAR Y : integer);

7-10. Which of the following are value parameters and which are variable parameters?
   a. PROCEDURE Prob1 (VAR A, B : char; X : real; Y : Boolean);
   b. PROCEDURE Prob2 (Num1, Num2, Num3 : integer; VAR Avg : real);
   c. PROCEDURE Prob3 (X : real; VAR A, B : char; Y : integer);

7-11. Write the appropriate heading for the following procedures:
   a. Cause the printer to skip a given number of lines.
   b. Swap the values of two integer variables obtained from the calling program.
   c. Print the cube of three integer variables obtained from the calling program without affecting the original uncubed values.

7-12. Write Pascal statements that will call the three procedures n question 7-11.

7-13. Given the following procedure,

```
PROCEDURE Swap (VAR X,Y : integer);

VAR
    Temp : integer;

BEGIN
    Temp := X;
    X := Y;
    Y := Temp
END;
```

show the output for each of the following segments of code in the main program.
   a. A := 2;
      B := 10;
      Writeln ('A = ',A,' B = ', B);   *(Continued)*

```
        Swap (A, B);
        Writeln ('A = ',A,' B = ', B);
b.   A := 20;
     B := -5;
     Writeln ('A = ',A,' B = ', B);
     IF A < B THEN
         Swap (A, B)
     ELSE
         Swap (B, A);
     Writeln ('A = ',A,' B = ', B);
c.   Num1 := 1;
     Num2 := 5;
     FOR Count := 1 TO 5 DO
         BEGIN
             Swap (Num1, Num2);
             Writeln ('Num1 = ',Num1, ' Num2 = ', Num2);
             Num1 := Num1 + 1;
             Num2 := Num2 - 1
         END;
```

7-14. Explain the difference between a local and a global variable.

7-15. What is meant by the scope of a variable?

7-16. What is a side effect?

7-17. True or False: Variables should be declared as locally as possible and constants as globally as possible.

7-18. Look at the block structure in Figure 7-8.
  a. Identify the global variables.
  b. Identify the local variables.
  c. Write a declaration section for the program and subprograms.

7-19. Explain recursion.

7-20. When should you consider a recursive solution to a problem?

Programming Problems

Write functions to perform the following tasks:

7-1. Convert a temperature in $°F$ to $°C$.

7-2. Find x^y, where x is a real value and y is an integer value.

7-3. Calculate $tan(\theta)$, for some angle θ in degrees.

7-4. Find $n!$, where $n! = n * (n - 1) * (n - 2) * \ldots * 1$ using iteration. Example: $5! = 5 * 4 * 3 * 2 * 1 = 120$

7-5. Find $n!$ using recursion.

7-6. Find the minimum of two integer values.

7-7. Return the Boolean result of a 2-bit XNOR operation.

7-8. Return the Boolean result of a 3-bit NAND operation.

Main Program Block

```
VAR
    X : integer;
    Inp, Out : char;



  Procedure 1 Block

    VAR
        Y : real;



      Procedure 2 Block

        VAR
            A : real;
            Flag : Boolean;




  Function 1 Block

    VAR
        X : real;
```

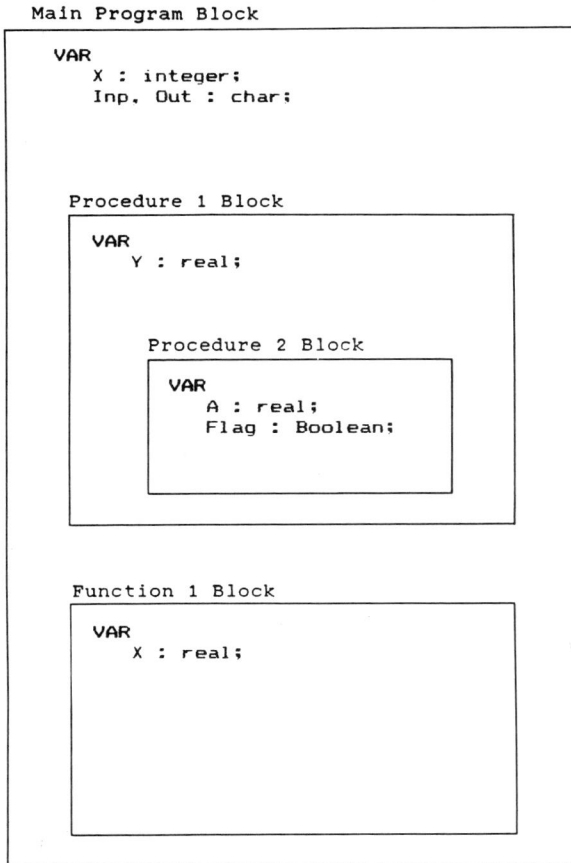

Figure 7-8 Block structure for question 7-18.

7-9. Examine a voltage range and return the Boolean value TRUE if a value is within the range and FALSE if the value is outside the range.

7-10. Calculate period, given frequency.

7-11. Calculate the time constant of an *RC* circuit, given the values of *R* and *C*.

7-12. Find the resonant frequency of the *RLC* circuit in Figure 7-9.

Write procedures to perform the following tasks:

7-13. Print your name, class, instructor, and hour.

7-14. Cause the printer to skip a given number of lines, where the number of lines to be skipped is passed to the procedure.

7-15. Swap, or exchange, any two integer values.

7-16. Compare some new integer value to a maximum integer value obtained from the calling program. Replace the maximum value with the new value if the new value

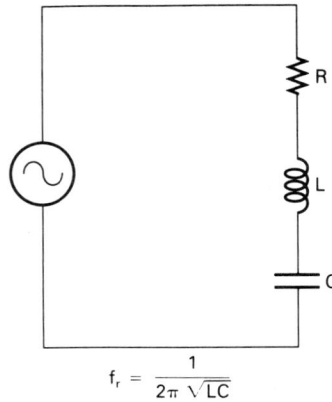

$$f_r = \frac{1}{2\pi \sqrt{LC}}$$

Figure 7-9 A series RLC circuit for problem 7-12.

is greater than the maximum value. Use the *Swap* procedure in problem 7-15 for the exchange operation.

In problems 17 through 25, employ the principles of structured top/down design discussed in this chapter.

7-17. Determine the cut-off frequencies for the active bandpass filter shown in Figure 7-10. Notice that both cut-off frequencies are obtained using the same relationship, or function. This is an ideal application for a function in Pascal. As a result, use a nested function to perform the frequency calculations within a calculation procedure.

7-18. Find the height at which the ladder in Figure 7-11 makes contact with the wall, given the length of the ladder and the distance the base of the ladder is from the wall.

7-19. Find the load current in Figure 7-12. Use nested functions to calculate the Thévènin voltage and resistance.

7-20. Find the output of the Wheatstone bridge circuit in Figure 7-13.

7-21. Given any two vectors as shown in Figure 7-14, find the resultant vector using the law of cosines.

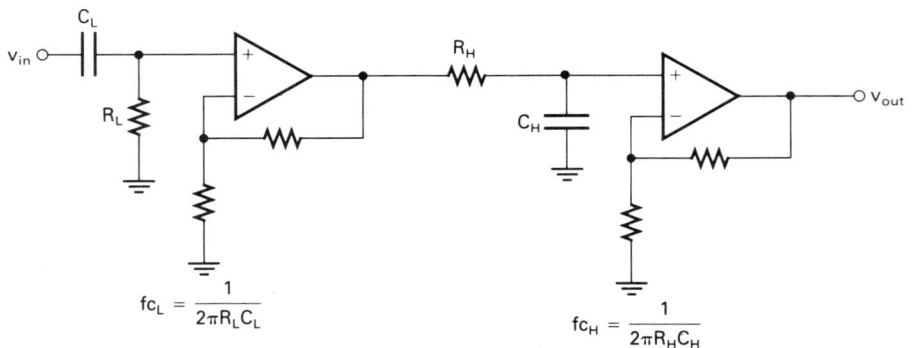

$$fc_L = \frac{1}{2\pi R_L C_L}$$

$$fc_H = \frac{1}{2\pi R_H C_H}$$

Figure 7-10 A bandpass filter for problem 7-17.

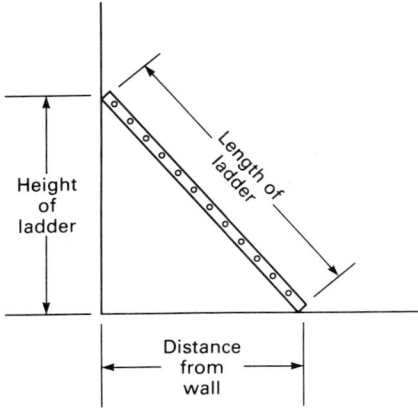

Figure 7-11 A ladder for problem 7-18.

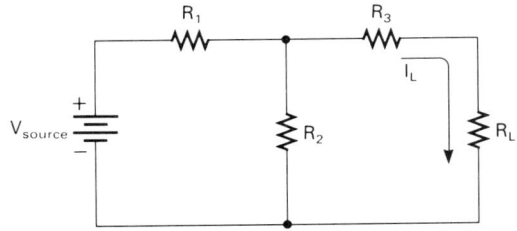

$$V_{TH} = \frac{R_2}{R_1 + R_2} V_{source}$$

$$R_{TH} = \frac{R_1 R_2}{R_1 + R_2} + R_3$$

$$I_L = \frac{V_{TH}}{R_{TH} + R_L}$$

Figure 7-12 A circuit for the Thévènin procedure in problem 7-19.

7-22. Find the total circuit impedance and current for any number of impedances in parallel with a source voltage as shown in Figure 7-15. Assume that the user will enter the impedance values in polar form and that the program must display the circuit values in polar form.

7-23. A Fibonacci sequence of numbers is defined as follows:

$$F_0 = 0$$

$$F_1 = 1$$

$$F_n = F_{n-1} + F_{n-2}, \text{ for } n > 1$$

This says that the first two numbers in the sequence are 0 and 1. Then each additional Fibonacci number is the sum of the two previous numbers in the sequence. Thus, the first ten Fibonacci numbers are

$$0, 1, 1, 2, 3, 5, 8, 13, 21, 34$$

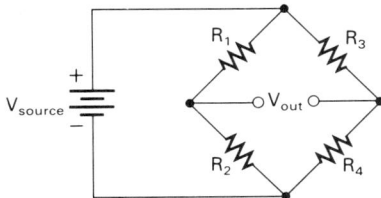

$$V_{out} = (\frac{R_2}{R_1 + R_2} - \frac{R_4}{R_3 + R_4}) V_{source}$$

Figure 7-13 A Wheatstone bridge for problem 7-20.

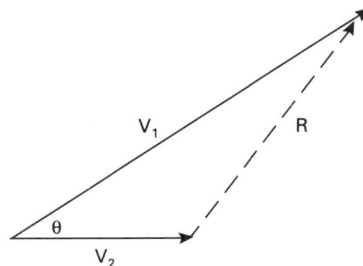

$$R^2 = V_1^2 + V_2^2 - 2V_1 V_2 \cos\theta$$

Figure 7-14 Vector diagram for problem 7-21.

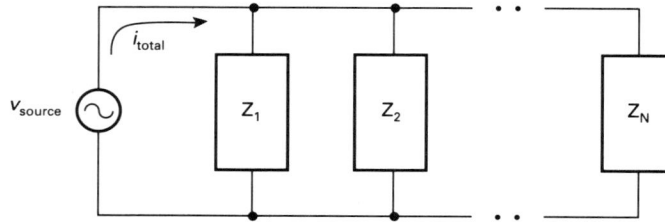

Figure 7-15   A parallel impedance circuit for problem 7-22.

Here we say that the first number occupies position 0 in the sequence, the second number position 1 in the sequence, and so on.   Thus, the last position in a ten number sequence is position 9.

Develop a program that employs a recursive function to generate a Fibonacci sequence of all numbers up to some position, n, entered by the user.

7-24. Develop a program that employs an iterative function to generate a Fibonacci sequence of all numbers up to some position, n, entered by the user.

7-25. Measure the amount of time it takes each of the programs in problems 7-23 and 7-24 to generate a Fibonacci sequence of fifty elements.

What do you conclude about the efficiency of recursion versus iteration?

Why does the recursive program take so long?

chapter eight

User-Defined Data and Arrays

INTRODUCTION

As the chapter title suggests, this chapter will introduce you to two very important topics in any programming language: user-defined data types and arrays.

One distinct advantage of using Pascal is that it allows you, the programmer, to create your own types of data. Up to this point, you have been using the standard data types of integer, real, character, and Boolean. As you have seen, these data types have been adequate for many programming applications. Although these predefined data types can be used for nearly any programming task, they often are insufficient to describe a problem clearly. You will soon discover that user-defined data types enhance the readability of your program by making it more clear and application oriented—something that we are especially concerned about in solving technical problems. The more clearly we can express a problem as related to its application, the easier it is for us and others to understand and solve the problem.

Once you learn how to create user-defined data, you will learn how to create user-defined data structures called *arrays*. Arrays simply provide an organized means for locating and storing data, just as the post office boxes in your local post office lobby provide an organized means of locating and storing mail. There are many technical applications for arrays. As a result, it is important that you obtain a solid understanding of how to create and use them.

8-1 USER-DEFINED DATA TYPES

User-defined data types consist of a set of data elements that you, the programmer, define for a particular application. The idea of defining your own data type might seem awkward to you at first, but you will soon discover that it provides a convenient means of working with real-world problems. There will be times when none of the four standard data types (integer, real, character, or Boolean) will work conveniently for certain applications. For example, suppose that an application problem required the manipulation of the days of the week. Since none of the standard data types include the days of the week as elements within their predefined range, you might suggest that each day of the week be set to an integer value using the **CONST** declaration, as follows:

```
CONST
    Sun  = 1;
    Mon  = 2;
    Tue  = 3;
    Wed  = 4;
    Thur = 5;
    Fri  = 6;
    Sat  = 7;
```

Then, using this declaration, you could actually manipulate the days within your program. For instance, assuming that the variable *Day* is declared as an integer, a program might include the following statement:

```
IF Day = Fri THEN
    Writeln ('Its pay day!');
```

Since you have set the days of the week to integer values, the above **IF/THEN** statement is simply comparing the value of *Day* to the integer value assigned to *Fri* (6). If *Day* = 6, then the message is written.

Pascal allows a more convenient way to work with nonstandard data through the use of a data **TYPE** declaration. Rather than using numeric assignments as in the preceding example, you can define the set of days using the **TYPE** declaration as follows:

```
TYPE
    DaysOfWeek = (Sun, Mon, Tue, Wed, Thur, Fri, Sat);
```

Here, the word **TYPE** declares the data type *DaysOfWeek* to include the set of seven elements *Sun, Mon, Tue, Wed, Thur, Fri*, and *Sat. DaysOfWeek* is called a ***user-defined*** data type since you, the user, have defined it.   That's all there is to it!

Declaring User-Defined Data

The general format and syntax for declaring user-defined data is as follows:

```
USER-DEFINED DATA DECLARATION FORMAT  **************************************
TYPE
    data type identifier = (element #1, element #2, . . . , element #n);
VAR
    variable identifier : data type identifier;
  *************************************************************************
```

As you can see, user-defined data requires a two-part declaration.   First, you must declare the data elements using a **TYPE** declaration.   Here, the user-defined data type is given a name (data-type identifier).   The data-type identifier is followed by an equals sign, and the elements that make up the data type are listed within parentheses.   Second, one or more variables are declared using the **VAR** declaration in order to operate with the data type.   A variable identifier, or name, is listed followed by a colon and the same data-type identifier used in the **TYPE** declaration.   For instance, let's go back to our days-of-the-week data type.   The days in the week are first declared as a user-defined **TYPE** declaration like this:

```
TYPE
    DaysOfWeek = (Sun, Mon, Tue, Wed, Thur, Fri, Sat);
```

Then a variable must be declared for the data type using a **VAR** declaration, as follows:

```
VAR
    Day : DaysOfWeek;
```

Any operations with the user-defined data in the statement section of your program will then use the variable identifier (*Day*), like this:

```
IF Day = Fri THEN
    Writeln ('Its pay day!');
```

The Location of TYPE Declarations

All **TYPE** declarations in a Pascal program must be located after any constant declarations and before any variable declarations, as follows:

```
*******************************************************************
        ┌─ PROGRAM name (input, output);
        │  CONST
        │       {Any constants declared here}
Declaration │  TYPE
 Section  ─┤       {User-defined data types declared here}
        │  VAR
        └─      {Variables and subprograms declared here}

        ┌─ BEGIN {main program}
Statement │    ⋮
 Section  ─┤      {main program statements here}
        │    ⋮
        └─ END. {main program}
*******************************************************************
```

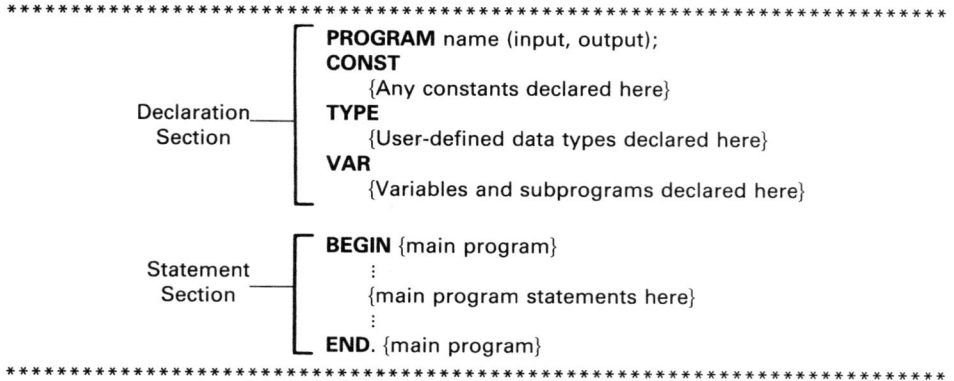

Putting it all together, here's how our days-of-the-week user-defined data type would be declared in a program:

```
PROGRAM  ShowMe (output);

CONST
    Space = ' ';

TYPE
    DaysOfWeek = (Sun, Mon, Tue, Wed, Thur, Fri, Sat);

VAR
    Day : DaysOfWeek;

BEGIN
    .
    .

IF Day = Fri THEN
    Writeln ('Its pay day!');
    .
    .

END.
```

The Ordering of User-Defined Data

Recall from Chapter 2 that a user-defined data type is also a scalar, or ordered, data type. As a result, the Pascal compiler assigns an order to the user-defined elements such that element 1 < element 2 < . . . < element n. This means that, in the *DaysOfWeek* data type, *Sun* < *Mon* < *Tue* < *Wed* < *Thur* < *Fri* < *Sat*. As a result, relational operations involving the user-defined data type are perfectly legitimate. For instance, consider the following segment of code:

```
BEGIN
    .
    .

IF (Day > Sun) AND (Day < Sat) THEN
    Writeln ('Its a weekday!');

    .
    .
    .

END.
```

Here, the value of *Day* is compared with *Sun* and *Sat*.   Using the declaration for *DaysOfWeek, Day* must be a weekday if it's between *Sun* and *Sat*, right?

EXAMPLE 8-1:

Declare the following as user-defined data types.   Provide an appropriate variable declaration to go along with the type declaration.

a. *MonthsOfYear* consisting of the twelve months of the year.

b. *TestGrades* consisting of the five common letter grades.

c. *ArmyRanks* consisting of the eight common ranks found in the army.

Solution:

a. **TYPE**
```
    MonthsOfYear = (Jan, Feb, Mar, Apr, May, Jun, Jul,
                    Aug, Sep, Oct, Nov, Dec);

    VAR
      Month : MonthsOfYear;
```

b. **TYPE**
```
      TestGrades = (F, D, C, B, A);

    VAR
      Test : TestGrades;
```

c. **TYPE**
```
    ArmyRanks = (Private, Corporal, Sergeant, Lieutenant
                 Captain, Major, Colonel, General);

    VAR
      Rank : ArmyRanks;
```

Observe the syntax in the foregoing declarations.   First, the data-type name must be all one word.   No spaces or punctuation are allowed.   Also, notice that individual words within the data-type name begin with a capital letter.   This is not a requirement of Pascal, but has been done for clarity.   Next, you see that the elements are contained in parentheses and separated by commas.   Finally, a semicolon is required at the end of the element listing to mark the end of a given data-type declaration.

You should also note the ordering of each declaration.   The *TestGrade* data type is ordered such that an $F < D < C < B < A$.   This represents a natural ordering, when you consider the application of grading.   In addition, the *ArmyRank* data type is ordered according to the natural order of ranks from the lowest rank (Private) to the highest rank (General).

Finally, notice that an appropriate variable has been declared for each data type using the **VAR** declaration.

When several different user data types must be declared for a program, they can all be listed under one **TYPE** declaration. Using this idea, all three data types in Example 8-1 could be listed under the single reserved word **TYPE** like this:

```
TYPE

    MonthsOfYear = (Jan, Feb, Mar, Apr, May, Jun,
                    Jul, Aug, Sep, Oct, Nov, Dec);

    TestGrades = (F, D, C, B, A);

    ArmyRanks = (Private, Corporal, Sergeant, Lieutenant,
                 Major, Colonel, General);
```

Notice that the different data types are separated using a semicolon after each element listing.

EXAMPLE 8-2:

Given the following list of technical courses—dc Circuits, ac Circuits, Digital, Micro, Statics, Dynamics, Drawing, and Surveying—declare a data type called *TechCourses* to include these courses, and include an appropriate variable declaration.

Solution: Using the **TYPE** declaration, the above set of technical courses would be declared as follows:

```
TYPE
    TechCourses = (DC_Circuits,  AC_Circuits, Digital,
                   Micro, Statics, Dynamics, Drawing,
                   Surveying);

    VAR
        Course : TechCourses;
```

Notice the "trick" that was used to list the dc circuits and ac circuits courses. Pascal requires that the listing consist of single-word elements. Since these courses require two words, a "_" was inserted between the two words to allow for normal word spacing and still meet the requirements of the Pascal compiler. Consequently, the element *DC_Circuits* is interpreted as a single word by the compiler.

Standard Subrange Types

The **TYPE** declaration can also be used to specify a subrange, or subset, of the standard integer and character data types. Here's how it works. Suppose that your programming application requires you to divide the last fifty years into decades of the forties, fifties, sixties, seventies, and eighties.   Each decade is represented by a subrange of integers.   For example, the forties consists of the integers 1940 through 1949.   Using the **TYPE** declaration, you can label these decades as follows:

```
Forties = 1940 .. 1949;

Fifties = 1950 .. 1959;

Sixties = 1960 .. 1969;

Seventies = 1970 .. 1979;

Eighties = 1980 .. 1989;
```

Here, the identifier *Forties* only includes the integers 1940 through 1949, the *Fifties* identifier includes all the integers 1950 through 1959, and so on.

Notice the syntax employed in the declaration.   The reserved word **TYPE** is followed by each *subrange* declaration.   Each subrange definition consists of a name, or identifier, followed by an equals sign, followed by the lower range limit, two dots, the upper range limit, and a semicolon.   Observe that the range is *not* enclosed in parentheses.   If it were, a syntax error would result.   In addition, only two dots are used between the lower and upper range limits.   Any more or less will cause a syntax error.

One final point: To use the subrange within your program, you must declare a variable for that subrange.   For instance, the variable *Fourth_Decade* might be appropriate for the *Forties* subrange and would be declared as follows:

```
VAR
     Fourth_Decade : Forties;
```

The general format and syntax for a subrange declaration is as follows:

```
DECLARING SUBRANGES *****************************************************
TYPE
     subrange name = lower range limit .. upper range limit;
VAR
     variable identifier : subrange name;
************************************************************************
```

Subranges can also be declared for the standard character data type.   As an example, suppose that a programming application required you to separate the upper- and lowercase letters of the alphabet.   This can be done using two subrange declarations, as follows:

```
TYPE
     LowerCase = 'a' .. 'z';
     UpperCase = 'A' .. 'Z';
```

```
VAR
     Small  :  LowerCase;
     Big    :  UpperCase;
```

That's all there is to it! The name *LowerCase* refers only to the lowercase letters from 'a' through 'z', and the *UpperCase* identifier refers only to the uppercase letters 'A' through 'Z'. Of course, character data must be enclosed in quotes as shown or a syntax error will result. The variables *Small* and *Big* are used within the statement section of the program to access their respective subranges.

The two subrange declarations just discussed created subranges of the standard integer and character data types. You might be wondering about declaring subranges for the real and Boolean data types. For instance, could you define a subrange of reals from 3.5 to 10.5? Think about it! How many possible real numbers are there from 3.5 to 10.5? You're right—there are an infinite number of reals between these two limits. In fact there are an infinite number of reals between any two range limits. For this reason, you *cannot* declare subranges for the real data type.

What about the Boolean data type? Well, you could declare a Boolean subrange, but it would make little sense because the entire Boolean data type only consists of two values (TRUE and FALSE).

User-Defined Subrange Types

You can also create subranges of user-defined data types. For instance, in Example 8-1 you declared a data type called *MonthsOfYear*. Suppose that a business program requires you to divide the months into calendar-year quarters. This can be done easily using the subrange declaration like this:

```
TYPE

    MonthsOfYear = (Jan, Feb, Mar, Apr, May, Jun, Jul,
                    Aug, Sep, Oct, Nov, Dec);

    FirstQuarter = Jan .. Mar;

    SecondQuarter = Apr .. Jun;

    ThirdQuarter = Jul .. Sep;

    FourthQuarter = Oct .. Dec;

VAR
    Month : MonthsOfYear;
    First : FirstQuarter;
    Second : SecondQuarter;
    Third : ThirdQuarter;
    Fourth : FourthQuarter;
```

The major requirement here is that the entire set of user-defined elements must be declared prior to the subrange definition.   In our example, the data type *MonthsOfYear* must be declared prior to declaring the quarterly subranges.   In addition, the subrange order must be the same as that specified in the original data-type declaration.   A subrange defined as *FirstQuarter = Mar . . Jan* is illegal, since *Jan* comes before *Mar* in the original *MonthsOfYear* declaration.

Example 8-3:

Using the *TechCourses* data type defined in Example 8-2, declare subranges for the *Electrical, Mechanical,* and *Civil* courses.

Solution: Using the **TYPE** declaration, the original set of courses must be declared first, followed by the respective subranges as follows:

```
TYPE
    TechCourses = (DC_Circuits, AC_Circuits, Digital,
                   Micro, Statics, Dynamics, Drawing,
                   Surveying);

    Electrical = DC_Circuits .. Micro;

    Mechanical = Statics .. Drawing;

    Civil = Statics .. Surveying;
VAR
    Course : TechCourses;
    E_Tech : Electrical;
    M_Tech : Mechanical;
    C_Tech : Civil;
```

Notice that the *Mechanical* and *Civil* subranges overlap.   The *Mechanical* subrange does not include the *Surveying* course, but the *Civil* subrange does.

8-2 ONE-DIMENSIONAL ARRAYS

Recall from the chapter introduction that an array is a ***data structure***.   In other words, an array consists of data that are organized, or structured, in a particular way.   This array structure provides a convenient means of storing large amounts of data in primary, or user, memory.   There are both one-dimensional and multidimensional arrays.   In this section you will learn about one-dimensional arrays. Then, in the next section you will literally expand this knowledge into multidimensional arrays.

The Array Structure

To get the idea of an array, look at the illustration in Figure 8-1.   Here you see a single row of post office boxes as you might find in any typical post office lobby. As you know, each box has a post office box number.   In Figure 8-1, our post

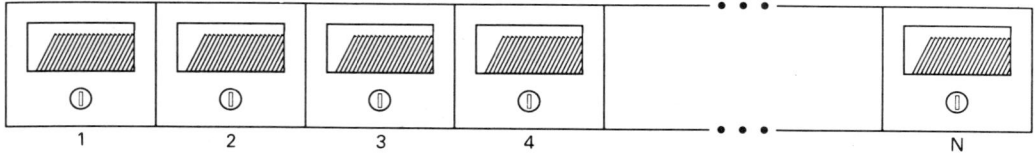

Figure 8-1 A one-dimensional array is like a row of post office boxes.

office box numbers begin with 1 and go up to some finite number *N*. How do you locate a given box? Of course, by using its post office box number, right? However, the post office box number has nothing to do with what's inside the box. It is simply used to locate a given box. Of course, the contents of a given box are the mail delivered to that box. The reason the postal service uses the post office box method is that it provides a convenient, well-organized method of storing and accessing the mail for its postal customers. An array does the same thing in a computer program: It provides a convenient, well-organized method of storing and accessing data for you, the programmer.

You can think of a one-dimensional array as a row of post office boxes like those shown in Figure 8-2. This array consists of a single row of storage locations, each labeled with a number called an ***index***. Each index location is used to store a given type of data. The data stored at a given index location is referred to as an array ***element***. Thus, a one-dimensional array is a sequential ***list*** of storage locations that contain individual data elements that are located, or accessed, via indices. As you can see, the post office box analogy is very fitting.

The two major components of any array are the elements stored in the array and the indices that locate the stored elements. Don't get these two array components confused! Although array elements and indices are related, they are completely separate quantities—just as the contents of a post office box are something different from its post office box number. With this in mind, let's explore array elements and indices a bit further.

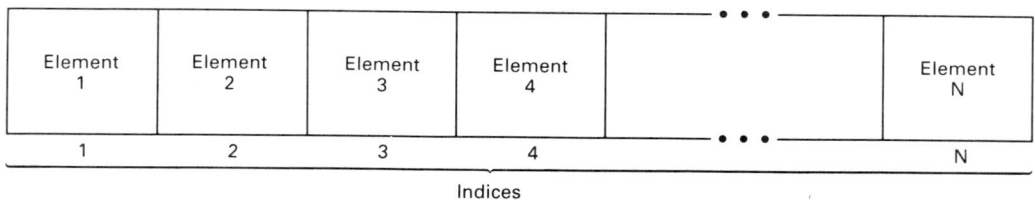

Figure 8-2 A one-dimensional array, or list, is a sequential list of storage locations that contain data elements located via indices.

The Array Elements

The elements of an array are the data stored in the array. These elements can be any type of data that you have seen so far. Thus, a given array can store integer elements, real elements, character elements, string elements, and Boolean elements. In addition to these standard data-type elements, an array can also be used to store user-defined data elements. In fact, the elements in an array can even be other arrays. However, there is one major restriction that applies to the array elements in Pascal: The elements in a given array *must all be of the same data type*.

As you will see shortly, you must declare arrays in a Pascal program. Part of the declaration is to specify the data type of the elements that the array will store. Once a given array is declared for a certain data type, only elements of that data type may be stored in the array. One exception is that integers can be stored in an array of reals, since the integers are a natural subset of the reals.

The Array Indices

The array indices locate the array elements. These indices can be any scalar, or ordered, data type *except real*. Thus, indices can be integers, characters, Boolean, or user-defined data. For example, look at the arrays illustrated in Figure 8-3. Each array can hold seven elements. In Figure 8-3a, the indices are integers,

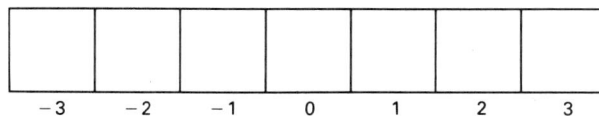

(a)

(b)

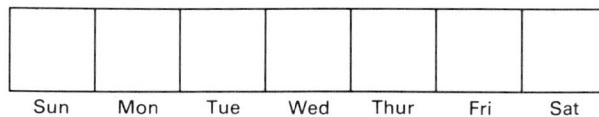

(c)

Figure 8-3   Three 1 × 7 lists with different indexing schemes.

ranging from -3 to 3. Notice that there are seven indices, including 0. In Figure 8-3b, the indices are characters ranging from 'A' to 'G'. Again, there are seven unique elements located by these seven indices. Finally, in Figure 8-3c the elements are located using the seven user-defined indices "Sun" to "Sat."

The Dimensions of an Array

As you have seen, the indices of an array range between two limits. The lower range limit, or minimum value, is called the **lower bound** of the index range, and the upper range limit, or maximum value, is called the **upper bound** of the range. Clearly, the index range dictates how many elements the array can store.

Moreover, the index range of an array gives it its **dimensions**. Just like the dimensions on a part drawing indicate the size of the part, the dimensions of an array indicate the size of an array and how many elements it can store. The arrays in Figure 8-3 are all 1×7 arrays. This means that there is one row of seven elements in the array. When there is only one row of elements in the array, the array is said to be a one-dimensional array, or **list**. Obviously, multidimensional arrays include multiple rows. More about these in Section 8-3.

Declaring One-Dimensional Arrays in Pascal

All arrays in Pascal must be declared. To declare an array, you must specify three things using a **TYPE** declaration:

1. The name of the array
2. The index range of the array
3. The data type of the array elements

Furthermore, to use the array, you must declare a variable for that array using the **VAR** declaration. Here's the general format:

```
ONE-DIMENSIONAL ARRAY FORMAT ********************************************
TYPE
     array name = ARRAY [index range] OF element data type;
VAR
     array variable identifier : array name;
     ********************************************************************
```

Under the **TYPE** declaration, you first see the array name. The array name is followed by an equals sign and the reserved word **ARRAY**. This tells the compiler that it is an array declaration. Following the reserved word **ARRAY,** you find the index range enclosed within brackets [ ]. Here, you will usually specify a subrange of the integers, characters, or a user-defined data type. For instance, the index ranges for the the arrays in Figure 8-3 would be specified as [-3 . . 3], ['A' . .

'G'], and [Sun . . Sat].   In the first two cases, the index ranges are subranges of the standard data types integer and character.   In the last case, the index range is a subrange of the user-defined data type, *DaysOfWeek*, that we discussed earlier. To use this index range, the user-defined data type *DaysOfWeek* must be declared prior to the array declaration so that the compiler knows the meaning of [Sun . . Sat].   Notice that in all three cases the lower range limit is specified first, followed by two periods; then the upper range limit is specified.

The index range specification must be followed by the reserved word **OF**, which is followed by the array element data type and a semicolon to end the declaration. As you know, the element data type can be any standard or user-defined data type. Thus, the words *integer, real, char, Boolean*, and **STRING** [   ] are all legal here.   In the case of a user-defined data type, the data type must be declared prior to the array declaration, and the data-type identifier is used here.

Finally, an array variable must be declared using the **VAR** declaration.   The variable identifier is followed by a colon, which is followed by the array name used in the **TYPE** declaration.   I think it's time to look at some examples to get comfortable with array declarations.

Example 8-4:

Declare the arrays shown in Figure 8-3.   Assume that the array in Figure 8-3a will store characters, that the array in Figure 8-3b will store integer data, and that the array in Figure 8-3c will hold Boolean data.

Solution: Following the general format for declaring arrays, you get the following:

a. **TYPE**
        Fig8_3a = ARRAY [-3 .. 3] OF char;

   VAR

        List1 : Fig8_3a;

b. **TYPE**
        Fig8_3b = ARRAY ['A'.. 'G'] OF integer;

   VAR
        List2 : Fig8_3b;

c. **TYPE**
        DaysOfWeek = (Sun, Mon, Tue, Wed, Thur, Fri, Sat);
        Fig8_3c = ARRAY [Sun .. Sat] OF Boolean;

   VAR
        List3 : Fig8_3c;

   or

   TYPE
        DaysOfWeek = (Sun, Mon, Tue, Wed, Thur, Fri, Sat);
        Fig8_3c = ARRAY [DaysOfWeek] OF Boolean;

   VAR
        List3 : Fig8_3c;

Notice that in each case the array names refer to the respective diagrams in Figure 8-3. Your array names and variable identifiers should be as descriptive as possible, depending on the application. Also, notice that in each case the index ranges have been specified using the subrange notation. However, in the last case the index range could also be specified using the single word *DaysOfWeek*, as shown. This can be done, since the index range comprises the entire user-defined data type, *DaysOfWeek*. Of course, this user-defined data type must be declared prior to the array declaration as shown. Finally, the respective element data types are listed following the reserved word **OF**, as specified in the example.

Under the **VAR** declaration you see a variable identifier, followed by a colon, followed by the respective array name. The array name used here must be identical to that used in the **TYPE** declaration. However, the variable must be different but conform to the rules for identifiers in Pascal. As you will soon see, the variable identifier is used to access the array.

Accessing the Array

Accessing the array means to insert elements into the array for storage or to get stored elements from the array. Inserting elements into the array is sometimes referred to as *filling* the array, and getting elements out of the array is sometimes referred to as *extracting* the array elements.

Filling One-Dimensional Arrays

There are basically three major ways to insert elements into an array: by using a direct assignment statement, by reading, or by using loops.

Direct Assignment

Here's the general format for inserting an element into an array using a direct assignment:

DIRECT ASSIGNMENT FORMAT (INSERTING ARRAY ELEMENTS) **********************
array variable identifier [array index value] := element value;
****

Using the array declarations in Example 8-4 (Figure 8-3) direct assignments might go something like this:

```
List1 [-3] := 'k';

List2 ['A'] := -17;

List3 [Sun] := FALSE;
```

In each of these instances, an element is placed in the first storage position of the array: A 'k' is placed in the first position of the array in Figure 8-3a, a -17

is placed in the first position of the array in Figure 8-3b, and the Boolean value FALSE is placed in the first array position in Figure 8-3c.

Observe that the respective array variable is listed, followed by the first array index within brackets. An assignment statement ($:=$) is then used and followed by the element to be inserted. It is very important that the element being inserted is the same data type as declared for the array elements in the **TYPE** declaration. Otherwise, you will get a "data type mismatch" error when the program is compiled.

How might you insert elements into the middle array positions of each of the arrays declared in Example 8-4? How about this:

```
List1 [0] := 'A';

List2 ['D'] := 37;

List3 [Wed] := TRUE;
```

Notice from Figure 8-3 that each index employed locates the middle position in its respective array. Also, the element assignments conform to the type of data declared for the respective array.

Reading Elements into the Array

You can also use a *Readln* statement to insert array elements, as follows:

```
Readln (List1 [1]);

Readln (List2 ['G']);
```

Here, the user must type the respective array element value on the keyboard and press the **ENTER** key to execute each *Readln* statement. A character must be entered for the first *Readln* statement and an integer for the second *Readln* statement. (Why?) The character will be stored in the fifth position (index [1]) of the array in Figure 8-3a, and the integer will be stored in the last position (index ['G']) of the array in Figure 8-3b. Why can't a *Readln* statement be used to insert a Boolean value in the array in Figure 8-3c? Because, as you recall, Boolean data cannot be entered directly via the keyboard.

Inserting Array Elements Using Loops

The obvious disadvantage to using direct assignments to insert array elements is that a separate assignment statement is required to fill each array position. You can automate the insertion process by using a loop structure. Although any of the three loop structures (**WHILE/DO, REPEAT/UNTIL, FOR/DO**) can be employed, the **FOR/DO** structure is the most common.

Consider the following program:

```
PROGRAM ShowMe (input);

USES
  Crt;

CONST
   Max = 10;
TYPE
   Sample = ARRAY [1 .. Max] OF real;
VAR
   A : Sample;
   I : integer;

BEGIN
   Clrscr;
   Writeln ('Enter a list of ', Max, ' numbers and');
   Writeln ('press the ENTER key after each entry.');
   Writeln;
   Writeln;
   FOR I := 1 TO Max DO
      Readln (A[I])
END.
```

First, you see a constant called *Max* declared. Notice where *Max* is used in the program. It is the upper bound of the array index range and the final counter value in the **FOR/DO** loop. Using a constant like this allows you to easily change the size of the array. Here, the array size is ten elements, since the indices range from 1 to *Max*, where *Max* = 10. To change the size of the array, you need to make a change in only one place in the program, under the constant declaration.

Next, look at the array declaration. The array *Sample* is declared as an array of real elements. The array variable identifier is *A*.

Now look at the statement section of the program. After the screen is cleared, the user is told to "enter a list of *Max* (where *Max* is 10) values and press the **ENTER** key after each entry." Once this prompt is displayed, the program enters a **FOR/DO** loop. The loop counter variable is *I*, which ranges from 1 to *Max*. Thus, the loop will be executed *Max*, or ten, times. Notice that the loop counter range is the same as the array index range. With each loop iteration, a single *Readln* statement is executed.

Let's analyze the *Readln* statement. First the array variable, *A*, is listed with the loop counter variable, *I*, as the array index in brackets. What does *I* do with each loop iteration? It increments from 1 to *Max*. As a result, the first loop iteration reads a value into *A[1]*, the second iteration reads a value into *A[2]*, and so on, until the last loop iteration reads a value into the last array position *A[Max]*. That's all there is to it! The array is filled!

You can also use loops for assigning values to array elements. For instance, using the foregoing declarations, consider this loop:

```
FOR I := 1 TO Max DO
   A[I] := 2 * I;
```

This time the array elements are assigned to twice the loop counter value with each loop iteration. What values are actually inserted into the array? How about the ten even integers from 2 through 20?

Extracting Elements from an Array

First, let me caution you that the word *extract* is not a good term here. Why? Because, in general, the word *extract* means to remove something. When we extract an element from an array, we don't actually remove it. We simply copy its value. It remains stored in the array until it is replaced by another value using an insertion operation.

As with insertion, you can extract array elements using one of three general methods: direct assignment, writing, or looping.

Direct Assignment

Extracting array elements using assignment statements is just the reverse of inserting elements using assignment statements. Here's the general format:

DIRECT ASSIGNMENT FORMAT (EXTRACTING ARRAY ELEMENTS) ********************
variable identifier : = array variable identifier [array index value];
****

As an example, suppose that we make the following declarations:

```
CONST
   Max = 10;

TYPE
   Sample = ARRAY [1 .. Max] OF integer;

VAR
   A : Sample;
   X : integer;
```

As you can see, the array consists of ten integer elements. In addition, *A* is the array variable and *X* is an integer variable. Now, assuming that the array has been filled, what do you suppose the following statements do?

```
X := A[1];

X := A[Max];

X := A[3] + A[5];

X := 2 * A[2] - 3 * A[7];
```

The first statement assigns the element stored in the first array position to the variable *X*. The second statement assigns the element stored in the last array position to the variable X. The third statement assigns the sum of the third and fifth array elements to X. Finally, the fourth statement assigns two times the second element minus three times the seventh element to X. The last two statements illustrate how arithmetic operations can be performed on array elements.

In all of the foregoing cases, the array element values are not affected by the assignment operations. The major requirement is that X must be declared the same data type as the array elements or a "data type mismatch" error will occur when the statements are compiled.

As a final example, consider these assignment statements:

```
A[1] := A[Max];

A[2] := A[3] + A[4];
```

Can you determine what will happen here? In the first statement, the first array element is replaced by the last array element. Is the last array element affected? No, since it appears on the right side of the assignment statement. In the second case, the second array element is replaced by the sum of the third and fourth array elements. Again, the third and fourth array elements are not affected by this operation, since they appear on the right side of the assignment statement.

Writing Array Elements

Write and *Writeln* statements can be used to display or print array elements. Let's use the same array to demonstrate how to write array elements. Here's the array declaration again:

```
CONST
    Max = 10;

TYPE
    Sample = ARRAY [1 .. Max] OF integer;

VAR
    A : Sample;
```

Now, what do you suppose the following *Writeln* statements will do?

```
Writeln (A[1]);

Writeln (1st,A[Max]);

Writeln (A[2] DIV A[3]);

Writeln (Sqr(A[7]);
```

The first statement will display the element contained at index 1 of the array. With our array definition, this is the first array element. The second statement will *print* the last array element located at index *Max*. The third statement will divide the element located at index 2 by the element located at index 3 and display the integer quotient.   Finally, the fourth statement will display the square of the element located at index 7.   None of the array element values are affected by these operations.

Extracting Array Elements Using Loops

As with inserting elements into an array, extracting array elements using loops requires less coding, especially when extracting multiple elements.   Again, any of the loop structures can be used for this purpose, but **FOR/DO** loops are the most common.

Consider the following program:

```
PROGRAM ShowMe (output);

USES
  Crt;

CONST
   Max = 10;

TYPE
   Sample = ARRAY [1 .. Max] OF integer;

VAR
   A : Sample;
   I : integer;

BEGIN
   Clrscr;
   Writeln ('This program will fill a ',Max, ' element array');
   Writeln (' called Sample, then display the element values.');
   Writeln;
   Writeln;
   FOR I := 1 TO Max DO
      A[I] := Sqr(I);
   FOR I := 1 TO Max DO
      Write (A[I], ' ')
END.
```

Here, the array is declared as an array of *Max* (10) integer values.   The array name is *Sample* and the array variable is *A*.   Notice that the loop counter variable, *I*, is used as the array index in both **FOR/DO** loops.   The first loop will fill the array locations with the square of the loop counter value.   Then the second loop will display each of the array elements located from index 1 to index *Max*.   A *Write* statement has been used instead of a *Writeln* statement so that the array elements will appear horizontally across the face of the display.   A *Writeln* statement would cause the elements to appear vertically down the left-hand side of the screen.   Think about it!   Notice also that each time an element is displayed, a space is written after the element to separate it from the next sequential element. Here is what you would see on the display:

```
This program will fill a 10 element array
called Sample, then display the element values.

1 4 9 16 25 36 49 64 81 100
```

Example 8-5:

Write a program that uses an array to store a maximum of twenty-five test scores and calculate their average. Use one procedure to fill the array with the scores, a function to calculate the average, and a second procedure to display all the scores along with the calculated average.

Solution: First, we will construct the declaration section of the program. Here is where the array will be declared as well as any global variables, the two procedures, and the function. Let's begin with the array and global variable declarations:

```
PROGRAM  Test_Average (input, output);

USES
  Crt;

CONST
  Max = 25;

TYPE
  Scores = ARRAY [1 .. Max] OF real;

VAR
  Score : Scores;
  Number : integer;
  Avg : real;
```

As you can see, a global constant (*Max*) is first declared. This will be the maximum number of elements in the array. The array, called *Scores*, is then declared to be an array of *Max*, or twenty-five, real elements. I have chosen the real data type here to allow for decimal score values. The array variable is *Score*. This is the identifier that must be used when accessing the array. In addition to the array variable, there are two global variables called *Number* and *Avg*. *Number* will be the number of test scores that the user wishes to average. *Avg* will be the average of the test scores.

The next step is to write the procedures and function. The first procedure must get the test scores from the user and fill the array with those scores. Here's the procedure:

```
PROCEDURE Get_Scores (VAR Score : Scores);

VAR
  I : integer;
```

```
BEGIN
   Write ('How many scores do you want to average?  Number = ');
   Readln (Number);
   Writeln;
   Writeln;
   Writeln ('Enter each score, and press ENTER after each entry.');
   Writeln;
   Writeln;
   FOR I := 1 TO Number DO
      Readln (Score[I])
END;   {procedure Get_Scores}
```

Looking at the procedure heading, you find that it is called *Get_Scores*, an appropriate name. Then you see a single parameter in the parameter list. The parameter, *Score*, is a variable parameter, since it is preceded by the word **VAR**. The data type of the parameter is *Scores*, which is the array we declared in the main program declaration section. What this means is that the array, *Scores*, is passed to the procedure, then passed back to the main program. Isn't this what you must do to fill the array within the procedure: pass it to the procedure, then pass the filled array back to the main program for use by subsequent operations? By the way, the variable parameter (*Score*) could be called something else. In other words, it doesn't have to be the same as the array variable. I have just chosen to use it here for consistency. Finally, a local variable (*I*) is declared in the procedure. This variable will be used as a loop counter when filling the array.

In the statement section of the procedure, the user is first prompted to indicate how many scores are to be averaged. This value is assigned to the global variable *Number*. Then the user is prompted to enter one score at a time, pressing the **ENTER** key after each score entry. A **FOR/DO** loop is used to fill the array with the scores. Notice that the loop counter increments from 1 to *Number* and acts as the array index as elements are being inserted into the array.

The next task is to calculate the average of the test scores using a function. Here's the function:

```
FUNCTION Average (Score : Scores) : real;

VAR
   J : integer;
   Total : real;

BEGIN
   Total := 0;
   FOR J := 1 TO Number DO
      Total := Total + Score[J];
   Average := Total / Number
END;   {function Average}
```

The function name, or identifier, is *Average*. Again, the only formal parameter is *Score*, which is of data type *Scores*. Thus, the array *Scores* is passed to the function so that it can be used to provide the scores for the average calculation. However, this time *Score* is a value parameter, since the array only needs to be passed one way, to the function. It does not have to be passed back to the main program because the function does not alter any of the array elements. The data type of the function is real, since it will return the average of several real-valued test scores.

There are two local function variables declared: *J* and *Total*. The variable *J* will be a loop counter variable and *Total* will act as a temporary variable to accumulate the sum of the scores.

The statement section of the function employs a **FOR/DO** loop to sum all the test scores. The variable *Total* is first initialized to 0. Then the loop is used to extract the array elements, one at a time, and add them to *Total*. Observe that the loop counter (*J*) acts as the array index within the loop. Thus, the array elements, from index 1 to *Number*, are sequentially extracted with each loop iteration and added to *Total*. The last test score is located at index *Number*. This is a global variable and, therefore, accessible to the function.

Once the loop calculates the sum total of all the test scores, an assignment statement is used to calculate the average and assign it to the function identifier (*Average*).

The last procedure in our program must display all the scores and their average. Here's one that should do the job:

```
PROCEDURE Display_Results(Score : Scores);

VAR
  K : integer;

BEGIN
   Clrscr;
   Writeln ('Test Scores');
   Writeln ('-----------');
   Writeln;
   FOR K := 1 TO Number DO
     Writeln (Score[K]:5:2);
   Writeln;
   Writeln;
   Writeln ('Average');
   Writeln ('-------');
   Writeln;
   Writeln (Avg :5:2)
 END;   {procedure Display_Results}
```

The procedure name is *Display_Results*. Again, the parameter is *Score*, whose data type is the array *Scores*. In addition, the array is being passed to the procedure by value. (Why?) A local variable, *K*, is declared and will act as a loop counter.

In the statement section of the procedure, a heading, 'Test Scores', is first displayed, followed by a listing of the individual scores. The scores are obtained from the array using a **FOR/DO** loop. With each loop iteration, a score is displayed in decimal format. A *Writeln* statement is used so that the scores will be listed in a single column under the 'Test Scores' heading. Again, the loop counter is used as a variable index for the array as it increments from 1 to *Number*. The variable *Number* is also accessible to this procedure, since it is a global variable.

Finally, a heading is displayed for the average, and the average (*Avg*) is written to the display in decimal form.   Notice that the global variable *Avg* is employed here. You will see why shortly.

Now let's put everything together and look at the entire program.   Here it is:

```
PROGRAM  Test_Average (input, output);
USES
  Crt;
CONST
  Max = 25;

TYPE
  Scores = ARRAY [1 .. Max] OF real;

VAR
  Score : Scores;
  Number : integer;
  Avg : real;


{*****************************************************************

          This procedure will get the test scores.

*****************************************************************}

  PROCEDURE Get_Scores (VAR Score : Scores);

  VAR
    I : integer;

  BEGIN
    Write ('How many scores do you want to average?  Number = ');
    Readln (Number);
    Writeln;
    Writeln;
    Writeln ('Enter each score, and press ENTER after each entry.');
    Writeln;
    Writeln;
    FOR I := 1 TO Number DO
      Readln (Score[I])
  END;   {procedure Get_Scores}

{*****************************************************************

   This function will calculate the average of the test scores.

*****************************************************************}

FUNCTION Average (Score : Scores) : real;

VAR
  J : integer;
  Total : real;
```

(Continued)

```
BEGIN
  Total := 0;
  FOR J := 1 TO Number DO
    Total := Total + Score[J];
  Average := Total / Number
END;   {function Average}



{**************************************************************

         This procedure will display the results.

**************************************************************}

PROCEDURE Display_Results(Score : Scores);

VAR
  K : integer;

BEGIN
   Clrscr;
   Writeln ('Test Scores');
   Writeln ('------------');
   Writeln;
   FOR K := 1 TO Number DO
     Writeln (Score[K]:5:2);
   Writeln;
   Writeln;
   Writeln ('Average');
   Writeln ('--------');
   Writeln;
   Writeln (Avg :5:2)
 END;   {procedure Display_Results}

 BEGIN   {main program}
   Clrscr;
   Writeln ('This program will average any number of test scores.');
   Writeln;
   Writeln;
   Get_Scores (Score);
   Avg := Average (Score);
   Display_Results (Score)
 END.   {main program}
```

First, you see the main program declarations, along with the two procedures and one function that we developed. Now look at the statement section of the main program. Are you surprised at its simplicity? The main program is relatively short, since all the work is done in the subprograms. This is the "beauty" of structured programming! All the main program does is to write a program description message and then simply call the three subprograms in the order that they are needed. The procedure *Get_Scores* is first called to obtain the scores from the user and insert them into the array. Notice that the array variable, *Score*, must be used in the call to pass the array to the procedure. The procedure fills the array and passes it back to the main program for use by the next two subprograms.

Next, the function (*Average*) is invoked using an assignment statement. Notice that the array variable (*Score*) is used again to pass the array to the function. The global variable, *Avg*, receives the average test score value returned by the function.

Finally, the display procedure is called. Again, the array variable (*Score*) is listed as the actual parameter during the call so that the array is passed to the procedure.

Example 8-6:

Write a program that uses an array to store the names of all the students in your class. Use one procedure to insert the student names into the array and a second procedure to display the contents of the array once it is filled. Assume that there are no more than twenty characters in any student name and that the maximum class size is twenty students.

Solution: Again, the first task is to write the declaration section of the program. How about this:

```
PROGRAM   Student_Array (input, output);

USES
  Crt;

CONST
  Max = 20;

TYPE
  Students = ARRAY [1 .. Max] OF STRING [Max];

VAR
  Number : integer;
  Student : Students;
```

As you can see, the name of the array is *Students*. It is declared as an array of *Max* (20) string elements. Each string element has a maximum of *Max* (20) characters. The array variable is *Student*. A global variable, *Number*, is declared and will be used to represent the actual number of students in the array.

The first procedure must fill the array with student names provided by the user. Here's the procedure:

```
PROCEDURE Fill_Array (VAR Student : Students);

VAR
  I : integer;
BEGIN
  Write ('How many students do you wish to enter?  Number = ');
  Readln (Number);
  Writeln;
  Writeln;
  Writeln ('Enter the ', Number, ' student names and press');
  Writeln ('the ENTER key after each entry.');
  Writeln;
  Writeln;                                              (Continued)
```

```
    FOR I := 1 TO Number DO
        Readln (Student[I])
END;   {procedure FillArray}
```

Here you see that the student array is passed by variable to the procedure. As you know, this means that the array is received by the procedure, then passed back to the main program. In the statement section, the user is first asked to enter the number of students that will be entered. A **FOR/DO** loop is then employed to fill the array with the student names. Each time the loop executes, it inserts a name of up to twenty characters into the array at the index location specified by the loop counter.

The final task is to write a procedure to display the student array contents. Here it is:

```
        PROCEDURE Display_Array (Student : Students);

        VAR
          I : integer;

        BEGIN
          Clrscr;
          Writeln ('The students in this class are: ');
          Writeln;
          Writeln;
          FOR I := 1 TO Number DO
              Writeln (Student[I])
        END;   {procedure Display_Array}
```

This time, the array is passed to the procedure by value. The statement section of the procedure employs a **FOR/DO** loop to extract the array elements via a *Writeln* statement.

Putting everything together, the complete program is as follows:

```
PROGRAM Student_Array (input, output);

USES
  Crt;

CONST
  Max = 20;

TYPE
  Students = ARRAY [1 .. Max] OF STRING [20];

VAR
  Number : integer;
  Student : Students;

{****************************************************************

     This proceedure will fill the student array

****************************************************************}
```

```
PROCEDURE Fill Array (VAR Student : Students);

VAR
  I : integer;
BEGIN
  Write ('How many students do you wish to enter?  Number = ');
  Readln (Number);
  Writeln;
  Writeln;
  Writeln ('Enter the ', Number, ' student names and press');
  Writeln ('the ENTER key after each entry.');
  Writeln;
  Writeln;
  FOR I := 1 TO Number DO
     Readln (Student[I])
END;   {procedure FillArray}


{*****************************************************************

       This procedure will display the class students.

*****************************************************************}


  PROCEDURE Display_Array (Student : Students);

  VAR
    I : integer;

  BEGIN
    Clrscr;
    Writeln ('The students in this class are: ');
    Writeln;
    Writeln;
    FOR I := 1 TO Number DO
       Writeln (Student[I])
  END;   {procedure Display_Array}

  BEGIN  {main program}
    Clrscr;
    Writeln ('This program will fill an array with up to ', Max);
    Writeln ('student names then display the array contents.');
    Writeln;
    Writeln;
    Fill_Array (Student);
    Display_Array (Student)
  END.   {main program}
```

As you can see, the two procedures are declared in the main program declaration section. The main program statement section simply writes a program description message and calls the two procedures. That's all there is to it!

8-3 MULTIDIMENSIONAL ARRAYS

A multidimensional array is simply an extension of a one-dimensional array. The most common multidimensional array is the *two-dimensional* array shown in Figure 8-4. Here you see that a two-dimensional array contains multiple rows. It's as if several one-dimensional arrays are combined to form a single rectangular structure of data. As a result, you can think of this rectangular data structure as a *table* of elements.

Observe that the two-dimensional array in Figure 8-4 is composed of elements that are located by rows and columns. The rows are labeled on the vertical axis, and in this array they range from 1 to m. The columns are labeled on the horizontal axis and range from 1 to n. As a result, we say that this two-dimensional array has a dimension of "m rows by n columns," written as $m \times n$.

How many elements are in the array? You're right—m times n elements! How do you suppose a given element is located? You're right again—by specifying its row and column index number. For instance, the element in the upper left-hand corner is located at the intersection of row 1 and column 1, or index [1,1]. Likewise, the element in the lower right-hand corner is located where row m meets column n, or index [m,n]. With this notation, the row index is listed first, followed by the column index. Get the idea?

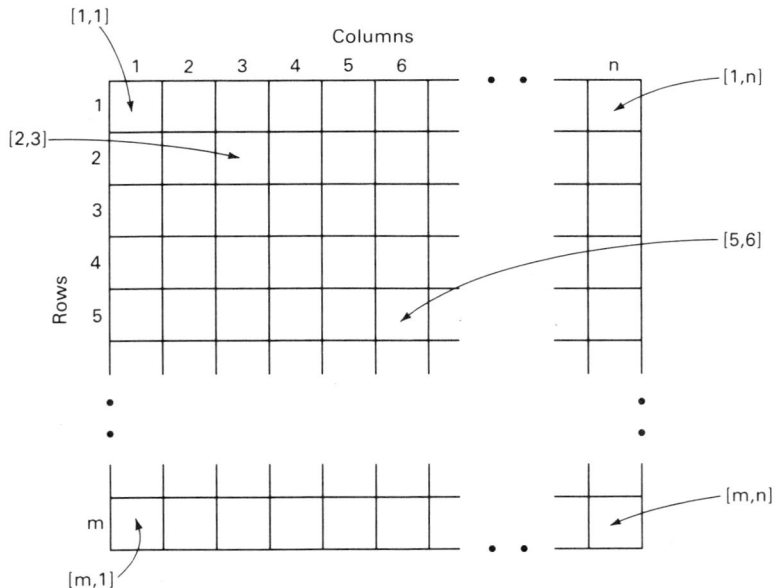

Figure 8-4 The structure of a two-dimensional array.

Declaring Two-Dimensional Arrays in Pascal

You declare two-dimensional arrays in Pascal in almost the same way that you declare one-dimensional arrays. Here's the general format:

TWO-DIMENSIONAL ARRAY FORMAT ★★★
TYPE
    array name = **ARRAY** [row range, column range] **OF** element type;
VAR
    array variable identifier : array name;
★★

The only difference between this declaration and that required for one-dimensional arrays is found within the index range specification. You must specify both the row and column ranges as shown.

Example 8-7:

Given the following two-dimensional array declarations, sketch a diagram of the array structures showing the respective row and column indices.

a. **TYPE**
       Table1 = **ARRAY** [1 .. 5, 1 .. 7] **OF** real;

    VAR
      Percent : Table1;

b. **TYPE**
     Row = 1 .. 5;
     Col = 1 .. 7;
     Table1 = **ARRAY** [Row, Col] **OF** real;

    VAR
     Percent : Table1;

c. **TYPE**
     Voltage = −12 .. 12;
     Resistance = 1 .. 1000;
     Ohms_Law = **ARRAY** [Voltage, Resistance] **OF** real;

    VAR
     Current : Ohms_Law;

d. **TYPE**
     Week = 1 .. 5;
     DaysOfWeek = (Sun, Mon, Tue, Wed, Thur, Fri, Sat);
     Month = **ARRAY** [Week, DaysOfWeek] **OF** integer;

    VAR
     December : Month;

(Continued)

e. **TYPE**
       Row = 1 .. 57;
       Seat = 'A' .. 'E';
       SeatOccupied = ARRAY [Row, Seat] OF Boolean;

   VAR
       Flight_327, Flight_423 : SeatOccupied;

Solution:

a. See Figure 8-5a. This is a rectangular array, or table, of reals whose rows range from 1 to 5 and whose columns range from 1 to 7. The array name is *Table1* and the array variable is *Percent*

b. See Figure 8-5a again. This array is identical to the first array. The only difference

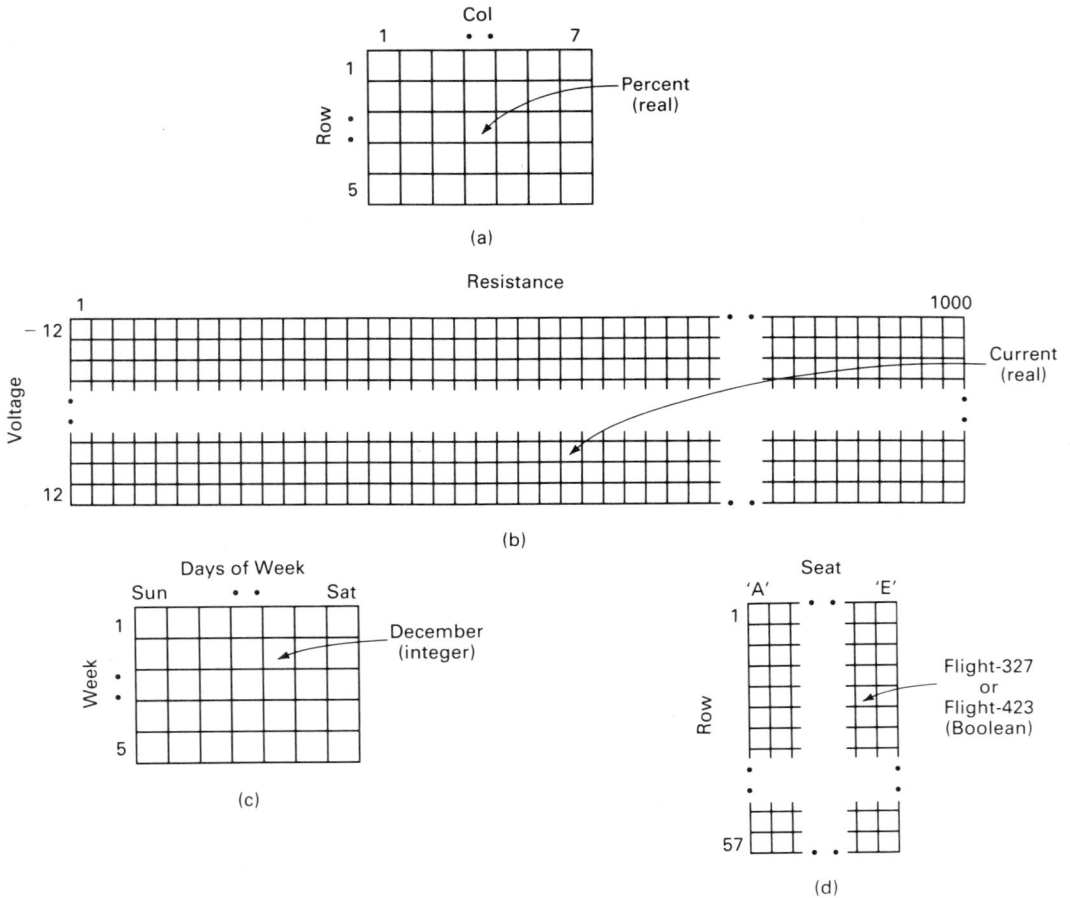

Figure 8-5 Four two-dimensional arrays: (a) Table1, (b) Ohms Law, (c) Month, (d) Seat Occupied.

here is in the way in which the array is declared. Notice that the row and column indices are declared as simply [*Row, Col*], where *Row* and *Col* are declared as integer subranges from 1 to 5 and 1 to 7, respectively

c. See Figure 8-5b. Here the rows are called *Voltage* and range from −12 to 12. The array columns are labeled *Resistance* and range from 1 to 1000. The array name is *Ohms_Law* and the array variable is *Current*. Obviously, the array will store the *Current* values corresponding to *Voltage* values from −12V to +12V and *Resistance* values from 1 Ω to 1000 Ω, using Ohm's law.

d. See Figure 8-5c. This array is constructed to store the dates for the month of December just like a calendar. Look at a common calendar if you have one handy. Isn't a given month simply a table of integers whose values are located by a given week (1 . . 5) and a given day (Sun . . Sat) within that week? As you can see from Figure 8-5c, the array structure duplicates a monthly calendar. The rows are labeled 1 through 5, representing the five possible weeks in any given month. The columns of the array are labeled "Sun" through "Sat," representing the seven days of the week.

Notice the use of user-defined variables in the array declaration to make the array more meaningful to the task at hand. In addition, the identifiers have meaning related to the task. The array name is *Month* and the array variable is *December*. Additional array variables like *May, June,* and *July* could also be declared for the same array to store the dates of those respective months. Do different variables declared for the same array present a problem? No! Pascal will create a separate array in memory for each array variable.

e. See Figure 8-5d. This last array also has a practical application. Can you determine what it is from the declaration? Notice that it is an array of Boolean elements. The rows range from 1 to 57 and the columns range from 'A' to 'E' as shown. Now observe in the declaration that there are two array variables: *Flight_327* and *Flight_423*. What do you suppose the array *SeatOccupied* will store? You're right—it will store TRUE and FALSE Boolean values to indicate whether or not a given airline-flight seat is occupied. The obvious application here is for an airline reservation program.

Notice that two variables are declared for the same array. As a result, Pascal creates two arrays of the same type in memory. One array is accessed using the variable *Flight_327*, and the other is accessed using the variable *Flight_423*. The only common thing between the two is their name and structure, since they are both declared the same type. The elements within the two arrays can be completely different, as long as they are Boolean elements.

Example 8-8:

How many elements will each of the arrays in Example 8-7 store, and what type of elements will they store?

Solution (see Figure 8-5):

a. The array in Figure 8-5a will store 5 × 7, or 35 elements. The elements will be real values.

b. The array in Figure 8-5b has 25 rows, from −12 to 12 and 1000 columns, from 1 to 1000. Thus, the array will store 25 × 1000 = 25,000 real elements.

    c. The array in Figure 8-5c has 5 rows and 7 columns and, therefore, will store 5 × 7 = 35 integer elements.

    d. The array in Figure 8-5d has 57 rows and 5 columns and will store 57 × 5 = 285 Boolean elements.

Accessing Two-Dimensional Array Elements

You access two-dimensional array elements in very much the same way as one-dimensional array elements. The difference is that to locate the elements in a two-dimensional array you must specify a row index and a column index.

You can access the array elements using direct assignment, reading/writing, or looping.

Direct Assignment

The general format for direct assignment of element values is as follows:

```
DIRECT ASSIGNMENT FORMAT (INSERTING ARRAY ELEMENTS) *********************
array variable identifier [row index, column index] : = element value;
***********************************************************************


DIRECT ASSIGNMENT FORMAT (EXTRACTING ARRAY ELEMENTS) ********************
variable identifier : = array variable identifier [row index, column index];
***********************************************************************
```

First, you see the format for inserting elements into a two-dimensional array, followed by the format for extracting elements from the array. Notice that in both instances you must specify a row and column index to access the desired element position. The row index is specified first, followed by the column index. Using the arrays declared in Example 8-7, possible direct assignments for insertion might be

```
Percent [3,4] := 0.5;

Current [0,500] := 0;

December [2,Wed] := 10;

Flight_327 [12,'B'] := TRUE;
```

In the first case, the real element value 0.5 is placed in row 3, column 4 of the *Table1* array. In the second case, a *Current* value of 0 is inserted into row 0, column 500 of the *Ohms_Law* array. Notice that this value corresponds to a *Voltage* value of 0 and a *Resistance* value of 500. In the third case, a value of 10 is placed in the *Wed* position of *Week 2* in the *Month* array. Finally, the last case assigns the Boolean value TRUE to row 12, seat B of *Flight_327*, obviously indicating that this seat is occupied.

Using the same arrays, direct assignment statements to extract elements might be

```
Sales := Percent [1,1];

Amperes := Current [5,100];

Today := December [3,Thur];

Tomorrow := December [3,Fri];

SeatTaken := Flight_423 [3,'A'];
```

In each of the above statements, the element value stored at the row/column position within the respective array is assigned to a variable identifier. Of course, the variable identifier must be declared as the same data type as the array element. Consequently, *Sales* and *Amperes* must be declared as real variables, *Today* and *Tomorrow* as integer variables, and *SeatTaken* as a Boolean variable.

Remember that extraction operations have no effect on the array elements. In other words, the elements are not actually removed from the array; their values are simply "copied" to the assignment variable.

Reading and Writing Array Elements

Readln statements can be used to insert two-dimensional array elements, and *Writeln* statements can be used to extract array elements, as follows:

```
Readln (Percent [2,2]);

Writeln (Percent [2,2]);

Readln (Current [-5,100]);

Writeln (Current [-5,100]);

Readln (December [2,Wed]);

Writeln (December [2,Wed]);

Writeln (Flight_423 [3,'A']);
```

Again you see that both a row and column index must be specified. The *Readln* statements will insert elements obtained from a keyboard input. Of course, the user entry must be the correct data type or a run-time error will occur. A real or integer value can be entered for the first two *Readln* statements, but an integer must be entered for the third *Readln* statement. (Why?) The *Writeln* statements will then extract the array element just inserted and simply "echo" the user entry back to the display.   Notice that the last *Writeln* statement extracts an element from the Boolean array.   This statement will produce a TRUE or FALSE on the display, depending on the contents of location [3,'A'] of *Flight₂423*.   Yes, you can write Boolean values obtained directly from an array to the display or printer.   However, you cannot read Boolean values directly from the keyboard for insertion into the array.   Do you have any ideas on how you might provide user input to a Boolean array?   Think about it, as this will be left for an exercise at the end of the chapter.

Using Loops

As you know, loops provide a more efficient way to access arrays, especially when working with large multidimensional arrays.   The thing to remember with multidimensional arrays is that a separate loop is required *for each dimension* of the array.   In addition, the loops must be *nested*.   Thus, a two-dimensional array requires two nested loops.

Look at the calendar pictured in Figure 8-6.   As you have seen, this calendar can be stored in memory using a two-dimensional array.   How do you suppose you might go about filling the calendar with the dates required for a given month? A logical approach would be to fill in all the dates of *Week 1*, from "Sun" to "Sat," then go to *Week 2* and fill in its dates, then fill in the *Week 3* dates, and so on.

Think about what the array indices must do to perform this filling operation. The *Week* index would start at *Week 1*, then the *DaysOfWeek* index would begin at "Sun" and increment through the days of the week to "Sat."   This will fill the first week.   To fill the second week, the *Week* index must be incremented to 2, with the *DaysOfWeek* index starting at "Sun" and incrementing to "Sat" all over again.   To fill the third week, the *Week* index is incremented to 3 and the *DaysOfWeek* index incremented from "Sun" to "Sat" again.   In other words, you are filling in the dates week by week, one week at a time.   Each time the *Week* index is incremented, the *DaysOfWeek* index starts at "Sun" and increments to "Sat," before the *Week* index is incremented to the next week.

Does this suggest two loops, one to increment the *Week* index and a second to increment the *DaysOfWeek* index?   Moreover, doesn't this process suggest that

DECEMBER

	Sun	Mon	Tue	Wed	Thur	Fri	Sat
Week 1			1	2	3	4	5
Week 2	6	7	8	9	10	11	12
Week 3	13	14	15	16	17	18	19
Week 4	20	21	22	23	24	25	26
Week 5	27	28	29	30	31		

Figure 8-6   December calendar.

the *DaysOfWeek* loop must be nested within the *Week* loop, since *DaysOfWeek* must run through its entire range for each *Week*?

Here's the general loop structure for inserting elements into a two-dimensional array.

LOOPING FORMAT FOR ACCESSING TWO-DIM ARRAY ELEMENTS *******************
FOR row index = lower bound **TO** upper bound **DO**
    FOR column index = lower bound **TO** upper bound **DO**
        {Assign, Read, or Write Array Elements}
****

You see that the column index loop is nested within the row index loop. Thus, the column loop runs through all its iterations for each iteration of the row loop. The actual insertion takes place within the column loop. Let's look at an example to get the idea.

Example 8-9:

Write a procedure using loops to fill the calendar array for the month of December. Write another procedure to print the calendar.

Solution: We will begin by declaring the month array as before.

```
TYPE
    Week = 1 .. 5;
    DaysOfWeek = (Sun, Mon, Tue, Wed, Thur, Fri, Sat);
    Month = ARRAY [Week, DaysOfWeek] OF integer;

VAR
    December : Month;
```

Next, we must write a procedure to fill the array with the dates for December. This procedure should do the job:

```
PROCEDURE  Fill_Month (VAR Dates : Month);

VAR
  Row : integer;
  Col : DaysOfWeek;

BEGIN
  Writeln ('Enter the dates for the month, beginning with Sunday');
  Writeln ('of the first week in the month.  If there is no date');
  Writeln ('for a given day, enter a 0.  Press the ENTER key');
  Writeln ('after each date entry.');
  Writeln;
  Writeln;
  FOR Row := 1 TO 5 DO
    BEGIN
      Writeln;
      Writeln ('Enter dates for Week ',Row, ' beginning with Sunday:');
```

(Continued)

```
      FOR Col := Sun TO Sat DO
         Readln (Dates [Row, Col])
      END  {Row for}
END;  {procedure Fill_Month}
```

The first few lines of the procedure provide a few simple directions to the user. The array filling operation takes place within the two **FOR/DO** loops. Notice that the *Row* loop is the outer loop, while the *Col* loop is the inner loop. Here's how it works: The *Row* counter begins with 1 and the *Col* counter begins with "Sun." As a result, the first date is inserted into *Dates*[1,Sun] corresponding to Sunday of week 1 in the month.

Notice that the array variable is *Dates*. How can this be, since we declared *December* as the array variable in the declaration part of the main program? Well, *December* in the main program declaration is the actual parameter for the array. It will be used when calling this procedure. However, *Dates* is the formal parameter listed in the procedure heading. As you can see, it is a variable parameter. Thus, the procedure will receive the *December* array from the main program, fill it, and return it to the main program. The reason I used a different array variable identifier (*Dates*) in the procedure is to make it more general. For example, additional array variables, such as *May, June*, and *July* could be declared in the main program to create arrays for these months. Again, these would act as actual parameters when calling the procedure. The respective month arrays (*December, May, June, July*, etc.) could then be filled separately using separate calls to this same procedure. In each case, the variable parameter *Dates* would take on the actual array parameter used in the procedure call.

Now back to the loops. After an element is read into *Dates*[1,Sun], the inner **FOR/DO** loop increments the *Col* counter to "Mon" and an element is read into *Dates*[1,Mon]. Notice that the *Row* counter remains the same. What is the next array position to be filled? You're right! *Dates*[1,Tue]. In summary, the inner *Col* loop will increment from "Sun" to "Sat" for each iteration of the outer *Row* loop. Thus, the first iteration of the outer *Row* loop will fill

Dates[1,Sun]
Dates[1,Mon]
Dates[1,Tue]
Dates[1,Wed]
Dates[1,Thur]
Dates[1,Fri]
Dates[1,Sat]

The second iteration of the outer *Row* loop will fill the second week as follows:

Dates[2,Sun]
Dates[2,Mon]
Dates[2,Tue]
Dates[2,Wed]

      Dates[2,Thur]
      Dates[2,Fri]
      Dates[2,Sat]

This filling process will continue for weeks (*Rows*) 3, 4, and 5. The looping is terminated when a value is read into the last array position, *Dates*[5,Sat].

    Now let's look at a similar procedure to display our December calendar once it has been filled. Here it is:

```
PROCEDURE  Display_Month (Dates : Month);

VAR
  Row : integer;
  Col : DaysOfWeek;

BEGIN
  Clrscr;
  Writeln ('                    DECEMBER        ');
  Writeln;
  Writeln;
  Writeln ('    Sun    Mon    Tue    Wed    Thur    Fri    Sat');
  Writeln;
  FOR Row := 1 TO 5 DO
    BEGIN
      FOR Col := Sun TO Sat DO
        Write (' ',Dates [Row, Col] : 6);
      Writeln;
      Writeln
    END   {Row for}
END;   {procedure Display_Month}


BEGIN   {main program}
  Clrscr;
  Fill_Month (December);
  Display_Month (December)
END.   {main program}
```

Again, *Dates* is the formal parameter declared in the procedure heading. However, this time it is a value parameter, since the procedure does not alter the array contents and, therefore, does not need to communicate the array back to the main program. Two local variables, *Row* and *Col*, are declared and will be used as loop counters.

    The first part of the procedure statement section simply writes the header information required for the calendar. Then the nested **FOR/DO** loops are entered to display the array contents. The basic loop structures are the same as those we discussed for the filling operation: The *Col* counter is incremented from "Sun" through "Sat" for every iteration of the *Row* loop. Thus, the array contents are displayed in a row-by-row, or week-by-week, fashion. Notice that a *Write* statement is used to display the element values. This is so that the weekly dates are displayed across the face of the screen. The *Write* statement is the only statement within the inner **FOR/DO** loop. The two single *Writeln* statements after this loop are part of the outer

(*Row*) **FOR/DO** loop.   What are they used for?   To move down the cursor two lines before displaying the next row of dates, thus providing an appropriate calendar output.

Now, putting everything together here is the entire program:

```
PROGRAM Calendar (input, output);

USES
  Crt;

TYPE
   Week = 1 .. 5;
   DaysOfWeek = (Sun, Mon, Tue, Wed, Thur, Fri, Sat);
   Month = ARRAY [Week, DaysOfWeek] OF integer;

VAR
   December : Month;


(*****************************************************************

    This procedure will fill-in the dates of the month array.

*****************************************************************)

PROCEDURE  Fill_Month (VAR Dates : Month);

VAR
  Row : integer;
  Col : DaysOfWeek;

BEGIN
  Writeln ('Enter the dates for the month, beginning with Sunday');
  Writeln ('of the first week in the month.  If there is no date');
  Writeln ('for a given day, enter a 0.  Press the ENTER key');
  Writeln ('after each date entry.');
  Writeln;
  Writeln;
  FOR Row := 1 TO 5 DO
    BEGIN
      Writeln;
      Writeln ('Enter dates for Week ', Row, ' beginning with Sunday:');
      FOR Col := Sun TO Sat DO
        Readln (Dates [Row, Col])
    END  {Row for}
END;  {procedure Fill_Month}


(*****************************************************************

        This procedure will display a monthly calendar.

*****************************************************************)

PROCEDURE  Display_Month (Dates : Month);

VAR
  Row : integer;
  Col : DaysOfWeek;

BEGIN
  Clrscr;
  Writeln ('                    DECEMBER         ');
  Writeln;
  Writeln;
  Writeln ('   Sun    Mon    Tue    Wed    Thur    Fri    Sat');
  Writeln;
```

```
   FOR Row := 1 TO 5 DO
      BEGIN
         FOR Col := Sun TO Sat DO
            Write (' ',Dates [Row, Col] : 6);
         Writeln;
         Writeln
      END  {Row for}
   END;  {procedure Display_Month}


BEGIN  {main program}
   Clrscr;
   Fill_Month (December);
   Display_Month (December)
END.  {main program}
```

Notice that the statement section of the main program is short. The main program simply clears the screen and calls the two procedures. In each procedure call, the actual array variable, *December*, is employed. As stated earlier, other monthly variables could also be declared to create additional monthly calendars. In fact, all twelve months could be declared to create a yearly calendar. To fill or display a given month, you simply use that monthly variable in the respective procedure call.

Assuming that the user executes this program and keys in the proper dates for December, the program will generate the following calendar display:

DECEMBER

Sun	Mon	Tue	Wed	Thur	Fri	Sat
0	0	1	2	3	4	5
6	7	8	9	10	11	12
13	14	15	16	17	18	19
20	21	22	23	24	25	26
27	28	29	30	31	0	0

Of course, this calendar could also be printed by inserting the *lst* command in each *Write/Writeln* statement.

Arrays of More than Two Dimensions

Arrays of more than two dimensions are required for some applications. In this text, we will only consider three-dimensional arrays, since very few applications require larger arrays.

The easiest way to picture a three-dimensional array is to imagine a cube such as that shown in Figure 8-7. Think of a cube as several two-dimensional arrays combined together to form a third dimension, depth. The cube is made up of rows (vertical dimension), columns (horizontal dimension), and planes (depth

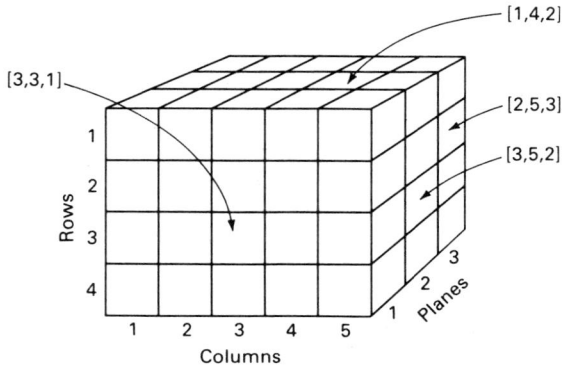

Figure 8-7   A 4 × 5 × 3 three-dimensional array.

dimension).   Thus, a given element within the cube array is located by specifying its row, column, and plane.   See if you can verify for yourself the element positions indicated in Figure 8-7.

Now let's look at a practical example of a three-dimensional array so that you can see how one is declared and accessed in Pascal.   Think of this excellent textbook as a three-dimensional array where each page of the book is a two-dimensional array made up of rows and columns.   The combined pages then form the planes within a three-dimensional array that make up the book.   Let's suppose that there are 45 lines on each page that form the rows for the array and 80 characters per line that form the columns of the array.   If there are 350 pages in the book, there are 350 planes in the array.   Thus, the book array is a 45 × 80 × 350 array. What are the array elements, and how many are there?   Well, the array elements must be characters, since characters form the words on a page.   In addition, there must be 45 × 80 × 350 = 1,260,000 of them, including blanks, since this is the size of the book in terms of rows, columns, and pages.

CAUTION ——————————————————————————————————

When you declare an array, Pascal actually sets aside enough read/write memory to store the array.   This memory is reserved exclusively for the declared array and cannot be used for other programming or system chores.   In other words, a large array "eats up" a lot of memory.   For instance, the foregoing book array contains 1,260,000 character elements. Since each character requires one byte of memory to store, Pascal will allocate about 1230K bytes of user memory for the book array.   This is much more than is available in many PC systems, and would create a "memory overflow" error during compilation.   So be careful that your arrays don't get too big for your system to store.   There are other, more memory-efficient ways to store large amounts of data.   If you're interested in exploring these techniques, I suggest that you take a course or read a book on the topic of Data Structures.

——

How might our book array be declared in Pascal?   How about this?

```
TYPE
  Line = 1 .. 45;
  Column = 1 .. 80;
  Page = 1 .. 350;
  Text_Book = ARRAY [Line, Column, Page] OF char;
VAR
  Technical_Pascal : Text_Book;
```

You should be able to understand this declaration from your work with one-and two-dimensional arrays.   There are three index ranges (*Line, Column,* and *Page*) that define the size of the *Text_Book* array.   The array data type is *char*, since the elements are characters.   Finally, the array variable is the book title, *Technical_Pascal*.   Of course, additional array variables could be used to create arrays for other books of the same general dimensions, right?   Well, theoretically yes, but just one of these book arrays would be too large for many PC systems. In many systems, the declaration would result in a "memory overflow" error when the program is compiled.

Next, how do you suppose that you might access the book information?   The easiest way is to use nested loops.   How should the loops be nested?   Although it is not critical, a logical way would be to place the page loop as the outermost loop, and the column loop as the innermost loop.   This leaves the row loop to be inserted between the page and column loops.   Translating this to our book array, you get the following:

```
FOR Plane := 1 TO 350 DO

    FOR Row := 1 TO 45 DO

        FOR Col := 1 TO 80 DO

            {Read, Write, or assign array elements}
```

Using this nesting approach, the *Col* loop is executed 80 times for each iteration of the *Row* loop, which is executed 45 times for each iteration of the *Plane* loop. Of course, the *Plane* loop is executed 350 times.   To fill or extract elements from the array, this **FOR/DO** structure would fill/extract elements one line at a time for a given page.   Notice the use of the variables *Row, Col,* and *Plane* as the loop counters.   These variables must be different from the variables (*Line, Column, Page*) used to declare the array.

EXAMPLE 8-10:

Given the foregoing *Text_Book* array declaration,
a. Write a program segment that could be used to fill the book
b. Write a program segment that could be used to print the entire book
c. Write a program segment that could be used to print page 200 of the book

Solutions:
a. Using the three foregoing nested loops, you could fill the book as follows:

```
FOR Plane := 1 TO 350 DO
    FOR Row := 1 TO 45 DO
        FOR Col := 1 TO 80 DO
            Read (Technical_Pascal[Row, Col, Plane]);
```

b. To print the contents of the book, a *Write* statement is employed in the innermost loop as follows:

```
FOR  Plane := 1 TO 350 DO
  FOR Row := 1 TO 45 DO
    BEGIN  {Row for}
      FOR Col := 1 TO 80 DO
          Write (1st. Technical_Pascal [Row. Col, Plane]);
        Writeln (1st)
    END;  {Row for}
```

Notice the single *Writeln* statement used in the middle loop to make the printer return to the beginning of the next line after a given line has been printed.

c. You only need two loops to print a given page number as follows:

```
FOR Row := 1 TO 45 DO
  BEGIN
    FOR Col := 1 TO 80 DO
        Write (1st. Technical_Pascal[Row. Col, 200]);
      Writeln (1st)
  END;
```

Observe that the *Plane* index is fixed at 200 within the *Write* statement in order to print page 200 of the book. How could this segment be modified to print any page desired by the user? (Think about it! This will be left as an exercise at the end of the chapter.)

8-4 AN APPLICATION FOR ARRAYS: SIMULTANEOUS EQUATION SOLUTION

In this section you will see how arrays can be used to perform a common task found in all branches of engineering and technology: the solution of simultaneous equations. Recall from your algebra class that a set of simultaneous equations exist when you have two or more equations with two or more common unknowns. For instance, consider the following:

$$7x - 5y = 20$$

$$-5x + 8y = -10$$

Here you have two equations and two unknowns. To solve the equations, you must find both x and y. This is impossible using just one of the equations alone but does not present a problem when both equations are solved "simultaneously," or together. One thing that you might remember from algebra class is that to solve simultaneous equations, there must be at least as many equations as there are unknowns. This is why you cannot solve for two unknowns using a single equation. However, two unknowns can be solved using two or more equations.

Determinants

A common way to solve simultaneous equations is by using determinants. You might recall from algebra that a ***determinant*** is simply a *square array*. By a square array, I mean an array that has the same number of rows and columns. Here is a simple 2 × 2 determinant:

$$\begin{vmatrix} A_1 & B_1 \\ A_2 & B_2 \end{vmatrix}$$

The elements are A_1, B_1, A_2, and B_2. (*Note:* These elements will be numeric values when we actually use determinants to solve simultaneous equations.) Notice the vertical "bars" on the left and right side of the array. These bars are used to indicate that the array is a determinant. This determinant is called a 2 × 2 determinant, since it has two rows and two columns. Determinants may also be 3 × 3, 4 × 4, 5 × 5, etc. In each case the determinant is a square array. Here is a 3 × 3 determinant:

$$\begin{vmatrix} A_1 & B_1 & C_1 \\ A_2 & B_2 & C_2 \\ A_3 & B_3 & C_3 \end{vmatrix}$$

Expansion of a Determinant

A determinant is said to be ***expanded*** when you replace the array with a single value. A 2 × 2 determinant expansion is the simplest. To get the idea, look at the diagram below:

$$\begin{matrix} \searrow & \nearrow \\ A_1 & B_1 \\ \times & = A_1B_2 - A_2B_1 \\ A_2 & B_2 \\ \nearrow & \searrow \\ & + \end{matrix}$$

Observe the arrows placed on the determinant. These arrows form the diagonals of the array. Comparing the arrows with the expansion on the right side of the equals sign, you see that the arrows indicate which elements are to be multiplied together to expand the determinant. In addition, the sign at the tip of each arrow indicates the sign of the product. As you can see, the arrow pointing up is subtracted from the arrow pointing down.

EXAMPLE 8-11:

Expand the following determinants:

a. $\begin{vmatrix} 20 & 5 \\ -10 & 8 \end{vmatrix}$

b. $\begin{vmatrix} 7 & 20 \\ -5 & -10 \end{vmatrix}$

c. $\begin{vmatrix} 7 & 5 \\ -5 & 8 \end{vmatrix}$

Solutions:

a. $\begin{vmatrix} 20 & -5 \\ -10 & 8 \end{vmatrix} = (20)(8) - (-10)(-5)$

$= 160 - (50) = 160 - 50 = 110$

b. $\begin{vmatrix} 7 & 20 \\ -5 & -10 \end{vmatrix} = (7)(-10) - (-5)(20)$

$= -70 - (-100) = -70 + 100 = 30$

c. $\begin{vmatrix} 7 & 5 \\ -5 & 8 \end{vmatrix} = (7)(8) - (-5)(5)$

$= 56 - (-25) = 56 + 25 = 81$

Expansion of a 3 × 3 determinant is a bit more challenging. Here is a general 3 × 3 determinant again:

$$\begin{vmatrix} A_1 & B_1 & C_1 \\ A_2 & B_2 & C_2 \\ A_3 & B_3 & C_3 \end{vmatrix}$$

To expand this determinant, you must rewrite the first two columns to the right of the determinant and then use the arrow (diagonal) method as follows:

$$= A_1B_2C_3 + B_1C_2A_3 + C_1A_2B_3 - A_3B_2C_1 - B_3C_2A_1 - C_3A_2B_1$$

This is called the "method of diagonals" for expanding 3×3 determinants. I should caution you, however, that the method of diagonals does not work for determinants larger than 3×3. This will not present a problem in this text, since we will not need to use larger determinants.

EXAMPLE 8-12:

Expand the following 3×3 determinant:

$$\begin{vmatrix} 6 & -2 & -4 \\ 15 & -2 & -5 \\ -4 & -5 & 12 \end{vmatrix}$$

Solutions: Rewriting the first two columns to the right of the determinant and forming the diagonals you get

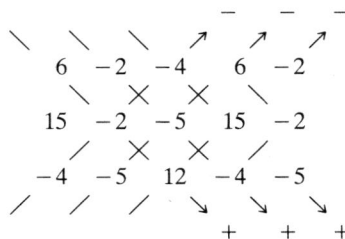

Now, multiplying the diagonal elements and applying the appropriate sign you get

$$+ \ (6)(-2)(12) \ + \ (-2)(-5)(-4) \ + \ (-4)(15)(-5)$$

$$- \ (-4)(-2)(-4) \ - \ (-5)(-5)(6) \ - \ (12)(15)(-2)$$

Finally, performing the required arithmetic gives you

$$+ \ (-144) \ + \ (-40) \ + \ (300)$$

$$- \ (-32) \ - \ (150) \ - \ (-360)$$

$$= \ -144 \ - \ 40 \ + \ 300 \ + \ 32 \ - \ 150 \ + \ 360$$

$$= \ 358$$

As you can see from the above example, expanding a 3×3 determinant can get a bit tricky! You have to pay particular attention to the signs. One simple sign error during your arithmetic will result in an incorrect expansion. Wouldn't it be nice if a computer program could be written to perform the expansion? This is an ideal application for a Pascal function, since the expansion operation returns a single value.

A 2 × 2 Determinant Expansion Function

Let's write a Pascal function to expand a 2×2 determinant. We will assume that the elements in the determinant are stored in a 2×2 array called *Determinant*.

This array must be passed to the function, then the function must evaluate the array and return a single expansion value. Here is the function heading:

```
FUNCTION  Expand (K : Determinant) : real;
```

The function name is *Expand*. The formal parameter is a value parameter, *K*. It is of type *Determinant*, since this is the array name that will be declared in the main program. The data type of the returned expansion value is real. Let's assume that the 2 × 2 *Determinant* array has row indices of 1 and 2, and column indices of 1 and 2. Here is the array showing the row/column indices layout:

$$\begin{vmatrix} [1,1] & [1,2] \\ [2,1] & [2,2] \end{vmatrix}$$

Remember that these are only the array indices and not the elements stored in the array. Now recall that to expand the determinant, the up diagonal must be subtracted from the down diagonal. Thus, the product of indices [2,1] and [1,2] must be subtracted from the product of [1,1] and [2,2]. Using this idea in our function, we get a single statement as follows:

```
Expand := (K[1,1] * K[2,2]) - (K[2,1] * K[1,2]);
```

That's all there is to it! Here is the complete function:

```
FUNCTION  Expand (K : Determinant) : real;

BEGIN
   Expand := (K[1,1] * K[2,2]) - (K[2,1] * K[1,2])
END;
```

Writing a function to expand a 3 × 3 determinant will be left as an exercise at the end of the chapter.

Cramer's Rule

Cramer's rule allows you to solve simultaneous equations using determinants. Let's begin with two equations and two unknowns.

I will define an equation to be in **standard form** when all the variables are on the left-hand side of the equals sign and the constant term is on the right-hand side of the equals sign. Here is a general two-variable equation in standard form:

$$Ax + By = C$$

This equation has two variables, *x* and *y*. The *x* coefficient is *A* and the *y* coefficient is *B*. The constant is *C*.

Here is a set of two general simultaneous equations in standard form:

$$\text{Equation 1: } A_1x + B_1y = C_1$$

$$\text{Equation 2: } A_2x + B_2y = C_2$$

The common variables between the two equations are x and y. The subscripts 1 and 2 denote the coefficients and constants of equations 1 and 2, respectively. Cramer's rule allows you to solve for x and y using determinants like this:

$$x = \frac{\begin{vmatrix} C_1 & B_1 \\ C_2 & B_2 \end{vmatrix}}{\begin{vmatrix} A_1 & B_1 \\ A_2 & B_2 \end{vmatrix}} \qquad y = \frac{\begin{vmatrix} A_1 & C_1 \\ A_2 & C_2 \end{vmatrix}}{\begin{vmatrix} A_1 & B_1 \\ A_2 & B_2 \end{vmatrix}}$$

As you can see, the determinants are *formed* using the coefficients and constants from the two equations. Do you see a pattern? First, look at the denominator determinants. They are identical and are formed using the x and y coefficients directly from the two equations. However, the numerator determinants are different. When solving for x, the numerator determinant is formed by replacing the x coefficients with the constant terms. When solving for y, the numerator determinant is formed by replacing the y coefficients with the constant terms. Here's an example.

EXAMPLE 8-13:

Solve the following set of simultaneous equations using Cramer's rule:

$$7x - 5y = 20$$

$$-5x + 8y = -10$$

Solution: Forming the required determinants you get

$$x = \frac{\begin{vmatrix} 20 & -5 \\ -10 & 8 \end{vmatrix}}{\begin{vmatrix} 7 & -5 \\ -5 & 8 \end{vmatrix}} \qquad y = \frac{\begin{vmatrix} 7 & 20 \\ -5 & -10 \end{vmatrix}}{\begin{vmatrix} 7 & -5 \\ -5 & 8 \end{vmatrix}}$$

Expanding the determinants and dividing gives you x and y:

$$x = \frac{(20)(8) - (-10)(-5)}{(7)(8) - (-5)(-5)} \qquad y = \frac{(7)(-10) - (-5)(20)}{(7)(8) - (-5)(-5)}$$

$$x = \frac{110}{31} \qquad\qquad y = \frac{30}{31}$$

$$x = 3.55 \qquad\qquad y = 0.97$$

Implementing Cramer's Rule in Pascal

Think about the "procedures" that you just went through using Cramer's rule to solve the set of simultaneous equations. There are three major tasks to be performed:

Task 1: Obtain the equation coefficients and constants.
Task 2: Form the determinants: both numerator and denominator.
Task 3: Expand the determinants.

We have already developed a function to perform the third task. We must now develop Pascal procedures to accomplish the first two tasks. Functions are not appropriate here, since we are not returning single values to the calling program.

To perform task 1, we must write a procedure that will obtain the coefficients and constants of the equations to be solved. There are two equations and three items (two coefficients and a constant) that must be obtained from each equation. Does this suggest any particular data structure? Of course, a 2 × 3 array! So let's write a procedure to fill a 2 × 3 array from coefficient and constant terms of the two equations that will be entered by the user. Here it is:

```
PROCEDURE Fill (VAR A : Equations);

VAR
  Row, Col : integer;

BEGIN
  FOR Row := 1 TO 2 DO
    BEGIN
      Writeln;
      Write ('Enter the variable coefficients and constant');
      Writeln (' for equation ',Row, ':');
      Writeln    ('(Note:  The equation must be in standard form.)');
      Writeln;
      FOR Col := 1 TO 3 DO
        BEGIN
          IF  Col = 3 THEN
            Write ('Enter the constant term:   ')
          ELSE
            Write ('Enter the coefficient for variable ',Col,':   ');
          Readln (A[Row,Col]);
          Writeln
        END  {Col for}
    END;  {Row for}
END;  {procedure Fill}
```

Such a procedure should be nothing new to you, since it simply employs nested **FOR/DO** loops to fill an array. The procedure name is *Fill*. It fills an array called *Equations* that must be declared as a 2 × 3 array in the main program declaration section.   The array will be passed to the procedure by variable using the variable parameter *A*.   Thus, once the procedure fills the array, it is passed back to the main program.

Given the following two general equations in standard form,

$$\text{Equation 1: } A_1 x + B_1 y = C_1$$

$$\text{Equation 2: } A_2 x + B_2 y = C_2$$

the procedure will fill the 2 × 3 array as follows:

$$A_1 \quad B_1 \quad C_1$$

$$A_2 \quad B_2 \quad C_2$$

As you can see, the first equation coefficients and constant term are inserted into the first row of the array.   The second row of the array stores the coefficients and constant term of the second equation.   Of course, the procedure assumes that the user will enter the coefficients and constants in their proper order.

To accomplish task 2, we must develop a procedure to form the determinants from the equation coefficients and constants.   How can we obtain the coefficients and constants?   You're right—from the 2 × 3 array that was just filled!   Now, how many unique determinants does Cramer's rule require to solve two equations and two unknowns?   Three: a numerator determinant for the x unknown, a numerator determinant for the y unknown, and a denominator determinant that is the same for both the x and y unknowns.   All the determinants must be 2 × 2, right?

So, our procedure must obtain the single 2 × 3 array that was filled with coefficients and constants in the *Fill* procedure and then generate three 2 × 2 arrays that will form the two numerator and one denominator determinants required by Cramer's rule.   Here's the procedure:

```
PROCEDURE Form_Det (A : Equations; VAR N1, N2, D : Determinant);

VAR
   Row, Col : integer;

BEGIN
    N1[1,1] := A[1,3];
    N1[1,2] := A[1,2];
    N1[2,1] := A[2,3];
    N1[2,2] := A[2,2];

    N2[1,1] := A[1,1];
    N2[1,2] := A[1,3];
    N2[2,1] := A[2,1];
    N2[2,2] := A[2,3];
```

(*Continued*)

```
      FOR Row := 1 TO 2 DO
        FOR Col := 1 TO 2 DO
           D[Row,Col] := A[Row,Col]
   END;
```

First, look at the procedure heading. The procedure name is *Form_Det*. There are four parameters: *A*, *N1*, *N2*, and *D*. The parameter *A* is a value parameter. Its type is *Equations*, which is the 2×3 array containing the coefficients and constants from the *Fill* procedure. There are three variable parameters: *N1*, *N2*, and *D*. The *N1* parameter represents the numerator determinant for the *x* unknown. The *N2* parameter represents the numerator determinant for the *y* unknown. The *D* parameter represents the denominator determinant for both the *x* and *y* unknowns. These three parameters are of type *Determinant*, which must be declared as a 2×2 array in the main program. Furthermore, *N1*, *N2*, and *D* are variable parameters, since the resulting determinants must be passed back to the main program.

Now look at the statement section of the procedure. The two numerator determinants (*N1* and *N2*) are formed using direct assignments. The formation pattern results from Cramer's rule. The denominator determinant (*D*) is formed using nested **FOR/DO** loops. Notice that in all instances the determinants are formed using the elements from the 2×3 array (*A*) of coefficients and constants generated by the *Fill* procedure.

Now we have all the ingredients for a Pascal program that will solve two equations and two unknowns using Cramer's rule. Combining our *Fill* procedure, our *Form_Det* procedure, and our *Expand* function into a single program, we get the following:

```
PROGRAM Solve_Two_Equations (input, output);

USES
  Crt;

TYPE
   Equations = ARRAY [1..2,1..3] OF real;
   Determinant = ARRAY [1..2,1..2] OF real;

VAR
   Equ : Equations;
   Num1, Num2, Denom : Determinant;



{************************************************************

This procedure will fill an array with the equation coefficients.

************************************************************}
```

```
PROCEDURE Fill (VAR A : Equations);

VAR
  Row, Col : integer;

BEGIN
  FOR Row := 1 TO 2 DO
    BEGIN
      Writeln;
      Write ('Enter the variable coefficients and constant');
      Writeln (' for equation ',Row, ':');
      Writeln   ('(Note:  The equation must be in standard form.)');
      Writeln;
      FOR Col := 1 TO 3 DO
        BEGIN
          IF  Col = 3 THEN
            Write ('Enter the constant term:  ')
          ELSE
            Write ('Enter the coefficient for variable ',Col,':  ');
          Readln (A[Row,Col]);
          Writeln
        END  {Col for}
    END;  {Row for}
END;  {procedure Fill}


{*****************************************************************

          This procedure will form the determinants.

*****************************************************************}

PROCEDURE Form_Det (A : Equations; VAR N1, N2, D : Determinant);

VAR
  Row, Col : integer;

BEGIN
  N1[1,1] := A[1,3];
  N1[1,2] := A[1,2];
  N1[2,1] := A[2,3];
  N1[2,2] := A[2,2];

  N2[1,1] := A[1,1];
  N2[1,2] := A[1,3];
  N2[2,1] := A[2,1];
  N2[2,2] := A[2,3];

  FOR Row := 1 TO 2 DO
    FOR Col := 1 TO 2 DO
      D[Row,Col] := A[Row,Col]
END;
```

(Continued)

```
{**************************************************************

        This function will expand a 2x2 determinant.

**************************************************************}

FUNCTION  Expand (K : Determinant) : real;

BEGIN
  Expand := K[1,1] * K[2,2] - K[2,1] * K[1,2]
END;

BEGIN  {main program}
  Clrscr;
  Writeln ('This program will solve two simultaneous equations.');
  Writeln;
  Writeln;
  Fill(Equ);
  Form_Det (Equ,Num1,Num2,Denom);
  Writeln;
  Writeln;
  Write ('The value of the first variable is:   ');
  Writeln  (Expand(Num1) / Expand(Denom):5:2);
  Writeln;
  Write ('The value of the second variable is:   ');
  Writeln (Expand(Num2) / Expand(Denom):5:2)
END.
```

Observe the declaration section of the main program. Here is where the two arrays (*Equations* and *Determinant*) are declared. *Equations* is a 2×3 array that will store the coefficients and constants of the two equations. *Determinant* is a 2×2 array that will be used to form the required determinants. A single variable (*Equ*) is declared for the *Equations* array, and three variables (*Num1*, *Num2*, and *Denom*) are declared for the *Determinant* array. Three variables are declared for the *Determinant* array, since three separate 2×2 determinants must be formed.

You find our *Fill* and *Form_Det* procedures along with our *Expand* function placed in the declaration section of the main program. These are the procedures and function that we just developed.

Now look at the statement section of the main program. The *Fill* procedure is called first to obtain the coefficient and constant terms of the two equations. The actual parameter used for the procedure call is *Equ*. Next, the *Form_Det* procedure is called to form the required determinants. The actual parameters used in this procedure call are *Equ, Num1, Num2*, and *Denom*. The *Equu* parameter is required to pass the 2×3 array to the procedure. The *Num1, Num2*, and *Denom* parameters are required to receive the three determinants back from the procedure.

Finally, look at how the *Expand* function is invoked. It is invoked twice to calculate the first unknown (*x*) within a *Writeln* statement as follows: *Ex-*

pand(*Num1*) / *Expand*(*Denom*).   This expands the numerator determinant for the *x* unknown (*Num1*), expands the common denominator determinant (*Denom*), and divides the two to obtain the value of the first unknown (*x*).   The function is called twice again in a second *Writeln* statement to find the second unknown (*y*).

Given the following two equations,

$$7x - 5y = 20$$

$$-5x + 8y = -10$$

here is what you would see when the program is executed:

```
Enter the variable coefficients and constant for equation 1:
(Note:  The equation must be in standard form.)

Enter the coefficient for variable 1:  7

Enter the coefficient for variable 2:  -5

Enter the constant term:  20


Enter the variable coefficients and constant for equation 2:
(Note:  The equation must be in standard form.)

Enter the coefficient for variable 1:  -5

Enter the coefficient for variable 2:  8

Enter the constant term:  -10


The value of the first variable is:  3.5484

The value of the second variable is:  0.9677
```

Do you think that you could develop a similar program to solve a set of three simultaneous equations?   You now have all the required knowledge.   (Guess what you will be doing in the programming exercises at the end of the chapter?)

CHAPTER SUMMARY

In this chapter you learned how user-defined data types can be employed in your Pascal programs to make them more understandable and applications oriented. A user-defined data type is simply a set of elements that you, the programmer, declare using a **TYPE** declaration.

Aside from declaring user-defined data, the **TYPE** declaration is also used to declare subranges for both standard data types and user-defined data types. A subrange of a given data type is simply a subset of that type defined by a lower bound and an upper bound.

An array is an important structured data type used to locate and store elements of a given data type. The two components of any array are the elements that are stored in the array and the indices that locate the stored elements. Array elements can be any data type, and array indices can be any data type except real.

There are both one-dimensional and multidimensional arrays. A one-dimensional array, or list, is a single row of elements. It has dimensions of $1 \times n$, where n is the number of elements in the list. A two-dimensional array, or table, is a combination of two or more element rows. It has dimensions of $m \times n$, where m is the number of rows in the array and n is the number of array columns. A three-dimensional array is the combination of two or more two-dimensional arrays. It is comprised of rows, columns, and planes. Thus, a three-dimensional array has dimensions of $m \times n \times k$, where m is the number of array rows, n is the number of columns, and k is the number of planes in the array.

Arrays are declared using a combination **TYPE/VAR** declaration. The array name, size, and element data type are declared using the **TYPE** declaration. The array variable(s) is declared using the **VAR** declaration. To access the array elements, you must use direct assignment statements, read/write statements, or loops. The **FOR/DO** loop structure is the most common way of accessing multiple array elements. A separate **FOR/DO** loop is required for each array dimension. In addition, the loops must be nested when accessing multidimensional arrays.

There are many technical applications for arrays. One of the most common uses of an array is to store determinants that are used to solve systems of simultaneous equations using Cramer's rule.

QUESTIONS AND PROBLEMS

Questions

8-1. User-defined data are declared using the reserved word ＿＿＿＿＿＿＿＿＿＿＿.

8-2. Where must user-defined data types be located in a Pascal program?

8-3. Write declarations for the following user-defined data types. Make sure to provide an appropriate variable to go along with each data type.

   a. *This_Semester_Courses*, consisting of the courses you are taking this semester.

   b. *Resistor_Color_Code*, consisting of the colors of the resistor color code in their proper order.

   c. *Major_Courses*, consisting of the courses required in your major program.

   d. *My_Family*, consisting of all the members of your immediate family.

8-4. Write subrange declarations for the following. Make sure that you have declared the entire range before declaring a subrange if the data are not part of a standard data type.

    a. *Weekdays* and *Weekends*, each consisting of those days of the week that occur in these respective periods.

    b. *Spring, Summer, Fall*, and *Winter*, each consisting of those months that make up these respective seasons.

    c. *Percent_Score*, consisting of percentages 0 through 100.

    d. *LowerCase*, consisting of the lowercase letters of the alphabet.

8-5. Given the following declarations;

```
TYPE
   Colors = (Blue, Green, Yellow, Red, Orange);

VAR
   Color : Colors;
```

which of the following are TRUE and which are FALSE?

    a. Blue < Yellow

    b. Red > Orange

    c. (Green < Yellow) **AND** (Yellow > Blue)

    d. (Yellow > Orange) **OR** (Yellow > Blue)

8-6. Using the declaration in question 8-5, which of the following are valid statements? Explain why a particular statement is not valid.

    a. `Color := Purple;`

    b. `Colors := Red;`

    c. `Color := Blue + Green;`

    d. `Read (Color);`

    e. `Blue := Yellow + 2;`

8-7. What three things must be specified in order to declare an array?

Use the following array declarations to answer questions 8-8 through 8-18.

```
TYPE
   Semester_Scores = ARRAY [1..10] OF real;

VAR
   Score : Semester_Scores;



TYPE
   Voltage = -5 .. 5;
   Current =  0 .. 10;
   DC_Power = ARRAY [Voltage, Current] OF real;
```

(Continued)

```
VAR
  Power : DC_Power;


TYPE
  Cube = ARRAY [-3 .. 3, 0 .. 3, 1 .. 3] OF Boolean;

VAR
  Item : Cube;


TYPE
  Colors = (Brown, Black, Red, Orange, Yellow,
            Green, Blue, Violet, Gray, White);

  Color_Code = ARRAY [Colors, Colors, Colors] OF real;

VAR
  Value : Color_Code;
```

8-8. Sketch a diagram of each array structure showing its indices.

8-9. List the identifiers that must be used to access each array.

8-10. What are the dimensions of each array?

8-11. How many elements will each array store?

8-12. List all the possible element values for the *Cube* array.

8-13. Write a Pascal statement that will display the element in the fourth row and second column of the *DC_Power* array.

8-14. Write a Pascal statement that will assign any legal element to the second row and last column of the *DC_Power* array.

8-15. Write a Pascal statement that will print the element values in the third row, second column, and third plane of the *Cube* and *Color_Code* arrays.

8-16. Assuming that the purpose of the *Color_Code* array is to store all the possible resistor color-code values, write Pascal statements that will insert the proper resistor values for the following color-code combinations:
  a. Brown, Black, Red
  b. Brown, Black, Green
  c. Yellow, Violet, Red
  d. Red, Red, Red

8-17. Write the Pascal code required to fill each array from keyboard entries.

8-18. Write the Pascal code required to display each array, and include appropriate table headings.

Programming Problems

8-1. Write a short program to declare a user-defined data type of your choice. Insert statements to try to read and write the value of a variable of your user-defined data type. Explain what happens when the program is compiled.

8-2. Write a program to read a list of twenty-five elements from a keyboard input and display them in reverse order.

8-3. Write a program to read fifteen elements from the keyboard and store them in a 3 × 5 array. Once the elements have been read, display them as a 5 × 3 array. (*Hint:* Reverse the rows and columns.)

8-4. Write a procedure that will display any given page of the book array used in Example 8-10. Assume that the user will input the page number to be displayed.

8-5. Write a program that will store the state table for a 4-bit decade (BCD) counter. Write procedures to fill and display the state table.

8-6. Write a program that employs two procedures to fill and print a calendar for the current month.

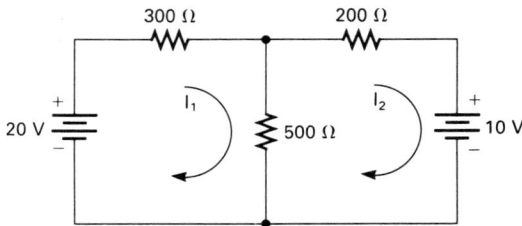

Figure 8-8   A two-loop circuit for problem 8-7.

Employ the *Solve_Two_Equations* program developed in Section 8-4 to solve problems 8-7 through 8-9. Modify the program to meet the given application.

8-7. Solve for the two loop currents, I_1 and I_2, in Figure 8-8. Assume that the user will write the two loop equations and enter the respective coefficients and constant terms via the keyboard.

8-8. Look at the lever in Figure 8-9. If you know one of the weights and all the distances of the weights from the fulcrum, you can calculate the other two weights using two simultaneous equations. The two equations have the following general form:

$$w_1 d_1 + w_2 d_2 = w_3 d_3$$

where w_1, w_2, w_3 are three weights
d_1, d_2, d_3 are the distances the three weights are located from the fulcrum

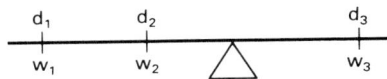

Figure 8-9   A lever/fulcrum arrangement for problem 8-8.

Using the above general equation format, you get two equations by knowing two balance points. Suppose that weight w_3 is 5 lb and that you obtain a balance condition for the following distance values:

Balance Point 1: $d_1 = 5$ in
$d_2 = 4$ in
$d_3 = 30$ in

Balance Point 2: d_1 = 3 in
d_2 = 6 in
d_3 = 36 in

Find the two unknown weights, w_1 and w_2.

8-9. The following equations describe the tension, in pounds, of two cables supporting an object. Find the amount of tension on each cable (T_1 and T_2).

$$0.5T_2 + 0.93T_1 - 120 = 0$$

$$0.42T_1 - 0.54T_2 = 0$$

8-10. Write a procedure to fill a 3 × 4 array with the coefficients and constant terms from three simultaneous equations expressed in standard form. Assume that the user will enter the array elements in the required order.

8-11. Write a procedure to display the equation array in problem 8-10.

8-12. Using Cramer's rule, write a procedure to form 3 × 3 determinants from the 3 × 4 equation array you filled in problem 8-10.

8-13. Write a function to expand a 3 × 3 determinant using the diagonal method.

8-14. Employ the procedures and function you developed in problems 8-10 through 8-13 to write a program that will solve a set of three simultaneous equations.

8-15. Use the program in problem 8-14 to solve the three loop currents (I_1, I_2, and I_3) in the Wheatstone bridge circuit shown in Figure 8-10. Assume that the user will write the loop equations and enter the required loop equation coefficients and constant terms.

8-16. Suppose the perimeter of a triangle is 14 inches. The shortest side is half as long as the longest side and 2 inches more than the difference of the two longer sides. Find the length of each side using the program you developed in problem 8-14.

8-17. Write a program that employs procedures to fill and print a calendar for the current year. (*Hint:* Declare a three-dimensional year array, as follows:

```
TYPE
  Months = (Jan,Feb,Mar,Apr,May,June,July,Aug,Sept,Oct,Nov,Dec);
  Week = 1 .. 5;
  DaysOfWeek = (Sun, Mon, Tue, Wed, Thur, Fri, Sat);
  Year = ARRAY [Months, Week, DaysOfWeek] OF integer;

VAR
  This_Year : Year;
```

Then write procedures to fill and display the array. Remember, these procedures must employ three nested loops, one for each dimension.)

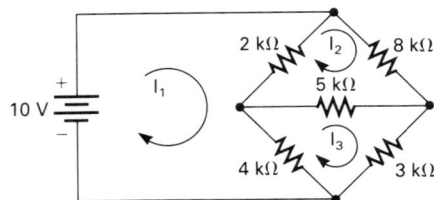

Figure 8-10 A three-loop Wheatstone Bridge circuit for Problem 8-15.

8-18. Assume that the array in the following table represents the monthly rental price of six resort cabins over a five-year period:

		YEAR				
		1983	1984	1985	1986	1987
	1	200	210	225	300	235
	2	250	275	300	350	400
CABIN	3	300	325	375	400	450
	4	215	225	250	250	275
	5	355	380	400	404	415
	6	375	400	425	440	500

Write a program that employs procedures and functions to perform the following tasks:

- Fill a two-dimensional array with information from the table.
- Compute the total rental income for each cabin by year and store the yearly totals in a second array.
- Compute the percentage increase/decrease in price between adjacent years for each cabin and store the percentages in a third array.
- Print a report showing all three arrays in table form with appropriate row and column headings.

chapter nine

Records

INTRODUCTION

The second important data structure that you need to learn about is the *record.* Like an array, a record is a structured data type, meaning that it provides a well-organized, convenient means of storing data. In many programming languages, such as BASIC and FORTRAN, the only structured data type available is the array. Recall that when you declare an array, you must specify the number of elements it contains (its dimensions) and the data type of the elements. The idea that all the elements must be the same data type is a serious limitation of an array. For instance, suppose an academic application requires a data structure for storing student information. Such information might include the student's name, student number, GPA, year enrolled, and whether or not the student has graduated. This information is composed of a variety of unique data types. As a result, an array would not be a suitable structure for this application. Fortunately, Pascal provides the record data type, which permits information of different data types to be conveniently stored, accessed, and manipulated.

In this chapter you will learn how to declare and access records. In addition, you will learn how to create very powerful complex data structures by building arrays of records.

9-1 RECORD STRUCTURE AND DECLARATION

A record is nothing more than a collection of fields.   Recall that a field is simply an item of meaningful data.   For example, the string of characters that form your name is a field, the collection of numbers that form your student number is a field, and the collection of numbers and the decimal point that form your GPA is a field. Thus, a student record might consist of a collection of student-related fields as follows:

STUDENT RECORD

Field identifier	Field data type
Name	A string of 25 characters
Student-Number	An integer value
GPA	A real value
Year-Enrolled	An integer value
Graduated	A Boolean value

Notice that each field within the record is a unique data type, whereas the collection of all the fields (the record) represents different data types.

A record can contain any number of fields, with each field having a unique name, called the *field identifier*.   Thus, the field identifiers in the above record are *Name, Student_Number, GPA, Year_Enrolled*, and *Graduated*.

Now that you have an idea of the structure of a simple record, you are ready to learn how to declare records in Pascal.

Declaring Records

Like an array, a record is a user-defined data structure that must be declared in Pascal using the **TYPE** declaration.   Here's the format:

RECORD DECLARATION FORMAT ***

TYPE
   record identifier = **RECORD**
                    field 1 identifier : field 1 data type;
                    field 2 identifier : field 2 data type;
                         ⋮
                    field n identifier : field n data type
              END; {record definition}
VAR
   record variable identifier : record identifier;

****

As you can see, the record declaration in Pascal literally shows that the record is a collection of individual fields, each identified by its field identifier and data type. Like an array, a record declaration is a two-part declaration: (1) a **TYPE** declaration that defines the record, and (2) a **VAR** declaration that defines a variable that will be used to access the record.

Under the **TYPE** declaration, you must first list the record identifier, or name. The identifier can be any valid identifier but should be descriptive of the record meaning. The record identifier is followed by an equals symbol (=), which is followed by the reserved word **RECORD**.

The individual fields are then defined using an indentation scheme below the reserved word **RECORD**. Here are some things that you will want to remember about the field definitions:

- Each field within the record must have a unique identifier. However, a given field identifier may be used again in another record declaration.
- A data type must be specified for each field. All the scalar and structured data types discussed so far are legal. Thus, a field can be an integer, a real, a char, a string, a Boolean, an array, or a user-defined data type. Of course, if a field data type is an array or user-defined data type, the array or user-defined data type must be declared prior to the record declaration.
- Fields of the same data type can be listed on the same line. Thus, the declaration

```
Mailing_List = RECORD
                 Name, Address : STRING [25];
                 Zip : integer
               END;
```

is a legal declaration. Notice that both the *Name* and *Address* fields are defined on the same line as a string data type.

The record **TYPE** declaration is concluded with the reserved word **END**. Observe that there is *no* corresponding **BEGIN,** since the record field definitions naturally begin with the reserved word **RECORD**. This is the second "case" in which an **END** is used without a corresponding **BEGIN.**

Like an array, a record is accessed using a variable that must be declared using the **VAR** declaration. Thus, each record declaration must include a variable declaration for that record. The variable is listed beneath the reserved word **VAR,** followed by a colon and the corresponding record identifier. You must use the same record identifier, or name, that you used under the **TYPE** declaration for that record. Clearly, the variable identifier must be different from the record identifier. Now let's declare some records.

Example 9-1:

Declare the following records:

a. A student record, consisting of the student's name, student number, year enrolled, GPA, and whether or not the student has graduated.

b. An automobile record, consisting of the automobile year, color (blue, black, yellow, red, or green), and price. Make provision for using this same record for a Ford, a Chevrolet, or a Chrysler.

c. A weather record, consisting of the date, temperature, barometric pressure, and conditions. Assume that there are three reportable conditions: clear, cloudy, and rain. Make provision for using this record for storing morning, afternoon, evening, and night weather information.

Solutions:

a. **TYPE**

```
Students = RECORD
              Name : STRING [25];
              Student_Number : integer;
              Year_Enrolled : integer;
              GPA : real;
              Graduated : Boolean
           END;
```

VAR
```
   Student : Students;
```

This record declaration is straightforward. The record identifier is *Students*, which contains five fields: *Name, Student_Number, Year_ Enrolled, GPA*, and *Graduated*. Observe that the *Student_Number* and *Year_Enrolled* fields are both integer data types but are defined on separate lines. They could be listed on the same line, but many software engineers prefer to use separate line definitions for clarity and program readability. Why is the *Graduated* field a Boolean field?

Finally, notice that the record variable is *Student*, which is different from the record identifier *Students*.

b. **TYPE**

```
Colors = (Blue, Black, Yellow, Red, Green);

Automobiles = RECORD
                 Year : integer;
                 Color : Colors;
                 Price : real
              END;
```

VAR
```
   Ford, Chevy, Chrysler : Automobiles;
```

You see two different twists in this record declaration. First, the user-defined data type *Colors* is used as the data type of the *Color* field. Thus, the automobile color can be blue, black, yellow, red, or green. Of course, the user-defined data type *Colors* must be declared prior to the record declaration.

Second, you see that the record has three variables: *Ford, Chevy*, and *Chrysler*. Like an array, different variables for the same record will create a separate record for each variable. Thus, three separate records can be stored in memory, one for each record variable.

c. **TYPE**

```
    Conditions = (Clear, Cloudy, Rain);
      Weather = RECORD
                   Date : STRING [15];
                   Temperature : real;
                   Pressure : real;
                   Condition : Conditions
                 END;
    VAR
      Morning, Afternoon, Evening, Night : Weather;
```

Here again, a user-defined data type is employed for the weather *Condition* field. In addition, four record variables are declared so that a separate weather record can be stored for morning, afternoon, evening, and night

9-2 RECORD ACCESS

When accessing a record, you will either store information into the record or retrieve information from the record. Of course, you are actually accessing the fields that make up the record when storing or retrieving record data.

Storing Information into Records

There are basically two ways to store information into a record: by using an assignment operation or by using a **WITH/DO** operation. As you will see, the **WITH/DO** operation is the most efficient when storing information into several fields within the record.

Assignment

When assigning information to a record, you must assign the information directly to the respective field within the record. How can you access a given field? Well, think about the record declaration. How do you access the record itself? By using the record variable right? Next, how do you suppose that you would access a given field within the record? Of course, by using its field identifier! So, the *path* to a given field within the record is via the record variable and the respective field identifier.

Consider the *Students* record in Example 9-1a. Suppose that you wish to store a name in the *Name* field. Ask yourself, What path must I take to get to the name field? Well, you must use the record variable, *Student*, to get to the record and the field identifier, *Name*, to get to the required field within the record.

Here's the required Pascal syntax:

ASSIGNMENT FORMAT (STORING RECORD INFORMATION) ∗∗∗∗∗∗∗∗∗∗∗∗∗∗∗∗∗∗∗∗∗∗∗∗∗∗∗∗

record variable identifier . field identifier : = data;

∗∗

Notice that the record variable identifier is listed first, followed by a dot, or period (.), followed by the required field identifier, an assignment symbol (: =), and the data to be stored.   Here are just a few examples of how you might store information into the records declared in Example 9-1.

```
Student . Name := 'Blaise Pascal';

Student . Graduated := TRUE;

Ford . Color := Yellow;

Chevy . Year := 1957;

Morning . Pressure := 30.02;

Afternoon . Condition := Clear;
```

As you can see, the "dot" notation provides a path directly to the field in which the information is to be stored.   One final point: The data being stored in a given field must be the same data type that has been declared for that field.   If not, a "DATA TYPE MISMATCH" error will occur when compiling the program. Thus, the following assignment would cause a data-type mismatch error (Why?):

```
Student . Graduated := 1643;
```

Using the **WITH/DO** Statement

The **WITH/DO** statement is specifically designed for record access in Pascal. It makes your coding much more efficient as compared with assignment.   For instance, suppose that you wish to fill the *Students* record declared in Example 9-1a.   Using assignment, such an operation would go something like this:

```
Student . Name := 'Blaise Pascal';

Student . Student_Number := 0001;

Student . Year_Enrolled := 1640;

Student . GPA := 4.00;

Student . Graduated := TRUE;
```

(Continued)

Notice how the record variable (*Student*) must be repeated for each assignment. This repetition can be eliminated using the **WITH/DO** statement. Here's the general format:

WITH/DO FORMAT FOR STORING INFORMATION INTO RECORDS ★★★★★★★★★★★★★★★★★★★★★

WITH record variable identifier **DO**
  BEGIN
    field identifier 1 := data;
    field identifier 2 := data;

         .
         .

    field identifier n := data
END;

★★★

So, using the **WITH/DO** statement, the *Students* record could be filled like this:

```
WITH Student DO
  BEGIN
    Name := 'Blaise Pascal';
    Student_Number := 0001;
    Year_Enrolled := 1640;
    GPA := 4.00;
    Graduated := TRUE
  END;
```

Observe the syntax. The record variable is listed between the reserved words **WITH** and **DO.** The **WITH/DO** assignment statements must *always* be framed with the words **BEGIN** and **END.** (It is a common source of error to forget this framing requirement.) Information is then assigned directly to the respective field identifiers of the record. Do you see how this method requires less coding than the assignment method when accessing multiple record fields?

You can also use a single **WITH/DO** statement to access several records. For instance, you can store information into the *Students* and *Automobiles* records using a single **WITH/DO** statement, like this:

```
WITH Student, Chevy DO
  BEGIN
    Name := 'Blaise Pascal';
    Year_Enrolled := 1640;
    Year := 1957;
    Price := 3495.39
  END;
```

As you can see, both record variables are listed in the statement heading, separated by a comma. With most systems, you can access up to nine records using a single **WITH/DO** statement. Of course, all the respective record variables must be listed in the statement heading.

There is one thing that you will want to watch when accessing multiple records in this way. If two or more records have a common field identifier, you will get an error. When this is the case, you are forced to use multiple **WITH/DO** statements.

Reading Information into a Record

Now suppose that you want the user to input the information into the record via the system keyboard. When this is desired, you simply insert the appropriate user prompts and *Read/Readln* statements within the **WITH/DO** statement. As an example, suppose that the user must input information into the *Students* record declared in Example 9-1a. Here's a statement that will do the job:

```
WITH Student DO
  BEGIN
    Write ('Enter student name ---> ');
    Readln (Name);
    Write ('Enter student number ---> ');
    Readln (Number);
    Write ('Enter year enrolled ---> ');
    Readln (Year_Enrolled);
    Write ('Enter grade point average ---> ');
    Readln (GPA);
    Write ('Has the student graduated? (Y/N) ---> ');
    Readln (Answer);
    CASE Answer OF
      'y','Y' : Graduated := TRUE;
      'n','N' : Graduated := FALSE
    END   {case}
  END;   {with}
```

As you can see, once the record variable is referenced on the first line, the field information is read into the record using *Readln* statements and the respective field identifiers. Why is the **CASE** statement required to read the *Graduated* field? Recall that Boolean data cannot be entered directly from the keyboard. Thus, a **CASE** statement is employed to make the correct Boolean assignment to the *Graduated* field. Of course, the variable *Answer* must be declared as a character variable in the declaration section of the program.

Retrieving Information from Records

You can retrieve record information using assignment or *Write/Writeln* statements. Here's the general format for both:

RETRIEVING RECORD INFORMATION USING ASSIGNMENT ***************************

variable identifier : = record variable identifier . field identifier;

****

RETRIEVING RECORD INFORMATION USING WRITE/WRITELN **************************

Write/Writeln (record variable identifier . field identifier);

****

Notice in each case that the "dot" notation is employed as before to get to the required record field. Here are some examples using the *Students* record declared in Example 9-1:

```
Number := Student . Student_Number;

Grad := Student . Graduated;

Writeln (Student . Name);

Writeln ('The GPA of ',Student . Name, ' is ',Student . GPA:4:2);
```

The first two statements show how assignment is used to assign the record information to another variable within the program. Clearly, the variable must be declared the same data type as the respective field information. Consequently, *Number* and *Student_Number* must be declared the same data type or a "DATA TYPE MISMATCH" error will occur.

The second two foregoing statements show how *Writeln* is employed to retrieve record information. Again the dot notation is used to get to the required record field. You might take special note of the last *Writeln* statement, which removes information from two fields in order to complete a sentence. In addition, observe that the *GPA* field is formatted for decimal output using the formatting technique discussed earlier in the text.

Lastly, notice that the record variable is repeated in all four of the foregoing statements. How do you suppose that you could make the coding more efficient? You're right—by using a **WITH/DO** statement, like this:

```
WITH Student DO
  BEGIN
    Number := Student_Number;
    Grad := Graduated;
    Writeln (Name);
    Writeln ('The GPA of ', Name, ' is ', GPA:4:2)
  END;
```

Example 9-2:

Your instructor needs a student record consisting of the following items:

- Student name
- Student number
- Major
- Semester test scores
- Semester test average
- Equivalent letter grade of the test average

a. Declare an appropriate record.
b. Write a procedure that will allow the instructor to fill the record.
c. Write a procedure that will print the contents of the record.

Solution:

a. The record is a student record for a given class. Consequently, let's give the record an appropriate name, such as *Student*. Then we can use the class name, such as *Pascal*, as the record variable to access the grades of a given class. Next, there are six fields that need to be declared as part of the record. Let's call them *Name*, *Student_Number, Major, Test_Scores, Test_Average*, and *Test_Grade*. The *Name*, *Student_Number*, and *Major* fields will be declared as a string.

Since several individual test scores must be stored, we will declare the *Test_Scores* field as an *array* of real elements. That's right, a field within a record can be an array!

Next, we will declare the *Test_Average* field an integer field, since we will use a rounded-off average of the test scores.

Finally, the *Grade* field must be a character field to represent a letter grade. Here's a record declaration that will work:

```
TYPE
   Student = RECORD
                Name : STRING [25];
                Student_Number : STRING [25];
                Major : STRING [20];
                Test_Scores :  ARRAY [1..15] OF real;
                Test_Average : integer;
                Test_Grade : char
             END;

VAR
   Pascal : Student;
   Test_Number : integer;
```

Notice in particular that the *Test_Scores* field is declared as an array of fifteen real elements. The value 15 was used to allow for a maximum of fifteen test scores. The record variable is *Pascal*, which has a data type of *Student*. In addition, the global variable *Test_Number* is declared as an integer. You will observe its use shortly.

b. Here's a procedure that will fill the record:

```
PROCEDURE  Fill_Record (VAR Pupil : Student);

VAR
  Count : integer;
  Test_Total : real;

BEGIN
  Test_Total := 0;
  WITH Pupil DO
    BEGIN
      Write ('Enter the student name ---> ');
      Readln (Name);
      Writeln;
      Write ('Enter the student number ---> ');
      Readln (Student_Number);
      Writeln;
      Write ('Enter the student major ---> ');
      Readln (Major);
      Writeln;
      Write ('How many test scores are there? ---> ');
      Readln (Test_Number);
      Writeln;
      FOR Count := 1 TO Test_Number DO
        BEGIN
          Write ('Enter test score ',Count,' and press return ---> ');
          Readln (Test_Scores [Count]);
          Test_Total := Test_Total + Test_Scores[Count];
          Writeln
        END;   {for}
      Test_Average := Round (Test_Total / Test_Number);
      CASE Test_Average OF
         0 .. 59  : Test_Grade := 'F';
        60 .. 69  : Test_Grade := 'D';
        70 .. 79  : Test_Grade := 'C';
        80 .. 89  : Test_Grade := 'B';
        90 .. 100 : Test_Grade := 'A'
      END {case}
    END {with}
END;  {procedure Fill_Record}
```

First, observe the procedure heading. The procedure name is *Fill_Record*. There is a single variable parameter, *Pupil*. Notice that *Pupil* has a data type of *Student*, which is the record we declared in part a. Thus, the *Student* record will be passed to the procedure, filled, then passed back to the calling program. The actual record variable in the calling program is *Pascal*, and the formal record variable in the procedure is *Pupil*. Consequently, any operations on the record within this procedure will employ the formal record variable, *Pupil*.

Next you see that two local procedure variables, *Count* and *Test_Total*, are declared. You will observe their use shortly.

Now look at how the record is being filled using the **WITH/DO** statement. The formal record parameter, *Pupil*, must be referenced here, since it has taken on the values of the actual record parameter, *Pascal*. The first field to be filled within the **WITH/DO** statement is the *Name* field. This is accomplished by prompting the user and reading the field identifier, *Name*. After the student name is read, the user is prompted to enter the student number and major. This information is read into the record and stored using the record variables *Student_Number* and *Major*, respectively.

Next, the user is prompted for the number of test scores that will be entered into the record. The global variable, *Test_Number*, receives this value. This value is needed to control the number of times that the subsequent **FOR/DO** loop will be executed.

The **FOR/DO** loop is used to fill the *Test_Scores* array. A local variable, *Count*, is incremented from 1 to the number (*Test_Number*) of test scores. With each loop iteration, the user is prompted for the respective score value, and the corresponding entry is read into the *Test_Scores* array. In addition to filling the array field, the **FOR/DO** loop calculates a running total (*Test_Total*) of the test scores as they are entered.

The next field to be filled is the *Test_Average* field. Observe that this field is filled using an assignment statement. The total sum of the test scores (*Test_Total*) is divided by the number of scores (*Test_Number*) and rounded off to the nearest integer value using the standard *Round* function. This rounded value is the value assigned to the *Test_Average* field.

Finally, the *Test_Grade* field is filled using a **CASE** statement. As you can see, the **CASE** statement translates the numerical average to a letter grade. A given case simply assigns the appropriate letter grade to the *Test_Grade* field.

Notice the **END**s. The **CASE** is ended, then the **WITH/DO,** then the procedure. Here is where ending can get confusing and commenting becomes important. This is what the user will see on the display as a result of the *Fill_Record* procedure.

```
Enter the student name --->

Enter the student number --->

Enter the student major --->

How many test scores are there? --->

Enter test score 1 and press return --->

Enter test score 2 and press return --->

Enter test score 3 and press return --->
```

c. A procedure to print the student record is as follows:

```
PROCEDURE Print_Record (Pupil : Student);

VAR
  Count : integer;

BEGIN
  Clrscr;
  WITH Pupil DO
    BEGIN
      Writeln (lst,'Student Name:   ', Name);
      Writeln (lst);
```

(Continued)

```
         Writeln (1st,'      Student Number:  ',Student_Number);
         Writeln (1st,'       Major:  ', Major);
         Write (1st,'      Test Scores:  ');
         FOR  Count := 1 TO Test_Number DO
            Write (1st,Test_Scores [Count]:4:1, ', ');
         Writeln (1st);
         Writeln (1st,'        Test Average:  ',Test_Average);
         Writeln (1st,'        Test Grade:  ', Test_Grade)
     END {with}
   END;  {procedure Print_Record}
```

Again, a **WITH/DO** statement is used to retrieve the record data. The procedure employs a value parameter, *Pupil*, that receives the record from the calling program. This becomes the record variable within the procedure and, therefore, is included on the first line of the **WITH/DO** statement. The student name is printed first along with an appropriate heading. Then the individual test scores are printed using a **FOR/DO** loop. Notice the use of the global variable *Test_Number*. *Test_Number* represents the number of test scores that have been entered. How is this value obtained by the *Print_Record* procedure? Well, *Test_Number* was declared a global variable. As a result, both procedures have access to its value. This is a classic use of a global variable.

After the individual test scores are printed, the *Test_Average* and *Test_Grade* fields are printed, respectively, using *Writeln* statements.

Here is a typical printout generated by the *Print_Record* procedure:

```
     Student Name:  Blaise Pascal

          Student Number:  12345
          Major:  Mathematics
          Test Scores:  98.0, 97.0, 92.0,
          Test Average:  96
          Test Grade:  A
```

Finally, you might be wondering what the main program looks like. Here it is!

```
          BEGIN
             Clrscr;
             Fill_Record (Pascal);
             Print_Record (Pascal)
          END.  {main program}
```

That's all there is to it! Once the screen is cleared, the two procedures are called to fill and print the record, respectively. Notice that the actual record variable, *Pascal*, must be used to pass the record to the corresponding procedures. Observe that the variable *Pascal* is declared as the record variable in the main program declaration section.

9-3 RECORD STRUCTURES

Now that you know how to work with single records, it is time to literally build on this knowledge and create structures of records. The first record structure that we will discuss is a record of records, or nested records. That's right, we can create a record that contains other records. The second record structure that you need to learn about is an array of records, where individual records form the elements of an array. This structure allows for internal storage of multiple related records.

Nested Records

A nested record is a record within a record. In other words, a nested record is a field of another record. Let's expand on our *Student* record of Example 9-2 to illustrate this idea.

Suppose that your instructor needs a more complete student record that will include lab as well as test results. Let's structure the record so that the test and lab results form two separate nested records within the student record. In addition, we will include a third nested record to store the semester totals. Thus, our new student record will contain the following fields:

- A student name field
- A student number field
- A major field
- A nested record field that contains test results
- A nested record field that contains lab results
- A nested record field that contains semester totals

Here's the declaration:

```
TYPE
  Student = RECORD
            Name : STRING [25];
            Student_Number : STRING [15];
            Major : STRING [20];

            Tests : RECORD
                    Test_Scores : ARRAY [1..15] OF real;
                    Test_Average : integer;
                    Test_Grade : char
                  END;  {Tests record}

            Lab : RECORD
                  Lab_Scores : ARRAY [1..15] OF real;
                  Lab_Average : integer;
                  Lab_Grade : char
                END;   {Lab record}

            Totals : RECORD
                     Sem_Average : integer;
                     Sem_Grade : char
                   END    {Totals record}
          END;   {Student record}
VAR
  Pascal : Student;
  Test_Number, Lab_Number : integer;
```

As you can see, the nested records are declared as fields within the main record. There are three nested record fields: *Tests, Lab*, and *Totals*. A colon separates the field identifier from its respective nested record declaration. The declaration for a nested record uses the same format as that of any record declaration. Each field within a nested record actually forms a subfield of the respective main record field.

You can actually have multiple levels of nesting. In other words, you can have a record within a record within a record, and so on. How many levels are allowed? That depends on what type of Pascal compiler you are using. TURBO allows for nine levels of record nesting. (*Note*: The CP/M-80 version of TURBO requires a special compiler directive to nest more than two record levels. See your TURBO reference manual for the details.)

Now you are probably wondering how you can gain access to the nested records. For instance, how can you get to the *Test_Scores* field within the nested *Tests* record? Well, the record variable, *Pascal*, will get you into the main record, then the nested field *Tests* will get you into the nested record, and finally the field identifier, *Test_Scores*, will get you into the required field. Thus, assignment statements such as

```
Pascal . Tests . Test_Scores [1] := 95;

Pascal . Tests . Test_Scores [2] := 87;

Pascal . Tests . Test_Scores [3] := 93;
```

would allow you to place three test scores into the *Test_Scores* field. Notice the repetition of identifiers. There must be an easier way, right? Of course, you can use the **WITH/DO** statement as follows:

```
WITH Pascal, Tests DO
  FOR Count := 1 TO Test_Number DO
    BEGIN
      Write ('Enter test score ',Count,' and press return ---> ');
      Readln (Test_Scores [Count]);
      Writeln
    END {for}
END;   {with}
```

Here, both the record variable (*Pascal*) and the nested record field identifier (*Tests*) *must* be listed between **WITH** and **DO**. This "opens up" any fields within the nested record *Tests*. The subfield *Test_Scores* is then used alone within the **FOR/DO** loop to fill the array with test scores. Now, using this idea, let's construct a procedure to fill this new student record.

```
PROCEDURE  Fill_Record (VAR Pupil : Student);

VAR
  Count : integer;
  Test_Total, Lab_Total : real;
```

```
BEGIN
  Test_Total := 0;
  Lab_Total := 0;
  WITH Pupil, Tests, Lab, Totals DO
    BEGIN
      Write ('Enter the student name ---> ');
      Readln (Name);
      Writeln;
      Write ('Enter the student number ---> ');
      Readln (Student_Number);
      Writeln;
      Write ('Enter the student major ---> ');
      Readln (Major);
      Writeln;
      Write ('How many test scores are there? ---> ');
      Readln (Test_Number);
      Writeln;
      FOR Count := 1 TO Test_Number DO
        BEGIN
          Write ('Enter test score ',Count,' and press return ---> ');
          Readln (Test_Scores [Count]);
          Test_Total := Test_Total + Test_Scores[Count];
          Writeln
        END;  {for}
      Test_Average := Round (Test_Total / Test_Number);
      CASE Test_Average OF
         0 .. 59  : Test_Grade := 'F';
        60 .. 69  : Test_Grade := 'D';
        70 .. 79  : Test_Grade := 'C';
        80 .. 89  : Test_Grade := 'B';
        90 .. 100 : Test_Grade := 'A'
      END;  {case}
      Writeln;
      Write ('How many lab scores are there? ---> ');
      Readln (Lab_Number);
      Writeln;
      FOR Count := 1 TO Lab_Number DO
        BEGIN
          Write ('Enter lab score ',Count,' and press return ---> ');
          Readln (Lab_Scores [Count]);
          Lab_Total := Lab_Total + Lab_Scores[Count];
          Writeln
        END;  {for}
      Lab_Average := Round (Lab_Total / Lab_Number);
      CASE Lab_Average OF
         0 .. 59  : Lab_Grade := 'F';
        60 .. 69  : Lab_Grade := 'D';
        70 .. 79  : Lab_Grade := 'C';
        80 .. 89  : Lab_Grade := 'B';
        90 .. 100 : Lab_Grade := 'A'
      END;  {case}
      Sem_Average := Round (0.8 * Test_Average + 0.2 * Lab_Average);
      CASE Sem_Average OF
         0 .. 59  : Sem_Grade := 'F';
        60 .. 69  : Sem_Grade := 'D';
        70 .. 79  : Sem_Grade := 'C';
        80 .. 89  : Sem_Grade := 'B';
        90 .. 100 : Sem_Grade := 'A'
      END  {case}
    END {with}
END;  {procedure Fill_Record}
```

The main thing that you should note here is how a single **WITH/DO** operation is used to fill the entire record. This requires that the record variable (*Pupil*), along with the nested record field identifiers (*Tests*, *Lab*, and *Totals*) be listed on the first line of the **WITH/DO** statement. Note that the record variable, *Pupil*, is employed, since it is the formal parameter for the *Fill_Record* procedure. Once the nested records are opened up using their respective identifiers within the **WITH/DO** statement, the subfields are filled directly using the respective subfield identifiers. Study the above procedure! You should now have all the prerequisite knowledge to understand its operation.

How about a procedure to print the foregoing record? Here's one:

```
PROCEDURE Print_Record (Pupil : Student);

VAR
  Count : integer;

BEGIN
  Clrscr;
  WITH Pupil, Tests, Lab, Totals DO
    BEGIN
      Writeln (1st,'Student Name:  ', Name);
      Writeln (1st);
      Writeln (1st,'      Student Number: ',Student_Number);
      Writeln (1st,'      Major:  ', Major);
      Writeln (1st);
      Write (1st,'     Test Scores:  ');
      FOR  Count := 1 TO Test_Number DO
        Write (1st,Test_Scores [Count]:4:1, ', ');
      Writeln (1st);
      Writeln (1st,'      Test Average:  ',Test_Average);
      Writeln (1st,'      Test Grade:  ', Test_Grade);
      Writeln (1st);
      Write (1st,'     Lab Scores:  ');
      FOR Count := 1 TO Lab_Number DO
        Write (1st,Lab_Scores [Count]:4:1, ', ');
      Writeln (1st);
      Writeln (1st,'      Lab Average:  ',Lab_Average);
      Writeln (1st,'      Lab Grade:  ', Lab_Grade);
      Writeln (1st);
      Writeln (1st,'SEMESTER AVERAGE:  ',Sem_Average);
      Writeln (1st);
      Writeln (1st,'SEMESTER GRADE:  ',Sem_Grade)
    END {with}
END;  {procedure Print_Record}
```

Again, you see the use of the nested record identifiers within the first line of the **WITH/DO** statement to open up the respective nested records for the output operation.

Arrays of Records

Up to this point you have been storing a single record within the primary memory of your system. This isn't very practical, since most applications require the storage of multiple records. For instance, consider the foregoing *Student* record. Don't you think that your instructor would want to store the records of all the students in a particular class, rather than just a single student record?

Multiple records can be stored in primary memory by creating an array of records. That's right, we will create an array whose elements are individual records! The diagram in Figure 9-1 illustrates this idea. Using this array-of-records structure, your instructor can store all the student records for an entire class in a single array. Of course, all the records within the array must have the same record structure.

Now, how can this structure be declared and accessed in Pascal? We will employ the same nested record structure that we used earlier for the individual student records. Then all we need to do is to add an array declaration to the program declaration section, as follows:

```
CONST
  Max = 25;

TYPE
  Student = RECORD
               Name : STRING [25];
               Student_Number : STRING [15];
               Major : STRING [20];

               Tests : RECORD
                          Test_Scores : ARRAY [1..15] OF real;
                          Test_Average : integer;
                          Test_Grade : char
                       END;

               Lab : RECORD
                        Lab_Scores : ARRAY [1..15] OF real;
                        Lab_Average : integer;
                        Lab_Grade : char
                     END;  {Lab record}

               Totals : RECORD
                           Sem_Average : integer;
                           Sem_Grade : char
                        END    {Totals record}
            END;  {Student record}

  Students = ARRAY [1..Max] OF Student;

VAR
  Pascal : Students;
  Number, Test_Number, Lab_Number : integer;
```

What has been added to the previous declaration? Well, first a constant (*Max*) has been declared to represent the maximum number of students in a class. This is followed by a declaration of the same nested record structure that we used previously. The record name is *Student*. After the record declaration is ended, the array of records is declared. As you can see, the array name is *Students*, which is declared as an array from 1 to *Max* of *Student*. So the array is defined as a twenty-five-element array of *Student* records. That's all there is to it! One major

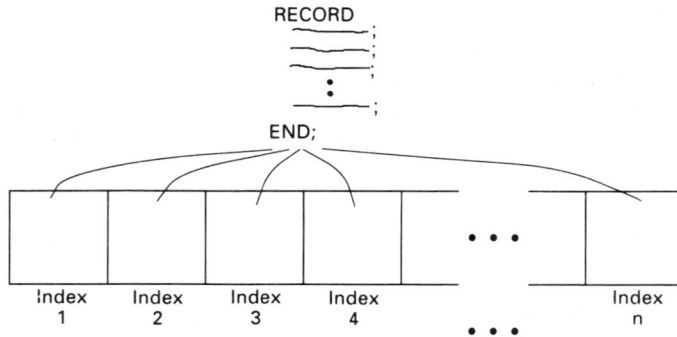

Figure 9-1 An array of records.

point; The record must be declared prior to the array, since the array declaration uses the record.

Finally, an array variable must be declared.   I have chosen to use the variable *Pascal* to represent the students in my Pascal course.   Notice the absence of a record variable.   It is not needed, since the array variable will get us into the array, which gets us into the individual records.

Now how do you suppose you could fill this array?   Why not employ a **FOR/DO** loop to fill the array, just as you would fill any other array?   Here's a procedure that will do the job:

```
PROCEDURE  Fill_Class_Array (VAR Pupils : Students);

VAR
  I, Count : integer;
  Test_Total, Lab_Total : real;

BEGIN
  Write ('How many students are in the class? ----> ');
  Readln (Number);
  Clrscr;
  FOR I := 1 TO Number DO
    BEGIN
      Test_Total := 0;
      Lab_Total := 0;
      WITH Pupils [I], Tests, Lab, Totals DO
        BEGIN
          Write ('Enter the name of student ',I,' ---> ');
          Readln (Name);
          Writeln;
          Write ('Enter ',Name,''s student number ---> ');
          Readln (Student_Number);
          Writeln;
          Write ('Enter ',Name,''s  major ---> ');
          Readln (Major);
          Writeln;
          Write ('How many test scores are there? ---> ');
          Readln (Test_Number);
          Writeln;
```

```
            FOR Count := 1 TO Test_Number DO
              BEGIN
                Write ('Enter test score ',Count,' and press return -> ');
                Readln (Test_Scores [Count]);
                Test_Total := Test_Total + Test_Scores[Count];
                Writeln
              END;  {for}
            Test_Average := Round (Test_Total / Test_Number);
            CASE Test_Average OF
                 0 .. 59  : Test_Grade := 'F';
                60 .. 69  : Test_Grade := 'D';
                70 .. 79  : Test_Grade := 'C';
                80 .. 89  : Test_Grade := 'B';
                90 .. 100 : Test_Grade := 'A'
            END;  {case}
            Writeln;
            Write ('How many lab scores are there? ---> ');
            Readln (Lab_Number);
            Writeln;
            FOR Count := 1 TO Lab_Number DO
              BEGIN
                Write  ('Enter lab score ',Count,' and press return -> ');
                Readln (Lab_Scores [Count]);
                Lab_Total := Lab_Total + Lab_Scores[Count];
                Writeln
              END;  {for}
            Lab_Average := Round (Lab_Total / Lab_Number);
            CASE Lab_Average OF
                 0 .. 59  : Lab_Grade := 'F';
                60 .. 69  : Lab_Grade := 'D';
                70 .. 79  : Lab_Grade := 'C';
                80 .. 89  : Lab_Grade := 'B';
                90 .. 100 : Lab_Grade := 'A'
            END;  {case}
            Sem_Average := Round (0.8 * Test_Average + 0.2 * Lab_Average);
            CASE Sem_Average OF
                 0 .. 59  : Sem_Grade := 'F';
                60 .. 69  : Sem_Grade := 'D';
                70 .. 79  : Sem_Grade := 'C';
                80 .. 89  : Sem_Grade := 'B';
                90 .. 100 : Sem_Grade := 'A'
            END  {case}
          END; {with}
          Clrscr
        END {for}
  END; {procedure Fill_Class_Array}
```

This is basically the same procedure that we used before to fill the individual student record. What's different? First, the procedure name has been changed to reflect the application. Next, notice that the formal parameter is *Pupils*, which has a data type of *Students*. The data type *Students* is the array that we declared. Thus, the *Students* array is passed to the procedure, filled, and then passed back to the main program.

Next you see a prompt for the user to enter the number of students in the class. Then a **FOR/DO** loop is constructed to fill the *Students* array with the individual student records. Notice the loop counter (*I*) ranges from 1 to *Number*, where *Number* is the number of students in the class. The first thing that you see in the body of the loop is a **WITH/DO** statement. Look at the statement header. The formal array parameter, *Pupils* [*I*], is listed first, followed by the nested record identifiers (*Tests, Lab*, and *Totals*). The *Pupils* [*I*] parameter is required to access the *Students* array, where *I* references the particular array index being filled according to the loop counter. The nested record identifiers (*Tests, Lab, Totals*) are listed to gain access into these respective nested records. Although a record variable is not listed here (since the array variable provides access to the records), you must list any nested record field identifiers to gain access to the nested records. If there were no nested records, you would simply list the array variable (parameter) here. The body of the **WITH/DO** statement is identical to the one we used before to fill an individual student record.

How about a procedure to print the records of all the students in the class? Here it is:

```
PROCEDURE Print_Class_Array (Pupils : Students);

VAR
  I, Count : integer;

BEGIN
  Clrscr;
  FOR I := 1 TO Number DO
    BEGIN
      WITH Pupils [I], Tests, Lab, Totals DO
        BEGIN
        Writeln (lst,'Student Name:  ', Name);
        Writeln (lst);
        Writeln (lst,'       Student Number:  ',Student_Number);
        Writeln (lst,'       Major:  ', Major);
        Writeln (lst);
        Write (lst,'     Test Scores:  ');
        FOR  Count := 1 TO Test_Number DO
          Write (lst,Test_Scores [Count]:4:1, ', ');
        Writeln (lst);
        Writeln (lst,'       Test Average:  ',Test_Average);
        Writeln (lst,'       Test Grade:  ', Test_Grade);
        Writeln (lst);
        Write (lst,'     Lab Scores:  ');
        FOR Count := 1 TO Lab_Number DO
          Write (lst,Lab_Scores [Count]:4:1, ', ');
        Writeln (lst);
        Writeln (lst,'       Lab Average:  ',Lab_Average);
        Writeln (lst,'       Lab Grade:  ', Lab_Grade);
        Writeln (lst);
        Writeln (lst,'SEMESTER AVERAGE:  ',Sem_Average);
        Writeln (lst);
        Writeln (lst,'SEMESTER GRADE:  ',Sem_Grade)
        END; {with}
      Writeln (lst);
      Writeln (lst);
      Writeln (lst)
    END {for}
END;  {procedure Print_Class_Array}
```

The idea here is the same as for the fill procedure. The procedure header contains a value parameter (*Pupils*) that receives the array from the main program for the printing operation. Notice that the data type of *Pupils* is *Students*, which is the array we declared. Again a **FOR/DO** loop is created to sequentially access each of the array elements. Since the array elements are the individual student records, a student record is printed with each loop iteration. The record data are accessed via a **WITH/DO** statement that references the array parameter (*Pupils* [*I*]) and the nested record identifiers. The body of the **WITH/DO** statement simply prints the record fields.

Finally, here's how the main program will call the fill and print procedures:

```
BEGIN   {main program}
  Clrscr;
  Fill_Class_Array (Pascal);
  Print_Class_Array (Pascal)
END.  {main program}
```

As you can see, the actual array parameter (*Pascal*) is listed in each procedure call to pass the array to the respective procedure. Notice that *Pascal* is declared as the array variable in the declaration section of the main program. How might your instructor store student records for other classes? By simply declaring additional array variables for those classes.

9-4 VARIANT RECORDS

All the records that you have dealt with up to this point have had a fixed set of fields. Sometimes it it desirable to create a general record structure in which the number and type of fields vary according to how the record is being used. For instance, let's make your English professor happy by considering a footnote record. When you write a research paper, the various references employed during your research must be footnoted within the body of the paper. You will often have both book and periodical references to footnote. However, did you know that the format for a book footnote is different from that for a periodical footnote? Here is the accepted format for each:

Book Footnote:
   Author, Title, Edition, (City of Publication: Publisher, Year Published), pp. Pages Referenced.
Periodical Footnote:
   Author, "Title," Name of Periodical, Issue, pp. Pages Referenced.

Notice that, aside from the format, some of the information in each footnote is different. Which information is the same, or *fixed*, in both footnotes, and which information is different, or *variant*, within the footnotes? Well, notice that both footnotes require an author, title, and pages referenced. However, the book footnote requires the edition, city of publication, publisher, and year published. On the other hand, the periodical footnote requires the name of the periodical and its issue. Thus, each footnote has a fixed part (author, title, and pages) and each has a variant part, which depends on the particular type of footnote (book or periodical).

Declaring Variant Records

Not let's declare a general reference record whose field structure will "vary," depending on whether the reference is a book or a periodical. Such a record is called a *variant record*. Here it is:

```
TYPE

    Ref_Type = (Book, Periodical);

    Reference = RECORD

                    Author : STRING [60];
                    Title  : STRING [70];
                    Pages  : STRING [10]

                    CASE Kind : Ref_Type OF

                        Book : (City : STRING [25];
                                Publisher : STRING [30];
                                Year_Published : integer;
                                Edition : integer);

                        Periodical : (Name : STRING [30];
                                      Issue : STRING [25])
                    END; {record}

    VAR
        Footnote : Reference;
```

Here I have first declared a user-defined data type called *Ref_Type* that has two elements, *Book* and *Periodical*. Next, a record, called *Reference*, is declared. Look at the body of the record. It consists of two parts: a fixed part and a variant part. The fixed part consists of those fields that are the same in both applications. They are the *Author, Title,* and *Pages* fields. The variant part consists of those fields that are different, or variant, for the book and periodical references. Notice that a **CASE** statement is employed to define these fields. In the **CASE** header, you see the identifier *Kind*. This is called a *tag field* and identifies which set of variant fields is selected. Here, the tag field (*Kind*) is of type *Ref_Type*. Thus, the tag field can take on a value of either *Book* or *Periodical*, the two elements defined in *Ref_Type*.

Book Footnote

Periodical Footnote

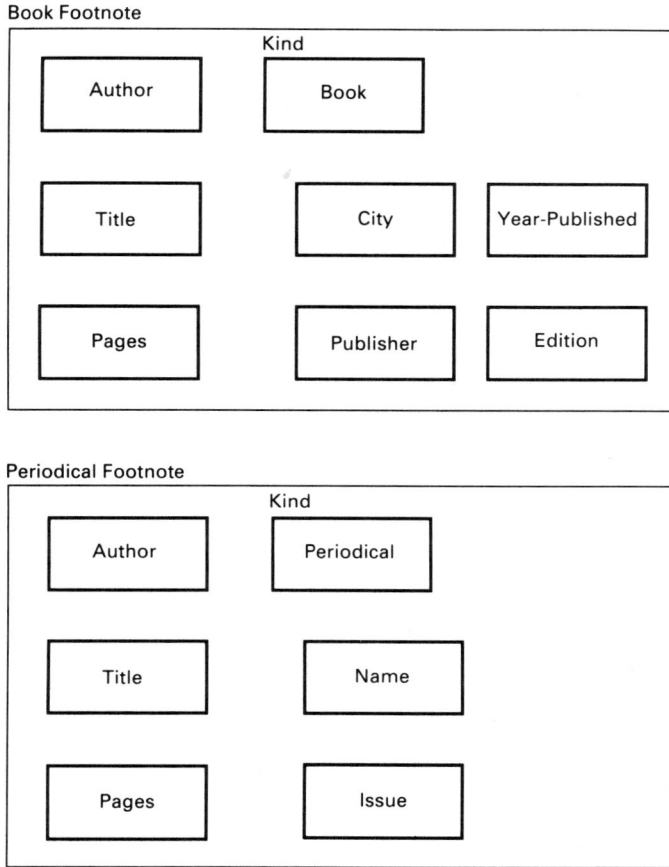

Figure 9-2 The structure of a variant record changes for (a) a book or (b) a periodical footnote.

Next, the required fields for a *Book* versus a *Periodical* reference are listed. Notice the syntax: The *Book* or *Periodical* identifiers are followed by a colon, then the respective fields are defined *within parentheses*. Here's how it works: If *Kind* has the value *Book*, the record structure is that shown in Figure 9-2a. However, if *Kind* has the value *Periodical*, the record structure is that shown in Figure 9-2b. Notice that each record has the same fixed information (*Author, Title*, and *Pages*) and different variant information, depending on the value of the tag field (*Kind*).

Finally, you see a record variable called *Footnote* declared for the *Reference* record. As before, the record variable provides access to the record.

Here's the general format for declaring variant records:

VARIANT RECORD DECLARATION FORMAT ✶✶✶
TYPE
  record identifier = **RECORD**

fixed part
$$\begin{cases} \text{field 1 identifier : data type;} \\ \text{field 2 identifier : data type;} \\ \qquad\qquad\vdots \\ \text{field n identifier : data type} \end{cases}$$

variant part
$$\begin{cases} \textbf{CASE}\ \text{tag field : tag type } \textbf{OF} \\ \quad \text{tag value 1 : (field list);} \\ \quad \text{tag value 2 : (field list);} \\ \qquad\qquad\vdots \\ \quad \text{tag value m : (field list)} \end{cases}$$

           END; (record declaration)
VAR
  record variable : record identifier;
✶✶

The following rules govern the declaration of variant records:

1. Only *one* variant part (**CASE**) can be declared in a given record.
2. The variant part must be the *last* part declared in the record, after the fixed part.
3. The fixed part is optional.
4. The tag field must be a scalar data type.
5. A single **END** terminates both the **RECORD** and the **CASE.**

Accessing Variant Records

Accessing variant records is basically the same as accessing nonvariant records. A **WITH/DO** statement is employed to open up the record to get information in and out of the record. However, the *tag field must be assigned a tag value* so that the compiler knows which variant fields make up the record. Here's a procedure that will fill the *Reference* record that we declared earlier:

```
PROCEDURE Fill_Reference (VAR Ref : Reference);

VAR
  Answer : char;

BEGIN
  WITH Ref DO
    BEGIN
      Write ('Enter the author name ---> ');
      Readln (Author);
      Writeln;
```

(Continued)

```
Write ('Enter the title of the book or article ---> ');
Readln (Title);
Writeln;
Write ('Enter the pages you are referencing ---> ');
Readln (Pages);
Writeln;
Writeln;
Write ('Is the reference a book or periodical?  (B/P) ----> ');
Readln (Answer);
Writeln;
CASE Answer OF

    'b', 'B' : BEGIN
                  Kind := Book;
                  Write ('Enter the city of publication ---> ');
                  Readln (City);
                  Writeln;
                  Write ('Enter the publisher ---> ');
                  Readln (Publisher);
                  Writeln;
                  Write ('Enter the year published ---> ');
                  Readln (Year_Published);
                  Writeln;
                  Write ('Enter the edition of the book ---> ');
                  Readln (Edition);
                  Writeln
               END; {case B}

    'p', 'P' : BEGIN
                  Kind := Periodical;
                  Write ('Enter the name of the periodical ---> ');
                  Readln (Name);
                  Writeln;
                  Write ('Enter the issue of the periodical ---> ');
                  Readln (Issue);
                  Writeln
               END {case P}

    END {case}
  END {with}
END; {procedure Fill_Record}
```

The procedure employs a variable parameter (*Ref*) to receive the record from and return the filled record to the calling program. Notice that the data type of *Ref* is the *Reference* record that we declared earlier. The body of the procedure employs a **WITH/DO** statement using the variable parameter *Ref* to access the record. The user is first prompted to enter the fixed record information. Then the user is asked whether the reference is a book or periodical. A **CASE** statement is used to select the appropriate set of fields, depending on the user's response. Observe that the first thing that is done in each case is to assign the tag field (*Kind*) a tag value that represents the type of reference being entered. This is required to create the appropriate record structure. Within each case, the user is prompted to enter the respective field information.

How about a procedure to print the variant record. Here's one that will do the job:

```
PROCEDURE Print_Footnote (Ref : Reference);

BEGIN
  WITH Ref DO
    BEGIN
      CASE  Kind OF

        Book :  BEGIN
                  Writeln (1st, Author,', ',Title,', Edition ',
                          Edition,', (',City,': ',Publisher,', ',
                          Year_Published,'), pp. ',Pages,'.')
                END;   {Book case}

        Periodical : BEGIN
                       Writeln (1st, Author,', ','"',Title,'," ',
                               Name,', ',Issue,', ','pp. ',Pages,'.')
                     END {Periodical case}
      END {case}
    END {with}
END; {procedure Print_Footnote}
```

This time *Ref* is a value parameter, since the record only needs to be passed one way to the procedure. Again a **WITH/DO** statement is employed using the value parameter *Ref* to open up the record. The body of the **WITH/DO** statement uses a **CASE** statement to print the footnote in the required format. The key to the whole operation is the tag field (*Kind*). The **CASE** statement selects one of two footnote formats (*Book* or *Periodical*) depending on the value of *Kind*. If the value of *Kind* is *Book*, the book footnote is printed. If the value of *Kind* is *Periodical*, the periodical footnote is printed. Of course, *Kind* is assigned a value in the *Fill_Reference* procedure.

The *Writeln* statements within each case are constructed to generate the accepted footnote format. (Consult your English composition book.)

Finally, here is a main program that will call the two foregoing procedures:

```
BEGIN {main program}
  Clrscr;
  Fill_Reference(Footnote);
  Print_Footnote(Footnote)
END. {main program}
```

Here are two sample outputs generated by the program. The first is a book footnote and the second a periodical footnote.

Andrew C. Staugaard, Jr., Robotics and AI: An Introduction To Applied Machine Intelligence, Edition 1, (Englewood Cliffs, N.J.: Prentice-Hall, Inc., 1987), pp . 201 - 213.

Edwin C. Jones, Jr. and Michael C. Mulder, "Accreditation in the Computer Profe ssion," COMPUTER, April, 1984, pp. 24 - 27.

How might you create a structure to store a bibliography containing several *Reference* records. You're right if you thought an array of *Reference* records. This bibliography problem will be left for you as an exercise at the end of the chapter.

CHAPTER SUMMARY

A record is a structure of field data. Unlike an array, the elements that make up a record, the fields, can be different data types. Records must be declared in Pascal under the **TYPE** declaration using the reserved word **RECORD.** In addition, a record variable must be declared to access the record information.

There are basically two ways to access record information: by using dot notation or a **WITH/DO** statement. To gain access to a field using dot notation, the record variable is listed first, followed by a dot, followed by the field identifier. The **WITH/DO** statement simplifies the coding by listing the record variable once, within the **WITH/DO** header. Then the field identifiers are used directly within the body of the **WITH/DO** statement. Always remember to **BEGIN** and **END** your **WITH/DO** statements.

Nested records are records within records. Thus, a nested record is actually a field of another record. Nested records are declared as fields within another record using the standard record declaration format. When accessing nested records, the nested record identifier must be listed in the dot notation string or the **WITH/DO** header.

You must use an array to store multiple records of the same type. When this is done, the individual records form the elements of the array. However, all the records must be the same type and the record type must be declared prior to the array declaration. Once declared, the individual records within the array are accessed using **FOR/DO** loops. The fields within a given record are then accessed using dot notation or **WITH/DO** statements.

Finally, a variant record is a record whose field structure can vary, depending on the application. A variant record consists of an optional fixed part and a variant part. The fixed part contains fields that are present for all variations of the record. The variant part defines the fields that are different for each variation of the record. The variant part of a variant record is declared within the record declaration using a **CASE** statement. The **CASE** statement employs a tag field whose value determines the field structure of the record. Only one variant part (**CASE**) can be declared in a given record and the variant part must be declared after the optional fixed part of the record.

A **WITH/DO** statement is employed to access variant records in the same way that it is used to access nonvariant records. However, when filling a variant record, the tag field must be assigned a legal value so that the compiler knows which variant fields to fill. Likewise, when retrieving variant record information, a **CASE** statement is used on the tag field to determine which variant fields are to be retrieved.

QUESTIONS AND PROBLEMS

Questions

9-1. What is a record?

9-2. How do the contents of a record differ from the contents of an array?

9-3. The data structure used to store multiple records in primary memory is the _____ .

9-4. The Pascal statement that is commonly used for record I/O is the _____ statement.

9-5. True or False: Records cannot be part of other records.

9-6. True or False: A given record is limited to one variant (**CASE**) part.

9-7. Discuss the two general ways in which records can be accessed.

9-8. What is a tag field and how is it used when accessing variant record information?

9-9. True or False: A given record can contain fields of any legal data type.

Given the following declaration,

```
TYPE
    Days = (Sun,Mon,Tue,Wed,Thur,Fri,Sat);
    Months = (Jan,Feb,Mar,Apr,May,Jun,Jul,Aug,Sep,Oct,Nov,Dec);

    Date = RECORD
             Day : Days;
             Month : Months;
             This_Date : 1 .. 31;
             Year : integer
           END;

VAR

    Yesterday, Today, Tomorrow, Christmas : Date;
```

determine which of the following statements are valid and which are invalid. Correct the invalid statements.

9-10. Today . Day := Wed;

9-11. Record . Day := Sat;

9-12. Date . Today . This_Date := 15;

9-13. Today . Month := 'Jun';

9-14. Yesterday := Today;

Programming Problems

9-1. Write a program segment to assign the proper values for Christmas of this year in the above record.

9-2. Declare a name record consisting of a person's last name, first name, and middle initial.

9-3. Declare an address record consisting of a street number, street name, city, state, and zip code.

9-4. Declare a person record consisting of the name and address records declared in problems 9-2 and 9-3. Use nested records.

9-5. Declare an array that will store ten of the person records declared in problem 9-4.

9-6. Declare a bibliography array that will store *Max* of the *Reference* records developed in Section 9-4. (*Note*: Declare *Max* as a constant to represent the maximum number of records in the array).

9-7. Declare a variant record for major-league baseball players. Assume that the fixed information in the record is the player's name and his team name. The variant information must be categorized as pitcher or nonpitcher. If the player is a pitcher, you must store his number of wins, number of losses, and ERA. If the player is not a pitcher, you must store his number of times at bat, number of home runs, number of hits, number of RBIs, and batting average.

9-8. Write two procedures for each of the declarations in problems 9-2 through 9-7: one procedure to allow for user input of the record information, and another procedure to display the record contents. Execute the procedures using the proper procedure calls via a main program.

chapter ten

Files

INTRODUCTION

All the data structures that you have learned about so far have provided you with a means of organizing and storing data in primary memory. However, recall that primary memory is volatile. In other words, when the system is turned off or power is lost for any reason, all information stored in primary memory goes to "bit heaven." The obvious solution to this problem is to store any long-term data in secondary memory, since secondary memory is nonvolatile.

In this chapter you will learn how to create files. A file provides you with a means of storing information in a convenient and organized manner in secondary memory, such as a magnetic disk. You will find that files can be used to store individual data elements such as integers, reals, and characters as well as data structures such as arrays and records. Now, let's complete your learning journey in *Technical Pascal* with a discussion of files.

10-1 FUNDAMENTAL CONCEPTS AND IDEAS

A *File* is a data structure that consists of a sequence of components of the same data type. There are two important aspects of this definition. First, a file is a *sequence* of components.   This means that the data elements, called ***components,*** are arranged within the file sequentially, or serially, from the first component to the last component.   As a result, when accessing files, the file components must be accessed in a sequential manner from one component to the next.   Second, all the components of a file must be the *same data type*.   As you will soon discover, Pascal requires you to declare the data type of the file.   Any of the data types discussed so far are legal candidates for files, including the structured data types of arrays and records.   The only way that a file can contain different data types is by creating a file of records.   The file components will still be of one data type (record), but the fields within the record can be of different data types.

A common analogy for a file is an audio cassette tape.   Think of the songs on the tape as the file components.   How are they stored on the tape?   Right— sequentially from the first song to the last.   How must you access a given song? Right again—by sequencing forwards or backwards through the tape until the desired song is found.   Thus, like a cassette tape, a file is a sequential, or serial, storage medium.   This makes file access relatively slow as compared with other random-access storage mediums.

You might be tempted to think of a file as a one-dimensional array, but there are some important differences.   First, files provide a means for you to store information within a program run, as do arrays.   But, unlike arrays, files also allow you to store information *between* program runs.   Second, many versions of Pascal require you to access the file components in sequence, starting with the first file component.   You cannot jump into the middle of a file as you can with an array, to access a given component.   However, TURBO Pascal does provide a means of semirandom access using the *Seek* procedure (more about this later). Third, files are not declared with specific dimensions as arrays are.   Once you declare a file, its size is theoretically unlimited.   Of course, the file size is actually limited by the amount of storage space available in secondary memory, such as a disk.

Creating Files in Pascal: The Declaration

Declaring files in Pascal requires a two-part **TYPE/VAR** declaration very much like declaring arrays and records.   Here's the general format:

FILE DECLARATION FORMAT ***

TYPE
   file identifier = **FILE OF** component data type;
VAR
   variable identifier : file identifier;

****

As you can see, the type declaration of a file employs the reserved words **FILE OF**. A file type identifier is followed by an equals sign (=), followed by the reserved words **FILE OF,** which are followed by the data type of the file components. Any scalar or structured-component data type is legal here, *except file*. In other words, you can have a **FILE OF** integer, char, real, Boolean, string, array, or record. However, you cannot have a **FILE OF** another file. After the **TYPE** declaration, you must declare a variable to access the file. The data type of the file variable must be the file-type identifier listed in your **TYPE** declaration. Here are a few declaration examples:

```
TYPE
    Keyboard = FILE OF char;


VAR
    Character : Keyboard;
```

In this declaration, the file type identifier is *Keyboard*. The file *Keyboard* is a "file of" characters. Thus, the component data type is char. The file variable is *Character*, whose data type is *Keyboard*. You will soon discover that the file variable must be used to access the file components. In this example, the variable *Character* must be used to access the *Keyboard* file components.

How about this one:

```
TYPE
    Scores = 0 .. 100;
    TestScores = FILE OF Scores;

VAR
    Score : TestScores;
```

The only twist here is the use of a user-defined data type called *Scores*. Notice that *Scores* is defined as a subrange of the integers from 0 through 100. The file is *TestScores*, whose components are *Scores*. Thus, the file components can be any integer from 0 through 100. The file variable is *Score*, whose data type is the file *TestScores*.

Here's another:

```
TYPE
    Row = 1 .. 3;
    Col = 1 .. 3;
    Tic_Tac_Toe = FILE OF ARRAY [Row,Col] OF Boolean;

VAR
    Game : Tic_Tac_Toe;
```

This time I have declared a file of arrays. Notice that the array declaration is part of the file declaration. The *Tic_Tac_Toe* file consists of a 3 × 3 array of components that contain Boolean elements. (Why do you suppose I chose to use Boolean elements?) The file variable is *Game*, which must be used to access the individual *Tic_Tac_Toe* array components.

Here is another way to declare the same file:

```
TYPE
  Row = 1 .. 3;
  Col = 1 .. 3;
  Board = ARRAY [Row,Col] OF Boolean;
  Tic_Tac_Toe = FILE OF Board;

VAR
  Game : Tic_Tac_Toe;
```

What's different? The array, *Board*, is declared prior to the *Tic_Tac_Toe* file. Thus, the file declaration simply lists the array identifier, *Board*, as the component data type.

Finally, let's consider the most common type of file, a file of records:

```
TYPE
  Student = RECORD
              Name : STRING [25];
              Student_Number : STRING [15];
              Major : STRING [20];

              Tests : RECORD
                        Test_Scores : ARRAY [1..15] OF real;
                        Test_Average : integer;
                        Test_Grade : char
                      END;

              Lab : RECORD
                      Lab_Scores : ARRAY [1..15] OF real;
                      Lab_Average : integer;
                      Lab_Grade : char
                    END;   {Lab record}

              Totals : RECORD
                         Sem_Average : integer;
                         Sem_Grade : char
                       END    {Totals record}
            END;   {Student record}

  Students = FILE OF Student;

VAR
  Pascal, Assembler, COBOL : Students;
```

Does the record look familiar? Of course, this is the student record that we developed in Chapter 9. Notice that the file declaration is made *after* the record declaration. A *Students* file is declared by simply making it a file of *Student* records. Thus, each of the *Students* file components will be a complete *Student* record. The *Students* file has three variables: *Pascal, Assembler*, and *COBOL*. As a result, we can use the *Students* file structure to store different student records for these three courses. Of course, the individual course files must be accessed via their respective file variable (*Pascal, Assembler,* or *COBOL*). You are now ready to learn how to access file information.

10-2 ACCESSING FILE INFORMATION

Before getting into specific file access routines, let's take a minute to discuss the more important overall concept of file access.

The File Window

Files can be thought of as a means for a program to communicate with the "outside world." Information can be input to the program by placing it in a file and having the program *read* that file. In the same way, the program can output information to the outside world by *writing* to a file. Did you know that TURBO Pascal treats a keyboard as an input file and a CRT display as an output file? Thus, think of a file as a means for your program to communicate with the outside world.

Now the question is: How can your program communicate with the file? The answer is, through something called a ***file window***. In other words, your program "sees" the outside file components through a window. This concept is illustrated by Figure 10-1. Here, the file consists of a sequence of record components. To access a given record, the window must be positioned over that record so that it can be seen. Once the window is positioned over the desired record, information can be *read from* or *written to* that record component.

When you declare a file, a window is automatically created to access the file components. This window is technically referred to as a ***file buffer variable***. Consequently, the file buffer variable, or window, is the link between the program and the file components.

File Operations

Now that you know how a file is structured, you need to learn about some general operations that will allow you to work with files. The following discussion will center on TURBO Pascal. I should caution you, however, that file operations in TURBO Pascal differ somewhat from file operations in other versions of Pascal. There are operations available in TURBO that are not available in Standard or

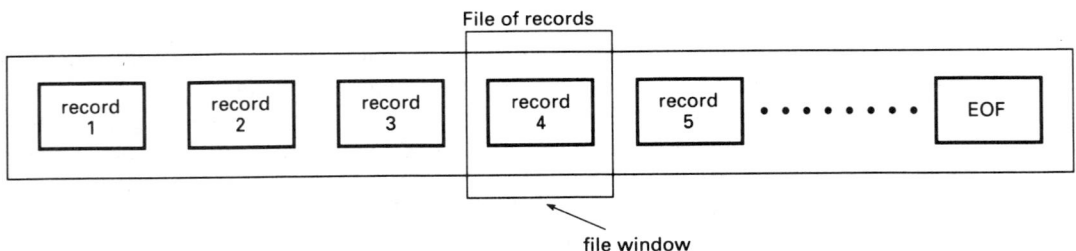

Figure 10-1 File components are accessed through a file window.

UCSD Pascal, and vice versa. You should consult a Standard or UCSD Pascal text before working with files, should you ever have occasion to use these versions of Pascal.

Standard Functions Used with Files

TURBO Pascal employs three standard functions that are applicable to files: *FileSize, FilePos*, and *EOF*.

File Size (*FileSize*)   **
FORMAT: *FileSize* (file variable)

The *FileSize* function returns the size, or number of components, in the file. As an example, suppose that there were twenty-five student records in the *Pascal* class of the *Students* file that we declared earlier. The statement

```
Writeln (FileSize(Pascal));
```

would display the value 25. Clearly, an empty file has a size of 0. Notice that the file variable, *Pascal*, is the required function argument, not the file type identifier, *Students*.

File Position (*FilePos*) ***
FORMAT: *FilePos* (file variable)

FilePos returns the current position of the file window. The first position in the file is always position 0. Thus, a statement such as

```
Writeln (FilePos(Pascal));
```

will display the current position of the window in the *Pascal Students* file that was declared earlier. Again, the function argument must be the file variable (*Pascal*).

End of File (*EOF*)   ***
FORMAT: *EOF* (file variable)

This is a Boolean function that returns the value TRUE if the window is positioned at the end of the file; otherwise, it returns the value FALSE. The end of the file is considered to be one position beyond the last component of the file. The end-of-file function is useful in a loop when sequencing through the contents of a file like this:

```
WHILE NOT EOF (file variable) DO

   BEGIN

        {loop statements}

   END;
```

Here, the loop is executed as long as *EOF* is FALSE. In other words, the loop is executed until the file window passes the last component position within the file. Of course, something must happen within the loop to move the window toward the end of the file, or an infinite loop will result. You will see the application of this loop later when you learn how to read files.

Standard Procedures Used with Files

The standard file procedures employed by TURBO are used when working with files. Unlike the file functions, these procedures perform a given file-related task. Study them, as you will need to use them when writing file access routines.

Seek ***

FORMAT: *Seek* (file variable, n)

The *Seek* procedure is unique to TURBO Pascal and allows semirandom access to file information. This procedure moves the file window to the *n*th component position within the file. Thus, the statement

Seek (Pascal, 0);

will move the file window to the first component in the Pascal file. How about this one:

Seek (Pascal, FileSize(Pascal));

FileSize returns the number of components in the file, and the first component in the file is at position 0. Thus, this statement will position the window one position beyond the last component in the file. Think about it! Such a statement could be used to add components to the file, right?

Assign ***

FORMAT: *Assign* (file variable, name)

This procedure is used to assign a name to your disk file. The name you assign is the file name that will appear in the disk directory for that file. Thus, the *Assign* procedure must be used prior to any file access so that the proper disk file is obtained. Here's an example:

Assign (Pascal, Pascal.F87);

This statement will create a file name of *Pascal.F87* on your disk, obviously standing for the fall 1987 Pascal course. You must use this statement prior to any operations on the *Pascal.F87* file.   However, you will still use the file variable (*Pascal*) when accessing the file components.   One final point: The disk file name can be up to eight characters, with a three character extension after the dot.   Any additional characters in the name will not cause an error; they are simply dropped from the file directory.

Rename **

FORMAT: *Rename* (file variable, new name)

The *Rename* procedure is used to rename an existing disk file.   Furthermore, the disk directory is automatically updated to show the new disk-file name.   Any subsequent operations on the file variable will access the newly named disk file.

Rewrite **

FORMAT: *Rewrite* (file variable)

The *Rewrite* procedure must be used prior to writing to a new disk file.   Thus, you will use *Rewrite* after *Assign* to prepare a new disk file for processing, as follows:

```
Assign (Pascal, Pascal.F87);
Rewrite (Pascal);
        .
        .


{write operations to Pascal.F87 disk file}
        .
        .
```

The *Rewrite* procedure initializes the file window to position 0 and assumes that the file is empty.   Any current disk file with the same name is erased.   Thus, in the above example, the *Pascal.F87* disk file is erased.   This is why you must be careful only to use *Rewrite* when creating a new disk file or replacing a current disk file with completely new information.

Reset **

FORMAT: *Reset* (file variable)

The *Reset* operation positions the file window at the beginning of the file (position 0).   It does not erase the file as does *Rewrite*.   The *Reset* operation is normally used after the *Assign* statement and prior to any file read operations, as follows:

```
Assign (Pascal, Pascal.F87);
Reset (Pascal);
        .
        .

{read operations on Pascal.F87 disk file}
        .
        .
```

The file variable must always have a name assigned to it as a result of the *Assign* procedure. Otherwise, an I/O error will occur.

Close ***

FORMAT: *Close* (file variable)

The *Close* procedure should always be used as the last statement in a file access routine. In other words, *always close the file* after working with it, even if you have only read from the file.

Erase ***

FORMAT: *Erase* (file variable)

The *Erase* procedure does exactly what it says: It erases the disk file associated with the file variable. You should always close a file prior to erasing it, so that you are sure that the entire disk file is erased.

Now it is time to learn how to put information into a file and get information from a file. Putting information into a file is called *writing* to the file, and getting information from a file is referred to as *reading* from the file.

Writing to Files

When you write to a file, you are storing information to the file. There are two fundamental tasks that might require this operation: (1) creating a new file or (2) updating an old file. In either case, the TURBO Pascal statement that must be used to store information to the file is the *Write* statement. Here's the general format:

WRITING TO FILES FORMAT **

Write (file variable, information to be written);

****

As you can see, the general format requires the *Write* statement to be followed by parentheses, which include the file variable identifier listed first, followed by the information to be written to the file. For instance, suppose that we declare the following general-purpose file:

```
TYPE
  FileIdent = FILE OF STRING [20];

VAR
  FileVariable : FileIdent;
  Component : STRING [20];
```

Here, the file is declared as a file of strings of twenty characters each. The file-type identifier is *FileIdent*, and the file variable is *FileVariable*. In addition, I have declared a variable, *Component*, to be a string of twenty characters. Now, suppose that an application for this file is to store the names of the students in your class. To build the file, your program prompts a user to enter a student name, and the name is read like this:

```
Write ('Enter a name and press return ---> ');
Read (Component);
```

At this point, the name has been entered and is stored in primary memory using the twenty-character string variable *Component*. Now, the idea is to write the name to the file. This is done with a *Write* statement using the above format like this:

```
Write (FileVariable, Component);
```

Notice that the file variable is listed first, followed by the information to be written. That's all there is to it! This single *Write* statement causes the value of *Component* to be transferred from primary memory through the file window to the disk file. The component data is written to the current position of the file window. Furthermore, *after* the *Write* operation, *the file window is automatically moved forward one position*. Consequently, after execution of the *Write* operation, the file window is located one position beyond where it was located prior to the operation.

You have undoubtedly noticed the similarity between this *Write* operation and the standard *Write* operations that you have used before. What's the difference? When writing to a file, the file variable is listed first, right? However, when writing to the CRT screen, no file variable is listed. Earlier I told you that the CRT display is treated like a file. Thus, when you use the *Write* statement to write information to the display, you are actually writing to the display file. When no file variable is listed in the *Write* statement, the **default** file is the display file. Likewise, when you use the *Write* statement to write information to the printer, you are writing to the printer file. So, what do you suppose is the printer file variable? Right—the printer file variable is *lst*. This is why you must use the abbreviation *lst* as the first item in a *Write* statement when writing to the printer.

Now let's expand on the foregoing file declaration and write a general procedure that can be used to create, or build, a new file. Then we will write a general procedure that can be used to expand an existing file. The flowchart in Figure 10-2 shows the file operations that must be performed to build a new file using TURBO Pascal. As you can see, you must first assign a disk-file name to the file using the *Assign* procedure. Then the file must always be rewritten using the *Rewrite* procedure to initialize the file and place the file window at the beginning of the file. Once the file is rewritten, information can be written to the file using the *Write* procedure. Finally, after all information has been written to the file,

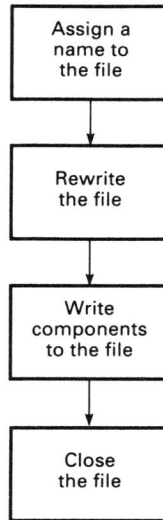

Figure 10-2 Procedures required to *create* a new disk file using TURBO Pascal.

the file must be closed using the *Close* procedure. Here's a procedure that will write names to the file:

```
PROCEDURE  WriteFile (VAR FileVar : FileIdent);

VAR
  Name : STRING [11];
  K, Number : integer;

BEGIN
  Clrscr;
  Writeln ('What name do you want to give your disk file?  ');
  Writeln ('Note:  Not more than 8 characters with a 3 ');
  Writeln ('character extension.');
  Writeln;
  Readln (Name);
  Writeln;
  Writeln;
  Assign (FileVar, Name);
  Rewrite (FileVar);
  Write ('How many components do you have to enter? ---> ');
  Readln (Number);
  Writeln;
  Writeln;
  FOR K := 0 TO Number - 1 DO
    BEGIN
      Write ('Enter component ',K,' and press return ---> ');
      Readln (Component);
      Writeln;
      Write (FileVar, Component)
    END;
  Close (FileVar)
END; {procedure WriteFile}
```

First, look at the procedure heading. The procedure name is *WriteFile*. A variable parameter, *FileVar*, is used to receive the file from the calling program. TURBO Pascal requires that you **must always use a variable parameter to pass files to procedures.** The variable parameter, *FileVar*, is of type *FileIdent*, which is the data-type identifier we declared earlier for the file.

Next, a local variable called *Name* is declared. This variable will be used to receive a name that the user desires for the file in the disk directory.

In the statement section of the procedure you see that the user is first prompted for a file name. Once entered, an *Assign* statement is used to assign the name to the variable parameter, *FileVar*. This causes a file to be created on the disk and the disk directory to be updated with the name received from the user.

The user is then prompted to indicate how many file components will be entered. For this application, a component is declared as a string of up to twenty characters. The number of file components is required to control the subsequent **FOR/DO** loop, which receives the individual components and writes them to the file. Notice that the loop counter, *K*, is incremented from 0 to *Number*-1 so that the counter value corresponds to the file component number. The components are written to the file by simply using a *Write* statement to write *Component* to *FileVar*.

Once all the components have been written to the file in the **FOR/DO** loop, the file is closed using the *Close* procedure. This is when the file information will actually be transferred to the disk.

Now suppose that we have stored a student-name file on the disk using the foregoing *WriteFile* procedure, and that we wish to expand the file with some additional student names. A flowchart for an expansion routine is shown in Figure 10-3. Here you see again that a file name must be first assigned to the file variable so that the compiler knows which disk file is to be expanded. Then the file must be reset using the *Reset* procedure. Next, to add components to the file, the file window must be positioned to one position beyond the last component in the file, right? This is accomplished using the *Seek* procedure. After the window is positioned one position beyond the end of the file, the new components are written to the file and the file must be closed. Here's the procedure:

```
PROCEDURE ExpandFile (VAR FileVar : FileIdent);

VAR
  Name : STRING [11];
  Number, K : integer;

BEGIN
  Clrscr;
  Write ('What disk file do you wish to expand? ---> ');
  Readln (Name);
  Writeln;
  Assign (FileVar,Name);
  Reset (FileVar);
  Seek (FileVar,FileSize(FileVar));
```

(Continued)

```
Write ('How many components do you wish to add? ---> ');
Readln (Number);
Writeln;
FOR K := 1 TO Number DO
   BEGIN
      Write ('Enter component ',K,' and press return ---> ');
      Readln (Component);
      Writeln;
      Write (FileVar, Component)
   END;
Close (FileVar)
END;  {procedure ExpandFile}
```

Again, a variable parameter (*FileVar*) is used to pass the file to the procedure from the calling program. The user is first prompted to enter the disk file name that needs to be expanded. This name is then assigned to the variable parameter, *FileVar*, so that the compiler knows which disk file to access. The file is then reset using *Reset*, and the window is positioned using the *Seek* procedure. Note how the *FileSize* function is called within the statement, as we discussed earlier, to seek the end of the file. Once the window is in the proper position, the new file components are added to the file using a **FOR/DO** loop as before. Finally, the file *must* be closed using the *Close* procedure.

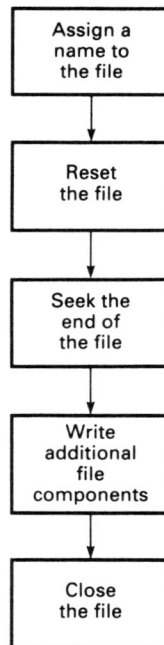

Figure 10-3 Procedures required to *expand* a file using TURBO Pascal.

Reading from Files

Reading from a file is very much like writing to a file. Here's the general format:

READING FROM FILES FORMAT **

Read (file variable, variable to receive data);

****

As you can see, a standard *Read* operation is employed. The file variable to be read is listed first within parentheses and followed by the variables to which the file data is to be assigned. As an example, let's use the general-purpose file we declared earlier. Here it is again:

```
TYPE
   FileIdent = FILE OF STRING [20];

VAR
   FileVariable : FileIdent;
   Component : STRING [20];
```

Now suppose that we have used the previous *WriteFile* procedure to store this file on a disk. How might you read a component of the file? Simple: by using a read statement, as follows:

```
Read (FileVariable, Component);
```

When executed, this operation will read the file component located at the current *FileVariable* window position. The component data is assigned to the variable *Component*. Of course, *Component* must be declared the same data type as the file components or a data-type mismatch error will occur. In addition, after the file component is read, **the file window is automatically moved forward one component position.** Thus, after the *Read* operation is executed, the file window is one position beyond where it was prior to the *Read* operation.

Now let's develop a general procedure to read an entire file. The required file operations are shown in the flowchart in Figure 10-4. First, a name must be assigned to the file using the *Assign* procedure. Then the file must be reset using the *Reset* procedure. Recall that this positions the file window at the first component position. Next, the file components are read using the *Read* procedure, and finally, the file must be closed using the *Close* procedure. Here is a general *ReadFile* procedure that incorporates these operations:

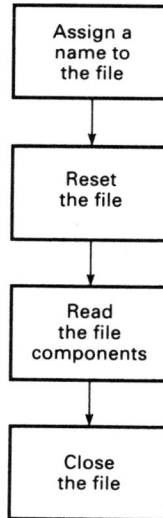

Figure 10-4 Procedures required to *read* an existing file using TURBO Pascal.

```
PROCEDURE ReadFile   (VAR FileVar : FileIdent);

VAR
   Name : STRING [11];


BEGIN
   Clrscr;
   Write ('What disk file name do you want to read and display? ---> ');
   Readln (Name);
   Writeln;
   Assign (FileVar, Name);
   Reset (FileVar);
   WHILE NOT EOF(FileVar) DO
     BEGIN
       Read (FileVar, Component);
       Writeln (Component)
     END;
   Close (FileVar)
END;   {procedure ReadFile}
```

The procedure heading requires that a variable parameter be declared for the file type. Again, I have chosen to use the parameter *FileVar*. The user is first prompted to enter the name of the disk file to be read. Once entered, this name is assigned to *FileVar* using the *Assign* procedure so that the compiler knows which disk file is to be accessed. The file is then reset using the *Reset* procedure to position the file window at the first component position. Observe that the file read operation is part of a **WHILE/DO** loop. Each time through the loop, a file component (*Component*) is read using the *Read* operation and written to the display using a *Writeln* statement. The file window begins at position 0 and is incremented through the file with each *Read* operation. (Why?) As long as the window is *not* at the end-of-file position, a file component is read and displayed. However, when the window reaches the *EOF* position, the loop is broken and the file is closed using the *Close* procedure.   Could a **REPEAT/UNTIL** loop be used in place of the **WHILE/DO** loop?   If so, how?

Finally, how do you suppose the procedure must be changed to print, rather than display, the file components.   Of course: by substituting a *Writeln (lst, Component)* statement for the *Writeln (Component)* statement within the procedure.

Changing a File

We have now developed three procedures: create a new disk file, add to an existing disk file, and read an existing disk file.   Now suppose that you need to change a file component.   Think about what has to be done to accomplish this task.   The file must first be opened to position the file window at the first component position. Then the file must be searched to find the component to be changed.   Once found, the new component information must be written to the same file position.   A general flowchart for a change-file procedure is shown in Figure 10-5.   Using this flowchart as a general guideline, we can develop a *ChangeFile* procedure as follows:

```
PROCEDURE ChangeFile (VAR FileVar : FileIdent);

VAR
  Name : STRING [11];
  NewComponent, OldComponent : STRING [20];
  Flag : Boolean;

BEGIN
  Clrscr;
  Write ('What disk file do you wish to change? ---> ');
  Readln (Name);
  Writeln;
  Assign (FileVar,Name);
  Reset (FileVar);
  Write ('What file component do you wish to change? ---> ');

  Readln (OldComponent);
  Writeln;
  Flag := FALSE;
  WHILE NOT EOF (FileVar) DO
    BEGIN
      Read (FileVar,Component);
      IF Component = OldComponent THEN
        BEGIN
          Flag := TRUE;
          Writeln (OldComponent,' has been found.  What do you ');
          Write ('wish to change it to? ---> ');
          Readln (NewComponent);
          Seek (FileVar, FilePos(FileVar) - 1);
          Write (FileVar, NewComponent)
        END{if statement}
    END;  {while loop}
  IF Flag = FALSE THEN
    Writeln (OldComponent,' was not found in this file.');
  Close (FileVar)
END;  {procedure ChangeFile}
```

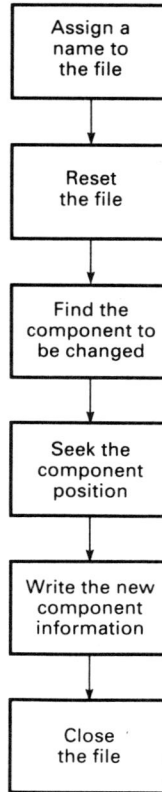

Figure 10-5 Procedures required to *change* a given file component using TURBO Pascal.

Again, a variable parameter called *FileVar* is employed. The user is first prompted to enter the name of the disk file that needs to be changed. Once the name is entered, it is assigned to *FileVar* so that subsequent references to *FileVar* access the proper disk file. The file is then reset to position the file window at the first component position. Next, the user is prompted to enter the component to be changed. This component value is assigned to the variable *OldComponent*. A Boolean flag (*Flag*) is then set to FALSE. This flag will be used to determine if the component is found in the file. A **WHILE/DO** loop is then executed to search for *OldComponent*. With each iteration of the loop, a file component (*Component*) is read and compared with the user entry (*OldComponent*). If the desired component is found, the Boolean flag is set to TRUE and the user is prompted for the new component information (*NewComponent*). At this point, the previous *Read* file operation has positioned the file window one position beyond the desired component position. (Why?) Consequently, the window needs to be moved back one position to locate the window in the correct position to write the new component. This is accomplished using a *Seek* procedure. The *Seek* procedure will position the window at the current window position minus 1, which is where it needs to be for the subsequent *Write* operation.   Once the window is in its proper position, the *Write* operation writes the new component (*NewComponent*) value over the old component value.   This completes the change operation.

Now, what happens if the old component value entered by the user is not found in the file?   Sure, the Boolean flag (*Flag*) would be FALSE and the last **IF/ THEN** statement would cause an appropriate message to be displayed.   By the way, even if the component is found, the **WHILE/DO** loop will continue to execute until the end of the file is reached.   Thus, the user will have the option of changing multiple entries of the same component.

We have now developed four general procedures to create, expand, read, and change a file.   Let's incorporate these procedures into a menu-driven main program that will give the user any one of the four procedure options.   All that the main program requires is a case operation to allow user selection of the desired procedure, as follows:

```
BEGIN   {main program}
  Clrscr;
  Writeln;
  Writeln;
  Writeln;
  Writeln;
  Writeln;
  Writeln ('                    Write and create a new file (W)');
  Writeln;
  Writeln ('                    Read and display an existing file (R)');
  Writeln;
  Writeln ('                    Add to an existing file (A)');
  Writeln;
  Writeln ('                    Change a file component (C)');
  Writeln;
  Writeln;
  Write    ('                         ENTER CHOICE ---> ');
  Readln (Choice);
  Writeln;
  CASE Choice OF
    'W', 'w' : WriteFile (FileVariable);
    'R', 'r' : ReadFile (FileVariable);

    'A', 'a' : ExpandFile (FileVariable);
    'C', 'c' : ChangeFile (FileVariable)
  ELSE
    Writeln ('Invalid entry, press R to run the program again.')
  END {case}
END.   {main program}
```

The first part of the main program displays a menu that prompts the user to enter one of the four file options.   The **CASE** statement then selects the corresponding procedure.   Notice that the file variable, *FileVariable*, is listed in each procedure call.   This is the variable that we originally declared for the *FileIdent* file.   That's all there is to it!

The file we have just been working with was declared as a file of string data. You only need to make minor changes to the foregoing file declaration and procedures to work with files of other scalar data types such as integer, real, character, and Boolean. However, one of the most common structures is a file of records. Let's look at a comprehensive example that shows the procedures required to work with such a file.

Example 10-1:

Modify the foregoing file declaration and procedures to perform the following tasks:
a. Declare a file of address records which consist of the names, addresses, and telephone numbers of your friends.
b. Write procedures to create, expand, read, and change your address file.

Solution:

a. The record must be declared first, followed by the file declaration like this:

```
TYPE

Address_Record = RECORD
                     Name : STRING [25];
                     Address : RECORD
                                  Street : STRING [20];
                                  City : STRING [20];
                                  State : STRING [15];
                                  Zip : STRING [10]
                               END;
                     Phone : STRING [15]
                  END;


      FileIdent = FILE OF  Address_Record;

VAR
   FileVariable : FileIdent;
   Person : Address_Record;
   Choice : char;
```

The declaration is straightforward. The *Address_Record* consists of a *Name* field, an *Address* field, and a *Phone* field. Notice that the *Address* field is a nested record. The file identifier is *FileIdent*, which is declared as a file of the *Address_Record*. The file variable is *FileVariable*, and the record variable is *Person*. The character variable, *Choice*, will be used for the user response to a menu prompt.

b. The first procedure that we need to write is a procedure that will create a new file. I have altered the earlier *WriteFile* procedure to operate on the address file as follows:

```
PROCEDURE  WriteFile (VAR FileVar : FileIdent);

VAR
   Name : STRING [11];
   K, Number : integer;
```

```
BEGIN
  Clrscr;
  Writeln ('What name do you want to give your disk file?  ');
  Writeln ('Note:  Not more than 8 characters with a 3 ');
  Writeln ('character extension.');
  Writeln;
  Readln (Name);
  Writeln;
  Writeln;
  Assign (FileVar, Name);
  Rewrite (FileVar);
  Write ('How many addresses do you have to enter? ---> ');
  Readln (Number);
  Writeln;
  Writeln;
  FOR K := 1 TO Number  DO
    BEGIN
      Writeln ('Enter address ',K,' as follows ---> ');
      WITH Person, Address DO
        BEGIN
          Write ('Enter the person's name ---> ');
          Readln (Name);
          Writeln;
          Write ('Enter street address ---> ');
          Readln (Street);
          Writeln;
          Write ('Enter city ---> ');
          Readln (City);
          Writeln;
          Write ('Enter state ---> ');
          Readln (State);
          Writeln;
          Write ('Enter Zip Code ---> ');
          Readln (Zip);
          Writeln;
          Write ('Enter phone number ---> ');
          Readln (Phone);
          Writeln;
          Writeln
        END; {with}
      Write (FileVar, Person)
    END; {for};
  Close (FileVar)
END; {procedure WriteFile}
```

What do you find different in this procedure from the previous *WriteFile* procedure? The major difference is the **WITH/DO** operation employed to fill the record.   The **WITH/DO** statement references the record variable (*Person*) and the nested record field (*Address*).   Notice that once a record is filled using **WITH/DO,** the record variable (*Person*) is written to the file using a *Write (FileVar, Person)* statement. There are absolutely no differences between this and the earlier *WriteFile* procedure as far as the file operations are concerned.   The file operations of *Assign, Rewrite, Write*, and *Close* are performed as before (refer to Figure 10-2).

Next, we need a procedure to expand an existing address file.   Altering the earlier *ExpandFile* procedure to work with the *Address_Record* you get the following:

```
PROCEDURE ExpandFile (VAR FileVar : FileIdent);

VAR
   Name : STRING [11];
   Number, K : integer;

BEGIN
   Clrscr;
   Write ('What disk file do you wish to expand? ---> ');
   Readln (Name);
   Writeln;
   Assign (FileVar,Name);
   Reset (FileVar);
   Seek (FileVar,FileSize(FileVar));
   Write ('How many components do you wish to add? ---> ');
   Readln (Number);
   Writeln;
   FOR K := 1 TO Number DO
     BEGIN
       Writeln ('Enter person ',K,' as follows: ');
       Writeln;
       WITH Person, Address DO
         BEGIN
           Write ('Enter the person's name ---> ');
           Readln (Name);
           Writeln;
           Write ('Enter street address ---> ');
           Readln (Street);
           Writeln;
           Write ('Enter city ---> ');
           Readln (City);
           Writeln;
           Write ('Enter state ---> ');
           Readln (State);
           Writeln;
           Write ('Enter Zip Code ---> ');
           Readln (Zip);
           Writeln;
           Write ('Enter phone number ---> ');
           Readln (Phone);
           Writeln;
           Writeln
         END; {with}
       Writeln;
       Write (FileVar, Person)


     END; {for}
   Close (FileVar)
END;  {procedure ExpandFile}
```

Notice that the file operations of *Assign, Reset, Seek, Write*, and *Close* are performed as before to add a record to the end of the file (refer to Figure 10-3). Of course, a **WITH/DO** statement must be used to fill the record. The record is then transferred to the file using a *Write (FileVar, Person)* statement.

The next procedure we need to develop is a procedure to change an existing record within the file.   Again, adapting the earlier *ChangeFile* procedure to our address record, we get the following:

```
PROCEDURE ChangeFile (VAR FileVar : FileIdent);

VAR
  Name : STRING [11];
  OldComponent : STRING [25];
  Number, K : integer;
  Flag : Boolean;

BEGIN
  Clrscr;
  Write ('What disk file do you wish to change? ---> ');
  Readln (Name);
  Writeln;
  Assign (FileVar,Name);
  Reset (FileVar);
  Write ('What person address do you wish to change? ---> ');
  Readln (OldComponent);
  Writeln;
  Flag := FALSE;
  WHILE NOT EOF (FileVar) DO
    BEGIN
      Read (FileVar,Person);
      IF Person.Name = OldComponent THEN
        BEGIN
          Flag := TRUE;
          Write (OldComponent,' has been found.   ');
          Writeln ('Enter new information: ');
          WITH Person, Address DO
            BEGIN
              Write ('Enter the person's name ---> ');
              Readln (Name);
              Writeln;
              Write ('Enter street address ---> ');
              Readln (Street);
              Writeln;
              Write ('Enter city ---> ');
              Readln (City);
              Writeln;
              Write ('Enter state ---> ');
              Readln (State);
              Writeln;
              Write ('Enter Zip Code ---> ');
              Readln (Zip);
              Writeln;
              Write ('Enter phone number ---> ');
              Readln (Phone);
```

(Continued)

```
              Writeln;
              Writeln
            END; {with}
          Seek (FileVar, FilePos(FileVar) - 1);
          Write (FileVar, Person)
        END{if statement}
    END;   {while loop}
  IF Flag = FALSE THEN
    Writeln (OldComponent,' was not found in this file.');

    Close (FileVar)
  END;   {procedure ChangeFile}
```

Upon examining the file operations in this procedure, you will find that they are consistent with those used in the earlier *ChangeFile* procedure (refer to Figure 10-5).

Finally, we need a procedure to read the file. Again, we will adapt the earlier *ReadFile* procedure to this task. However, considering the address file application, we will give the user the option of listing the entire address file on a printer or displaying a single address record. Here's the procedure:

```
PROCEDURE ReadFile   (VAR FileVar : FileIdent);

VAR
  Nam : STRING [25];
  Name : STRING [11];
  Choice : char;
  Flag : Boolean;

BEGIN
  Clrscr;
  Write ('What disk file name do you want to read and display? ---> ');
  Readln (Name);
  Writeln;
  Assign (FileVar,Name);
  Reset (FileVar);
  Clrscr;
  Writeln;
  Writeln;
  Writeln;
  Writeln ('                        Print entire address file (P)    ');
  Writeln;
  Writeln ('                        Display a given address (D)     ');
  Writeln;
  Writeln;
  Write   ('                        ENTER CHOICE ---> ');
  Readln (Choice);
  CASE Choice OF
    'P', 'p' : BEGIN
                 WHILE NOT EOF(FileVar) DO
```

```
            BEGIN
              Read (FileVar, Person);
              WITH Person, Address DO
                BEGIN
                  Writeln (1st,Name);
                  Writeln (1st,Street);
                  Writeln (1st,City,', ',State,'  ',Zip);
                  Writeln (1st,'PHONE:   ',Phone);
                  Writeln (1st);
                  Writeln (1st)
                END  {with}
            END {while/do}
        END; {case P}

'D', 'd' : BEGIN
             Clrscr;
             Write ('What person address do you wish to ');
             Write ('display? ---> ');
             Readln (Nam);
             Writeln;
             Flag := FALSE;
             WHILE NOT EOF (FileVar) DO
               BEGIN
                 Read (FileVar,Person);
                 IF Person.Name = Nam THEN
                   BEGIN

                       Flag := TRUE;
                       WITH Person, Address DO
                         BEGIN
                           Writeln (Name);
                           Writeln (Street);
                           Writeln (City,', ',State,'  ',Zip);
                           Writeln ('PHONE:   ',Phone);
                           Writeln;
                           Writeln
                         END {with}
                   END  {if}
               END {while}
           END {case D}
  ELSE
    Writeln ('Invalid choice, press R to run again.')
  END; {case}
  IF Flag = FALSE THEN
    Writeln (Nam, ' was not found in this file.');
  Close (FileVar)
END;  {procedure ReadFile}
```

The file operations are basically the same as in the earlier *ReadFile* procedure. We must *Assign, Reset, Read*, and *Close* the file as indicated in the flowchart in Figure 10-4.   Notice, however, that when a file component is read, it is read to the record variable using a *Read (FileVar, Person)* statement. Once the record variable (*Person*) receives a file component, it can be printed or displayed using a **WITH/DO** statement just as if it were any record in primary memory.

Now notice how the user is given the option of printing the entire file or displaying a single address record within the file. These options are provided via a **CASE** statement.

The print option is simple: Each record component within the file is read and printed until the end of the file is reached. The display option, on the other hand, requires the user to enter the name of the person to be displayed. The first record component in the file is then read and the person name within that record (*Person.Name*) is compared with the name entered by the user (*Nam*) using an **IF/ THEN** statement. If the names are the same, the record is displayed. If not, another record component is read from the file, the names are compared, and so on, until either the two names match or the end of the file is reached. If the name is not found, the user is told that the name he or she entered was not found in the file.

10-3 TEXT FILES

The final type of file that we need to discuss is a ***text file***. Think of a text file as a file of characters where the characters are divided into lines using *end-of-line* (*EOLN*) markers. In other words, you can imagine the text you are reading on this page as a text file. It is a continuous sequence of characters, where each line is terminated by an end-of-line marker. Of course, the blanks are considered as characters within the character sequence. As its name implies, a text file is commonly used to store written text.

To declare a text file, you employ a single variable declaration as follows:

DECLARING TEXT FILES   **

VAR
    file variable : **text;**

****

As you can see, no **TYPE** declaration is required, since **text** is already predefined by Pascal as a file of characters similar to

```
TYPE
   text = FILE OF char;
```

Text files have basically the same properties of other files. However, they must be processed sequentially from beginning to end. Thus, semirandom file operations available in TURBO, such as *Seek, FilePos,* and *FileSize cannot* be used

on text files.   Otherwise, you operate on text files basically the same way that you
do any other file.

Let's develop a procedure to write some text to a text file.

Writing to Text Files

We will first declare the file as follows:

```
VAR
      FileVariable : text;
```

Here, the file variable is *FileVariable*.   Of course, the file is **text,** which is
predefined as a file of characters.   Now here is a procedure that will write some
fixed text to the file:

```
PROCEDURE  WriteText (VAR FileVar : text);

VAR
  Name : STRING [11];


BEGIN
  Clrscr;
  Writeln ('This procedure will simply write text to a text file.');
  Writeln;
  Write ('What do you want to call this text file? ---> ');
  Readln (Name);
  Writeln;
  Assign (FileVar,Name);
  Rewrite (FileVar);
  Writeln (FileVar, 'This is a text file.  A text file has the');
  Writeln (FileVar, 'same properties of other files, however they');
  Writeln (FileVar, 'are divided into lines with an end-of-line');
  Writeln (FileVar, 'marker placed at the end of each line.');
  Writeln (FileVar);
  Writeln (FileVar, 'Text files must be processed sequentially as  ');
  Writeln (FileVar, 'as series of characters.  Thus, the TURBO file ');
  Writeln (FileVar, 'operations of FilePos, FileSize and Seek ');
  Writeln (FileVar, 'do not apply to text files.');
  Write ('The text contained in the procedure has now been written ');
  Writeln ('to the ',Name, ' file.');
  Close (FileVar)
END;   {procedure WriteText}
```

You see that the procedure header lists the variable parameter *FileVar* as a
type **text.**   Remember, file parameters must always be variable parameters.   Thus,
the parameter *FileVar* will receive the text file from the calling program and be
used when writing text to the file.   In the statement section of the procedure, you
first see that the user is prompted to enter a disk-file name (*Name*).   This name

is then assigned to the file variable (*FileVar*) using an *Assign* statement.   Next, the file is rewritten using *Rewrite* in preparation for the write operation.   Up to this point, the file processing is identical to that of any other file.   Now, how do you write text to the file?   Simple: by using *Write/Writeln* statements as shown. Notice that the procedure employs *Writeln* statements to write individual lines to the file.   Each *Writeln* statement first lists the variable file parameter (*FileVar*), followed by the text to be written to the file, enclosed within single quotes.   In addition, the statement *Writeln* (*FileVar*) in the middle of the procedure writes a blank line to the file to separate the two paragraphs.   That's all there is to it!   It's like writing text to the display or printer, except that the file variable (*FileVar*) is listed in the *Writeln* statement.

Now, what do you suppose is the difference between using *Write* versus *Writeln* to write text information to the file?   Well, *Writeln* places an end-of-line (*EOLN*) marker at the end of the respective line, whereas *Write* does not.   For instance, the first line to be written to the above file is

'This is text file. A text file has the'

This same line could be written to the file using the following two statements:

```
Write (FileVar,'This is a text file.   ');
Writeln (FileVar,'A text file has the');
```

This way, the *Write* statement writes the text 'This is a text file.' to the file but does not insert an *EOLN* marker after the text.   The *Writeln* statement then adds 'A text file has the' to the same line and inserts an *EOLN* marker at the end of the line, so that the next write operation begins writing text on the next line. Get the idea?

After all of the text is written to the file, the final operation is to close the file using a *Close* procedure.   Remember, files must always be closed after any kind of processing, even text files.

Reading Text Files

You read text files just as you would read a file of characters.   The basic file operations of *Assign, Reset, Read*, and *Close*, are employed just as before.   Here's a procedure that will read our text file:

```
PROCEDURE ReadText (VAR FileVar : text);

VAR
  Name : STRING [11];
  Character : char;

BEGIN
  Clrscr;
  Write ('What is the name of the text file that ');
```

```
    Write ('you want to read? ---> ');
    Readln (Name);
    Writeln;
    Assign (FileVar,Name);
    Reset (FileVar);
    WHILE NOT  EOF (FileVar) DO
      BEGIN
        Read (FileVar,Character);
        Write (Character)
      END;
  Close (FileVar);
  Writeln;
  Writeln;
  Writeln;
  Writeln ('That's all folks!')
END;  {procedure ReadText}
```

Again, a variable file parameter (*FileVar*) is listed in the procedure header as type **text.** The user is prompted for the disk file name, and the name entered by the user is assigned to *FileVar* using the *Assign* procedure. Next, the file is reset and a **WHILE/DO** loop is executed to read the text file characters. Notice that a single character is read each time the loop executes using the statement *Read* (*FileVar, Character*). Once read, the character is displayed using a normal *Write* statement. Of course, the variable *Character* is declared as a local character variable. The **WHILE/DO** loop continues to execute, reading and displaying one character at a time, until the end-of-file (*EOF*) marker is encountered. Here is what you would see on the display:

```
This is a text file.  A text file has the
same properties of other files, however they
are divided into lines with an end-of-line
marker placed at the end of each line.

Text files must be processed sequentially as
as series of characters.  Thus, the TURBO file
operations of FilePos, FileSize and Seek
do not apply to text files.
```

Now, does the display know when to end a given line and begin a new one? Sure, by detecting the *EOLN* marker. Recall that the *Writeln* statements in the *WriteText* procedure place an *EOLN* marker at the end of each line. Finally, you see that the file is closed after all the text characters have been read.

CHAPTER SUMMARY

A file is a sequential data structure used to store components of the same data type. The most common application for a file is for storing information on disk. Thus, files provide a means of storing information between program runs. You can think of a file as a means for your program to communicate with the outside world.   In fact, all I/O operations in TURBO Pascal are handled via files, even keyboard, CRT, and printer operations.

To declare a user-defined file in Pascal, you must use a two-part **TYPE/VAR** declaration.   The file identifier and component data type are declared using the **TYPE** declaration, while the file variable, used to access the file components, is declared using the **VAR** declaration.

File components are accessed via a file window.   The file window must be positioned over the component to be accessed.   When you declare a file, the window, sometimes called a file buffer variable, is automatically created to access the file components.

File processing in TURBO Pascal is quite different from other versions of Pascal.   TURBO includes file operations that are not included in other versions of Pascal and vice versa.   There are three standard file functions available in TURBO: *FileSize*, *FilePos*, and *EOF*.   In addition, there are several predefined file procedures available in TURBO, including *Seek*, *Assign*, *Rename*, *Rewrite*, *Reset*, *Close*, *Erase*, *Read/Readln*, and *Write/Writeln*.

Before processing any files in TURBO, the file variable must be assigned a file name using the *Assign* procedure.   To create new files, you must rewrite the file using the *Rewrite* procedure.   To process an existing file, the file must be reset using the *Reset* procedure.   You use *Write* statements to store information to a file and *Read* statements to get information from a file.   You employ the *Seek* procedure to locate the file window at a given component position for reading or writing.   Remember, files must always be closed after any file processing.

A special type of file available in all versions of Pascal is the **text** file.   A text file is a predefined file of characters in which the characters are divided into lines using end-of-line (*EOLN*) markers.   As its name implies, a text file is commonly used to store written text information.   All text files must be processed sequentially as a series of characters.   Thus, the TURBO operations of *FilePos*, *FileSize*, and *Seek* cannot be applied to text files.

QUESTIONS AND PROBLEMS

Questions

10-1. Describe the structure of a file.

10-2. What is a file window and how is it used during file processing?

10-3. The statement used to retrieve data from a file is the _____ statement.

10-4. True or False: Both the *Write* and *Read* statements post-increment the file window position.

10-5. True or False: TURBO Pascal does not support random file access.

10-6. A file that is predefined as a file of characters is a _____ file.

10-7. Which of the following statements will locate the file window at the beginning of the file?

    a. `Reset (file variable);`

    b. `Rewrite (file variable);`

    c. `Seek (file variable,0);`

    d. Both a and b above

    e. All of the above

    f. None of the above

10-8. True or False: All the components in a given file must be the same data type.

10-9. Which of the following file declarations are illegal?

    a. `FileIdent = FILE OF char;`

    b. `FileIdent = FILE OF ARRAY [1..3,1..5] OF real;`

    c. `FileIdent = FILE OF text;`

    d. `FileIdent = FILE OF FILE`

    e. They are all legal in TURBO Pascal.

Indicate which TURBO Pascal functions/procedures you would use to perform the following operations:

10-10. Terminate the processing of a file.

10-11. Obtain a component from a file.

10-12. Insert a component into a file.

10-13. Determine the current position of the file window.

10-14. Test to see if the entire file has been read.

10-15. Prepare a new file for writing.

10-16. Prepare a file for reading.

10-17. Position the file window at the end of the file.

10-18. Position the file window at the position of a component that has just been read.

10-19. Change the name of an existing disk file.

10-20. Create a disk file name.

Programming Problems

10-1. Modify the *ReadFile* procedure in Section 10-2 to employ a **REPEAT/UNTIL** loop.

10-2. Write the code for a main program that will call the text-file procedures developed in Section 10-3.

10-3. Write a menu-driven program that could be used to call the procedures developed in Example 10-1.

10-4. Write a procedure that will determine if two integer files are identical.

10-5. Write a procedure that will copy an old file to a new file.

10-6. Write a procedure that will create a new file of reals by multiplying all the components of an old file of reals by 10.

10-7. Write a procedure to erase a disk file.

10-8. Declare a parts-inventory file consisting of the following information:
Part Name
Part Number
Price
Quantity

10-9. Write a procedure to create the parts-inventory file declared in question 10-8.

10-10. Write a procedure to expand the parts-inventory file declared in question 10-8.

10-11. Write a procedure to change the information for a given part in the parts-inventory file declared in question 10-8.

10-12. Write a procedure to allow a user to print the entire parts-inventory file declared in question 10-8 or to display the information for a given part.

Appendix A

Getting Started with TURBO

INTRODUCTION

This appendix has been provided as an aid in getting you started with TURBO Pascal. It has been divided into two sections, one for earlier versions of TURBO Pascal and one for TURBO 4.0 and beyond. Both sections are only intended to provide a quick reference quide. For further information, consult your TURBO reference manual or your instructor if you have specific problems with your system or cannot get TURBO to execute properly.

In addition to the operating-system disk, you will need two disks to write and store Pascal programs: the TURBO Pascal compiler disk and a work disk. Make sure that the TURBO disk is compatible with the operating system (CP/M-80, CP/M-86, MS/DOS, or PC/DOS) employed by your system. In addition, your work disk must be properly formatted for the system you are using. Consult your operating-system manual or lab instructor for directions on how to format a blank work disk. **DO NOT FORMAT THE TURBO DISK!!!**

TURBO 2 AND 3

STEP 1: Turn the system power on and insert the operating-system diskette into the primary disk drive, A. For dual drive systems, drive A will be the left or top disk drive.

STEP 2: Boot the system using the operating-system disk as follows: With
           IBM PCs and most compatibles, the system will automatically boot
           from the system disk after a short delay.

           With some systems, especially those using the CP/M operating
           system, you must press the B key followed by the **ENTER** or
           RETURN key to boot the system.

           Once the system is booted, the following system prompt should
           appear on the display:

                              A>

           Note: At this point you should format your work disk if it has not
           already been formatted.

STEP 3: Remove the system disk.

STEP 4: Insert your TURBO disk into drive A.

STEP 5: Type-in the word TURBO and press the **ENTER** OR **RETURN**
           key.   The following message should appear on the display:

```
-----------------------------------------
TURBO Pascal system        Version 3.01A
                                   PC-DOS

Copyright (C) 1983,84,85    BORLAND Inc.
-----------------------------------------

Default display mode


Include error messages (Y/N)?
```

STEP 6: The TURBO disk includes an editing feature that generates error
           messages when compiling your program.   This is a helpful aid when
           debugging programs.   If you want to use this feature, press the Y
           key.   Press the N key if you do not desire this option.

           The following main TURBO menu should now appear on the dis-
           play:

```
         Logged drive: A
         Active directory: \

         Work file:
         Main file:

         Edit      Compile  Run    Save

         Dir       Quit  compiler Options

         Text:      0 bytes
         Free: 62024 bytes
```

STEP 7: Place a formatted work disk in drive B. Drive B is the right or bottom disk drive.
Note: If you only have a single drive, remove the TURBO disk and insert your work disk in the same disk drive.

STEP 8: (For dual drive systems only) Press the L key and the following prompt will appear:

New drive:

Type-in B and press the **ENTER** key. This will log you onto drive B.

STEP 9: Press the W key and the following prompt will appear

Work file name:

Type-in a file name, not to exceed eight characters, and press the **ENTER** key. For this trial run, let's use the file name SAMPLE. The file name is what TURBO uses to locate your program on your work disk. Once a file name has been assigned to a program, the same name must be used for subsequent access to that program. When writing a new program, create a new file name that has not already been used on your work disk. To edit an old program already stored on your work disk, you must use the file name that was previously assigned to that program.

STEP 10: Press the E key for edit. You are now in the Edit mode of TURBO and can begin entering a program. Just for practice, enter the following program:

```
PROGRAM Sample (input, output);

BEGIN
  Writeln ('Congratulations, you have just entered, compiled,');
  Writeln ('and ran your first TURBO Pascal program.')
END.
```

STEP 11: Next, simultaneously press the CTRL, K, and D keys. This operation is designated as ^KD. You should see the TURBO prompt (⟩) at the bottom of the screen.

STEP 12: Press the S key to save your sample program. You should observe that the disk drive activates, indicating that your program is being saved.

STEP 13: Now that your program is saved, press the C key to compile your program. If you made any errors entering the program, the compiler will ask you to press the Escape (ESC) key. This will return you to the Edit mode and place the cursor close to the place it found the error. At this point, you must correct the error and repeat STEPS 11 through 13. When the program compiles successfully, you will get a compiled message at the bottom of the screen along with the TURBO prompt (⟩).

STEP 14: Now that your program has successfully compiled, press the R key to run the program. The program should display the message:

Congratulations, you have just entered, compiled, and ran your first TURBO Pascal program.

STEP 15: If you have a printer and want to get a hard copy of your sample program, refer to the section of this appendix titled LISTING A PROGRAM WITH TURBO 3.

You have several options from the main TURBO menu. Here is a short summary of these options. (*Note*: To get to the main menu from anywhere within TURBO, simultaneously press the CTRL, K, and D keys (^KD). Then press the spacebar.)

Dir----⟩ Press D

Dir stands for Directory. This option will allow you to view the file directory of a disk. Press the D key and the following message will appear:

Dir mask:

Now press the **ENTER** key to view the file directory on the disk in the logged drive. To view the directory on a disk in another drive, type-in the drive designation, a colon, and press the **ENTER** key. For instance, to view the directory of the disk in drive A, type in

A: **ENTER**

Edit ----⟩ Press E

This option is used to write a new Pascal program or edit an old one. To write a new program, simply press the E key and begin entering the program. When editing an old program, pressing the E key will cause the program whose work file name you entered to appear on the display.

TURBO Pascal employs the Wordstar® word processing editing commands and operations. If you are familiar with Wordstar®, your editing task is a much simpler one. If you are not familiar with Wordstar®, you must consult your TURBO reference manual for the various editing commands. It's a good idea to learn these commands to make your editing more efficient.

To exit the editing mode and return to the main menu, simultaneously press the control (CTRL), K, and D keys. This operation is commonly designated as

^KD, where the carrot (^) stands for CTRL. The ^KD operation causes the
TURBO prompt (>) to appear on the screen as follows:

>

Whenever you see this prompt, press the space bar to return to the main
TURBO menu.

Compile ----> Press C

To compile your program, press the C key. When the program is being compiled
the TURBO compiler checks for various errors. When an error is found, TURBO
will generate an error message. Write down the message and then press the escape
(ESC) key. TURBO will then automatically return to the editing mode and place
the cursor near that point in the program where the error was found. You must
correct the error and return to the main menu (^KD and space bar) and attempt
to compile (C) the program again. This compile/error/edit process must be repeated until the program is successfully compiled. When the program compiles
successfully, you will get a display like the following:

```
Compiling
   210 lines

Code:        0068 paragraphs (  1664 bytes), OCCO paragraphs free
Data:        0015 paragraphs (   336 bytes), OFC7 paragraphs free
Stack/Heap: 85B4 paragraphs (547648 bytes)

>
```

Notice that the display indicates how many lines of code have been compiled. In
addition, the message tells how much memory is used by the program and how
much memory remains free.

Save ----> Press S

It is always a good idea to save your program on your work disk before running
it. Pressing the S key from the main menu accomplishes this task. The program
is saved on the disk located in the logged drive. Furthermore, it will be saved
under the work file name that you have assigned to it.

Run ----> Press R

Pressing the R key when you see the TURBO prompt (>) will execute your program.
TURBO will detect and display an error message if a run-time error is detected
during program execution. When this happens, you must return to the editing
mode and correct the program. However, some run-time errors, such as infinite

loops, will not be detected by TURBO. When this happens, the system "locks-up" and must be reset or turned off to get out of the lock-up condition. Hopefully, you have saved your program prior to running it. If not, it is lost! If the program has been saved, you can get back to it by rebooting the system and entering the TURBO editing mode, as described in steps 1–9 above.

Once a program has been successfully executed the TURBO prompt (⟩) will reappear on the screen. You can get back to the main TURBO menu by pressing the space bar at this point.

Compiler Options ----⟩ Press O

The compiler options allow you to compile your program in different ways. For example, you can compile your program onto a disk as a .COM file so that it can be run directly from the operating system, without using TURBO. Consult your TURBO reference manual for further details.

Quit ----⟩ Press Q

Pressing the Q key from the main menu exits TURBO and returns you to the operating system. The system prompt will appear on the screen.

Listing a Program with TURBO 3

Your version 3 TURBO disk contains a Pascal program called LISTER that will allow you to get a hard copy of your program. Make sure that your TURBO disk is in drive A, then press the W key from the main TURBO menu. Type-in the following:

> **A:LISTER**

Next press the R key to run LISTER. You will observe the following message on the display:

> **Enter Filename:**

Make sure that your printer is on. Now type-in the drive designation, a colon, the program name, the extension .PAS, and press the **ENTER** key. For example, if the program is named SAMPLE and is located on a disk in drive B you would enter the following:

> **B:SAMPLE.PAS**   **ENTER**

Once the program is listed, press the space bar to return to the main TURBO menu.

TURBO 4 AND BEYOND

This section has been written to get you started with the TURBO *integrated environment*. The command-line mode is not covered here. In addition, it is assumed that TURBO has been installed on your system.

STEP 1: Turn the system power on and insert the operating system diskette into the primary disk drive, A. For dual drive systems, drive A will be the left or top disk drive.

With IBM PCs and most compatibles, the system will automatically boot from the system disk after a short delay.

Once the system is booted, the following system prompt should appear on the display:

A>

Note: At this point you should format your work disk if it has not already been formatted. To do this, simply enter the word FORMAT and follow the system instructions.

STEP 2: Remove the system disk.

STEP 3: Insert your TURBO *Compiler* diskette into drive A.

STEP 4: Type-in the word TURBO and press the **ENTER** key. What you see is the main menu screen for the integrated environment of TURBO.

Main Menu Command Line

The main menu command line at the top of the screen shows the menu options that can be selected at this point. Use the highlighted capital letter to select a particular option. Alternatively, use the arrow keys on your keyboard to move to the desired menu option and press the **ENTER** key. To get back to the main menu from any point in TURBO, simply press the F10 key.

Function Key Line

The bottom line of the main menu screen indicates the function of several "hot" keys. Pressing any of these hot keys from anywhere within TURBO will cause the respective operation to be performed.

STEP 5: Now place a formatted work disk in drive B. Drive B is the right or bottom disk drive.

Note: If you only have a single drive, remove the TURBO compiler disk and insert your work disk in the same disk drive.

STEP 6: (For dual drive systems only) Press the F key to enter the file menu. Now press the C key to Change the logged drive. A window will appear on the screen. Enter the following:

B: **ENTER**

Press the F10 key to return to the main menu screen.

You have just logged onto your work disk located in drive B. This means that any disk reference operations will automatically access drive B. Thus, any programs that you save will be saved on your work disk in drive B. Likewise, any programs on your work disk can now be loaded directly from drive B using the TURBO Load command.

STEP 7: Now let's enter, compile, and run a sample TURBO Pascal program. Press the F3 key, and the load program window will appear on the screen. Enter the following:

SAMPLE   **ENTER**

STEP 8: You are now in the TURBO Edit mode and can begin entering a Pascal program. Enter the following program:

```
PROGRAM Sample (input,output);

USES
  Crt;

BEGIN
  Clrscr;
  Writeln ('Congratulations, you have just entered, compiled,');
  Writeln ('and ran your first TURBO Pascal program.');
  Writeln;
  Writeln ('Press ENTER to return to TURBO.');
  Readln
END.
```

STEP 9: Press the F2 key to save your program. You should observe that the disk drive activates, indicating that your program is being saved.

STEP 10: Press the F9 key to compile your program. If you made any errors entering the program, the compiler will return you to the Edit mode and position the cursor near the error. At this point, you must correct the error and repeat steps 9 and 10. When the program compiles successfully, a window will appear with the words *Success: Press any key* flashing within the window.

STEP 11: Now that your program has successfully compiled, simultaneously press the Alternate (Alt) and R keys. This operation is designated as Alt-R. The program execution will cause the following message to appear

(*Note:* some later versions of TURBO require you to press the R key at this point to run the program):

```
Congratulations, you have just entered, compiled,
and ran your first TURBO Pascal program.

Press ENTER to return to TURBO.
```

STEP 12: If you have a printer and want to get a hard copy of your sample program, refer to the section of this appendix entitled LISTING A PROGRAM WITH TURBO 4 AND LATER.

You have several options available to you from the main menu. Here are some guidelines when selecting the various main menu options. (*Note:* Press the F10 hot key to return to the main menu from anywhere within TURBO.)

File ---⟩ Press F

Selecting this main menu option causes a file option window to be displayed on the screen. From within this window you have several file-related options:

Change (C) Option

Use the Change (C) option to change the logged drive as you did in step 6.

Directory (D) Option

Use the Directory (D) option to view the file directory of a disk. To view the directory of the logged disk drive, simply press the D key followed by the **ENTER** key. To view the directory of another drive, press the D key, followed by the drive designation (A, B, or C), a colon, and press the **ENTER** key.

Load (L) Option

The Load (L) option allows you to load an existing program from your work disk or enter a new program. From within the file menu, press the L key. A window will appear on the screen. Type-in an existing program file name or new file name and press the **ENTER** key. When an existing file is being loaded, the file program is displayed and TURBO automatically enters the Edit mode. When a new file name is entered, TURBO will automatically enter the Edit mode so that you can begin entering your program. This new file name is the name that TURBO will use to locate your program on your work disk. Once a file name has been assigned to a program, the same name must be used for subsequent access to that program. Pressing the F3 hot key from anywhere within TURBO allows you to load a program.

Save (S) Option

Pressing the S key from within the file menu allows you to save the file you are editing. Pressing the F2 hot key from anywhere within TURBO saves the file you are editing.

OS (O) Option

Pressing the O key from within the file menu temporarily returns you to the operating system. Use this option when you want to run an operating system program (such as FORMAT) within TURBO. Type-in Exit **ENTER** to return to TURBO from the operating system.

Quit (Q) Option

Pressing the Q key from within the file menu returns you to the operating system. Pressing Alt-X from anywhere within TURBO also returns you to the operating system.

Consult your TURBO reference manual for information on the other file menu options.

Edit ---〉 Press E

Pressing the E key from the main menu invokes the built-in text editor. You can also enter the Edit mode by pressing Alt-E from anywhere within TURBO.

The TURBO text editor employs the Wordstar® word-processing editing commands and operations. If you are familiar with Wordstar® your editing task is a much simpler one. If you are not familiar with Wordstar®, you must consult your TURBO reference manual for the various editing commands. It's a good idea to learn these commands to make your editing more efficient.

Edit Mode Options

Any of the "hot" keys can be pressed within the edit mode to perform the following options:

F1   Help: Opens a window that provides information about the TURBO editor commands.

F2   Save: Saves the file being edited.

F3   Load: Loads a new file.

F5   Zoom: Toggles the screen between Edit only and Edit/Output windows (TURBO 4) or Edit/Watch windows (TURBO 5).

F6   Output: Toggles screen between Edit only and Output only windows (TURBO 4) or Edit only/Watch only windows (TURBO 5).

F9   Make: Invokes the compiler to compile your Pascal program.

F10   Main Menu: Returns you to the main menu.

Run ---⟩ Press R

Pressing the R key from the main TURBO menu invokes the compiler and runs the program that you are currently editing. After your program has executed, a *Press any key to return to Turbo Pascal* message will be displayed at the bottom of the screen.

Pressing Alt-R from anywhere within TURBO will accomplish the same thing. Thus, pressing Alt-R within the Edit mode will compile and run the program you are editing without having to return to the main menu. (*Note*: Some later versions of TURBO require you to press the R key after Alt-R to run the program.)

Compile ---⟩ Press C

Pressing the C key from the main menu will enter you into the compile menu, from which you have several options:

Compile (C) Option

Pressing the C key from within the Compile menu will compile the last program loaded into the editor. Pressing the F9 hot key from anywhere within TURBO will accomplish the same thing.

Consult your TURBO reference manual for an explanation of the other compile options.

Options ---⟩ Press O

Pressing the O key from the main menu will generate an Options menu that contains settings that control the operation of the integrated environment. Consult your TURBO reference manual for information on the Options menu.

Listing a Program with TURBO 4 and Later

Your TURBO *Utilities* diskette contains a Pascal program called LISTER that will allow you to get a hard copy of your program. Make sure that the program has been saved before you attempt to print it.

To execute LISTER, you must have entered the TURBO integrated environment via your TURBO *Compiler* diskette. To execute LISTER, insert your TURBO *Utilities* diskette into drive A and press the F3 hot key. The load program window will appear on the screen. Type-in

A: LISTER   **ENTER**

Now press Alt-R to run LISTER. You will observe the following message in the Output window:

Enter filename:

Make sure the printer is on. Now type-in the drive designation, a colon, the program name, the program extension (normally .PAS), and press the **ENTER** key. For example, if the program is named SAMPLE and is located on a disk in drive B you must enter the following:

B:SAMPLE.PAS   **ENTER**

Once a program is listed, press any key to return to the main TURBO menu. At this point, pressing the R key will allow you to run LISTER again to print a hard copy of another program. Of course, any other of the main menu options are also available to you.

A summary of the hot key functions for TURBO 4 and later is provided in Table A-1.

TABLE A-1   TURBO 4 AND LATER HOT KEY FUNCTIONS

Key	Function
F1	Generates a help window with information about the current position within the integrated environment
F2	Saves the file currently in the editor
F3	Loads a new or existing file
F5	Zooms and unzooms the active window
F6	Switches to the active window
F9	Compiles the program in the editor
F10	Displays the main menu
Alt-F1	Displays the last help screen referenced
Alt-F3	Allows you to load a file
Alt-F5	Generates the saved screen
Alt-F9	Compiles the file currently in the editor
Alt-F10	Generates the version screen
Alt-C	Displays the Compile menu
Alt-E	Enters the Edit mode
Alt-F	Displays the File menu
Alt-O	Displays the Options menu
Alt-R	Runs the program currently in the editor
Alt-X	Quits TURBO and takes you to the operating system

appendix b

Odd-Numbered Question and Problem Solutions

CHAPTER 1

Questions

1. ALU: Performs all arithmetic and logic operations.
   Control Unit: Directs and coordinates the activity of the CPU.
   Internal Registers: Used to temporarily store program instructions and data during fetch and execute.

3. Firmware.

5. Machine Language: Consists of binary 1s and 0s that can only be easily understood by the CPU.
   Assembly Language: Consists of instruction abbreviations called mnemonics that are easily understood by the programmer.
   High-Level Language: Consists of English-like instructions that are very easily understood by people.

7. Source program to an object program.

9. An algorithm is a step-by-step sequence of well-defined, effective instructions that will generate problem solutions in a finite amount of time.

11. Output, input, and processing.

13. Coding.

15. A narrative description of the problem definition.
A algorithm and/or flowchart.
A program listing.
Samples of input and output data.
Testing and debugging results.
User instructions.

17. Flowchart.

Problems

```
{P1-1.PGM}
BEGIN

    Write a program description message to the user.

    Write a user prompt message to input the first integer (A).

    Read (A).

    Write a user prompt message to input the second integer (B).

    Read (B).

    Add A to B.

    Write the sum.

    Subtract B from A.

    Write the difference.

    Multiply A times B.

    Write the product.

    Divide A by B.

    Write the quotient.

  END.

{P1-3.PGM}
BEGIN

    Write a program description message to the user.

    Write a user prompt to enter the current (I).

    Read (I).
```

```
    Write a user prompt to enter the resistance (R).

    Read (R).

    Calculate V = I * R.

    Write the voltage (V).

  END.
{P1-5.PGM}
BEGIN

    Write a program description message to the user.
                       -8
    Set p = 1.72 x 10  .

    Write a user prompt to enter the conductor length (1)  in
    inches.

    Read (1)

    Divide 1 by 39.37 to get meters.

    Write a user prompt to enter the cross-sectional area (A) of
    the conductor in square inches.

    Read (A).
                      2
    Divide A by (39.37) , or 1550, to get square meters.



                       1
    Calculate  R =  p -------
                       A

    Write the conductor resistance (R).
```

CHAPTER 2

Questions

1. The four standard data types defined in Pascal are integer, real, character, and Boolean. String can also be considered as a standard data type in TURBO Pascal.

3. **a.** -32.0 is not an integer value, since it contains a decimal point.
   d. 3,240 cannot be used as an integer value in Pascal, since it contains a comma.
   f. 40000 cannot be used as an integer value in TURBO Pascal, since it is larger than

the maximum allowed integer value.   The exception is the long integer data type in later versions of TURBO.

5. c. .456 is not a valid real number, since the decimal point is not preceded by an integer. This must be written as 0.456.

e. $-2.5-E3$ is not a valid real number, since the minus sign before the E is illegal. It must be written as $-2.5E-3$.

g. You might suggest that the value 25 is not a valid real number, since it is an integer value.   However, the integers are actually a subset of the reals.   This means that integer values are also real values.   As a result, the TURBO Pascal compiler will accept whole number integer values as reals.   The compiler will automatically convert the integer value to exponential form. Be aware, however, that you can't go the other way!   In other words, real values cannot be used as integers.

7. a. 0.000000345
   b. -0.0000225
   c. 2220000.0
   d. -34500.0

9. a. 0.001 A
   0.032 V
   0.000100 V
   0.000000125 A

   b. $1E-3$
   $32E-3$
   $100E-6$
   $125E-9$

Problems

{P2-1.PGM}

1.   **a.** 16   **b.** 1.6E+01   **c.** 4.0E+00   **d.** 4.0E+00

   e. Error   **f.** Error   **g.** 121   **h.** 89

   i. 53   **j.** False   **h.** True   **l.** Error

   m. Error

{P2-3.PGM}

   a. **CONST**

      MaxValue = 100;

   b. **CONST**

      Milli = 0.001;

c. **CONST**

    Kilo = 1000;

d. **CONST**

    Age = 39;

e. **CONST**

    Period = '.';

f. **CONST**

    Birthdate = '5/16/47';

g. **CONST**

    School = 'The School of the Ozarks';

{P2-5.PGM}

a. **VAR**

    GPA : real;

b. **VAR**

    CourseGrade : char;

c. **VAR**

    GrossPay : real;

d. **VAR**

    LogicOutput : Boolean;

e. **VAR**

    Rth , Vth : real;

f. **VAR**

    StudentName, CourseName : **STRING** [25];

    CourseNumber : **STRING** [7];

{P2-7.PGM}

```
a.  BEGIN
        x := 25;
        b := Sqrt(x);
        Write (b)
    END.


b.  BEGIN
        y := 5;
        a := Sqrt(Sqr(y));
        Write (a)
    END.

c.  BEGIN
        x := 1;
        x := x + 1;
        y := Sqr(x);
        Write (y)
    END.


d.  BEGIN
        x := 2;
        y := x + x;
        a := (y + 1) * Value;
        Write (a)
    END.

e.  BEGIN
        x := 2;
        y := x + x;
        a := y + 1 * Value;
        Write (a)
    END.
```

CHAPTER 3

Questions

1. **a.** Generates two blank lines on the display.
   b. Displays HELLO right justified to column 40.
   c. Displays -36.200 right justified to column 12.
   d. Displays:
   3.7500000000E + 00.
   e. Displays:
   1 2 3 4 5
   Note that the value 1 is displayed in column 5, then each subsequent value has a field width of 5.
   f. Displays:
   My test score is: 97.50

g. Displays:
TEST SCORE97.5

h. Displays:
TEST SCORE
97.5

i. Prints:
TEST SCORE
97.5

3. It does the same thing as question 3-2: The output will space over twenty spaces, then display the word HELLO.

5. a. A run-time error will occur, since there is no space between the 6 and the F. Without a space, Pascal tries to assign a letter digit (F) as part of the integer variable A.

b. 6F

c. A run-time error will occur, since the letter "F" has been entered for the integer variable A.

7. Generate a blank line, called a line feed, on the printer.

9. You must count the number of blank lines from the end of the first table to the end of the page. Then insert that number of *Writeln* statements in your program prior to generating the second table. For example, if the last line of the first table was line 18, then the number of blank lines required is 25 − 18, or 7. Thus seven *Writeln* statements must be inserted between the first and second table outputs.

Note: Standard Pascal includes a command called *Page* which automatically generates the required number of blank lines to get the print head to the beginning of the next page. TURBO Pascal does not include this command.

11. No problem. Pascal will accept any string input that is less than or equal to the declared string length.

Problems

```
{P3-1.PGM}

    PROGRAM Name (input, output);

USES
  Crt;

    BEGIN
        Clrscr;
        Writeln;
        Writeln;
        Writeln;
        Writeln;
        Writeln;
        Writeln;
        Writeln;
        Writeln;
        Writeln;
        Writeln;
        Writeln;
        Writeln('Andy':42)

    END.
```

```
{P3-3.PGM}

PROGRAM Rectangle (output);

USES
  Crt;

BEGIN
    Clrscr;
    Writeln;
    Writeln;
    Writeln;
    Writeln;
    Writeln;
    Writeln;
    Writeln;
    Writeln;
    Writeln ('XXXXXXXXXXXXXXXXXXXX':50);
    Writeln ('X':31,'X':19);
    Writeln ('X':31,'X':19);
    Writeln ('X':31,'X':19);
    Writeln ('X':31,'X':19);
    Writeln ('X':31,'X':19);
    Writeln ('X':31,'X':19);
    Writeln ('XXXXXXXXXXXXXXXXXXXX':50)

END.
```

```
{P3-5.PGM}

PROGRAM Simple_Interest (input, output);

USES
  Crt;

CONST
  Loan = 2000.00;
  Rate = 0.125;
  Term = 2.0;

VAR
  Interest : real;

BEGIN
  Clrscr;
  Writeln ('This program will calculate simple interest.');
  Writeln;
  Writeln;
  Interest := Loan * Rate * Term;
  Writeln ('LOAN':10,'TERM':10,'INTEREST RATE':20,'INTEREST AMOUNT':20);
  Writeln ('----':10,'----':10,'--------------':20,'---------------':20);
  Writeln;
  Writeln ('$',Loan:9:2,Term:10:1,Rate*100:18:2,'%','$':14,Interest:6:2)
END.
```

```
{P3-7.PGM}

PROGRAM Power (output);

USES
  Crt;

VAR
    Power. Voltage, Current :real;

BEGIN
    Clrscr;
    Voltage := 12;
    Current := 0.00125;
    Power := Voltage * Current;
    Writeln;
    Writeln;
    Writeln;
    Writeln;
    Writeln ('VOLTAGE':20,'CURRENT':20,'POWER':20);
    Writeln ('(volts)':20,'(amperes)':20,'(watts)':20);
    Writeln ('-------':20,'-------':20,'-----':20);
    Writeln;
    Writeln (Voltage:20:0,Current:20:5,Power:20:5)

END.


{P3-9.PGM}

PROGRAM Series (input, output);

USES
  Crt;

VAR
    R_equiv, R1, R2, R3, R4, R5 : real;

BEGIN
  Clrscr;
  Writeln ('This program will calculate the equivalent series ');
  Writeln ('resistance of five resistor values that you must enter.');
  Writeln ('Please enter all values in decimal form.');
  Writeln;
  Writeln;
  Writeln;
  Write ('Enter the first resistor value:  R1 = ');
  Readln (R1);
  Writeln;
  Write ('Enter the second resistor value:  R2 = ');
  Readln (R2);
  Writeln;
  Write ('Enter the third resistor value:  R3 = ');
  Readln (R3);
```

(Continued)

```
Writeln;
Write ('Enter the fourth resistor value:  R4 = ');
Readln (R4);
Writeln;
Write ('Enter the fifth resistor value:  R5 = ');
Readln (R5);
R_equiv := R1 + R2 + R3 + R4 + R5;
Writeln;
Writeln;
Writeln;
Writeln ('R1':10,'R2':10,'R3':10,'R4':10,'R5':10,'R_equiv':15);
Writeln ('--':10,'--':10,'--':10,'--':10,'--':10,'-------':15);
Writeln;
Writeln (R1:10:0,R2:10:0,R3:10:0,R4:10:0,R5:10:0,R_equiv:15:0);
Writeln;
Writeln ('All values are in ohms.');
Writeln;
Writeln ('Press the R key if you wish to run the program again.')
END.



{P3-11.PGM}



PROGRAM TestAverage (input, output);

USES
  Crt;

VAR
    StudentName : STRING [30];
    CourseName : STRING [20];
    Score1, Score2, Score3, Score4, Average : real;

BEGIN
    Clrscr;
    Writeln ('This program will calculate the average of four ');
    Writeln ('test scores that you must enter.');
    Writeln;
    Writeln;
    Writeln;
    Write ('Enter the student name:  Name = ');
    Readln (StudentName);
    Writeln;
    Write ('Enter the course name: Course = ');
    Readln (CourseName);
    Writeln;
    Write ('Enter the first test score:  Test #1 = ');
    Readln (Score1);
    Writeln;
    Write ('Enter the second test score:  Test #2 = ');
```

```
Readln (Score2);
Writeln;
Write ('Enter the third test score:  Test #3 =  ');
Readln (Score3);
Writeln;
Write ('Enter the fourth test score:  Test #4 = ');
Readln (Score4);
Average := (Score1 + Score2 + Score3 + Score4) / 4;
Writeln;
Writeln;
Writeln;
Writeln ('Student Name:  ',StudentName);
Writeln;
Writeln ('Course:  ',CourseName);
Writeln;
Write    ('Test #1':10,'Test #2':10,'Test #3':10,'Test #4':10);
Writeln ('Average':10);
Write    ('-------':10,'-------':10,'-------':10,'-------':10);
Writeln ('-------':10);
Writeln;
Write    (Score1:10:2,Score2:10:2,Score3:10:2,Score4:10:2);
Writeln (Average:10:2);
Writeln;
Writeln ('Press the R key if you wish to run the program again.')
```

END.

CHAPTER 4

Questions

1. a. -2
   b. -5
   c. -5
   d. 0
   e. -20
   f. 0

3. a. Is valid.
   b. Is valid but will produce an incorrect result due to integer overflow.
   c. Is not valid, since **DIV** is only defined for integers.
   d. Is valid (you can mix real and integer operations).
   e. Is valid.
   f. Is not valid, since -33000 is an integer out of bounds.

5. a. FALSE
   b. TRUE
   c. FALSE
   d. TRUE
   e. FALSE

7.

A	B	(A **AND NOT** B) **OR** (**NOT** A **AND** B)
FALSE	FALSE	FALSE
FALSE	TRUE	TRUE
TRUE	FALSE	TRUE
TRUE	TRUE	FALSE

9.

A	B	(**NOT** A) **OR** (**NOT** B)
FALSE	FALSE	TRUE
FALSE	TRUE	TRUE
TRUE	FALSE	TRUE
TRUE	TRUE	FALSE

11. Arithmetic, scalar, and transfer.

13. a. 4
   b. b
   c. FALSE
   d. FALSE

15. The relationship is not true and can be disproven by substituting FALSE for *A* and TRUE for *B*. (*Note:* substituting TRUE for *A* and FALSE for *B* will also disprove the relationship.)

Problems

{P4-1.PGM}

```
PROGRAM TempConv (input, output);

USES
  Crt;

VAR
  C, F : real;

BEGIN
  Clrscr;
  Writeln ('This program will convert degrees Farenheit to');
  Writeln ('degrees Celsius.');
  Writeln;
  Writeln;
  Write ('Enter degrees Farenheit:  F = ');
  Read (F);
  Writeln (' degrees.');
  Writeln;
  C := 5/9 * (F - 32);
  Writeln (F:6:2,' degrees Farenheit is equivalent to ',C:6:2,
           ' degrees Celsius.');
  Writeln;
  Writeln ('Press the R key if you want to run the program again.')

END.
```

{P4-3.PGM}

```pascal
PROGRAM Parallel_Current (input, output);

USES
  Crt;

VAR
    R1, R2, I, V_source : real;

BEGIN
    Clrscr;
    Writeln;
    Writeln;
    Writeln ('This program will calculate the total current in a');
    Writeln ('two-resistor parallel circuit.');
    Writeln;
    Writeln;
    Write ('Enter the first resistor value in kilohms: R1 = ');
    Read (R1);
    Writeln (' kilohms.');
    Writeln;
    Write ('Enter the second resistor value in kilohms: R1 = ');
    Read (R2);
    Writeln (' kilohms.');
    Writeln;
    Write ('Enter the source voltage value in volts:  V_source = ');
    Read (V_source);
    Writeln (' volts.');
    Writeln;
    I := V_source / ((R1 * R2) / (R1 + R2));
    Writeln ('The total current with R1 and R2 in parallel is ',I:5:2,
             ' milliamperes.');
    Writeln;
    Writeln;
    Writeln ('Press the R key if you want to run the program again.')
END.
```

{P4-5.PGM}

```pascal
PROGRAM Linear_Equation (input, output);

USES
  Crt;

VAR
    x, y : real;

BEGIN
    Clrscr;
    Writeln ('This program will solve the equation 3x - 5y + 2 = 35');
```

(Continued)

```
      Writeln ('for x.   You must enter values for y.');
      Writeln;
      Writeln;
      Write ('Enter a value for y:   y = ');
      Readln (y);
      Writeln;
      x := (5 * y + 33) / 3;
      Writeln ('The value of x is: ',x:5:2);
      Writeln;
      Writeln ('Press the R key if you want to run the program again.')

  END.
```

{P4-7.PGM}

```
PROGRAM Rectangular_to_Polar (input, output);

USES
   Crt;

VAR
   M, Angle, x, y : real;

BEGIN
   Clrscr;
   Writeln ('This program will convert rectangular vector coordinates');
   Writeln ('to polar vector coordinates.');
   Writeln;
   Writeln;
   Write ('Enter the real coordinate of the vector:   x = ');
   Readln (x);
   Writeln;
   Writeln;
   Write ('Enter the imaginary coordinate of the vector:   y = ');
   Readln (y);
   Writeln;
   Writeln;
   M := Sqrt (Sqr(x) + Sqr(y));
   Angle := (Arctan (y/x)) * (180/Pi);
   Writeln ('POLAR COORDINATE':25,'RECTANGULAR COORDINATE':40);
   Writeln ('----------------':25,'----------------------':40);
   Writeln;
   Writeln (M:10:2, ' @ ', Angle:6:2,' degrees', x:23:2, ' + j', y:5:2);
   Writeln;
   Writeln ('NOTE:   The above polar coordinate angle is the reference');
   Writeln ('angle in the given quadrant.')

END.
```

```
{P4-9.PGM}


PROGRAM Cap_Charge (input, output);

USES
  Crt;

VAR
   Charge, R, C, t : real;

BEGIN
   Clrscr;
   Writeln ('This program will calculate the % charge across a');
   Writeln ('capacitor in a series RC circuit at any given point');
   Writeln  ('in time.');
   Writeln;
   Writeln;
   Write ('Enter the series resistance value in kilohms:  R = ');
   Read (R);
   Writeln (' kilohms.');
   Writeln;
   Write ('Enter the capacitor value in microfarads:  C = ');
   Read (C);
   Writeln (' microfarads.');
   Writeln;
   Write ('Enter the charge time in milliseconds:  t = ');
   Read (t);
   Writeln (' milliseconds.');
   Writeln;
   Charge := (1 - Exp (-t/(R*C))) * 100;
   Write ('The capacitor will be ', Charge:5:2,' percent ');
   Writeln ('charged after ',t:5:3, ' milliseconds.')

 END.



{P4-11.PGM}



PROGRAM Op_Amp (input,output);

USES
  Crt;

VAR
   Gain, R1, R2 : real;

BEGIN
   Clrscr;
   Writeln ('This program will calculate the gain of the op amp ');
```

(Continued)

```
Writeln ('circuit shown below.');
Writeln ('                               *                                 ');
Writeln ('                               *   *                             ');
Writeln ('V_in  o-----------* +     *                                      ');
Writeln ('                               *           *                     ');
Writeln ('                               *             * -------------o V_out');
Writeln ('                               *         *         :                 ');
Writeln ('            -----------* -     *                   :                 ');
Writeln ('            :               *   *                  :                 ');
Writeln ('            :               *                      :                 ');
Writeln ('            :                                      :                 ');
Writeln ('            :-----------XXXXXX----------------:              ');
Writeln ('            :               R1                          ');
Writeln ('            X                                          ');
Writeln ('            X                                          ');
Writeln ('            X R2                                       ');
Writeln ('            X                                          ');
Writeln ('            :                                          ');
Writeln ('            :                                          ');
Writeln ('     -------                                          ');
Writeln ('      ---                                             ');
Writeln ('       -                                              ');
Write ('Enter a value for R1 in kilohms:  R1 = ');
Read (R1);
Writeln (' kilohms.');
Write ('Enter a value for R2 in kilohms:  R2 = ');
Read (R2);
Writeln (' kilohms.');
Gain := R1/R2 +1;
Clrscr;
Writeln;
Writeln;
Writeln ('                               *                                 ');
Writeln ('                               *   *                             ');
Writeln ('V_in  o-----------* +     *                                      ');
Writeln ('                               *           *                     ');
Writeln ('                               *             * -------------o V_out');
Writeln ('                               *         *         :                 ');
Writeln ('            -----------* -     *                   :                 ');
Writeln ('            :               *   *                  :                 ');
Writeln ('            :               *                      :                 ');
Writeln ('            :                                      :                 ');
Writeln ('            :-----------XXXXXX----------------:              ');
Writeln ('            :               R1 = ',R1:5:2, 'K              ');
Writeln ('            X                                          ');
Writeln ('            X                                          ');
Writeln ('            X R2 = ',R2:5:2, 'K                         ');
Writeln ('            X                                          ');
Writeln ('            :               Gain = ', Gain:6:2          );
Writeln ('            :                                          ');
Writeln ('     -------                                          ');
Writeln ('      ---                                             ');
Writeln ('       -                                              ')

END.
```

CHAPTER 5

Questions

1. When X is negative and not divisible by 5.
3. **a.** Yes, the fourth line must be Y := Y − 1 and there must not be a semicolon after the **END** prior to the **ELSE.**
   b. When both X and Y are greater than 0.
   c. When only X is less than or equal to 0.
5. False, you never begin a **CASE** statement.
7. False, a no-match condition within a **CASE** does not result in an error in TURBO, but it does in Standard Pascal.
9. **a.** 1
   b. 2
   c. 4
   d. 8
   e. 16
   f. No match exists for this Power.
11.
   CASE Score **OF**
       90 . . 100: Lettergrade: = 'A';
       80 . . 89 : Lettergrade: = 'B';
       70 . . 79 : Lettergrade: = 'C';
       60 . . 69 : Lettergrade: = 'D';
        0 . . 59 : Lettergrade: = 'F'
   END;

Problems

```
{P5-1.PGM}

PROGRAM Power_Supply_Test (input, output);

USES
  Crt;

VAR
  Voltage : real;

BEGIN
  Clrscr;
  Write ('Enter the measured supply output:  Voltage = ');
  Read (Voltage);
  Writeln (' volts.');
  Writeln;
  Writeln;
   IF Voltage >= 4.5 THEN
     IF Voltage <= 5.5 THEN
         Writeln ('ACCEPTABLE')
```

(Continued)

```
        ELSE
            Writeln ('UNACCEPTABLE')
      ELSE
        Writeln ('UNACCEPTABLE')
    END.
```

{P5-3.PGM}


```pascal
PROGRAM Digital_Simulator (input, output);

USES
  Crt;

VAR
    Entry, Output :integer;
    A, B, C, y : Boolean;

BEGIN
    Clrscr;
    Writeln ('This program will simulate the operation of the');
    Writeln ('digital circuit shown in Figure 5-8.  You must');
    Writeln ('enter a logic 1 or 0 for the three digital inputs');
    Writeln ('A, B, and C.  The program will then generate the');
    Writeln ('circuit output.');
    Writeln;
    Writeln;
    Write ('Enter a logic 1 or 0 for the A input:  A = ');
    Readln (Entry);
    IF Entry = 1 THEN
        A := TRUE
    ELSE
        A := FALSE;
    Writeln;
    Write  ('Enter a logic 1 or 0 for the B input:  B = ');
    Readln (Entry);
    IF Entry = 1 THEN
        B := TRUE
    ELSE
        B := FALSE;
    Writeln;
    Write ('Enter a logic 1 or 0 for the C input:  C = ');
    Readln (Entry);
    IF Entry = 1 THEN
        C := TRUE
    ELSE
        C := FALSE;
    Writeln;
    Writeln;
    y := NOT (NOT (A OR B) AND C);
    IF y = TRUE THEN
        Output := 1
    ELSE
        Output := 0;
    Writeln ('The circuit output for the above logic inputs is ', Output)
END.
```

{P5-5.PGM}

```
PROGRAM   Color_Code (input,output);

USES
  Crt;

VAR
   Entry : integer;

BEGIN
  Clrscr;
  Writeln ('This program will display the color which corresponds');
  Writeln ('to an integer entry from 0 to 9 using the resistor');
  Writeln ('color code.');
  Writeln;
  Writeln;
  Write ('Enter an integer value between 0 and 9:  Entry = ');
  Readln (Entry);
  Writeln;
  CASE Entry OF
    0 : Writeln ('The color is Black.');
    1 : Writeln ('The color is Brown.');
    2 : Writeln ('The color is Red.');
    3 : Writeln ('The color is Orange.');
    4 : Writeln ('The color is Yellow.');
    5 : Writeln ('The color is Green.');
    6 : Writeln ('The color is Blue.');
    7 : Writeln ('The color is Violet.');
    8 : Writeln ('The color is Gray.');
    9 : Writeln ('The color is White.')
  ELSE
    Writeln ('This is an invalid entry, press the R key');
    Writeln ('to run the program again.')
  END    {case}
END.   {program}
```

{P5-7.PGM}

```
PROGRAM   Power_Supply (input, output);

USES
  Crt;

VAR
  Choice : char;
  N1, N2, V_sec, R_load, V_load, I_load : real;

BEGIN
  Clrscr;
  Writeln ('This program will calculate the load values for a ');
  Writeln ('half- or full- wave power supply.');
  Writeln;
```

(Continued)

```
Writeln;
Writeln;
Writeln ('                         Enter H for Half-wave supply.');
Writeln;
Writeln ('                         Enter F for Full-wave supply.');
Writeln;
Write ('             Enter you choice:   ');
Readln (Choice);
Clrscr;
CASE Choice OF

   'H','h' : BEGIN
                Write ('Enter the primary turns:   N1 = ');
                Read (N1);
                Writeln (' turns');
                Writeln;
                IF N1 = 0 THEN
                  BEGIN
                    Write ('You cannont enter a value of 0 for N1, ');
                    Writeln ('press R to run the program again.')
                  END {then clause}
                ELSE
                  BEGIN
                    Write ('Enter the secondary turns:   N2 = ');
                    Read (N2);
                    Writeln (' turns');
                    Writeln;
                    Write ('Enter the load resistance value in ');
                    Write ('kilohms:  R_load = ');
                    Read (R_load);
                    Writeln (' kilohms');
                    Writeln;
                    V_sec := (115 * N2 * 1.414 ) / N1;
                    V_load := 0.318 * V_sec;
                    I_load := V_load / R_load;
                    Write ('The load voltage is ',V_load:5:2);
                    Writeln (' volts.');
                    Writeln;
                    Write ('The load current is ',I_load:5:2);
                    Writeln (' millamperes.')
                  END   {else clause}
                END; {case H}

   'F','f' : BEGIN
                Write ('Enter the primary turns:   N1 = ');
                Read (N1);
                Writeln (' turns');
                Writeln;
                IF N1 = 0 THEN
                  BEGIN
                    Write ('You cannont enter a value of 0 for N1, ');
                    Writeln ('press R to run the program again.');
                  END {then clause}
                    ELSE
                      BEGIN
```

```
                    Write ('Enter the secondary turns:  N2 = ');
                    Read (N2);
                    Writeln (' turns');
                    Writeln;
                    Write ('Enter the load resistance value in ');
                    Write ('kilohms:  R_load = ');
                    Read (R_load);
                    Writeln (' kilohms');
                    Writeln;
                    V_sec := (115 * N2 * 1.414 ) / N1;
                    V_load := 0.636 * V_sec;
                    I_load := V_load / R_load;
                    Write ('The load voltage is ',V_load:5:2);
                    Writeln (' volts.');
                    Writeln;
                    Write ('The load current is ',I_load:5:2);
                    Writeln (' milliamperes.')
                 END    {else clause}
             END    {case F}
    END   {case}
END.  {program}
```

CHAPTER 6

Questions

    1. While/Do, Repeat/Until, and For/Do.

    3. While/Do.

    5. d. Never.

    7.

        1 0
        2 1
        3 2
        4 1
        5 2

    9.

        2   0
        4   0
        8   1
       16 3

    11.

```
    Enter a string of characters, ending them with
    an asterisk.  Press the ENTER key after each entry.

    a
    b
    c
    d
    *

    The character count is 4
```

13.

```
10
9
8
7
6
5
4
3
2
1
```
That's all folks!

15.

```
1,1  1,2  1,3  1,4  1,5  1,6  1,7  1,8  1,9  1,10
2,1  2,2  2,3  2,4  2,5  2,6  2,7  2,8  2,9  2,10
3,1  3,2  3,3  3,4  3,5  3,6  3,7  3,8  3,9  3,10
4,1  4,2  4,3  4,4  4,5  4,6  4,7  4,8  4,9  4,10
5,1  5,2  5,3  5,4  5,5  5,6  5,7  5,8  5,9  5,10
```

17.

```
1
12
123
1234

1
12
123
1234

1
12
123
1234
```

Problems

```
{P6-1.PGM}

PROGRAM  Test Average (input, output);

USES
  Crt;

VAR
  Number, Count : integer;
  TestScore, Sum, Average : real;
```

```
BEGIN
   Clrscr;
   Writeln ('This program will compute the average of any number');
   Writeln ('of test scores using a While/Do loop.');
   Writeln;
   Writeln;
   Write ('Enter the number of scores you wish to average:  Number = ');
   Readln (Number);
   Writeln;
   Writeln;
   Sum := 0;
   Count := 0;
   WHILE Count < Number DO
      BEGIN
         Count := Count + 1;
         Write ('Enter test score #',Count,':  ');
         Readln (TestScore);
         Sum := Sum + TestScore
      END;   {while}
   Average := Sum/Number;
   Writeln;
   Writeln;
   Writeln ('The average of ',Number,' scores is ',Average:5:2)
END.


{P6-3.PGM}


PROGRAM   Test_Average (input, output);

USES
  Crt;

VAR
  Number, Count : integer;
  TestScore, Sum, Average : real;


BEGIN
   Clrscr;
   Writeln ('This program will compute the average of any number');
   Writeln ('of test scores using a For/Do loop.');
   Writeln;
   Writeln;
   Write ('Enter the number of scores you wish to average:  Number = ');
   Readln (Number);
   Writeln;
   Writeln;
   Sum := 0;
```

(Continued)

```
        FOR Count := 1 TO Number DO
            BEGIN
                Write ('Enter test score #',Count,':  ');
                Readln (TestScore);
                Sum := Sum + TestScore
            END;  {for loop}
        Average := Sum/Number;
        Writeln;
        Writeln;
        Writeln ('The average of ',Number,' scores is ',Average:5:2)
    END.


{P6-5.PGM}

PROGRAM Series_Resistance (input, output);

USES
  Crt;

VAR
  Number, Count : integer;
  R_equiv, R1, R : real;

BEGIN
  Clrscr;
  Writeln ('This program will calculate the total resistance');
  Writeln ('of a  series circuit.');
  Writeln;
  Writeln;
  Write ('Enter the number of resistors in the circuit:  Number = ');
  Readln (Number);
  Writeln;
  Count := 0;
  REPEAT
      Count := Count + 1;
      Write ('Enter resistor value #',Count,' in ');
      Write ('kilohms:  R',Count,' = ');
      Read (R);
      Writeln (' kilohms.');
      Writeln;
      IF  Count = 1 THEN
        R_equiv := R
      ELSE
        R_equiv := R_equiv + R
  UNTIL Count = Number;
  Write ('The equivalent resistance of the series circuit');
  Writeln (' is ', R_equiv:6:2,' kilohms.')
END.  {program}


{P6-7.PGM}

PROGRAM Series_Or_Parallel (input, output);
```

```
USES
  Crt;
VAR
  Number, Count : integer;
  R_equiv, R : real;
  Answer : char;

BEGIN
  Clrscr;
  Writeln ('This program will calculate the total resistance');
  Writeln ('of a series or parallel circuit.');
  Writeln;
  Writeln;
  Writeln ('Select the appropriate circuit:');
  Writeln;
  Writeln ('              Enter S for Series');
  Writeln;
  Writeln ('              Enter P for Parallel');
  Readln (Answer);
  Clrscr;
  Writeln;
  Writeln;
  CASE Answer OF

    'S','s' :   BEGIN
                Write ('How many resistors are in series?  Number = ');
                Readln (Number);
                Writeln;
                FOR Count := 1 TO Number DO
                  BEGIN
                    Write ('Enter resistor value #',Count,' in ');
                    Write ('kilohms:  R',Count,' = ');
                    Read (R);
                    Writeln (' kilohms.');
                    Writeln;
                    IF Count = 1 THEN
                      R_equiv := R
                    ELSE
                      R_equiv := R_equiv + R
                  END;  {for}
                Write ('The equivalent resistance of the series');
                Writeln (' circuit is ', R_equiv:6:2,' kilohms.')
              END; {case S}

    'P','p' : BEGIN
                Write ('How many resistors are in parallel? Number =');
                Readln (Number);
                Writeln;
                Writeln;
                FOR Count := 1 TO Number DO
                  BEGIN
                    Write ('Enter resistor value #',Count,' in ');
```

(Continued)

```
                          Write ('kilohms:  R',Count,' = ');
                          Read (R);
                          Writeln (' kilohms.');
                          Writeln;      '
                          IF Count = 1 THEN
                            R_equiv := R
                          ELSE
                            R_equiv := (R_equiv * R) / (R_equiv + R)
                      END;  {for}
                    Write ('The equivalent resistance of the parallel');
                    Writeln (' circuit is ', R_equiv:6:2,' kilohms.')
                  END  {case P}


        ELSE
          BEGIN
            Writeln ('Your entry is invalid.  Please press the R key to');
            Writeln ('run the program again.')
          END    {else}
        END    {case}
      END.  {program}




{P6-9.PGM}

PROGRAM Temp_Conv (input, output);

USES
  Crt, Printer;

VAR
  F : integer;
  C : real;

BEGIN
  Clrscr;
  Writeln ('This program will generate a Celsius conversion table for');
  Writeln ('all even temperatures from 32 to 212 degrees Fahrenheit.');
  Writeln;
  Writeln;
  Writeln (lst, 'DEGREES FAHRENHEIT':20, 'DEGREES CELSIUS':20);
  Writeln (lst, '-------------------':20, '---------------':20);
  Writeln (lst);
  FOR F := 32 TO 212 DO
    IF NOT Odd(F) THEN
      BEGIN
        C := 5/9 * (F - 32);
        Writeln (lst, F:12,C:23:2);
      END {Then clause}
END. {program}
```

```
{P6-11.PGM}

PROGRAM Op_Amp_Gain (output);

USES
  Crt;

CONST
  R2 = 1;

VAR
  R1 : integer;
  A : real;

BEGIN
  Clrscr;
  Writeln ('This program will generate a table of voltage gain (A)');
  Writeln ('versus feedback resistance (R1) for the op amp circuit');
  Writeln ('in Figure 6-5.');
  Writeln (lst, 'FEEDBACK RESISTANCE (R1)':20, 'GAIN (A)':20);
  Writeln (lst, '------------------------':20, '--------':20);
  Writeln (lst);
  FOR R1 := 9 TO 99 DO
    BEGIN
      A := R1/R2 +1;
      Writeln (lst,R1:12,A:30:2)
    END  {for}
END.  {program}


{P6-13.PGM}

PROGRAM Binary_Counter (output);

USES
  Crt;

VAR
  Q3, Q2, Q1, Q0 : integer;

BEGIN
  Clrscr;
  Writeln ('This program displays the output of the binary');
  Writeln ('counter shown in Figure 6-6.');
  Writeln;
  Writeln ('PRESS THE ENTER KEY REPEATEDLY TO APPLY CLOCK PULSES');
  Writeln;
  Writeln;
  Writeln;
  Writeln ('Q3':10, 'Q2':5, 'Q1':5, 'Q0':5);
  Writeln;
  FOR Q3 := 0 TO 1 DO
```

(*Continued*)

```
BEGIN
  GotoXY (10,9);
  Write (Q3);
  FOR Q2 := 0 TO 1 DO
    BEGIN
      GotoXY (15,9);
      Write (Q2);
      FOR Q1 := 0 TO 1 DO
        BEGIN
          GotoXY (20,9);
          Write (Q1);
          FOR Q0 := 0 TO 1 DO
            BEGIN
              GotoXY (25,9);
              Writeln (Q0);
              Readln
            END     {Q0 for}
        END     {Q1 for}
    END     {Q2 for}
  END     {Q1 for}
END.  {program}
```

```
{P6-15.PGM}

PROGRAM Step (output);

USES
  Crt;

VAR
  STEP, Counter, Aux_Counter : integer;

BEGIN
  Clrscr;
  Writeln ('This program will demonstate a STEP operation ');
  Writeln ('within a For/Do loop.');
  Writeln;
  Writeln;
  Write ('By what step do you wish the loop counter to increment?  ');
  Readln (STEP);
  Writeln;
  FOR Counter := 1 TO 100 DIV STEP DO
    BEGIN
      Aux_Counter := Counter * STEP;
      Writeln (Aux_Counter)
    END {for}
END.  {program}
```

CHAPTER 7

Questions

1. Function

3. **a.** Invalid: Parameter and function data type missing.
   b. Invalid: Function data type missing.
   c. Valid
   d. Valid

5. False: You do not specify a data type for procedures, only functions.

7. **c.** The actual parameter is altered after the subprogram execution.

9. **a.** Valid
   b. Invalid: No data type is specified for a procedure.
   c. Valid
   d. Invalid: You cannot list the value parameter (X) and the variable parameter (Y) in the same data-type statement. They must be typed separately and separated by a semicolon as follows:
   PROCEDURE OutData (X:integer; **VAR** Y : integer);

11. **a.** **PROCEDURE** Skiplines (Number : integer);
    b. **PROCEDURE** Swap (**VAR** X, Y : integer);
    c. **PROCEDURE** Cubes (X, Y, Z : integer);

13. **a.** $A = 2\ B = 10$
    $A = 10\ B = 2$
    b. $A = 20\ B = -5$
    $A = -5\ B = 20$
    c. $Num1 = 5\ Num2 = 1$
    $Num1 = 0\ Num2 = 6$
    $Num1 = 5\ Num2 = 1$
    $Num1 = 0\ Num2 = 6$
    $Num1 = 5\ Num2 = 1$

15. The scope of a variable refers to the largest block in which the variable is accessible.

17. True

19. A recursive operation is an operation that calls itself until a primitive state is reached. During each recursive call, all information required to complete the calculations after the recursive call is saved by the CPU in a memory area called a stack. As the recursive calls continue, information is saved on the memory stack until the primitive state is reached. Then the CPU works backwards from the primitive state, retrieving the stack information to determine the final result.

Problems

```
{P7-1.PGM}


PROGRAM Problem1 (input, output);

VAR
  F : real;

{****************************************************************

This function will convert a temperature in degrees F to degrees C.

****************************************************************}

FUNCTION Celsius (F : real) : real;

BEGIN
   Celsius :=  5/9 * (F - 32)
END;   {function Celsius}

BEGIN   {main program}
  Clrscr;
  Write ('Enter degrees Fahrenheit:  F = ');
  Readln (F);
  Writeln;
  Writeln ('Degrees Celsius are:  C = ', Celsius(F):5:2)
END.   {main program}
```

```
{P7-3.PGM}

PROGRAM Problem3 (input,output);

USES
  Crt;

VAR
  Angle : real;

{********************************************************************

    This function will calculate the tangent of an angle.

********************************************************************}

FUNCTION Tan (Theta : real) : real;
  BEGIN
    Tan := (Sin (Theta * Pi / 180)) / (Cos (Theta * Pi / 180))
  END;   {function Tan}
```

```
BEGIN  {main program}
  Clrscr;
  Write ('Enter the angle:  Angle = ');
  Readln (Angle);
  Writeln;
  Writeln ('The Tangent is:  Tan(',Angle:5:2,') = ',Tan (Angle):5:4)
END.  {main program}
```

```
{P7-5.PGM}


PROGRAM Problem5 (input, output);

USES   {TURBO 4 only}
   Crt;

VAR
  Value : integer;


{*****************************************************************

This function will find the factorial (N!) of an integer value, N.

*****************************************************************}

FUNCTION  Factorial (N : integer) : real;

BEGIN
  IF N = 1 THEN
    Factorial := 1
  ELSE
    Factorial := N * Factorial (N-1)
END; {function Factorial}

BEGIN  {main program}
  Clrscr;
  Writeln ('This program employs a recursive function to find the');
  Writeln ('factorial (N!) of an integer value, N.');
  Writeln;
  Writeln;
  Write ('Enter an integer value:  N = ');
  Readln (Value);
  Writeln;
  Writeln (Value,'! = ',Factorial(Value):0:0)
END.  { main program }
```

{P7-7.PGM}

```
PROGRAM Problem7 (input, output);

USES
  Crt;

VAR
  Entry : char;
  X, Y : Boolean;


{*********************************************************************

This function will return the Boolean result of a 2-bit XNOR operation.

*********************************************************************}

FUNCTION XNOR (A,B : Boolean) : Boolean;

BEGIN
  XNOR := NOT (A XOR B)
END; {function XNOR}

BEGIN  {main program}
  Clrscr;
  Write ('Enter a Boolean value (T for TRUE or F for FALSE): ');
  Readln (Entry);
  IF (Entry = 'T') OR (Entry = 't') THEN
    X := TRUE
  ELSE
    X := FALSE;
  Writeln;
  Write ('Enter a second Boolean value (T for TRUE or F for FALSE): ');
  Readln (Entry);
  IF (Entry = 'T') OR (Entry = 't') THEN
    Y := TRUE
  ELSE
    Y := FALSE;
  Writeln;
  Writeln ('The XNOR result is:  ',XNOR(X,Y))
END.  {main program}
```

{P7-9.PGM}

```
PROGRAM Problem9 (input, output);

USES
  Crt;
```

```
VAR
   Minimum, Maximum, Voltage : real;


{****************************************************************

This function will determine if a voltage value is within range.

****************************************************************}

FUNCTION  Within_Range (Min, Max, V : real) : Boolean;

BEGIN
   IF (V >= Min) AND (V<= Max) THEN
     Within_Range := TRUE
   ELSE
     Within_Range := FALSE
END;  {function Within_Range}

BEGIN  {main program}
   Clrscr;
   Write ('Enter the lower range limit:  Minimum = ');
   Readln (Minimum);
   Writeln;
   Write ('Enter the upper range limit:  Maximum = ');
   Readln (Maximum);
   Writeln;
   Write ('Enter the voltage value:  Voltage = ');
   Readln (Voltage);
   Writeln;
   IF Within_Range (Minimum,Maximum,Voltage) = TRUE THEN
     Writeln ('The voltage is within range.')
   ELSE
     Writeln ('The voltage is out of range.')
END.  {main program}



{P7-11.PGM}


PROGRAM Problem11 (input,output);

USES
   Crt;

VAR
   Resist, Cap : real;

{****************************************************************

   This function will return the time constant of an RC circuit.

****************************************************************}
```

```pascal
FUNCTION Time_Constant (R,C : real) : real;

BEGIN
  Time_Constant := R * C
END;   {function Time_Constant}

BEGIN  {main program}
  Clrscr;
  Write ('Enter the series resistance in kilohms:  Resistance = ');
  Read (Resist);
  Writeln (' kilohms');
  Writeln;
  Write ('Enter the series capacitance in microfarads: Capacitance =
  Read (Cap);
  Writeln (' microfarads');
  Writeln;
  Writeln ('The RC time constant is ',Time_Constant(Resist,Cap):4:2,
           ' milliseconds')
END.   {main program}
```

```
{P7-13.PGM}
```

```pascal
PROGRAM  Problem13 (output);

USES
  Printer;


{*****************************************************************

  This procedure will print my name, class, instructor and hour.

*****************************************************************}

PROCEDURE PrintHeader;

BEGIN
  Writeln (lst,'      Name:  Andrew C. Staugaard, Jr.');
  Writeln (lst,'     Class:  Technical Programming');
  Writeln (lst,'Instructor:  Prof. Leonard');
  Writeln (lst,'      Hour:  9:00 A.M.')
END;   {procedure PrintHeader}

BEGIN  {main program}
  PrintHeader
END. {main program}
```

```
PROGRAM Problem15 (input, output);

USES
  Crt;

VAR
  A, B : integer;


{****************************************************************

        This procedure will swap any two integer values.

****************************************************************}

PROCEDURE Swap (VAR X,Y : integer);

VAR
  Temp : integer;

BEGIN
  Temp := X;
  X := Y;
  Y := Temp
END; {procedure Swap}

BEGIN   {main program}
  Clrscr;
  Write ('Enter an integer value:  A = ');
  Readln (A);
  Writeln;
  Write ('Enter a second integer value:  B = ');
  Readln (B);
  Writeln;
  Swap (A,B);
  Writeln ('The value of A is now ',A);
  Writeln ('The value of B is now ',B)
END.   {main program}




{P7-17.PGM}


PROGRAM Problem17 (input, output);

USES
  Crt;

VAR
  R_low, C_low, R_high, C_high : real;
  Low_Cut, High_Cut : real;
```

(Continued)

```
{****************************************************************

          This function will determine cut-off frequency.

*****************************************************************}

FUNCTION Cut_Off (R,C : real): real;

BEGIN
  Cut_Off := 1 / (2 * Pi * R * C)
END;


{****************************************************************

  This procedure will read the bandpass filter component values.

*****************************************************************}

PROCEDURE Get_Data (VAR R_l, C_l, R_h, C_h : real);

BEGIN
  Clrscr;
  Write ('Enter the value for R_low in kilohms:  R_low = ');
  Read (R_l);
  Writeln (' kilohms');
  Writeln;
  Write ('Enter the value for C_low in microfarads:  C_low = ');
  Read (C_l);
  Writeln (' microfarads');
  Writeln;
  Write ('Enter the value for R_high in kilohms:  R_high = ');
  Read (R_h);
  Writeln (' kilohms');
  Writeln;
  Write ('Enter the value of C_high in microfarads:  C_high = ');
  Read (C_h);
  Writeln (' microfarads');
  Writeln;
  Writeln;
  Writeln
END;  {procedure Get_Data}


{****************************************************************

This procedure will calculate the cut-off frequencies for the
Bandpass filter shown in Figure 7-8.

*****************************************************************}

PROCEDURE Calculate (R_l,C_l,R_h,C_h : real; VAR L_Cut, H_Cut : real);

BEGIN
  L_Cut := Cut_Off (R_l,C_l);
  H_Cut := Cut_Off (R_h,C_h)
END;  {procedure Calculate}
```

```
{****************************************************************

This procedure will display the lower and upper cut-off frequencies
for the Bandpass filter in Figure 7-8.

****************************************************************}


PROCEDURE Out_Data (L_Cut, H_Cut : real);

BEGIN
  Writeln ('The lower cut-off frequency is ',L_Cut:5:2,' kilohertz.');
  Writeln;
  Writeln ('The upper cut-off frequency is ',H_Cut:5:2,' kilohertz.')
END;   {procedure Out_Data}

BEGIN {main program}
  Get_Data (R_low, C_low, R_high, C_high);
  Calculate (R_low, C_low, R_high, C_high, Low_Cut, High_Cut);
  Out_Data  (Low_Cut, High_Cut)
END.   {main program}

  {P7-19.PGM}


  PROGRAM Problem19 (input, output);

  VAR
    V_Source, R_1, R_2, R_3, R_Load, I_Load : real;


  {****************************************************************

         This function will return the Thevenin voltage.

  ****************************************************************}

  FUNCTION  V_th (R1, R2, V : real) : real;

  BEGIN
    V_th := (R2 / (R1 + R2)) * V
  END;   {function V_th}



  {****************************************************************

         This function will return the Thevenin resistance.

  ****************************************************************}

  FUNCTION   R_th (R1, R2, R3 : real) : real;

  BEGIN
    R_th := ((R1 * R2) / (R1 + R2)) + R3
  END;   {function R_th}
```

(Continued)

```
{*********************************************************************

     This procedure will get the circuit component values.

*********************************************************************}

PROCEDURE Get_Data (VAR R1, R2, R3, RL, V : real);

BEGIN
  Write ('Enter the value for R_1 in kilohms:  R_1 = ');
  Read (R1);
  Writeln (' kilohms');
  Writeln;
  Write ('Enter the value for R_2 in kilohms:  R_2 = ');
  Read (R2);
  Writeln (' kilohms');
  Writeln;
  Write ('Enter the value for R_3 in kilohms:  R_3 = ');


  Read (R3);
  Writeln (' kilohms');
  Writeln;
  Write ('Enter the value for R_Load in kilohms:  R_Load = ');
  Read (RL);
  Writeln (' kilohms');
  Writeln;
  Write ('Enter the value for V_source in kilohms:  V_source = ');
  Read (V);
  Writeln (' volts');
  Writeln;
  Writeln
END;   {procedure Get_Data}




{*********************************************************************

This procedure will calculate the load current for the circuit
in Figure 7-10.

*********************************************************************}

PROCEDURE Calculate (R1, R2, R3, RL, V : real; VAR I : real);

VAR
  V_thev, R_thev : real;

BEGIN
  V_thev := V_th (R1, R2, V);
  R_thev := R_th (R1, R2, R3);
  I := V_thev / (R_thev + RL)
END;   {procedure Calculate}
```

```
{*****************************************************************

          This procedure will display the load current.

*****************************************************************}

   PROCEDURE Out_Current (I : real);

   BEGIN
     Writeln ('The load current is ',I:5:2, ' milliamps.')
   END;   {procedure Out_Current}


   BEGIN {main program}
     Clrscr;
     Get_Data (R_1, R_2, R_3, R_Load, V_Source);
     Calculate (R_1, R_2, R_3, R_Load, V_Source, I_Load);
     Out_Current (I_Load)
   END.   {main program}

{P7-21.PGM}

PROGRAM Vectors (input,output);


{USES        TURBO 4 and Later
   Crt;                                       }


VAR
  Vector1, Vector2, Angle : real;


{*****************************************************************

          This procedure will get the vector data.

*****************************************************************}

PROCEDURE  Get_Data (VAR V1, V2, Ang : real);

BEGIN
  Clrscr;
  Write ('Enter the magnitude of the first vector:  V1 = ');
  Readln (V1);
  Writeln;
  Write ('Enter the magnitude of the second vector:  V2 = ');
  Readln (V2);
  Writeln;
  Write ('Enter the angle between V1 and V2:  Angle = ');
  Readln (Ang)
END;   {Procedure Get_Data}
```
(Continued)

```
{****************************************************************

This function will use the Law of Cosines to calculate the resultant
vector.

****************************************************************}

FUNCTION  Resultant (V1, V2, Ang : real) : real;

BEGIN

  Resultant := Sqrt(Sqr(V1) + Sqr(V2) - 2*V1*V2*Cos(Angle*(Pi/180)))

END;   {Function Resultant}


{****************************************************************
           This procedure will display the results.

****************************************************************}

PROCEDURE  Display (V1, V2, Ang : real);

BEGIN
  Clrscr;
  Writeln ('Given two vectors with magnitudes of ',V1:5:2,
           ' and ',V2:5:2);
  Writeln;
  Writeln ('at an angle of ',Ang:5:2,
           ' degrees, the resultant vector magnitude is:');
  Writeln;
  Writeln (Resultant(V1,V2,Ang):5:2)

END;   {Procedure Display}



BEGIN   {main}
  Get_Data (Vector1,Vector2,Angle);
  Display  (Vector1,Vector2,Angle)

END.   {main}


  {P7-23.PGM}

  PROGRAM Problem_19 (input, output);

  USES   {TURBO 4 only}
    Crt;
```

```
VAR
  Position: integer;

{****************************************************************

          This procedure will get the input.

****************************************************************}
PROCEDURE  Input (VAR n : integer);
  BEGIN
    Clrscr;
    Write ('Enter the maximum Fibonacci element position ');
    Write ('you desire:  n = ');
    Readln (n)
  END;   {Procedure Input}


{****************************************************************

      This function will generate the Fibonacci number.

****************************************************************}

FUNCTION Fib (I: integer) : integer;
  BEGIN
    IF I > 1 THEN
      Fib := Fib (I-1) + Fib (I-2)
    ELSE
      IF I = 1 THEN
        Fib := 1
      ELSE
        Fib := 0
END; {Function Fib}




{****************************************************************

      This procedure will generate the Fibonacci sequence.

****************************************************************}


PROCEDURE Output (n : integer);

VAR
  Count : integer;
```

(Continued)

```
BEGIN
  Writeln;
  Write ('0');
  FOR Count := 1 TO n DO
    Write (', ', Fib (Count))
END;  {Procedure Output}


BEGIN  {main program}
  Clrscr;
  REPEAT
    Input (Position);
  UNTIL Position > 0;
  Output (Position)
END.  {main program}
```

{P7-25. PGM}

In this application, iteration is much more memory and time efficient than is recursion. The recursive operation takes so long because the entire set of recursive calls is repeated to generate each Fibonacci number in the sequence. Thus, to generate, say, the fourth number in the sequence, the third number must be generated, then the second, then the first all over again, even though these numbers have been found previously.

CHAPTER 8

Questions

1. TYPE

3. a. TYPE
      This _Semester_Courses = (Tech_Progr, DC, AC, Digital);
   VAR
      Course: This_Semester_Courses;
   b. TYPE
      Resistor_Color_Code = (Brown, Black, Red, Orange, Yellow, Green, Blue,
                             Violet, Gray, White);
                  VAR
                     Color: Resistor_Color_Code;
   c. TYPE
      Major_Courses = (DC, AC, Digital, Micro, Semiconductors, Linear,
                       Elect_Machines, Tech_Programming);
                  VAR
                     Major_Course: Major_Courses;

    d. TYPE
        My_Family = (Andy, Janet, Ron, Dave, Zane, Andrew);
    VAR
        Member: My_Family;

5. a. TRUE
   b. TRUE
   c. FALSE
   d. TRUE

7. The array name, the index range(s) of the array, and the data type of the array elements. In addition, an array variable must be declared to access the array.

9. *Score*, *Power*, *Item*, and *Value*.

11. 10, 121, 72, and 1000.

13. Writeln (Power[−2, 1]);

15. Writeln (lst, Item[−1, 1, 3],Value[Red, Black, Red]);

17. FOR K: = 1 **TO** 10 **DO**
    Readln (Score[K]);

    {Note: Assumes that *K* has been declared as an integer variable.}

    FOR V := −5 **TO** 5 **DO**
      FOR I := 0 **TO** 10 **DO**
        Readln (Power[V,I]);

    {Note: Assumes that *V* and *I* have been declared as a variables of the data types *Voltage* and *Current*, respectively.}

    FOR Row := −3 **TO** 3 **DO**
      FOR Col := 0 **TO** 3 **DO**
        FOR Plane := 1 **TO** 3 **DO**
          BEGIN
            Write ('Enter T for TRUE or F for FALSE: ');
            Readln (Entry);
            IF (Entry = 'T') **OR** (Entry = 't') **THEN**
              Item[Row,Col,Plane] := TRUE
            ELSE
              Item[Row,Col,Plane] := FALSE
          END; {Plane for}

    {Note: Assumes that *Row*, *Col*, and *Plane* have been declared as integer variables and *Entry* as a character variable.}

    FOR Color1 := Brown **TO** White **DO**
      FOR Color2 := Brown **TO** White **DO**
        FOR Color3 := Brown **TO** White **DO**
          Readln (Value[Color1,Color2,Color3]);

    {Note: Assumes that *Color1*, *Color2*, and *Color3* have been declared as variables of data type *Colors*.}

Problems

{P8-1.PGM}
When you try to read or write the value of your user-defined data type, you will get
an "I/O are not allowed" error when the program is compiled. A way to get around
this problem is to read and write user-defined data via **CASE** statements, as you do
Boolean data.

```
{P8-3.PGM}

PROGRAM  Problem3 (input, output);

USES
  Crt;

TYPE
  Reverse = ARRAY [1..3, 1..5] OF char;

VAR
  A : Reverse;
  Row, Col : integer;

BEGIN
  Clrscr;
  Writeln ('This program will form a 3 x 5 array of elements');
  Writeln ('in memory and display them as a 5 x 3 array with');
  Writeln ('the rows and columns reversed.');
  Writeln;
  Writeln;
  FOR Row := 1 TO 3 DO
    BEGIN
      Writeln;
      Writeln;
      Writeln ('Enter five elements for row ',Row,'.  Press the ENTER');
      Writeln ('key after each element entry.');
      Writeln;
      FOR Col := 1 TO 5 DO
        Read (A[Row, Col])
    END;  {Row for}
  Clrscr;
  Writeln ('Here is the original array:  ');
  FOR Row := 1 TO 3 DO
    BEGIN
      Writeln;
      FOR Col := 1 TO 5 DO
        Write (A[Row,Col]);
    END;  {Row for}
  Writeln;
```

```
Writeln;
Writeln ('Here is the array with the rows and columns reversed:');
Writeln;
    FOR Row := 1 TO 5 DO
      BEGIN
        Writeln;
        FOR Col := 1 TO 3 DO
          Write (A[Col, Row])
      END  {Row for}
  END.  {program}



  {P8-5.PGM}

  PROGRAM Problem5 (input, output);

  USES
    Crt;

  TYPE
    BCD Counter = ARRAY [0..9,0..3] OF char;

  VAR
    State_Table : BCD Counter;


  {****************************************************************

            This procedure will fill the state table.

  ****************************************************************}

  PROCEDURE  Fill_Table (VAR Table : BCD_Counter);

  VAR
    State, Bit : integer;

  BEGIN
    FOR State := 0 TO 9 DO
      BEGIN
        Writeln;
        Writeln;
        Writeln ('Enter the 4-bit value for state ', State,':');
        Writeln ('Press the ENTER key after each single bit entry.');
        FOR  Bit := 3 DOWNTO 0 DO
          Read (Table[State, Bit])
      END {State for}
  END;  {procedure Fill_Table}
```

(Continued)

```
{****************************************************************

          This procedure will display the state table.

****************************************************************}

PROCEDURE Display_Table (Table : BCD_Counter);

VAR
  State, Bit : integer;

BEGIN
  Clrscr;
  Writeln ('The BCD counter state table is:');
  Writeln;
  FOR State := 0 TO 9 DO
    BEGIN
      Write ('State ',State,':   ');
      FOR Bit := 3 DOWNTO 0 DO

        Write (Table[State,Bit]);
      Writeln
    END   {State for}
END;   {procedure Display_Table}

BEGIN   {main program}
  Clrscr;
  Writeln ('This program will store and display the state table');
  Writeln ('for a 4-bit decade (BCD) counter.');
  Writeln;
  Fill_Table (State_Table);
  Writeln;
  Writeln;
  Display_Table (State_Table)
END.   {main program}


{P8-7.PGM}

PROGRAM Problem7 (input, output);

USES
  Crt;

TYPE
  Equations = ARRAY [1..2,1..3] OF real;
  Determinant = ARRAY [1..2,1..2] OF real;

VAR
  Equ : Equations;
  Num1, Num2, Denom : Determinant;
```

```
{********************************************************************

This procedure will fill an array with the equation coefficents.

*******************************************************************}

PROCEDURE Fill (VAR A : Equations);

VAR
   Row, Col : integer;

BEGIN
   FOR Row := 1 TO 2 DO
     BEGIN
       Writeln;
       Write ('Enter the variable coefficients and constant');
       Writeln (' for equation ',Row, ':');
       Writeln ('(Note:  The equation must be in standard form.)');
       Writeln;
       FOR Col := 1 TO 3 DO
         BEGIN
           IF Col = 3 THEN
             Write ('Enter the constant term:  ')
           ELSE
             Write ('Enter the coefficient for I',Col,':  ');
           Readln (A[Row,Col]);
           Writeln
         END {Col for}
     END   {Row for}
END;   {procedure Fill}




{********************************************************************

            This procedure will form the determinants.

*******************************************************************}

PROCEDURE Form_Det (A : Equations; VAR N1, N2, D : Determinant);


VAR
   Row, Col : integer;

BEGIN
    N1[1,1] := A[1,3];
    N1[1,2] := A[1,2];
    N1[2,1] := A[2,3];
    N1[2,2] := A[2,2];
```

(*Continued*)

```
   N2[1,1] := A[1,1];
   N2[1,2] := A[1,3];
   N2[2,1] := A[2,1];
   N2[2,2] := A[2,3];

   FOR Row := 1 TO 2 DO
     FOR Col := 1 TO 2 DO
       D[Row.Col] := A[Row.Col]
END;   {procedure Form_Det}



{****************************************************************

        This function will expand a 2x2 determinant.

 ****************************************************************}

FUNCTION  Expand (K : Determinant) : real;

BEGIN
  Expand := K[1,1] * K[2,2] - K[2,1] * K[1,2]
END; {function Expand}


BEGIN  {main program}
  Clrscr;
  Writeln ('This program will solve for the currents (I1 and I2)');
  Writeln ('in a two loop circuit.');
  Writeln;
  Writeln;
  Fill(Equ);
  Form_Det (Equ,Num1,Num2,Denom);
  Writeln;
  Writeln;
  Write ('The value of I1 is:   ');
  Writeln  (Expand(Num1) / Expand(Denom):5:4,' amperes.');
  Writeln;
  Write ('The value of of I2 is:   ');
  Writeln (Expand(Num2) / Expand(Denom):5:4,' amperes.')
END.   {main program}


{P8-9.PGM}

PROGRAM Problem9 (input, output);

USES
  Crt;

TYPE
   Equations = ARRAY [1..2,1..3] OF real;
   Determinant = ARRAY [1..2,1..2] OF real;
```

```
VAR
   Equ : Equations;
   Num1, Num2, Denom : Determinant;


{*****************************************************************

This procedure will fill an array with the equation coefficents.

*****************************************************************}

PROCEDURE Fill (VAR A : Equations);

VAR
  Row, Col : integer;

BEGIN
  FOR Row := 1 TO 2 DO
    BEGIN
      Writeln;
      Write ('Enter the variable coefficients and constant');
      Writeln (' for equation ',Row,':');
      Writeln ('(Note:  The equation must be in standard form.)');
      Writeln;
      FOR Col := 1 TO 3 DO
        BEGIN
          IF Col = 3 THEN
            Write ('Enter the constant term:  ')
          ELSE
            Write ('Enter the coefficient for T',Col,':  ');
          Readln (A[Row,Col]);
          Writeln
        END {Col for}
    END  {Row for}
END;  {procedure Fill}



{*****************************************************************

            This procedure will form the determinants.

*****************************************************************}

PROCEDURE Form_Det (A : Equations; VAR N1, N2, D : Determinant);
```

(Continued)

```
VAR
  Row, Col : integer;

BEGIN
    N1[1,1] := A[1,3];
    N1[1,2] := A[1,2];
    N1[2,1] := A[2,3];
    N1[2,2] := A[2,2];

    N2[1,1] := A[1,1];
    N2[1,2] := A[1,3];
    N2[2,1] := A[2,1];
    N2[2,2] := A[2,3];

    FOR Row := 1 TO 2 DO
      FOR Col := 1 TO 2 DO
        D[Row,Col] := A[Row,Col]
END;   {procedure Form_Det}



{*****************************************************************

        This function will expand a 2x2 determinant.

*****************************************************************}

FUNCTION  Expand (K : Determinant) : real;

BEGIN
  Expand := K[1,1] * K[2,2] - K[2,1] * K[1,2]
END; {function Expand}


BEGIN   {main program}
  Clrscr;
  Writeln ('This program will solve for the tension, in pounds,');
  Writeln ('of two cables (T1 and T2) supporting an object.');
  Writeln;
  Writeln;
  Fill(Equ);
  Form_Det (Equ,Num1,Num2,Denom);
  Writeln;
  Writeln;
  Write ('The value of T1 is:  ');
  Writeln  (Expand(Num1) / Expand(Denom):5:4,' pounds.');
  Writeln;
  Write ('The value of of T2 is:  ');
  Writeln (Expand(Num2) / Expand(Denom):5:4,' pounds.')
END.   {main program}
```

{P8-11.PGM}

```
{*****************************************************************

This procedure will display the array of equation coefficents.

*****************************************************************}

PROCEDURE Display (A : Equations);

VAR
  Row, Col : integer;

BEGIN
  Clrscr;
  Writeln ('The equation array is:');
  FOR Row := 1 TO 3 DO
    BEGIN
      Writeln;
      FOR Col := 1 TO 4 DO
        Write (A[Row,Col]:5:2,' ')
    END   {Col for}
END; {procedure Display}
```

{P8-13.PGM}

```
{*****************************************************************

        This function will expand a 3x3 determinant.

*****************************************************************}

FUNCTION  Expand (K : Determinant) : real;

BEGIN
  Expand := K[1,1]*K[2,2]*K[3,3] + K[1,2]*K[2,3]*K[3,1] +
            K[1,3]*K[2,1]*K[3,2] - K[3,1]*K[2,2]*K[1,3] -
            K[3,2]*K[2,3]*K[1,1] - K[3,3]*K[2,1]*K[1,2]
END; {function Expand}
```

{P8-15.PGM}

     Using the program in problem 14, you get:

     I1 = 2.76 milliamperes

     I2 = 0.78 milliamperes

     I3 = 1.25 milliamperes

{F8-17.PGM}

```
PROGRAM Calendar (input, output);

USES
  Crt, Printer;

TYPE
    Months = (Jan,Feb,Mar,Apr,May,June,July,Aug,Sept,Oct,Nov,Dec);
    Week = 1 .. 5;
    DaysOfWeek = (Sun, Mon, Tue, Wed, Thur, Fri, Sat);
    Year = ARRAY [Months, Week, DaysOfWeek] OF integer;

VAR

  This_Year : Year;
  This_Month : STRING [8];
  Calendar_Year : integer;




{****************************************************************

    This procedure will fill-in the dates of the year array.

****************************************************************}

PROCEDURE  Fill_Year (VAR Dates : Year);

VAR
  Month : Months;
  Week : integer;
  Day : DaysOfWeek;

BEGIN
  FOR Month := Jan TO Dec DO
    BEGIN
      CASE Month OF
        Jan  : This_Month := 'January';
        Feb  : This_Month := 'February';
        Mar  : This_Month := 'March';
        Apr  : This_Month := 'April';
        May  : This_Month := 'May';
        June : This_Month := 'June';
        July : This_Month := 'July';
        Aug  : This_Month := 'August';
        Sept : This_Month := 'September';
        Oct  : This_Month := 'October';
        Nov  : This_Month := 'November';
        Dec  : This_Month := 'December'
```

```
      END;   {case}
      Clrscr;
      Writeln ('Enter the dates for ',This_Month,' beginning with');
      Writeln ('Sunday of the first week in the month.  If there is');
      Writeln ('no date for a given day, enter a 0.  Press the ENTER');
      Writeln ('key after each date entry.');
      Writeln;
      Writeln;
      FOR Week := 1 TO 5 DO
        BEGIN
          Writeln;
          Writeln ('Enter the dates for Week ', Week,
                   ' beginning with Sunday:');
          FOR Day := Sun TO Sat DO
          Readln (Dates [Month,Week,Day])
        END   {Week for}
    END   {Month for}
END;   {procedure Fill_Year}




  {****************************************************************

        This procedure will display the year calendar.

  ****************************************************************}

  PROCEDURE   Display_Year (Dates : Year);

  VAR
    Month : Months;
    Week : integer;
    Day : DaysOfWeek;

  BEGIN
    Clrscr;
    FOR Month := Jan TO Dec DO
      BEGIN
        CASE Month OF
          Jan  : This_Month := 'January';
          Feb  : This_Month := 'February';
          Mar  : This_Month := 'March';
          Apr  : This_Month := 'April';
          May  : This_Month := 'May';
          June : This_Month := 'June';
          July : This_Month := 'July';
          Aug  : This_Month := 'August';
          Sept : This_Month := 'September';
          Oct  : This_Month := 'October';
          Nov  : This_Month := 'November';
          Dec  : This_Month := 'December'                    (Continued)
```

```
END;  {case}
Writeln (1st);
Writeln (1st);
Writeln (1st);
Writeln (1st,'                    ',This_Month,', ',Calendar_Year);
Writeln (1st);
Writeln (1st);
Writeln (1st,'   Sun    Mon    Tue    Wed    Thur    Fri    Sat');
Writeln (1st);
FOR Week := 1 TO 5 DO
        BEGIN
          FOR Day := Sun TO Sat DO
            Write (1st,' ',Dates [Month,Week, Day] : 6);
          Writeln (1st);
          Writeln (1st)
        END {Week for}
    END {Month for}
END;  {procedure Display_Month}


BEGIN   {main program}
  Clrscr;
  Write ('Enter the year for this calendar:  Year = ');
  Readln (Calendar_Year);
  Fill_Year (This_Year);
  Display_Year (This_Year)
END.  {main program}
```


CHAPTER 9

Questions

1. A record is a collection of fields.

3. Array.

5. False

7. There are two ways to access record information: by using dot notation or a **WITH/DO** statement. To gain access to a field using dot notation, the record variable is listed first, followed by a dot, followed by the field identifier. The **WITH/DO** statement simplifies the coding by listing the record variable once, within the **WITH/DO** header. Then the field identifiers are used directly within the body of the **WITH/DO** statement.

9. True

11. Invalid, should be
    Today . Day : = Sat;

13. Invalid, should be
    Today . Month : = Jun;

Problems

9-1.

```
WITH  Christmas DO
  BEGIN
    Day := Sun;
    Month := Dec;
    This_Date := 25;
    Year := 1988;
  END;

{OR}

Christmas . Day := Sun;
Christmas . Month := Dec;
Christmas . This_Date := 25;
Christmas . Year := 1988;
```

9-3.

```
TYPE
  Address = RECORD
              Street_Number : STRING [10];
              Street_Name   : STRING [10];
              City          : STRING [15];
              State         : STRING [12];
              Zip           : STRING [10]
            END;

VAR
  This_Address : Address;
```

9-5.

```
CONST
  Max = 10;

TYPE
  Person = RECORD

             Name : RECORD
                      Last        : STRING [25];
                      First       : STRING [10];
                      Middle_Init : STRING [2]
                    END;

             Address : RECORD
                         Street_Number : STRING [10];
                         Street_Name   : STRING [10];
                         City          : STRING [15];
                         State         : STRING [12];
                         Zip           : STRING [10]
                       END
           END;

  Persons = ARRAY [1..Max] OF Person;
```

(Continued)

```
     VAR
       This_Person : Persons;
```

9-7.

```
TYPE
  Status = (Pitcher, Non_Pitcher);

  Player = RECORD
               Name : STRING [35];
               Team : STRING [25];

               CASE Kind : Status OF

                  Pitcher : (Wins, Losses : integer;
                              ERA : real);

                  Non_Pitcher : (Bats, Runs, Hits, RBI : integer;
                                  Avg : real)


            END;   {record}
VAR
  Ball_Player : Player;
```

9-9.

```
PROGRAM  Address_Record (input,output);

USES
  Crt;

TYPE
  Address = RECORD
               Street_Number : STRING [10];
               Street_Name   :STRING [10];
               City          : STRING [15];
               State         : STRING [12];
               Zip           : STRING [10]
            END;

VAR
  This_Address : Address;


{*****************************************************************

   This procedure will input the address record information.

****************************************************************)

PROCEDURE  Get_Address (VAR Addr : Address);

BEGIN
  Clrscr;
  Writeln ('Please input the address record information as follows: ');
  Writeln;
  WITH Addr DO
```

```
    BEGIN
      Write ('Enter street number ---> ');
      Readln (Street_Number);
      Writeln;
      Write ('Enter street name ---> ');
      Readln (Street_Name);
      Writeln;
      Write ('Enter city ---> ');
      Readln (City);
      Writeln;
      Write ('Enter state ---> ');
      Readln (State);
      Writeln;
      Write ('Enter zip code ---> ');
      Readln (zip)
    END {with}
  END; {procedure}


{**************************************************************

  This procedure will display the address record information.

**************************************************************}

PROCEDURE  Display_Address (Addr : Address);

BEGIN
  Clrscr;
  Writeln;
  WITH Addr DO
    BEGIN
      Writeln ('Here is the address record you entered:');
      Writeln;
      Writeln;
      Writeln (Street_Number,'  ',Street_Name);
      Writeln;
      Writeln (City,', ',State,'  ',Zip)
    END  {with}
  END;  {procedure}

BEGIN {main}
  Get_Address (This_Address);
  Display_Address (This_Address)
END.
```

9-11.

```
{$W9}
{Note:  This compiler directive only required for CPM/80 systems.}

PROGRAM  Problem11 (input,output);

USES
  Crt;

CONST
  Max = 10;
TYPE
  Person = RECORD
```

(Continued)

```
            Name : RECORD
                        Last          : STRING [25];
                        First         : STRING [10];
                        Middle_Init : STRING [2]
                    END;

            Address : RECORD
                            Street_Number : STRING [10];
                            Street_Name   : STRING [10];
                            City          : STRING [15];
                            State         : STRING [12];
                            Zip           : STRING [10]
                        END;
            END;

    Persons = ARRAY [1..Max] OF Person;


VAR
  Count : integer;
  This_Person : Persons;



{*************************************************************

    This procedure will input the person record information.

*************************************************************}


PROCEDURE  Get_Person (VAR Per : Persons);

BEGIN
  Clrscr;
  Writeln ('Please input  person ',Count, ' information as follows: ');
  Writeln;
  WITH Per[Count], Name, Address DO
    BEGIN
      Write ('Enter last name ---> ');
      Readln (Last);
      Writeln;
      Write ('Enter first name ---> ');
      Readln (First);
      Writeln;
      Write ('Enter middle initial ---> ');
      Readln (Middle_Init);
      Writeln;
      Write ('Enter street number ---> ');
      Readln (Street_Number);
      Writeln;
      Write ('Enter street name ---> ');
      Readln (Street_Name);
      Writeln;
      Write ('Enter city ---> ');
      Readln (City);
      Writeln;
      Write ('Enter state ---> ');
      Readln (State);
      Writeln;
```

```
        Write ('Enter zip code ---> ');
        Readln (zip)
    END {with}
  END; {procedure}



{*************************************************************

   This procedure will display the address record information.

*************************************************************}


PROCEDURE  Display_Person (Per : Persons);

BEGIN
  Writeln;
  Writeln;
  WITH Per[Count], Name, Address DO
    BEGIN
      Writeln;
      Writeln (First,' ',Middle_Init,'. ',Last);
      Writeln;
      Writeln (Street_Number,'  ',Street_Name);
      Writeln;
      Writeln (City,', ',State,'  ',Zip);
      Writeln
    END; {with}
    Writeln ('Press the ENTER key to display next record.');
    Readln
  END;  {procedure}

BEGIN {main}
  FOR Count := 1 TO Max DO
    Get_Person (This_Person);
  Clrscr;
  Writeln ('Here are the person records that you entered:  ');
  Writeln;
  FOR Count := 1 TO Max DO

    Display_Person (This_Person)
  END.
```

9-13.

```
PROGRAM  Problem13 (input, output);

USES
  Crt;

TYPE
  Status = (Pitcher, Non_Pitcher);

  Player = RECORD
             Name : STRING [35];
             Team : STRING [25];
```

(Continued)

```
            CASE Kind : Status OF

              Pitcher : (Wins, Losses : integer;
                          ERA : real);

              Non_Pitcher : (Bats, Runs, Hits, RBI : integer;
                              Avg : real)        .

          END;   {record}

VAR
  Ball_Player : Player;


{************************************************************

      This procedure will fill the player record.

************************************************************}


PROCEDURE Get_Player (VAR Ball : Player);

VAR
  Answer : char;

BEGIN
  WITH Ball DO
    BEGIN
      Write ('Enter the player name ---> ');
      Readln (Name);
      Writeln;
      Write ('Enter the team name ---> ');
      Readln (Team);
      Writeln;
      Write ('Is the player a pitcher? (Y/N) ----> ');
      Readln (Answer);
      Writeln;
      CASE Answer OF

        'y', 'Y' : BEGIN
                     Kind := Pitcher;
                     Write ('Enter wins ---> ');
                     Readln (Wins);
                     Writeln;
                     Write ('Enter losses ---> ');
                     Readln (Losses);
                     Writeln;
                     Write ('Enter ERA ---> ');
                     Readln (ERA);
                     Writeln;
                   END; {case B}

        'n', 'N' : BEGIN
                     Kind := Non_Pitcher;
                     Write ('Enter times at bat ---> ');
                     Readln (Bats);
                     Writeln;
```

```
                              Write ('Enter home runs ---> ');
                              Readln (Runs);
                              Writeln;
                              Write ('Enter hits ---> ');
                              Readln (Hits);
                              Writeln;
                              Write ('Enter RBI's ---> ');
                              Readln (RBI);
                              Writeln;
                              Avg := ((Runs + Hits) / Bats) * 1000;
                          END {case P}
          END {case}
        END {with}
    END; {procedure Fill_Player}


{**************************************************************

            This procedure display the player record.

 *************************************************************}


 PROCEDURE Display_Player (Ball : Player);

 BEGIN
    WITH Ball DO
      BEGIN
        CASE Kind OF

            Pitcher : BEGIN
                          Writeln ('Pitcher  ');
                          Writeln ('Name:  ',Name);
                          Writeln ('Team:  ',Team);
                          Writeln ('Wins:  ',Wins);
                          Writeln ('Losses:  ',Losses);
                          Writeln ('ERA:  ',ERA:5:2)
                      END; {Pitcher case}


            Non_Pitcher : BEGIN
                          Writeln ('Non-pitcher  ');
                          Writeln ('Name:  ',Name);
                          Writeln ('Team:  ',Team);
                          Writeln ('At bats:  ',Bats);
                          Writeln ('Home runs:  ',Runs);
                          Writeln ('Hits:  ',Hits);
                          Writeln ('RBI's:  ',RBI);
                          Writeln ('Batting average:  ',Avg:5:3)
                      END {Non-pitcher case}
        END {case}
      END {with}
 END; {procedure Print_Player}

 BEGIN {main program}
   Clrscr;
   Get_Player (Ball_Player);
   Clrscr;
   Writeln ('Here is the baseball player record that you entered.');
```

(Continued)

```
      Writeln;
      Writeln;
      Display_Player (Ball_Player)
END. {main_program}
```

CHAPTER 10

Questions

1. A file is a sequential data structure used to store components of the same data type in secondary memory.

3. Read

5. False

7. e. All of the above.

9. d. FileIdent = **FILE OF FILE**

11. Read/Readln

13. FilePos

15. Rewrite

17. Seek(file variable, FileSize(file variable));

19. Rename

Problems

10-1.

```
PROCEDURE ReadFile  (VAR FileVar : FileIdent);

USES
  Crt:

VAR
  Name : STRING [11];

BEGIN
  Clrscr;
  Write ('What disk file name do you want to read and display? ---> ');
  Readln (Name);
  Writeln;
  Assign (FileVar,Name);
  Reset (FileVar);
  REPEAT
      Read (FileVar, Component);
      Writeln (Component)
```

```
  UNTIL EOF(FileVar);
  Close (FileVar)
END;   {procedure ReadFile}
```

10-3.

```
BEGIN   {main program}
  Clrscr;
  Writeln;
  Writeln;
  Writeln;
  Writeln;
  Writeln;
  Writeln ('              Write and create a new address file (W)');
  Writeln;
  Writeln ('              Read and display an existing address file (R)');
  Writeln;
  Writeln ('              Add to an existing file address (A)');
  Writeln;
  Writeln ('              Change an address file component (C)');
  Writeln;
  Writeln;
  Write    ('                    ENTER CHOICE ---> ');
  Readln (Choice);
  Writeln;
  CASE Choice OF
    'W', 'w' : WriteFile (File_Variable);
    'R', 'r' : ReadFile (File_Variable);
    'A', 'a' : ExpandFile (File_Variable);
    'C', 'c' : ChangeFile (File_Variable)
  ELSE
    Writeln ('Invalid entry, press R to run the program again.')
  END {case}
END.   {main program}
```

10-5.
```
  PROGRAM Problem5 (input, output);

  USES
    Crt;

  TYPE
    CharFile= FILE OF char;

  VAR
    OldFile, NewFile : CharFile;


  PROCEDURE CopyFile (VAR Old,New : CharFile);

  VAR
  Name : STRING [12];
  Character : char;

  BEGIN

    Write ('Enter the old file name:  ');
    Readln (Name);
```

(Continued)

```
   Writeln;
   Assign (Old,Name);
   Write ('Enter new file name:  ');
   Readln (Name);
   Writeln;
   Assign (New,Name);
   Reset (Old);
   Rewrite (New);
   WHILE NOT eof(Old) DO
     BEGIN
        Read (Old,Character);
        Write (New,Character)
     END;
 Close (Old);
 Close (New)
END; {procedure Copy}


BEGIN  {main}
  Clrscr;
  Writeln ('This procedure will copy an old file to a new file.');
  Writeln;
  Writeln;
  CopyFile (OldFile,NewFile)

END.  {main}
```

10-7.

```
      PROGRAM Problem7 (input, output);

      USES
        Crt;

      TYPE
        CharFile = FILE OF char;

      VAR
        OldFile : CharFile;

      PROCEDURE EraseFile (VAR Old : CharFile);

      VAR
      Name : STRING [12];

      BEGIN
        Write ('Enter the disk file name to be erased:  ');
        Readln (Name);
        Assign (Old,Name);
        Reset (Old);
        Erase (Old);
        Close (Old)
      END; {procedure EraseFile}


      BEGIN  {main}
        Clrscr;
        Writeln ('This procedure will erase a disk file.');
        Writeln;
```

```
            Writeln;
            EraseFile (OldFile)
        END.  (main)
```

10-8-10-12.

```
{***************************************************************

  Problem 8:  Here is the parts inventory file declaration.

***************************************************************}


PROGRAM Problems_8_Through_12 (input, output, inventory);

USES
  Crt, Printer;

TYPE

  Part = RECORD
            Name : ·STRING [25];
            Number : STRING [10];
            Price  : STRING  [10];
            Quantity : STRING [3]
         END;


  Inventory = FILE OF  Part;

VAR
  Inven : Inventory;
  Apart : Part;
  Choice : char;


{***************************************************************

Problem 9:  This procedure will create a parts inventory file.

***************************************************************}


PROCEDURE  CreateFile (VAR Inv : Inventory);

VAR
  FileName : STRING [11];
  K, Number : integer;

BEGIN
  Clrscr;
  Writeln ('What name do you want to give your disk file?  ');
  Writeln ('Note:  Not more than 8 characters with a 3 character');
  Writeln ('extension.');
  Readln (FileName);
  Writeln;
  Writeln;
  Assign (Inv, FileName);
  Rewrite (Inv);
  Write ('How many parts do you have to enter? ---> ');
  Readln (Number);                                    (Continued)
```

```
      Writeln;
      Writeln;
      FOR K := 1 TO Number  DO
        BEGIN
          WITH Apart DO
            BEGIN
              Writeln ('ENTER THE FOLLOWING PART DESCRIPTION:  ');
              Writeln;
              Write ('Part Name ---> ');
              Readln (Name);
              Writeln;
              Write ('Part Number ---> ');
              Readln (Number);
              Writeln;
              Write ('Part Price ---> ');
              Readln (Price);
              Writeln;
              Write ('Part Quantity ---> ');
              Readln (Quantity);
              Writeln
            END; {with}
          Write (Inv, Apart)
        END; {for};
    Close (Inv)
  END; {procedure CreateFile}


  {**************************************************************

  Problem 10:  This procedure will expand the parts inventory file

  **************************************************************}

  PROCEDURE ExpandFile (VAR Inv : Inventory);

  VAR
    FileName : STRING [11];
    Number, K : integer;

  BEGIN
    Clrscr;
    Write ('What disk file do you wish to expand? ---> ');
    Readln (FileName);
    Writeln;
    Assign (Inv,FileName);
    Reset (Inv);
    Seek (Inv,FileSize(Inv));
    Write ('How many components do you wish to add? ---> ');
    Readln (Number);
    Writeln;
    FOR K := 1 TO Number DO
      BEGIN
        WITH Apart DO
          BEGIN
            Writeln ('ENTER THE FOLLOWING PART DESCRIPTION:  ');
            Writeln;
            Write ('Part Name ---> ');
            Readln (Name);
            Writeln;
            Write ('Part Number ---> ');
```

```
              Readln (Number);
              Writeln;
              Write ('Part Price ---> ');
              Readln (Price);
              Writeln;
              Write ('Part Quantity ---> ');
              Readln (Quantity);
              Writeln
          END; {with}
        Write (Inv, Apart)
      END; {for}
    Close (Inv)
  END;   {procedure ExpandFile}



  {*****************************************************************

    Problem 11:   This procedure will change a part description.

  ****************************************************************}


  PROCEDURE ChangeFile (VAR Inv : Inventory);

  VAR
    FileName : STRING [11];
    PartNumber : STRING [10];
    Number, K : integer;
    Flag : Boolean;

  BEGIN
    Clrscr;
    Write ('What disk file do you wish to change? ---> ');
    Readln (FileName);
    Writeln;
    Assign (Inv,FileName);
    Reset (Inv);
    Write ('What part number do you wish to change? ---> ');
    Readln (PartNumber);
    Writeln;
    Flag := FALSE;
    WHILE NOT EOF (Inv) DO
      BEGIN
        Read (Inv,Apart);
        IF Apart.Number = PartNumber THEN
          BEGIN
            Flag := TRUE;
            Write ('Part number ',PartNumber,' has been found.  ');
            Writeln ('Enter new part information: ');
            WITH Apart DO
              BEGIN
                Writeln;
                Write ('Part Name ---> ');
                Readln (Name);
                Writeln;
                Write ('Part Number ---> ');
                Readln (Number);
                Writeln;
                Write ('Part Price ---> ');
```

(Continued)

```
                    Readln (Price);
                    Writeln;
                    Write ('Part Quantity ---> ');
                    Readln (Quantity);
                    Writeln
                END; {with}
              Seek (Inv, FilePos(Inv) - 1);
              Write (Inv, Apart)
          END  {if statement}
      END;  {while loop}
    IF Flag = FALSE THEN
      Writeln ('Part number ',PartNumber,' was not found in this file.');
    Close (Inv)
  END;  {procedure ChangeFile}


{*********************************************************************

  Problem 12:  This procedure will print the entire parts inventory
               or display information for a single part.

  ********************************************************************}


  PROCEDURE ReadFile  ( VAR Inv : Inventory);

  VAR
    PartNumber : STRING [10];
    FileName : STRING [11];
    Choice : char;
    Flag : Boolean;

  BEGIN
    Clrscr;
    Write ('What disk file name do you want to print or display? ---> ');
    Readln (FileName);
    Writeln;
    Assign (Inv,FileName);
    Reset (Inv);
    Clrscr;
    Writeln;
    Writeln;
    Writeln;
    Writeln ('                 Print parts inventory (P)    ');
    Writeln;
    Writeln ('                 Display a given part (D)    ');
    Writeln;
    Writeln;
    Write   ('                      ENTER CHOICE ---> ');
    Readln (Choice);
    CASE Choice OF
      'P', 'p' : BEGIN
                   WHILE NOT EOF(Inv) DO
                     BEGIN
                       Read (Inv, Apart);
                       WITH Apart DO
                         BEGIN
                           Writeln (lst,'PART NAME:  ',Name);
                           Writeln (lst,'PART NUMBER:  ',Number);
                           Writeln (lst,'PRICE:   ',Price);
```

```
                              Writeln (1st,'QUANTITY:   ',Quantity);
                              Writeln (1st);
                              Writeln (1st)
                        END  {with}
                  END {while/do}
               END; {case P}

      'D', 'd' : BEGIN
                   Clrscr;
                   Write ('What part number do you wish to display? -> ');
                   Readln (PartNumber);
                   Writeln;
                   Flag := FALSE;
                   WHILE NOT EOF (Inv) DO
                     BEGIN
                       Read (Inv,Apart);
                       IF Apart.Number = PartNumber THEN
                         BEGIN
                           Flag := TRUE;
                           WITH Apart DO
                             BEGIN
                               Writeln ('PART NAME:   ',Name);
                               Writeln ('PART NUMBER:   ',Number);
                               Writeln ('PRICE:  ',Price);
                               Writeln ('QUANTITY:   ',Quantity);
                               Writeln;
                               Writeln
                             END {with}
                         END  {if}
                     END; {while};
                   IF Flag = False THEN
                     Writeln ('Part number ',PartNumber,' was not found.')
                 END {case D}
  ELSE
    Writeln ('Invalid choice, press R to run again.')
  END; {case}
  Close (Inv)
END;  {procedure ReadFile}

  BEGIN  {main program}
    Clrscr;
    Writeln;
    Writeln;
    Writeln;
    Writeln;
    Writeln;
    Writeln ('        Create a new inventory file (N)');
    Writeln;
    Writeln ('        Print or display an existing inventory file (P)');
    Writeln;
    Writeln ('        Expand an existing inventory file (E)');
    Writeln;
    Writeln ('        Change a part information (C)');
    Writeln;
    Writeln;
    Write   ('        ENTER CHOICE ---> ');
    Readln (Choice);
    Writeln;
    CASE Choice OF
      'N', 'n' : CreateFile (Inven);                          (Continued)
```

```
      'P', 'p' : ReadFile (Inven);
      'E', 'e' : ExpandFile (Inven);
      'C', 'c' : ChangeFile (Inven)
    ELSE
      Writeln ('Invalid entry, press R to run the program again.')
    END {case}
END.   {main program}
```

Index